Too Great
a Burden to Bear

RECONSTRUCTING AMERICA
Andrew L. Slap, series editor

Too Great
a Burden to Bear

*The Struggle and Failure
of the Freedmen's
Bureau in Texas*

Christopher B. Bean

FORDHAM UNIVERSITY PRESS
NEW YORK 2016

Fordham University Press has no responsibility for the persistence or accuracy of URLs for external or third-party Internet websites referred to in this publication and does not guarantee that any content on such websites is, or will remain, accurate or appropriate.

Fordham University Press also publishes its books in a variety of electronic formats. Some content that appears in print may not be available in electronic books.

Visit us online at www.fordhampress.com.

Library of Congress Cataloging-in-Publication Data

Names: Bean, Christopher B.
Title: Too great a burden to bear : the struggle and failure of the
    Freedmen's Bureau in Texas / Christopher B. Bean.
Description: First edition. | New York : Fordham University Press, 2016. |
    Series: Reconstructing America | Includes bibliographical references and
    index.
Identifiers: LCCN 2015042262 (print) | LCCN 2016006934 (ebook) | ISBN
    9780823268757 (cloth : alkaline paper) | ISBN 9780823271764 (paper :
    alkaline paper) | ISBN 9780823268764 (ePub)
Subjects: LCSH: African Americans—Texas—History—19th century. |
    Freedmen—Texas—History. | Reconstruction (U.S. history,
    1865–1877)—Texas. | United States. Bureau of Refugees, Freedmen, and
    Abandoned Lands—Officials and employees—Biography. | United States.
    Bureau of Refugees, Freedmen, and Abandoned Lands—History. | Texas—Race
    relations—History—19th century. | BISAC: HISTORY / United States / Civil
    War Period (1850–1877). | SOCIAL SCIENCE / Ethnic Studies / African
    American Studies.
Classification: LCC E185.93.T4 B43 2016 (print) | LCC E185.93.T4 (ebook) |
    DDC 305.896/073076409034—dc23
LC record available at http://lccn.loc.gov/2015042262

Printed in the United States of America

18 17 16   5 4 3 2 1

First edition

Contents

TOO GREAT
A BURDEN TO BEAR

Introduction

Few eras in American history have a more profound and lasting imprint on this country as the decade or so that followed the Civil War. Reconstruction, as it's called, was an attempt to wipe away the vestiges of slavery and to reintegrate the former Confederate states into their normal places in the Union. By infusing the ideals of "free men, free soil, and free labor," Republicans hoped to shape the South in the image of the victorious North, with all remnants of the old order erased. Central to this restructuring was an organization created with much hope and optimism. Passed on March 3, 1865, the Bureau of Refugees, Freedmen, and Abandoned Lands, more commonly called the Freedmen's Bureau, was the first federal social-welfare organization. Functioning under the War Department, it operated in all the former Confederacy and slave states. According to historian John A. Carpenter, the "fact that the Freedmen's Bureau existed at all was a miracle." It had a multipurpose task: easing the transition of the freedpeople from servitude to freedom; implanting republican ideals of democracy and free labor in the ashes of the "peculiar institution;" and preventing any further attempts to break up the Union.[1]

Legislators wrestled with exactly how to empower it. While some worried the organization might create a permanent dependent class, others feared it might disrupt federalism. A few, however, prophesied the agency becoming a tool to control freed votes, with its agents being "overseers" and "negro drivers," who might "re-enslave" the emancipated. Still others doubted its constitutionality. With little consensus on how to address the needs of the former slaves, Congress was essentially experimenting. Congressman Robert C. Schenk of Ohio best summarized it as "experimental legislation," continuing with,

> it is better, from the very nature of the case, as it is a matter which relates to an emergency, to a necessity, to an accident, as it were of the times and the condition of the war in which we are, that the system should build itself up

and grow by accretion and development according to the necessities as they arise or are found to exist . . . If you attempt to provide in advance for every particular thing, if you have complicated machinery in this bill, or simple machinery even, running so much into detail, you run the risk of not accomplishing the object you seek, but, on the contrary, the further risk of defeating the very object which you are engaged in by raising endless questions as to the meaning or application of this particular provision of this law.[2]

Its work "must be left to the discretion of those engaged in [the footwork]. . . ."[3]

Without rigid guidelines and with uncertain "objectives" and "mandates," Bureau officials had to fill in the void. Much of their policy, consequently, resembled the Freedmen's Bureau bill itself: vague and, at times, confusing. Orders, letters, and instructions (often open to interpretation) filtered down the chain of command to field personnel. In his *Autobiography* the commissioner of the Bureau, Oliver Otis Howard, stated why he resisted "one minute system of rules": he wanted subordinates to improvise and adapt. A very decentralized and fluid system was created so that how orders would be interpreted, implemented, and enforced generally fell to the men in the field. These men literally dictated the agency's policy. As noted by historians Eileen Boris and Peter Bardaglio, "ultimately public policy is forged in the minute regulations, and in the interpreting them on a daily basis." Decentralization allowed for quick, decisive moves as well as ingenuity. Yet it also created much indecision and confusion. Such a framework resulted in field agents' truly becoming "The Bureau" within their respective areas.[4]

In its brief seven-year existence, the Freedmen's Bureau became the epicenter of the debate about Reconstruction. Cognizant of its responsibilities, Republicans and Democrats fiercely debated its necessity. Throughout the years, students have highlighted the agency's features. One facet, however, has been neglected until recently: the subassistant commissioners (SACs), the men in direct contact with Southern civilians. Scholars have begun recently to focus on the men historian Barry Crouch termed the "hearts of Reconstruction," but a number have examined only individual experiences, often neglecting other significant questions.[5]

Not ignoring individual experiences and attitudes, this work will go further, focusing on the agents at a more personal level. Were they Southern or Northern born? Could they be considered poor, middle-class, or wealthy? Were they married or single? Did the agency prefer young, middle-age, or older men as agents? Did these men have military experience or were they civilians? What occupations did the Bureau draw from? The answers to these questions will help us understand the type of man Bureau officials believed qualified—or not qualified—to oversee the freedpeople's transition to freedom. A brief chronicling of the image of the Bureau agent is in order. During their time in office, these men elicited varied reactions from the public. Where contemporaries left off, the academic community picked up, and the discussion of the SAC's role and effect, at times, became very heated. For nearly a century, the dominant view of the Bureau man was of occupier—one who descended on the prostrate South to meddle with race relations by filling freedpeople's heads with wild ideas contrary to their natural state in life and enriching himself at the expense of white Southerners, and to brutalize the former Confederate populace. These avaricious "carpetbaggers" unnecessarily antagonized the emancipated against their former masters, all the while benefiting from this tumult politically and financially.[6] Influenced by the events unfolding across the South during the 1960s, historians revisited the role of the Freedmen's Bureau in Reconstruction. Such works revised the agent as a product of his time, who was subject to the whole gamut of human characteristics, from honesty and compassion to greed and nefariousness, and whose efforts, for the most part, failed to live up to its promises.[7] At the same time, others were a little more critical. To them, they represented not a vehicle of liberation, but an instrument for oppression. Their lack of commitment to the needs of the freedmen, racial and gender predispositions, and desire for order and profitability at all costs "banked the fires of freedom." They achieved this by colluding with white Southern planters essentially to re-enslave the freedpeople.[8] Since the 1980s, however, a "new" image of the Bureau agent has appeared, one more balanced than previous interpretations. Appreciating the enormity of the task, contemporary historians "go beyond [their] limitations, weaknesses, and failures to underscore the significant role [these men] played in the former slaves' lives. . . ."[9]

A close examination reveals the typical SAC in Texas (with exceptions of course) was a well-intentioned, honest man toward the freedpeople. Although influenced by contemporary attitudes toward labor, dependency, and gender, for his time he engaged in work seen as quite philanthropic. The country asked them to do the unprecedented, and, despite falling short of some expectations (including some of their own), they achieved more than many thought possible. Sacrificing to help the former slaves, some men paid financially, some paid socially, and others paid with their lives. Whatever their motives and the obstacles placed before them, their attempts and sacrifices, in the words of Bureau historian Paul A. Cimbala, deserve "better than a summary dismissal . . . as being no more than the effort of a racist society attempting to define a subordinate kind of freedom for the ex-slaves."[10]

1

"A *Stranger* Amongst *Strangers*"

Who Were the Subassistant Commissioners?

Congress charged the Freedmen's Bureau with a multipurpose task. This task fell specifically to the subassistant commissioners, who were directly in contact with Southern whites and former slaves. Few subjects in Reconstruction history have more differing interpretations than of these men, considered everything from "avaricious harpies" and "honest and genuine vehicles of change" to "racist paternalists." Later scholars would credit SACs with transitioning, to a small extent, the former slave into postwar American society, while simultaneously indicting them for everything from stifling poverty and racial segregation to black degradation during Hurricane Katrina.[1] By doing so, their identities become more than faceless, abstract entities to be either loathed or applauded. Lost is the fact that a Texas Bureau man went on to lead United States military forces in Cuba in 1898 against the Spanish; or that one fired the first Union shots in defense at Fort Sumter; or that military officials initially had another tentatively scheduled to lead the expedition into Montana where he would have met his fate at the Little Big Horn; or that many others went on to productive (if less spectacular) lives. Was the "avaricious harpy" a wealthy man or from more common stock? Was he a Yankee or did he hail from Dixie? Did that "honest and genuine vehicle of change" have a family or was he single? What occupations were those "racist paternalists" drawn from? Was it from the civilian sector or the military? By focusing on such matters, interested readers can address the very important question of who were the agents of the Freedmen's Bureau. The answers will suggest the type of man high Bureau officials believed most qualified (or not) to guide the freedmen's journey from bondage to freedom.

The Bureau operated within all eleven former Confederate states as well as Maryland, Missouri, Kentucky, West Virginia, and the District of Columbia. A commissioner in Washington oversaw the entire organization. He delegated authority to subordinates known as assistant commissioners. Each one supervised actions within a particular state (sometimes several states fell under an

assistant commissioner's jurisdiction). Over time, each state was sectioned into
subdistricts, generally comprising one to several counties. Each subdistrict was
headed by a subordinate, an SAC. The responsibilities of the SACs extended to
"all subjects relating to refugees and freedmen" and empowered them "to exercise and perform within their respective subdistricts all the powers . . . of the
Assistant Commissioner." In effect, they held broad powers within their subdistricts. Agents had to be familiar with army regulations, engage in diplomacy,
marriage counseling, and education, and serve as judge and jury. As one Bastrop agent described his duties for one month, it entailed "[e]xamining, explaining and approving [labor] contracts, settlement of last year[']s contracts, visiting
plantations, addressing the freedmen, hearing complaints, giving advice etc."
To be sure, it required "an official jack-of-all-trades."[2]

From September 1865, when the agency arrived in Texas, to December 1868,
when its operations—excluding education—ceased in the state, 239 of these
jacks-of-all-trades served in Texas, a number approximately three times the
total in Arkansas (n=79). Some earlier accounts place the number of agents in
Texas at 202. Several reasons may explain the discrepancy. First, not all agents
were listed in the Freedmen's Bureau Roster of Officers and Civilians. Headquarters posted the roster on a monthly basis, but those who received their
appointments and were relieved all within the same month were not included.
SACs frequently exceeded their authority, appointing help to lessen their workload. In time, all would be filtered out by superiors, but this can be discerned
only by a thorough examination of the records. Past examinations also did not
include traveling agents, special agents, or assistant subassistant commissioners
(ASAC). Since these positions essentially had the same responsibilities as subassistant commissioners, they should be included in any agent study. Inherent
problems often found in any large bureaucracy also led to inaccurate record
keeping. Further, critics often mislabeled certain men as agents in order to castigate them within the white community. Former slaves, Richard Allen and
Charles Bryant, and county official Benjamin Franklin Barkley have all been
erroneously cited as agents.[3]

At the agency's high point in Texas, it counted 61 subassistant commissioners, 10 assistant subassistant commissioners, 1 traveling agent, 1 special agent, 1
assigned to "special duty," and 1 inspector (July 1867) manning 59 subdistricts.
As seen in Figure 1-1,[4] the high point for agents did not occur until nearly two
years after entering Texas, and came about because of the renewed effort when
Congress wrested the reconstruction process from the president in early 1867.
No matter who controlled the reconstruction process, the prevailing federal

attitude believed U.S. military experience and "Northern" lineage necessary for the work of the Freedmen's Bureau. See Figure 1-2 for a comparison of the number of military and civilian agents. At any time in the three-month interval sample there never exceeded more than seven (average 9.3 percent of agents each month were "Southern") men serving from the former Confederacy (see Figure 1-3). Only 23.4 percent of Bureau agents, in fact, lacked recent military service.

Texas thus had a high of more than six dozen agents (SACs, ASACs, inspectors, and traveling agents) in the field at one time, greatly exceeding the maximum in other Southern states like Alabama, Arkansas, and Mississippi. But considering Texas's immense size and the fact that the Freedmen's Bureau never employed more than nine hundred agents, including office staff, throughout the South at any given time, there never existed an adequate number of Texas agents to service the community. While some served more than two years, others lasted but days or a few weeks. More than half served six months or less (see Table 1-1). Turnover in Texas was high, resulting in an average tenure approximating seven

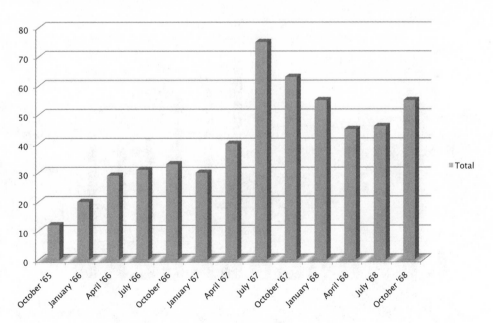

Figure 1–1. Total Number of Bureau Agents in Three-Month Intervals

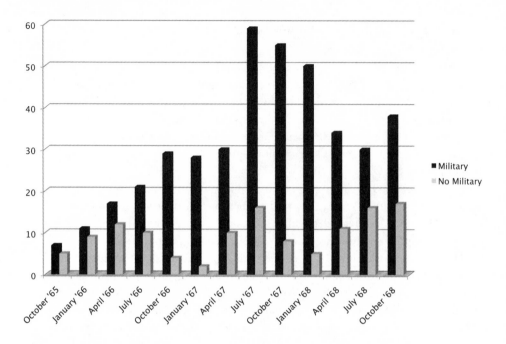

Figure 1–2. Total Number of Military-Civilian Agents in Three-Month Intervals

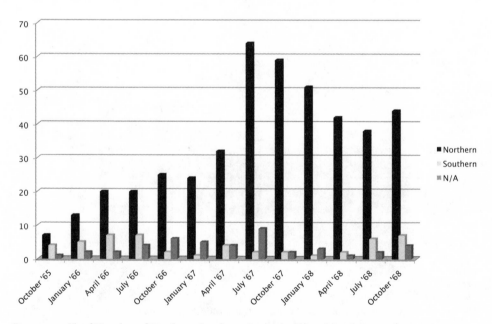

Figure 1–3. Total Number of Northern-Southern Agents in Three-Month Intervals

Table 1-1   Length of Tenure for Subassistant Commissioners in Texas

Length of Tenure w/Bureau	Number of Bureau Agents	Percentage
Less than Four Months Service	58	27.2
Four to Six Months Service	57	26.8
Seven to Nine Months Service	36	16.9
Ten to Twelve Months Service	24	11.3
More than Twelve Months Service	38	17.8
	n=213	100

Note: Dates came from Freedmen's Bureau Roster of Officers and Civilians.

and three-quarter months (7.8 months). This was below the nine and one-half months in the Arkansas Bureau and approximates the mean for Alabama.[5]

Civilians remained with the Bureau slightly more than their military counterparts. On average, their tenures lasted 8.1 months (n=48). As for those with military experience, they remained with the agency for 7.7 months (n=165). This discrepancy is likely explained by the revolving commanders at Bureau posts. This resulted in one- or two-month tenures. Whether because of the workload, revolving post commands, the low pay, or certain inherent dangers of the job, it is certain that few served long enough to establish any confidence, if that was ever possible, within the white community or greatly enhance their overall effectiveness for the freedpeople.

Of the 239 who served in Texas, all but one were white and all were men. Some sources have listed agents other than George T. Ruby as black, most notably Jacob C. DeGress. But none of these assertions can be substantiated, and, judging by DeGress's place of birth (Prussia), this seems unlikely. Officials in Washington, although never specifically prohibiting black men, warned of white reaction to them, noting they "created a hostility hard to overcome." Of those whose birthplace could be confirmed (n=185), 160 or 86.5 percent were born outside the former Confederacy (i.e., slaveholding states that did not secede, Union states, and foreign countries). Twenty-five men (13.5 percent) came from states that seceded (the former Confederacy).[6]

The Bureau in Texas preferred men born north of Dixie, with approximately two-thirds (120 of 185) coming from a non-slaveholding, Northern state. Men who came from the Upper South—slaveholding states that remained in the Union, including Delaware and D.C.—represented 6.5 percent (n=12). The remaining 28 men (15.1 percent) came from another country, a percentage noticeably less than the approximate 25 percent in the Union army. The numbers for those born in the non-slaveholding Union states (n=120) shows that about half (n=61, or 50.8

percent) were born in a Middle Atlantic State (New York, Pennsylvania, or New Jersey), with no agent being from New Jersey. Twenty-five percent (n=30) were born in New England, and the Great Lakes region produced 29 men (24.2 percent). Only 25 (13.5 percent of 185) were born in one of the eleven states that seceded. Surprisingly (or not), only one man came from Texas. A majority of men who came from states that "left" the Union came from Tennessee, Virginia, and Alabama, former Confederate states with large Unionist populations. The underrepresentation from seceded states corroborates findings in other studies: the agency hesitated to appoint men from the former Confederacy and desired men with Northern roots.[7]

Officials preferred Northern-born applicants. All regions except the Middle Atlantic States and New England were underrepresented. According to census records, slightly more than 22 percent (22.9) and 9 percent (9.1) of the country's population came from the Mid-Atlantic and New England. In Texas, 33 and 16.2 percent, respectively, came from these two regions, meaning nearly half of the Texas SACs came from the Northeast (see Table 1-2). Men from the Upper South and Great Lakes Region, however, represented 6.5 percent and 15.7 percent of Bureau men in Texas. That is noticeably lower than the general population from those areas: 10.6 and 26.8 percent. Not surprising, Bureau officials in Texas drastically underrepresented those born in the former Confederate states. That region represented a quarter of the population in 1870, but only 13.5 percent of Texas subassistant commissioners. Foreign-born agents approximated the general population as a whole: 15.1 percent in Texas and 14.4 percent for the general population.[8]

The small proportion of Southern-born agents demonstrates the first assistant commissioner for Texas E. M. Gregory's suspicion of anyone from former "secesh" states. His successors generally followed his lead, as did other ACs for other states. Manpower shortages sometimes forced officials to draw from the state's "scalawag" (i.e., Southern white Unionist) population. It is true that the organization occasionally turned to residents such as Hardin Hart, Albert Latimer, and James A. Hogue, all born in the South and residents of Texas prior to the war; but white Southern men were few, and they were greatly outnumbered by Northerners.[9]

Who were some of these so-called scalawags and carpetbaggers? Few could exactly be called heroes or villains. Most turned out to be quite unassuming men on the frontline of Reconstruction. But a few achieved some status and popularity for their time. For instance, "scalawag" Albert H. Latimer, a moderate Republican, was born in Tennessee either in 1800 or 1808 and arrived in Texas with his wife just prior to hostilities with Mexico. Although he served

Table 1-2 Origins of Subassistant Commissioners in Texas

Place of Origin	Number of Bureau Agents n=185	Percentage of Bureau Agents from Each Region
Outside the former Confederacy, including foreign born	160	86.5
Middle Atlantic States (New Jersey, New York, and Pennsylvania)	61	33
Upper South (Delaware, D.C., Kentucky, Missouri, and Maryland)	12	6.5
New England (Massachusetts, Vermont, Maine, Connecticut, Rhode Island, and New Hampshire)	30	16.2
Great Lakes (Michigan, Ohio, Indiana, Illinois, Wisconsin, and Iowa)	29	15.7
Foreign Countries (England, Prussia, Ireland, Sweden, Canada, and Scotland)	28	15.1
Confederate States (Virginia, Tennessee, Texas, Georgia, North and South Carolina, Florida, Mississippi, Alabama, Louisiana, and Arkansas)	25	13.5
	n=185	100

Note: The information in this table came from various sources, but much of it came from the U.S. Census and the agent's application to the Freedmen's Bureau.

in a military unit during the Texas Revolution, he became best known for representing his region at the Convention of 1836 at Washington-on-the-Brazos, where he signed the Texas Declaration of Independence. An ardent Unionist and owner of twenty-two slaves, Latimer resisted secession but remained in Texas throughout the war. He served in the provisional government of Governor Andrew Jackson Hamilton before being elected to the Constitutional Convention in 1866. With stints as a tax collector, voter registrar, and Freedmen's

Bureau agent in north Texas, Latimer in 1869 accepted an appointment to the Texas Supreme Court, but resigned later that year. Such positions helped him attain a high economic status, owning nearly nine thousand dollars in wealth in 1870. A moderate Republican, Latimer opposed the gubernatorial run of the more radical Edmund Jackson Davis in 1869, but still received an appointment by Davis as a district judge. It is uncertain exactly why Davis appointed Latimer, but his appointment might have had something to do with his reputation as one of the premier legal minds in the state, unquestioned Unionism during and after the war, and loyalty to the Republican party. The Radical Republicans had a tenuous hold on power in the state and never claimed a majority of support. Thus, Latimer's appointment could easily have been an attempt by Governor Davis to coalesce support by courting moderate Republicans. Considering the numerous fusion parties and tickets throughout Reconstruction, such an assertion is quite plausible. He would serve three years in Davis's administration before dying in Clarksville in 1877. Most citizen agents lived less conspicuous lives, going about with little fanfare or reason for people to notice.[10]

Born in New York, George T. Ruby was the only black SAC in Texas. There remains speculation concerning his parents, with some doubt about whether he was a "mulatto" or not. He came south, zealously committing himself to black education in Louisiana, where he became interested in politics. He arrived in Texas in the summer of 1866. Appointed as a traveling agent, he toured the state to encourage the establishment of freedmen schools and morality, particularly temperance. Ruby left Bureau service in late 1867, and through his political work, became a delegate at the Republican National Convention and later to the state's constitutional convention. Afterward, his constituents in Galveston elected him to the state legislature in 1869, where he furthered business interests and became one of the most important and influential black politicians during Reconstruction in Texas. With the Democrats regaining control of the state senate, Ruby decided not to run for reelection in 1873. Believing his political prospects better, he moved back to Louisiana, where he worked as a surveyor for New Orleans, agent for the Internal Revenue department, and editor of a local paper until his death from malaria in 1882. Although known as a radical carpetbagger (a label applied to about any Republican), his "personal qualities of tact and diplomacy . . . softened" some of his harshest critics.[11]

Another "carpetbag" agent was Ira Hobart Evans. A Vermont resident and an officer in several black units in the Army of the James, Evans served in the honor guard for President Abraham Lincoln's funeral cortège. For his actions at Hatcher's Run, Virginia, in the closing days of the war, he received the Medal of

Honor in 1895. He became a SAC in 1867, but resigned in disgust with superiors in late January 1868. Evans bounced around as a rancher along the Texas coast and as an Internal Revenue agent along the Texas border and coast until fellow Republican and gubernatorial candidate Edmund Jackson Davis convinced him to run for a seat in the next legislature. In 1870 his fellow legislators elected him speaker of the House of the Twelfth Legislature, thus making him the youngest ever to hold that position in Texas. The amity, however, did not last long, for he soon angered his own party by siding with the Democrats in opposition to a controversial election law. This break with the party resulted in his ouster from the speakership. After serving the remainder of his term, he left political office and worked for the Texas Land Company along with various railroads. His interest in the freedmen always remained, as he lent his support to the all-black Tillotson College in Austin. He served on its board for four decades. With failing health (a heart condition), Evans, on the recommendation of his doctor, moved to San Diego in 1920, where he died two years later.[12]

Charles F. Rand, from Batavia, New York, entered service for the Union with the 12th New York Volunteers. Congress officially recognized him as the first man to volunteer for the Civil War, when President Lincoln issued a call for volunteers after Confederates fired on Fort Sumter in April 1861. When an officer came to Batavia soliciting volunteers, Rand, stepping from the crowd, said, "I will." He served heroically, even winning the Medal of Honor at Blackburn's Ford, Virginia, in July 1861. As his "regiment broke in disorder," Rand remained in action, facing the fire of an entire Confederate company. With bullets whizzing all around, he continued to load and fire at the enemy. Impressed by this courage, Confederates withheld their fire from the lone gunmen and allowed him to retreat. Wounded in action at Gaines Mill in June 1862, Rand had a portion of the right humerus bone "excised." Doctors removed the head of the bone and four inches of the shaft so that the arm "hangs by the muscles and ligaments." Confederates captured the wounded soldier, and he spent three months in Libby prison. After being exchanged, he continued service in the Veteran Reserve Corps and finished the war on assignment at Douglas Hospital, where he became interested in medicine. After the Bureau, he enrolled at Georgetown Medical College and was graduated in 1870, practicing medicine in the nation's capital. He died in 1908 and, because he was the first to volunteer for the war effort, was buried in plot No. 1 at Arlington National Cemetery. These case studies highlight something worth noting: most were simply average nineteenth-century people who, although a few may have achieved extraordinary feats during the war, lived rather inconspicuous lives.[13]

The types of jobs agents in Texas held after the war ran the gamut for nineteenth-century America (see Table 1-3). In all, agents followed twenty-nine different occupations, ranging from contractor to law enforcer, from merchant to farmer, from editor to minister, from seaman to clerk. Of those whose occupations could be ascertained according to the 1870 census (n=139), 64.7 percent of the men listed a professional or personal service occupation (n=90). That equals almost four times the state average (17.2 percent), but the high number of U.S. military personnel in the table explains this. Twenty-nine men (20.9 percent) listed an occupation in the agricultural sector, significantly lower than the state's average approximating 70 percent and the Union army's 40 percent. Those who listed a trade or a commercial job equaled 10.1 percent (n=14) and manufacturing 4.3 percent (n=6). The former was almost two times the state's average (5.7 percent), but the latter was slightly less than the state's 6.7 percent.[14]

Of those who cited a professional or personal occupation in the 1870 census (n=90), Bureau men in Texas cited the United States Army most often as their employer (n=52, or 37.4 percent of 139). (When adjusted for those who served during the war [but not afterward] and for those who were still in the army in 1880 but could not be located in the 1870 census, the number who served in military service increases greatly [n=182, or 76.2 percent of 239 Bureau agents in Texas.]) The difference can best be explained by the high number of officers (either in the volunteer or regular army) in the Bureau in the state. From the entire population of agents who served in Texas (n=239), officers represented more than 66 percent (n=160), all of whom attained the rank of 2nd lieutenant

Table 1-3   Occupation of Subassistant Commissioners in Texas

Occupation[a]	Number of Bureau Agents	Percentage of Bureau Agents	Percentage of Texans
Professional/Personal Services	90	64.7	17.2
Agricultural Industry	29	20.9	70.4
Trade and Commerce	14	10.1	5.7
Manufacturing and Mechanical	6	4.3	6.7
	n=139	100	100

[a] The occupations are as follows: professional and personal services include military, legal professions, which includes attorneys, law/district clerks, judges, and sheriffs, physicians/druggists, ministers, domestics, insurers, academics, journalists/editors, and governmental employees. Agriculture includes all occupations pertaining to farming, including a beef manager, farmers, farm hands, and planters. Those within the trades and commerce are merchants, grocers, book dealers, printers, a painter, a seaman, a real estate agent, and a hotel keeper. Manufacturing includes a miner, a cooper, mill/paper manager, railroad worker, and a box shop employee.

Note: Texas's averages are from *Ninth Census, Wealth and Industry*, 3:808–823.

or higher. Characteristics of ideal officers—maturity, leadership, bravery, and the ability to abide by military protocol—could only be a benefit to agents, and the Bureau's belief that officers possessed these qualities perhaps influenced their appointments. The high percentage of military personnel and experience compares closely to the findings in other state studies of the Freedmen's Bureau. Considering that nearly three-quarters of Texas Bureau agents enlisted in the armed forces during the war and the agency came under military control, this hardly seems novel. But it appears that military service helped with an appointment and might be, like birthplace, a good indicator of Union sentiment.[15]

J. B. Kiddoo, Gregory's successor, believed the soldiers to be loyal, above reproach, and unlikely to cheat the freedpeople because he "is being paid his regular salary." With agents receiving no pay until the summer of 1866, Kiddoo believed civilian agents to be lazy and possibly shirkers. Personnel and applicants alike knew the importance of military service. Charles Haughn, a man headquarters called one of the "most efficient and reliable of the Bureau agents," understood the preference when he informed superiors about the large pool of discharged soldiers in his subdistrict. "There are many discharged soldiers here," he wrote, "but all of them are addicted to the use of intoxicating liquor." One former soldier, who never received an appointment, noted in his application "I think one that served during the whole war . . . should have precedence over one who [did not]." William H. Sinclair, a SAC and later Bureau inspector in Texas, presumed an application would be declined, for he had "never served in the army during the war. . . ."[16]

Other reasons, perhaps, help explain the high percentage of military men in the Bureau in Texas. In their groundbreaking study, LaWanda and John Cox found officials recognized the "prestige of the uniform aided the effectiveness of Bureau work," since these men "were more easily held to required military discipline and responsibility than were civilians." In the initial Bureau bill in 1865, Congress did not allocate funds to pay civilian agents. Thus out of necessity, the agency had to turn to the military for personnel. Commissioner Howard initially hesitated to appoint civilian agents, because he did not want to spend money on their salaries.[17]

Another reason might be the organization itself. Thirty-one agents, including the first two assistant commissioners, at one time or another, served as officers in regiments of the United States Colored Troops (U.S.C.T.). That means nearly one in five agents (n=31, or 17 percent) whose military status could be confirmed (n=182) served as officers in all-black regiments—that percentage greatly increases when applied to those who could be found in the 1870 but not the 1860 census (n=52, or 45.6 percent). The willingness of a white man to work with and lead black troops into combat was not lost on Bureau officials or those wanting an appointment. In addition to a man's possible "humanitarian" and "liberal" spirit, officials also believed those who commanded black regiments "pretty thoroughly acquainted with their [blacks'] nature. . . ."[18]

Although some agents never encountered a life-threatening situation in their subdistricts, others literally took their lives in their hands. Those stationed in northeast Texas, along the Red River and the frontier, and in the triangular "no man's land" between San Antonio, Corpus Christi, and Brownsville could face great danger, particularly from Indians, outlaws, or both. The work required battle-tested men who would not wilt. "Occasional collision," as one agent recognized, is "unavoidable." The father of one agent who served in Dallas concluded, "The [Bureau agent] must be willing to carry his life in his hand. . . ." Those who served in the armed forces also had experience following orders. Despite some leeway in their day-to-day operations, agents still had to abide by Bureau and military policies and guidelines. With critics watching for a misstep, the agency could ill-afford carelessness. Those with military service were familiar with the ins and outs of military paperwork. Finally, appointing soldiers essentially married the Bureau with the army. This allowed for protection, but it also was quite practical, since many in the North feared another war. This marriage then could be another means to prevent the former slaveholding states of the Confederacy from rising like a phoenix. Whatever the reason, the high number of soldiers suggests the Bureau was hardly engaged in work to "revolutionize" the South, but probably something more moderate, precise, and achievable.[19]

These men's military careers ranged from unremarkable to heroic and included four winners of the Medal of Honor.[20] Consider the career of William Rufus Shafter. He received the Medal of Honor for meritorious action at Fair Oaks during the war, but had a relatively obscure career as a Bureau agent on the Texas frontier. Following Reconstruction, however, his exploits and career could hardly be called ordinary. He became a renowned Indian fighter in West Texas, Arizona, and in South Dakota, where he commanded the expedition responsible for returning the Indians back to the reservation after the Wounded Knee massacre. In 1898, in spite of being considered incompetent, becoming the target of Theodore Roosevelt's backbiting and criticism, and being terribly overweight (305 pounds), he led the American expedition into Cuba during the Spanish-American War. At the time, it was the largest force ever to leave American soil. He left Cuba in 1898 and served in the Department of California, retiring from the military in 1901 and dying in San Francisco five years later. After a distinguished service in West Virginia, the battles of Chickamauga in Georgia and Chattanooga in Tennessee, and as a corps commander in the capture of Mobile, Joseph Jones Reynolds headed the District of Arkansas at war's end. Transferred shortly thereafter to Texas, he took over the Rio Grande military subdistrict. Assigned to command the Department of Texas, he oversaw the solidification of Republican rule in Texas. After a brief stint on the Montana frontier, where superiors offered him command of the ill-fated Little Big Horn expedition (but which he declined because of poor health), Reynolds was court-martialed for actions during another Indian campaign (subsequently found guilty, receiving a suspended sentence) and retired shortly afterward in 1877. He died in 1899 and is buried in Arlington National Cemetery.[21]

Although some were participants in some of the most famous battles of the Civil War and subsequent Indian campaigns, the vast majority of men appointed as agents had inconspicuous military careers and less-than-famous or historic lives after their tenures. The agent at Tyler, Gregory Barrett, entered military service in a Maryland volunteer unit before transferring to the 26th Infantry Regiment. A lieutenant at war's end, he remained in the army for more than a decade after Appomattox. Apparently he still yearned for martial life, because in 1884 he was recommissioned as a captain, dying on the field of battle at Santiago de Cuba in 1898. Oscar E. Pratt, a lieutenant colonel in the 7th U.S.C.T., partici-pated in the "hotly contested battles around Richmond and Petersburg." Luckily he never received a serious wound, but the same cannot be said for several of his hats and jackets. He had a relatively short stay as an agent in Indianola and even-tually returned home to northwest New York to resume his medical studies. For the next four decades, Pratt built a lucrative medical practice in New York, Illi-nois, and Michigan and distinguished himself as the president and secretary of several medical associations and societies. A native of Prussia, Jacob C. DeGress was a cavalry officer during the war. After Bureau service in Texas and Louisi-ana, he accepted a commission in the regular army and served until 1870. Having amassed a sizable amount of money (more than twelve thousand dollars in wealth in 1870), he soon entered Republican politics as Texas's first superinten-dent of public instruction. In this position he zealously performed his duties in the face of Democratic resistance. When Democrats regained control of the state, they removed him from office, but he remained active in local, state, and national Republican party politics until his death in Austin in 1894.[22]

Hiram Seymour Hall, a native New Yorker and lieutenant in the 43rd U.S.C.T., participated in every battle and campaign of the Army of the Potomac from July 1861 through April 1865, receiving the Medal of Honor for "gallantry in action" at Gaine's Mill. His bravery and skill brought him to the attention of Brigadier General Ambrose E. Burnside, who selected him to lead the ill-fated storming party after the explosion at the Battle of the Crater outside of Petersburg. Losing his right arm in the attack, he later lamented its effect: "No more for me to lead my command on the field of battle, no more for me the thrill of fire that I had felt with my comrades on two-score fields of patriotic glory." Post-Bureau, Hall resumed his private life in Missouri and Kansas to live out his days as a farmer. Another SAC, William H. Horton, lost his arm in battle and finished the war in the Veteran Reserve Corps. He left Texas after his tenure, retiring to Kentucky, where he worked for the Bureau of Internal Revenue until his death in 1893. A native of Pennsylvania, Frank Holsinger enlisted and eventually became a captain in the 19th U.S.C.T. While on picket duty, a bullet struck his right arm, completely shattering the bones in the forearm. His wound left "his right arm and hand . . . completely disabled." Holsinger, after leaving the Bureau, moved to Kansas with his family. There he lived a rather normal (yet financially successful) life (eleven thousand dollars total in wealth) as a farmer until his death in 1916.[23]

Farmers were the second largest group of agents (n=18, or 17.1 percent). According to the statistics for the state at that time, a little more than one in three Texans listed farming or planting (non-slave labor, of course) as an occupation in 1870. If added to those who listed some other agricultural-related occupation, the number climbs to more than 70 percent of Texans. The Bureau clearly underrepresented men from this occupation, a finding similar to another state study of the Bureau. In his study of the Freedmen's Bureau and local white leadership in Virginia, Richard G. Lowe found the agency demurred at selecting farmers when choosing suitable officeholders for that state. Of the 18 agents in Texas who listed farming as their occupation in the 1870 census, only 7 had owned slaves according to the 1860 census. All were Southern born, with only one coming from a non-Confederate state (Kentucky). All were also civilians and, with the exception of one, significantly older (51.3 to 36.33) than the average Bureau agent in Texas. From those who owned slaves, four qualified as planters in the pre-emancipation sense: 20 or more slaves. Approximately one in fifteen (6.7 percent) agents whose occupations were established (n=105) owned at least one slave prior to the war. These percentages differ greatly from those in Georgia, where almost half (49 percent) the agents had owned at least one slave. Texas numbers resembled those in Virginia, where only 10 percent of Bureau men were former slave owners. The paucity of former planters (slaveholders for that matter) in the agency in Texas reflected the opinions of those heading the organization in the state. Both E. M. Gregory and J. B. Kiddoo distrusted the planter class "with the interests of the freedmen." Bureau officials in Texas simply did not trust former masters with the welfare of their former slaves. It appears that personal preferences of each state's assistant commissioner, rather than any overall Bureau policy handed down from Washington, explain the disparities.[24]

Texas Bureau and census records indicate that Bureau men were generally in their late thirties (n=154, 36.33 years of age) in 1870. That would place the average individual generally in his early to mid thirties at the time of his appointment. In fact, nearly 44 percent of all agents were in their thirties at the time of their appointment (see Figure 1-4).[25] That holds steady when civilians are taken out of the study. Those with military service had an average age of 35.8 years (n=120). Civilians, however, were nearly a full decade older on average than their military counterparts, with an average age slightly more than 44 years of age (n=34). The discrepancy can best be explained by those who lacked military service due to age. Unfortunately, the census did not compute average age, so a comparison with the population as a whole is difficult. Further, such a comparison may not

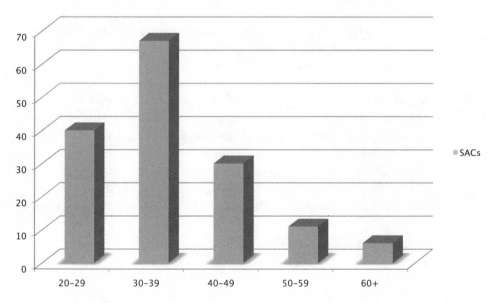

Figure 1–4.   Number of Bureau Agents by Age

be a meaningful item considering the entire population includes children. Comparison to the military, on the other hand, is possible, and since the Bureau came under military control and drew from its ranks, the comparison is useful. The average Union soldier, according to historian Bell I. Wiley, was 26.3 at the war's conclusion. The average SAC in Texas was about five to ten years older than his Billy Yank counterfpart.[26]

With many challenges inherent in Bureau work (long hours and inspection tours with little or no help), it was generally not a job for the old. Almost one-third (n=46, or 29.8 percent) in 1870 were forty or older, and of those whose age could be confirmed (n=154), slightly more than 10 percent (n=16, or 10.4 percent) had reached at least fifty. Despite the selection of officers, often older than the men they led, these men would still have been young enough to meet the agency's demands. Prewar politics might also have played a part. As noted by Richard G. Lowe's study, the Virginia Bureau avoided members of the Democracy, the party identified with secession and slavery. The average agent in Texas would have been barely voting age and less likely to have been identified with the state's (or the South's) slaveholding politics.[27]

The Bureau generally drew from the wealthy (real estate and personal property combined for the 1870 federal census) between $1,000 and $4,999.[28] On average, they held approximately $2,540 in real estate and slightly more than $1,427 in personal property, which totaled approximately $3,967 in wealth (n=110). While some were worth tens of thousands of dollars, 63 individuals listed their total wealth (real estate + personal property) below $1,000, with a significant portion with no valued wealth. Using measurements from the *Ninth Census, Statistics of Wealth and Industry*, and *Historical Statistics of the United States*, an average white head-of-household in 1870 had more than $2,141[29] in total wealth. Although SACs in Texas held almost twice the amount of wealth as the average head-of-household ($3,967 compared to $2,141) in the United States in 1870, nearly six in ten (n=63, or 57.3 percent) of Bureau men either had no wealth or were not financially well-off (below $1,000 in wealth).[30]

The numbers reveal a dichotomy in wealth between SACs in Texas. A student of wealth in nineteenth-century America, Lee Soltow defines very poor as hav-

Table 1-4   Wealth of Subassistant Commissioners in Texas

$ Value of Wealth	0	1–249	250–499	500–999	1,000–4,999	5,000–9,999	10,000+
Number of Agents	43	6	4	10	22	14	11
Percentage	39.1	5.5	3.6	9.1	20	12.7	10

Note: Determination of each agent's wealth came from the 1870 U.S. Census.

ing no real estate or personal property. He found that 61.6 percent of whites in 1870 had at least $100 or more in wealth. These numbers correspond with Bureau agents in Texas: 60.9 percent of Bureau men had real estate or personal property of at least $100. A closer look at asset holders shows that 40.9 percent held only real estate. That percentage corresponds with the 43.3 percent of white property holders in 1870. Slightly less than 42 percent (41.8) held only personal property. This equals almost 50 percent lower than the white male population in 1870 (61.6 percent). Broken down by age, those holding property in Texas corresponds with the country as a whole.[31]

These findings differ from those in other studies. Paul A. Cimbala, for instance, examining the Bureau in Georgia, discovered officials appointed men who, on average, were twice as wealthy as Texas agents (n~$8,000).[32] Cimbala's population (including a much higher percentage of former slaveholders) helps explain the difference. The varying findings for Texas and Georgia demonstrate that officials in Washington, D.C., did not impose one policy for the organization. Instead, officials in each state were free to implement policies of their choosing, according to conditions within their districts. Broken down by specific occupation, those in the farming profession averaged around $3,861 in real estate (not unexpected) and slightly less than $2,678 in personal wealth. Former slave owners far exceeded those yeomen farmers (those who did not own slaves) in both categories. Individuals in the legal profession (n=12)—lawyers, judges, and law enforcement—held just under $2,367 in real estate and around $1,583 in personal wealth. Soldiers (those whose wealth could be established in the 1870 census, n=43) possessed slightly more than $1,000 ($1,007) in real estate and slightly below $802 in personal (the average of other occupations was not included due to only one to three people).[33]

Why would the Freedmen's Bureau turn to such financially prosperous individuals? Certainly officials wanted those inspired to help the freedpeople, imbued with good Republican ideology, and steeled for the trials and tribulations that awaited them in Texas; but these characteristics were hardly limited to those with wealth. The answer might partially lie with the high percentage of heads-of-households (84 of 105, or 80 percent) or married men (n=62, or 59 percent), each contributing in its own way to increased wealth. The answer might be explained by the constant struggle for funds that plagued the agency from its inception. With restraints on spending, including salaries for civilian agents and allocations for supplies, Bureau officials wanted individuals not reliant upon the salary and men with some disposable income. Officials rarely countenanced complaints about pay (a red flag indicating commitment to money rather than to his duties), usually reminding the complainant of "[m]any requests for employment, the writers of which, are strongly recommended" and warning that "worthy and capable men can be procured to fill the vacancies." A perusal of the records uncovers few complaints about monthly salaries (ranging from slightly less than $100 a month to $150 a month) and noticeable instances of SACs purchasing supplies and providing charity out-of-pocket. The intense scrutiny of the Freedmen's Bureau and the nineteenth-century philosophy on government spending meant officials had to stretch every dollar, and solvent agents helped in this course.[34]

Measurements of wealth and demographic traits are revealing, but they do not explain *why* these men wanted to be Bureau agents. Despite the voluminous Bureau records for Texas, there existed only application letters for twenty-four men (these are only of those who received an appointment). As desirous as it would be to have many more, these two dozen applications, nonetheless, shed light onto what motivated someone to pursue Bureau service. References to military service, Northern origin, and other perceived indicators of Union sentiment and loyalty litter these applications and letters of recommendations. Highlights of upstanding character and intelligence likewise appear. Few applications referenced only one reason for qualification. Most, in fact, highlighted multiple reasons for applying (see Table 1-5).

Since the Bureau was a quasi-military organization, applicants naturally stressed their service during the war. With more than three-quarters of SACs for Texas having military experience, Bureau officials favored a martial background. The prevailing opinion of the professional military at the time explains this. Discipline and regimentation, among other attributes such as patriotism and unionism, were generally believed to accompany any applicant with military experience. Military service notwithstanding, an appeal to one's character and competence was the only other reason to appear in a majority of the appli-

Table 1-5   Primary Reason Agents in Texas Cited for Employment in Freedmen's Bureau

Reason	Military Service	Economic/ Job Reasons	Protecting the Freedmen	Character and Competence	Patriotism, Unionism, and Anti-Confederacy
Number of Agents Citing in Application	14	9	8	12	7
Percentage of Total Applications	58.3	37.5	33.3	50	29.2

Note: Reasons came from letter or application for employment to Assistant Commissioner in Texas.

cations. It surpassed free-standing appeals to one's patriotism, unionism, and hatred for the "so-called Confederacy" as well as clarion calls for protecting the freedmen. At first glance, considering the nature of the work, this lack of idealism and zealotry for the former slaves is surprising. But this quasi-military organization most likely preferred pragmatism and common sense above idealism and zealotry.

Such applicants fell into two main groups: those with military service and those without, with the former typically highlighting their service above all else. They definitely believed their sacrifice for the Union was qualification enough for an appointment. Those lacking this experience (usually too old for military service) expressed their loyalty through claims of persecution by the Confederate government or resistance to secession.[35]

Civilian applicants followed expressions of loyalty most of the time with claims of compassion for the freedpeople, an expression rarely seen in applicants with a martial background. The difference in the applications (besides the obvious fact of military service) might be explained by the applicant's locality. Civilians, by and large, applied from the South. They needed to lessen skepticism and doubts about their loyalty. Applicants from Union states, with military service and location attesting to their devotion to republican ideals, did not have to go as far in proving their loyalty. Such things certainly helped headquarters choose the "right kind of man": one committed to the ideals of the Old Flag. And certainly some of these men wanted to "reconstruct" a land seemingly devoid of such ideals. Patriotism and republicanism appear to have touched all the agents in one form or another, but ideals alone fall short in explaining deeper and more personal motives. More practical reasons motivated some.

The applicants stressed the opportunities Bureau service afforded to help the emancipated slaves. One of the first agents appointed, Eli W. Green, was moved by such a desire and "determined that the Negroes shall not be imposed upon" by unscrupulous whites. The agent at Liberty, A. H. Mayer, took great pride in his work, wanting "to make [the South] my home" and to protect the freedmen in their contractual rights, "particularly so, for the just payment of their labor." Freedom and justice for the freedpeople appeared to move George C. Abbott to service. The veteran of the United States Navy believed black men and women now "Free American Cittizens [sic]," and he "determined that no amount of ignorance, rage, or wretchedness" would "bias" him in favor of "sleek and well-fed ex-Rebels who for four years past have been amusing themselves by hunting down and hanging Americans, who[se] only crime was loyalty to Government

which had protected them when they were too weak to protect themselves."
He admitted never devoting much interest to them prior to emancipation,
and did not believe it "possible that I could become so deeply interested in
these people."[36]

"But now," he confessed, "Freed men as they are, they seem to me more
utterly friendless and defenceless [sic] than any people on the face of God's
earth." Consequently, Abbott followed the Golden Rule, "Do as you would be
done by." Through his and others' committed efforts, Abbott augured a not
too distant time when the freedpeople "shall gain the rights that white men
have. . . ." William H. Farner, a "scalawag" and resident of Brazos County,
promised "that the rights and interests of the freedmen, women [and] children
will be guarded with the same fidelity that I would those of my own household."
His future actions after leaving the Bureau, however, might cast doubt on his
words, when some accused him of abuse. Albert Evans, an officer in the 116th
U.S.C.T., disregarded the possibility of personal harm. The officer stated his
concern "for the condition of the freedmen and their cries for help." Evans
wanted "to render some real benefit to them," and believed any apathy on his
part would "hinder" the government's effort. With his muster out imminent,
Evans begged superiors to allow him to help solve the many problems the former slaves in Texas faced: "I would much prefer going north . . . than to remain
here so far as my personal comfort were it not for the condition of the freedmen
and their cries for help. I want to render some real benefit to them."[37]

"Scalawag" Philip Howard wanted to participate in the "best cause," helping
the "poor and oppressed negro." On several occasions, he helped poor freedpeople out of his own pocket. Regardless of his financial situation, Howard
knew he was "doing a good service." With a little tinge of patriotism, he stated
that his "convictions are to save the south from [another] Bloody Rebellion
[and] to arm the Blacks with armes [sic] and the Ballot. . . ." Former slave owner
James A. Hogue, who desired to protect "the freedmen from injustice and
fraud," claimed to have "no selfish motive" and wanted the appointment "without compensation." Hogue promised to have a strong "moral influence" on his
charges.[38]

John H. Morrison, a "scalawag" who called himself a refugee because he had
to leave the state during the war, also appeared moved by the plight of the
oppressed. Inspector and fellow Bureau agent William H. Sinclair described
him as an "out and out Union man," who was concerned about the harassment
and threats against the freedpeople in Anderson County. "I think these things
should be nipped in the bud," Morrison recommended, and he believed himself
the man to do so. "I feel an interest in the welfare of the freedmen," he stated; he

promised to always be "found battling for the rights of the unfortunate and the prosperity of my country."[39]

Along with equality for the former slaves, a few agents also wanted to promote Radical Republican ideology. This ideology certainly encompassed other motivating factors, like free labor and political expediency, but the plight of the freedpeople swayed most of those who called themselves Radical. William Price, former soldier in the 1st Texas Cavalry (Union) and refugee (which might show his loyalty to the Union through resistance to the Confederacy), came highly recommended by Texas Republicans like Edmund Jackson Davis, Andrew Jackson Hamilton, and Edward Degener for his Radical beliefs. So too were Hardin Hart, Mortimer H. Goddin, and Edwin Miller Wheelock, who was one of the few agents whose abolitionist past could be confirmed. Although some described themselves as Radical and others just subscribed to aspects of the ideology, the evidence shows their numbers were quite small compared to Texas Bureau agents who identified themselves as conservative or moderate Republicans.[40]

Many men answered the call to duty because of patriotism. John Dix, a strong Unionist from Corpus Christi, experienced great persecution during the war. Because of his opposition to secession and resistance to the state Confederate government, Dix had his property confiscated and had his life and freedom threatened when indicted for treason late in the war. Nonetheless, Dix claimed these actions "never in the slightest degree swerve[d] him from his loyalty." The same could be said of J. Orville Shelby, a "gentleman of the highest personal social and moral worth." (This is not the Confederate cavalry officer with the same name.) During the war, Confederates "insulted," "outraged," and "imprisoned" Shelby for his principles. He claimed to be a "stirling [sic] patriot who would rather have lost his life than seen the enemies of his country triumph." It seems men such as these two, having been persecuted for their Unionist beliefs during the war, wanted to serve the U.S. government and deliver the same values and ideology, which prompted his persecution, to former Confederates.[41]

Men like William H. Horton perhaps wanted Bureau service for a more practical reason. After losing an arm at Chancellorsville, he transferred to the Veteran Reserve Corps, a special branch of the military that allowed men with debilitating injuries to continue the war effort. The Freedmen's Bureau drew from the VRC to make up for those lost to mustering out. Edward Miller, who lost an arm at Williamsburg, seemed "anxious to remain in the Service. . . ." Samuel A. Craig, Henry H. E(d)dleson, J. Ernest Goodman, James F. Hutchison, Isaac M. Beebe, Lemuel K. Morton, and Albert A. Metzner also served as officers in the VRC. Fifteen men from the corps served as subassistant commissioners in

Texas. Motivated to some extent by patriotism, pride, and a desire to help the emancipated slaves, these men most certainly wanted to prove their continued worth to the country and society in general.[42]

Others simply wanted to continue with the government. Charles Schmidt wanted an appointment after clerking for the Bureau for an extended time. Henry Young, who aided the agent in Austin for nearly a year, wanted to move up the ladder with the agency. Michael Butler, former seaman with the U.S. Navy, came to Texas with his brother after the war. He assisted the SAC at Huntsville, becoming "somewhat acquainted with the people and the duties of the office." When that agent resigned, Butler asked to be considered as his replacement. George Eber, already employed with the Bureau of Internal Revenue, was told by his friend and Bureau man Charles Haughn that he could "get a situation in the employ of the U.S. Government." Robert McClermont wanted to bring his family to Texas, but his service in the cavalry prevented "having any permanent post [for his family] to remain at." In order to continue with the government and be at a post "two or more years," McClermont applied to the Bureau.[43]

Men like Jacob C. DeGress, one of the first agents in the state, on the other hand, were more influenced by the Northern ideal of free labor, for nearly every letter refers to the state of labor relations in his district. The agent at Indianola, Eugene Smith, noting few plantations in Indianola, also put high priority on protecting contractual rights. "I cannot do the good here," he stated, "that was intended by the Bureau." Some may claim that since the main objective of the Bureau was to regulate the labor situation in the state, it would be natural for these and other agents to include references to labor in their reports. A perusal of correspondences between agents and headquarters does not exactly show this, however, since not all field agents focused attention on the same issues. In fact, one way to help discern the motivations of applicants is to see what they focused on after their appointment. How they comprehended their duties perhaps sheds light into their motivations for entering the agency.[44]

In the emotionally and politically charged Reconstruction era, it is certain some entered Bureau service for other than noble motives. Some held a vengeful spirit toward the vanquished, or wished "to show my former oppressors that they were, and not I, 'wrong.'" Consider the case of William Longworth, the agent in Wilson County and author of that sentiment. He strove to make his district a "model one," by vigorously protecting the economic and civil interests of the freedpeople. In his pursuit of justice for the former slaves, however, superiors concluded "he has often done great injustice to them." A Unionist during the war, Longworth used his office to exact revenge: "I am always in the Front receiving the brunt of the battle, for me there is no recreation and to me there will be no mercy shown by my political opponents."[45]

As in war, Longworth believed one must never give quarter to or compromise with the enemy. "There is no word in the language that causes my [blood] to rise equal to that of, Conciliation," he declared. "[Y]ou might as well try to conciliate a pack of Hyenas by throwing one of your children to them with the hope of saving the rest." A later investigation found that Longworth unnecessarily antagonized the white community with his "vengeful spirit," often encouraging freedmen to continue suing employers in cases that had already been resolved to the satisfaction of both parties, and then would impose an "arbitrary and unjust" fine. Considering his actions, a Bureau inspector admitted being "truly surprised (considering the style in Texas) that he was not summarily dealt with by some one" for "in many communities he would have been." In his application letter Longworth yearned "to ameliorate the condition of the Negro," but his unwise course and vindictive manner appeared only to have worsened it.[46]

Finally, the reality was most applicants simply needed employment, no matter how selfless their other motives. John H. Morrison's application highlights a realistic aspect of applying to the agency. Concerned for the "welfare [sic] of the Freedmen" in Anderson County, Morrison nevertheless needed the appointment because he had "but little of this world's goods," informing he sacrificed "for the good of the cause," stating he had to leave his family, and "during my absence all my property was squandered. . . ." Mahlon E. Davis, David S. Beath, and a number of others also expressed desire for work as they faced financial uncertainty.[47]

After his muster out, Patrick F. Duggan, "with a view of becoming a resident of the South," wanted someone to "confer a favor on me by assisting me to a position in some of the offices of the other department of this State." George Johnson, needing such an appointment as his muster out neared, requested "the appointment . . . at any Station in Texas you may designate." He must have found a better offer, because shortly after receiving his appointment, Bureau headquarters revoked it due to his "having reconsidered his application." William Holt, willing to go anywhere in Texas, also was prompted by his impending discharge from the military. N. H. Randlett had a more pressing reason for his desire for employment. With his muster out imminent, Randlett worried about providing for his family, which he had brought to Texas, and pressed for reappointment as a civilian Bureau agent.[48]

Philip Howard also applied for monetary reasons. He complained the war "crippled me in the way of money." A. F. N. Rolfe, a graduate of Oxford University and college professor in the Northeast, found the academy "gave no [financial] prospects." An appointment in the Freedmen's Bureau would ease his financial problems. "I hope you may be able, without detriment to the Service," he wrote, "to please a stranger amongst strangers in a position of relief." A "scalawag" resident in Hill County, Edwin Finch professed to be "a thorough, out and out Union man," resulting in his destitution. Albert Evans, who yearned to return north at some time, lacked the immediate funds and requested employment until "I can get a settlement."[49]

Then there is the case of James Burke. A native of the South, he claimed to be an "<u>original</u> <u>union</u> man—a lifelong hater of slavery." He certified his unionism as he voted against secession and gave no willing aid to the Rebellion. Burke held a "deep interest in the education of Freedmen" and promised to "<u>honestly</u> and <u>earnestly</u>, to the best of my ability, endeavor to discharge my duty." Bureau officials later relieved him from duty when they discovered he ran (but lost) for local office in Confederate Texas during the war. Perhaps Burke might have been like countless other men who accepted change and embraced the current course from Washington. Reconstruction historian Richard G. Lowe finds such individuals in his study of prospective office holders in Virginia. But Burke himself shed light on his application when he informed Bureau officials that "I desire the office. I <u>need</u> it." To be sure, as shown by historian Lawrence Powell and viewed in the light of the importance of earning a living, these men's explicit solicitation for employment does not necessarily nullify their other motives.[50]

The evidence shows that many things motivated these men. But what most motivated them? Was it patriotism or an opportunity for revenge against former Confederates? Perhaps they were simply in need of employment? Or did they focus on the Bureau's mission, desiring to help the former slaves adjust to freedom? As with so many things involving people, there rarely is a single answer, but rather a combination. To ascribe this reason or that one to these men greatly oversimplifies the complicated. It appears several motives drove them to Bureau service.

Of course, each agent wanted employment. But it might well have been easier, safer, and, for most agents, financially better to have found a different occupation—for those whose wartime injuries inhibited their physical ability, service in the Bureau may have been their only plausible choice. There existed far deeper reasons for wanting the responsibilities than just employment. What appears to have motivated most Bureau men in Texas, to a great degree, was their honest desire to help the former slaves, something supported by the agency's records and small number of troublesome agents and complaints by freedpeople. Doubtless, these men had a strong philanthropic streak. They earnestly wanted to help the helpless, and, in the words of one agent, not allow them to be cast adrift. The white community knew this, as witnessed by the endemic antagonism toward Bureau men. More important, the former slaves knew this, as witnessed by their numerous requests for redress, their many appeals for assistance, and trust in the men of the Bureau. Too many examples exist of agents protecting the freedpeople from white abuse, and too few examples exist to the contrary to conclude anything else. "In sum total," stated William H. Heistand, the agent at Hallettsville, "my duties consist [in looking] over the interest of the Freedpeople and in acting as their adviser and protector." Whatever their reason, most who applied shared one thing in common: the proud satisfaction of doing one's best, regardless of the outcome. In a report to headquarters, John T. Scott, whose statement certainly embodied the opinion of many of his fellow agents, relayed that he had "tried to do the best I could for all parties, and it may be hard for any one not upon the spot to understand."[51]

In summary, in selecting agents, Bureau officials in Texas wanted men able to meet the challenges that arose from emancipation. That meant Northern-born, mature, white men from the middle and upper-middle class, and generally with military experience, while shying away from Southern-born men who had been part of the planter class of the Old South. Bureau officials, with their appointments, addressed not just the needs of the freedpeople, but also something else. In a very hopeful sense, Reconstruction was a process to remake the South in the image of the capitalistic and republican North. But it also was, in a much more practical sense, a time to prevent the South from trying to break up the country again and restore order where chaos had existed. This could be achieved only by wiping away the last vestiges of slavery and secession, and Northern patriotic Union men were more likely to advance the new order than anyone else.

2

"The Post of Greatest Peril"

The E. M. Gregory Era,
September 1865–April 1866

On March 3, 1865, after much debate, Congress created, according to W. E. B. DuBois, one of the most "singular and interesting of the attempts made by a great nation to grapple with vast problems of race and social condition." The Bureau was responsible for the freedpeople's transition from servitude to freedom during Reconstruction, a daunting task, the likes of which had never been tried before, and one that some people and forces would make very difficult.[1]

Such an undertaking required the right kind of man, someone imbued with patience and purpose, yet studied in managerial and bureaucratic ways. One who saw the emancipated "not as he was supposed to be in 1865—illiterate, childlike, improvident, inferior—but as a man with the same potentialities as any other man." Washington officials selected Oliver Otis Howard to head this unprecedented and ill-defined organization, and he would be its only commissioner in its seven-year existence. Many applauded but few envied this appointment. "I hardly know whether to congratulate you or not," Major General William T. Sherman admitted to his friend and former subordinate. "I cannot imagine [matters] that involve the future of 4,000,000 souls could be put in more charitable and more conscientious hands . . . I fear you have Hercules's task. . . ." A general and a devout Christian, Howard earned a reputation as a righteous, if not brilliant, soul. The agency existed only on paper. Years later in his *Autobiography*, Howard remembered. He recalled Secretary of War Edwin Stanton handing him a basket and remarking with a smile, "Here, general, here's your Bureau!"[2]

With his organization literally in both hands, Commissioner Howard began to man it with personnel. He initially appointed ten (later twelve) subordinates throughout the former slaveholding South. These men, called assistant commissioners (AC), oversaw Bureau operations within their specified jurisdictions. In July 1865 Howard requested and received approval from the War

Department to appoint sixty-one-year-old[3] Edgar Mandlebert Gregory for Bureau service. Prior to the war, he worked (and ultimately failed) as a lumber merchant and banker. Gregory did not let such failures dampen his spirits. A native New Yorker known for a caring nature, Gregory entered the army in 1861 with the 91st Pennsylvania Volunteer Regiment, a unit in the Army of the Potomac. Devoutly religious and a temperance advocate, he received the nickname "the Fighting Parson" during the war. After hearing about an encounter during the Siege of Petersburg where Gregory had two horses shot out from under him, General Charles Griffin, his superior and later an AC in Texas, humorously observed Gregory was advantaged since most men feared "both the Rebels and hell, whereas Gregory was in danger only from the Rebels!" He varied the "duties of military life by preaching and conducting prayer-meeting services at his own brigade headquarters." He fought at Antietam, was wounded at Fredericksburg and Chancellorsville, promoted for his action before Petersburg, and witnessed the Confederate surrender at Appomattox. Doubtless brave, later historians are not in consensus about the extent of his abolitionism. Less uncertain was his commitment to the emancipated. Howard believed him so genuine and "fearless of opposition or danger" he specifically sent him to Texas, an assignment believed to be "the post of greatest peril." After his removal from Texas in early 1866, Gregory was reassigned within the Bureau. He died in Philadelphia in 1871.[4]

Meanwhile, Gregory arrived in Galveston in early September 1865, and assumed responsibility from the military. Since mid-June 1865, when Brevet General Gordon Granger announced to Texans the Emancipation Proclamation, the military had responsibility for the freedpeople. Gregory kept much of what the military had started. Besides a few guidelines and some wise advice by Howard to refrain from "ill-advised" policies, the AC, for the most part, was free to use his best judgment. After setting headquarters in Galveston (the state's port of entry), Gregory toured the state. He relied on these tours for valuable information and took four in his nine months' service in Texas. What he discovered was the war had barely touched the state. In a few places, the "breakup" ushered in chaos. But in other areas life went on relatively unchanged, with some slaves in the interior having not yet been informed of emancipation.[5]

With information from his tours, Gregory began sifting through applications for positions, a process that was primarily his responsibility with little interference from superiors. It was important to choose wisely since these men would be the flesh and blood of the organization. But the prospective applicant pool was limited. With no funds allocated for civilian agents and few willing to do the work unpaid, officers were chosen from regiments already in Texas. The organization would have been nothing more than a dream without the military. Drawing from army personnel had certain disadvantages. Along with ongoing demilitarization, another hurdle was the military itself, as bureaucratic and self-serving as any other institution. More than a few detached duty with the Freedmen's Bureau, especially if he was simultaneously to serve as agent and commanding officer. Sometimes he was still enlisted and superiors were hesitant to lose their better personnel for such service. On the other hand, the armed forces could use the opportunity to purge some "troublesome" individuals from its ranks.[6]

Gregory initially asked for only fifteen officers. Inspector General of the Freedmen's Bureau William E. Strong, however, pressed for fifty, desiring a larger footprint. "The campaign of an army through the eastern part of the State, such as was made by General Sherman in South Carolina," Strong concluded, "would improve the temper and generosity of the people." Realizing the enormity of the task, Gregory asked his boss for an additional fifteen men a few months later—although he really wanted an additional seventy. Howard denied the request for even the smaller number, however. The initial twelve Bureau agents would have to do.[7]

Of the first twelve, who were generally assigned to places of greatest need or importance such as major cities or areas with larger black populations, seven served the Union in the war, including one in the navy. Most came from the volunteer services, and one served as an officer in a U.S.C.T. unit. To help offset the shortage, Gregory, with cautious encouragement from superiors, turned to civilians. William H. Farner was a physician, and Ira P. Pedigo was a lawyer and lumber businessman. John F. Brown, Johnathan F. Whiteside, and F. D. Inge worked in the agricultural business, with the latter two having owned slaves. All declared their willingness to serve without pay so long as they could remain in their current jobs and serve within their home counties. These men, at least on the surface, benefited the agency. First, they were no expense to the government; and second, they knew the community's surroundings and people (although some historians would not see this as a plus) and were viewed less as outsiders. On the other hand, they had to work other jobs for support, thus splitting their commitment. Doubtless, a small footprint, these assignments still helped to stabilize operations with the freedpeople.[8]

Because of the Freedmen's Bureau bill's "disfigured" and "loose and indefinite phraseology," Gregory himself had to ensure uniformity for his district—a difficult task considering his vague mandate. Agents were to oversee the transition to free labor and, at the same time, dispel any ideas the emancipated might have of not working. They also had to ensure their civil rights and inculcate respect for the law. White Texans also had to be disabused of old ways. When civil officials failed to render impartial justice, agents had authority to adjudicate "all cases arising between Freedmen themselves or between Freedmen and white persons" and "between whites when the matter in dispute relates to freedmen." SACs were to dispense color-blind justice, for only "a spirit of fairness and great discretion . . . may conquer the opposition of all reasonable men." The military would lend assistance upon request.[9]

Before beginning their work, they needed to establish an office and find quarters. The two often were the same. With complainants calling at all hours, rarely paying attention to office hours, this necessitated combining the two spaces. Rent ranged from three dollars to fifteen dollars a month, and any amount above, superiors often questioned. Requisitions for rent had to be sent to headquarters, where, if agreed to by officials in Washington (later by a board in Galveston), the proprietor received a monthly check. In no instance was the agent to pay out-of-pocket for official business (circumstance made that impractical). Superiors required the office to be in a convenient location, like a county seat or populous city. In districts comprising multiple counties, however, it generally was located in the most populous county in the district. Superiors required a posting of office hours. Complainants rarely respected set hours.[10]

Finding quarters appeared on the surface the easiest of tasks, and for many it was. But for others it proved quite troublesome. "[E]very where I stop to get meals and accommodation," one harassed agent reported, "they charge me the highest specie price." He described it as "humiliating." H. W. Allen at Hempstead in early 1866 wrote about his landlady. She complained, he reported, when he took business out in the hallway instead of in his room, and she "forbids its continuance." Allen believed he might be justified to secure another office, but he wanted permission before acting. A week later, after no response, a frustrated Allen reiterated his problems in another letter. His superiors took offense to his letter, as his frustration and aggravation was evident. "This communication is impertinent and uncalled for," they responded. "[A] repetition of such language will not be overlooked." Such conflicts between proprietors and agents continued throughout the agency's existence.[11]

Superiors sometimes frustrated subordinates more than white Texans. One example best highlights such frustration experienced by field agents. It further highlights the belief field agents had that superiors sometimes trivialized and ignored their problems. "The endorsement of the board [the one to determine office rent] in regard to the <u>little</u> matter of office rent is . . . calculated to cut," wrote a frustrated P. B. Johnson from Woodville in 1867. "When I find that I am not more respected by the officers of the Bureau, I shall not consider myself a proper person [to] fill the important functions of S.A. Com." Further underscoring his point, Johnson added: "I do not mind any of my applications to be simply disapproved; that, I can understand, and have no right to question. But in this, there seems to be query: 'Why an office at one place costs more than at another[?]' " Throughout the Bureau's existence, its field agents routinely complained about the difficulties in obtaining (as well as the lack of) office furniture and receiving from headquarters the required amount of office supplies (i.e., pens, ink, stationery, etc.). Problems arose not so much because of white Texans' actions or attitudes but because of bureaucracy's nature. The agency was supposed to draw supplies from the military. This caused much delay and confusion, since some army officers did not feel "authorized to serve the officers of this Bureau." Consider the case of William Longworth at Sutherland Springs. He worried that his lack of furniture will lead some "to suspect I am flinching in the cause." An exasperated Longworth reminded headquarters of his situation:

> Remember I am away in the wilderness, far from any post or district commander, and scarcely recognized by them when I presented myself, and have not yet had the assistance of as much as a bottle of ink. And all the while a disaffected community foaming and raging around me, I have to maintain a hospital and boarding house for all . . . under my cognizance, together with transportation for the sick and helpless, and all entirely out of my own pocket.[12]

With contract fees forbidden (for the time being), agents routinely used personal expenses, despite discouragement by superiors. Examples abound in out-of-pocket expenses for office supplies, horse feed, fuel, and assistance. "I have several times employed special agents when it was impossible for me to go myself," wrote one agent, "and in each instance have paid such agents myself." Congressional funds for agents' salaries in July 1866 went a long way to remedy this situation, but instances of men spending their own money to perform official duties continued throughout the organization's existence. John Dix at Corpus Christi in December 1867 had to pay for both his and a detachment of soldiers' supplies. "I have not been able to get one dollar refunded," he reminded superiors. "And therefore I respectfully ask your aid in pointing out some way for me to receive the amount I have expended."[13]

A few raised their superiors' ire with unauthorized expenses and instances of improper use of materials. Officials issued many a reprimand for excessive and improper use of stationery and unauthorized expenses for school books, scouts, guides, transportation, and requests for reimbursement for personal expenses. For example, A. P. Delano and A. H. Mayer, the SACs at Marlin Falls and Liberty, respectively, were reprimanded for what superiors believed to be repeated and flagrant disregard of policy. They repeatedly informed A. P. Delano that the Bureau lacked funds for hiring scouts or guides, only to have him request funds for such hired help. "I am surprised that you should still employ scouts and guides," replied assistant quartermaster Samuel I. Wright to the less-than-compliant agent, "after the conversation we had in regard to it." Wright's replacement, Charles Garretson, who appeared to enjoy reminding subordinates they had exceeded their authority and that there "is but one Disbursing Officer of the Bureau in this state," experienced similar problems when he questioned A. H. Mayer's postal expenditures. "The accounts of no SAC in the State, presented a corresponding increase" and with no explanation as to why, he noted. "There may be some circumstances connected with the Post of Liberty, which [would] justify a larger disbursement for Postage, than that which takes place at the much more important post of Marshall." The quartermaster responded to a request for fifty-three quires (unbound reams of paper) by suspiciously asking, "How [can you] require 10 times [the necessary] amount . . . in addition to the 3 quires allowed [each 5 months]?" Bureau records include numerous such admonishments and rejections. The actions by Delano and Mayer affected not only their dealings with superiors, but also the relations between those at headquarters and all those in the field. A select few cast suspicion on all and contributed to a perception at headquarters that subordinates lacked frugality. This contributed to a rift between superiors and their agents. Whether responsible or not, all complained about supply problems. In many instances, in fact, officials failed to provide subordinates with even the minimum monthly allowance of office supplies or basic furniture called for in the *Officers' Manual*, which superiors required all to have and refer to for guidance. They charged agents with what many believed an impossible task and never fully supplied them with the most basic aids.[14]

Insufficient supplies became such an issue that superiors sent William H. Sinclair, Bureau Inspector for Texas, to investigate in 1867. In his report, he discovered that many in the interior lacked the tools "for the proper and regular discharge of their duties." Sinclair admonished headquarters for the "discouraging and perplexing" feeling by subordinates. "This subject might to some seem a small matter," he warned, "but to the agents . . . it is not." The supply breakdown became quite frustrating at times; even boiling over into direct conflict with superiors. Drawing the most ire and seen by some as primarily responsible for the lack of supplies was Assistant Quartermaster Charles Garretson. Garretson and David L. Montgomery conflicted for several reasons, including Montgomery's requisition for stationery. In addition, in late summer of 1867, Montgomery complained about not receiving his pay. Garretson endorsed the letter as follows:

> Respectfully returned to Head Quarters . . . with the information that although certified accounts for Office Rent were transmitted to this office by Col. Montgomery his office [rent] has not been reported to this day on Form No. 21 and no account for services or Rent can be paid until reported. Col. Montgomery's report of Persons etc. for April & May were both received at this office 30th June 1867. The May report was returned for correction and was not received corrected until 9th August 1867. On . . . 8th July Col. Montgomery's first voucher in favor of B. H. Denson was returned for correction. On . . . 20th July his second voucher in favor of B. H. Denson was returned for correction. On . . . 27th July his certified accounts in favor of William J. Goodman for office rent were returned for correction and have not yet been received correct nor has Col. Montgomery's report of Persons for June 1867 been received corrected. Until Col. Montgomery's Reports of Persons for March, April, May & June have been perfected, William J. Goodman's account for Office Rent cannot be paid. My absence at San Antonio and the illness of the whole of the clerks with this office have prevented B. H. Denson's account from being paid between 14th Aug. & the present date. It is submitted that under the circumstances detailed above Col. Montgomery is scarcely in a position to complain of the non payment of his certified accounts. It is now 13th of Sept. and his report of Persons & articles for June is not on File in this office.[15]

Montgomery, angry about the whole ordeal, took matters into his own hands. He purchased stationery and sent the voucher to Garretson for reimbursement. The assistant quartermaster rejected it, noting the problem stemmed from the agent's "incompleteness or incorrectness of every Report." Montgomery accused Garretson of neglect and incompetence, only to have him ask who the true incompetent was, considering Montgomery could not follow orders or properly complete forms. These feuds, which continued until the agency's end, reflected a serious problem within the Bureau's chain of command in Texas.[16]

Those appointed by Gregory experienced many of the same problems as their successors. But they also faced unique problems, ones stemming from the immediate aftermath of the war. Of particular concern was a rumor among the freedpeople that they would receive land from the federal government. The government would supposedly confiscate and divide Southern plantations into forty-acre plots among the former slaves in late 1865. "The Negroes had left their old homes and were refusing to make contracts for the new year with any person," reported John T. Raper from Columbus. "They were waiting for a division of property." The freedpeople's refusal to contract threatened to derail free labor in Texas. The president's pardons of wealthy former Confederates, which reestablished their right to their land; Commissioner Howard's Circular No. 15, which rescinded his previous circular laying out procedures for distribution of confiscated land to ex-slaves; the almost sacrosanct belief Americans had toward private property; and Northern Republicans' unwillingness to "disturb the traditional relationships between capital and labor" all combined to quash land redistribution—if it ever was a realistic option. Gregory then instructed field personnel to immediately "remove so erroneous and injurious an impression." This was difficult, because even after the 1865 holiday season passed with no land distribution, the rumor persisted. At Liberty, for example, agent A. H. Mayer described freedpeople as late as 1868 still believing they would receive land, this time from the Radical Republicans with their election to office in Texas. "I regret to state," he frustratingly stated about his attempts to disabuse them of this belief, "that all my efforts have been abortive, and will continue to be so long as bad men control them. . . ."[17]

Further complicating matters, some white Texans feared once freedpeople realized no land was coming, they would rise up in rebellion. The holiday season of 1865 portended another Santo Domingo (i.e., a bloody slave uprising between 1791 and 1804) in the minds of many whites. Christmastime instilled hope for one group, but brought fear to another. All the hysteria, optimism, and, ultimately, frustration late in 1865 turned out to be nothing more than a momentary concern for Bureau men. Of more lasting importance was the implementation of free labor, something considered the "knottiest problem of modern times." With slavery's demise, a new labor system had to be implanted in the South. This objective constituted the basis of the Freedmen's Bureau operations and to a great extent, its success greatly hinged on its agents' efforts.

From late 1865 on, Bureau men would struggle with developing a system of free labor in Texas. The difficulties faced by agents in late 1865 and early 1866, although "fixed" at certain times and on certain occasions, remained to befuddle their successors.[18]

The agency's name disguises its true mission, for it could have been easily called the Labor Bureau. To nineteenth-century Americans, free labor meant economic mobility, equality before the law, contract labor, self-sufficiency, and property ownership, and, despite any flaws and contradictions, it exemplified what Northern society believed good, contrasted by what was wrong and backward about the slaveholding South. Northerners saw the war's outcome as a triumph of their economic system, and through the Bureau they planned to sow the seeds of free labor in slavery's ashes. "If federal troops introduced emancipation on the point of a bayonet during their war," declared Jeffrey R. Kerr-Ritchie, a student of Virginia Reconstruction, "their [Bureau] cousins were charged with imposing free labor negotiations under the nib of a pen."[19]

Influenced by the military's policies during the war, Commissioner Howard issued a circular letter that vaguely framed the agency's free labor system. He instructed subordinates in May 1865 to introduce "a practical system of compensated labor" and to dissuade the freed community that they did not have to work. In extreme cases exceptions could be made, but no aid was to be granted to the able-bodied. Howard realized this might cause some suffering, but that was to be expected. But idleness, a sinful, personal flaw contrary to man's existence on earth, must not to be tolerated. The commissioner believed their freedom would come through their labor and thus viewed the examination of contracts as "the most important duty of an agent upon being assigned." He hoped to "rehabilitate labor" in each state and "establish the actual freedom of the late slave." Freedom measured by "justice in settling past contracts and in making new ones." The policy turned Bureau agents into a vast army of "employment agents."[20]

Avoiding rigidity, which might stifle experimentation on the part of planters and the freedpeople, Howard left his subordinates to fill in the details. Gregory liked free labor's prospects in Texas and wanted to transfer the "spirit that has made the great states of the Northwest." Gregory put his optimism into details in late 1865. Labor relations were to be controlled through the labor contract, reconciling freedom on one hand and the state's authority on the other. It was a way to ensure freedom and equality—perhaps myopically, some claim—backed by federal protection. Contracts had to be made for at least a month, but not longer than one year. On plantations, contracts had to be made with the head of each worker's household and include all capable of working (specifically his wife and children). Gregory ordered agents not to set wages, but also not to approve any unfair wages: in Texas, wages ranged from two dollars to fifteen dollars per month according to the sex and quality of the worker. The employer, furthermore, provided food, quarters, fuel, and medical attendance for the entire family. Each contract was a lien upon no more than one half of the crop until the hands had been paid. Since freedmen "have not learned the binding force of a contract," it should stipulate punishment for unjust absence of work, which usually meant forfeiture of wages or treatment as a vagrant. Agents were to approve each contract, only if the freedman understood "what he was called upon to do, if the contract was not unfair, if the negro understood it, and gave consent." This understanding proved elusive, since "slavery proved a poor preparation for freedom."[21]

This responsibility, as noted, to educate Texans about what agent Eugene Smith called "the Yankee way of doing business" fell to Bureau men, who on many occasions also had to fill in the details. Gregory believed the only path for Texas economically was in getting the state back on its feet agriculturally. Agents urged freedpeople to work for their former owners. On the one hand, through the agent's guidance, they would learn diligence, frugality, and industry, capitalism's holy trinity. On the other hand, the white landed elite was to be reminded "of the golden rule," a very difficult task when many continued to "peer over their shoulder at a by gone era." SACs tried to convert Texans to a new religion, one based on economic productivity and cooperation. "If this crop fails," one agent informed those under his responsibility, "the country is bankrupt, and of necessity the Freedmen must become paupers. . . ."[22]

The first step toward conversion was the contract. Simply put, Bureau men had to affirm "the former slaves' rights to liberty" and warn them "that freedom barred dependence." By doing so, they hoped to "transform" both masters and slaves "into new people—employers and employees—whose relationship was mediated by an impersonal market rather than personal sovereignty." Through tours in late 1865 and early 1866, field agents concluded that the freedpeople neither respected the sanctity of the contract nor fully understood it. They noted how laborers refused to perform tasks outlined in their contracts. Others worked their own crops at the expense of their employer's. One agent told laborers they owed him their time "to plough, to hoe, to build gin houses, [and] to split rails," he added, "in fact any honest labor that you are called upon to do . . . He [the employer] has the right to sound the horn or ring the bell anytime after day break." For those unmoved by speeches, officials authorized more coercive measures such as fines and, if necessary, application of the state's vagrancy laws.[23]

Although many freedpeople resisted contracting, agents had to instruct them that free labor and contracting meant freedom. Wanting to make the "best of a bad situation," they eventually reconciled to contracting. SACs believed proper management meant instilling confidence in the free labor system, something achieved only by protecting contractual rights and disabusing the emancipated of verbal contracts with their former masters. Moreover, they advised come to the agency for protection and guidance. "Of course, the planter[s] think but little of the 'Bureau,'" stated Isaac Johnson at La Grange, "not so, however, with the Freedmen." Such comments would later be fodder for historians to indict the Bureau as "racist" and "paternalistic."[24]

Ensuring that the former slaves received their just compensation caused great resistance. If white resistance gauged whether SACs pursued justice, then some were very committed to their duties. For example, at Meridian in early 1866, Philip Howard forcibly settled one hundred cases between whites and their black employees. Byron Porter, while "busily engaged in discharging" his duties, encountered resistance from "the disloyal part of the citizens," which included "nearly the entire population" in his district. As with the freedpeople, agents not only had to "educate" whites about the new labor system, but also safeguard their rights as well. No matter how thoroughly it was explained, many freedpeople simply did not fully understand their contractual responsibilities. This only made enforcement more difficult. Bureau records offer a litany of instances of fines for breaking contracts, with agents either consulting or punishing (usually through fines) obstreperous, uncooperative, or ignorant laborers. Cases concerning contract settlement, wages or money owed, or contract violation or interference amounted to almost forty-five hundred (n=4,439)— more analysis of the cases will appear in later chapters. That comes to more than 65 percent of all complaints brought before Bureau agents. Even accounting for those complaints filed under money (debt for example) that might not have dealt with contracts per se, the overwhelming majority of complaints an agent investigated concerned labor disputes. "Bureau agents are entrusted with very sacred and responsible duties," remarked one field agent. "I understand the object to be not only to protect the freedmen in their rights but also to do justice to their employers." Historian Joe M. Richardson concluded they "were as vigorous in forcing the Negroes to adhere to their terms . . . as they were in compelling the planters to keep their part of the bargain." Although correct in his claim that they protected both parties to some extent, Richardson overestimated the "vigor" and "compulsion" toward the weaker party at least regarding Texas. Their protection of the planter went only so far. Since many realized the workers were the weaker party, most approached disputes with this in mind.[25]

When enforcing contracts, SACs took a more lenient approach toward the former slaves. Biased by their current status, both as the weaker party and their primary responsibility, these men generally held them to a different (lesser) standard. "In setting the claims of Freedmen for services during the past year," stated Samuel C. Sloan from Richmond in early 1866, "I am governed as far as possible by equity—paying little attention to the technical violations of contracts, as I find the employer has a decided advantage over the employee, and can with little difficulty get an abundance of evidence to prove this point." According to Mortimer H. Goddin, a farmer from Virginia, when adjudicating cases "my aim must be to be for the best [for] the freedmen as a general rule. . . ." Stanton Weaver "got pretty well acquainted with the manner in which the business between the freedmen and their employers was conducted." "If left to themselves entirely," he noticed, "the planter would reduce the freedmen to a worse state than slavery (if possible)—work them the whole year under a pretty fair contract (perhaps), and then, generally, have a bill large enough to swallow the wages, or scare the poor fellows off with threats. . . ." While holding the freedpeople more accountable as time passed, field agents extended greater leeway to the field hand compared to his white employer. This approach was lost on most white Texans. Thus, a considerable portion of the planters, but by no means all, resisted dealing with SACs, generally damning them at every opportunity.[26]

By making the freedpeople contract with their former masters and holding them accountable, Bureau agents did not return "the lamb to the wolf," as some later historians would claim. Nor were they responsible for (or even cognizant of) the inherent inequities and dependency endemic within the labor contract system during the nineteenth century. The freed community realized the agents' honesty, with the magnitude and significance of their work hardly misunderstood. Simply because Bureau men were "reestablish[ing] discipline toward labor" does not equate with the return of slavery in another form. Critics seem to overlook that they also "disciplined planters." Field personnel realized that in order for free labor to work in Texas, the interests of both parties had to be secured. What was good for the worker was also good for the employer. Albeit tempered, of course. Officials at headquarters warned subordinates about being too friendly to the freedpeople and overlooking the whites, wanting them to be circumspect in their behavior. In other words, be "as wise as a serpent as well as harmless." Commenting on how some employers had accepted the new situation and what that meant for obtaining good workers, one Bureau officer, placing his hopes in the planters' desire for profits, predicted "the plastic character of mind soon adapts itself to circumstances[,] as selfishness was the enslaver of the negro, it will now be one of the means of his elevation." In Leon County, for example, F. D. Inge observed planters in his district experiencing "pleasant disappointment." In its infancy during Gregory's administration, the policy of protecting the employees through the bottom line of the employer became more important as time passed.[27]

Overseeing the genesis of a new labor system, in and of itself, amounted to a full time job. But when added to the many other responsibilities of the Bureau man, the workload could prove too much for some. Such demands prompted one inspector in 1867 to declare, in answer to charges to the contrary, the position of SAC "is no sinecure nor are their duties of a pleasant and agreeable character." William H. Rock, one of the most respected and longest tenured of all Bureau men in Texas, and described by one official as "an agent that could not be easily replaced," adopted a most rigorous policy while at Richmond. Rather than conduct business in his office, he decided to "visit . . . every plantation" within his district, and not surprisingly, he found it "very <u>fatiguing</u> for I am in the saddle every day more or less." But he also found this way to be the most effective. Unlike Rock, some of the initial agents appointed by Gregory sometimes complained about the "fatiguing" workload (in one form or another, complaints persisted to the end, but were not nearly as frequent as field personnel increased and headquarters showed little patience for such complaints). From Crockett, Stanton Weaver, after only a couple of months on the job, found "the work of my office is more than I can attend to properly myself," admitting "I do not pretend to attend to anything but the approving of contracts and trying of cases when freedmen have been maltreated." George C. Abbott likewise groused about only "one or two nights sleep, and have often ridden forty miles in 24 hours besides attending to my office duties." He believed his duties beyond what one man could effectively handle, but reaffirmed to superiors his "splendid health." In contrast to Rock, who remained with the organization for years and thrived on the work, Abbott quickly tired of the workload, despite his claims of a steeled resolve. His self-evaluation proved premature, for shortly after his affirmation, he believed himself no longer "competent to the proper discharge of the duties of this office" and asked for and received a discharge in early 1866.[28]

Confusion about their purpose and authority made their already difficult task all the more difficult. In his study of Bureau men, John A. Carpenter concluded agents entered "upon his duties almost completely on his own." He had not "attended indoctrination school, had not in most cases been briefed by [superiors] concerning his duties, and usually assured on the scene of his labors with only a few verbal instructions or perhaps only some circulars from superiors." Officials, nonetheless, wanted subordinates "to be thoroughly introduced to their duties." Consider some examples. Writing from Sutherland Springs in January 1866, William Longworth wanted to know the "maximum of my jurisdiction [I already know] the minimum." Unfortunately, this did not always happen. Stanton Weaver and John T. Scott, the SACs at Crockett and Victoria, respectively, seemed confused about writing contracts, what specifics to include in them, and what fines to levy for breach of contract. Full of zeal, B. J. Arnold desired "some further and more definite instructions than those which you have given me." Such need for clarification existed throughout the agency's existence. In April 1866 Joseph Ferguson at San Antonio admitted the lack of direction has left "me at a loss as to my duty" and desirous for "some general information as to my duties and the authority vest in me." Byron Porter likewise admitted his "greatest difficulty" was "the want of definite instructions . . . [to] my jurisdiction and powers." John T. Raper at Columbus greatly desired direction dealing with apprenticing. "I have had no conversation with you upon this subject," he relayed. "I was simply told to do as was right and proper." That was the answer to many an inquiry for direction or clarification. As late as June 1868, Willis A. Bledsoe admitted "I am not Posted as regards my duties."[29]

In reply, superiors either deferred to subordinates ("use your best judgment" or "you must be your own judge in each particular case") or referred them to various general or circular orders, congressional statutes, or military and Freedmen's Bureau manuals. It was obvious many were ignorant of their jurisdiction and policies. The latter problem partly resulted from the first: many simply lacked the necessary instructional aids. In Colorado County, Eli W. Green requested "copies of all recent orders . . . in regard to this 'Bureau.'" Pennsylvanian native Byron Porter informed superiors "Scarcely a day passes in which I do not suffer annoyance and inconvenience from this want and this office [is] doubtless not the only one destitute of proper records." This situation remained a consistent problem, since SACs were never fully apprised of their authority and constantly in need of direction.[30]

On the surface, this disconnection looks like typical parsimonious, bureaucratic interplay. Yet it highlights a prevalent belief shared by many men in the field, a belief that persisted until the agency ceased operations in the state: superiors never *truly* understood the extent of conditions on the ground. Many unanswered requests from superiors, along with other slights (actual and perceived) only increased their frustration. Asked to carry out an unprecedented task in a hostile environment, Bureau men expected, at minimum, the confidence and support of their superiors. Too often, whether warranted or not, they believed support lacking. The responsibilities and being "a stranger amongst strangers" weighed on even the most resolute men. More than a few of the men appointed by Gregory severely underestimated the amount of time and effort necessary for the position. What was needed was an increase in agents.[31]

In late 1865 and early 1866 Bureau officials in Texas faced a dilemma: at the very time the organization was expanding its operations, it experienced a manpower shortage. Gregory (as well as his successor J. B. Kiddoo) had to turn to civilians as agents, regardless of his suspicions. When appointing "scalawags," all Bureau chiefs in Texas turned to the aid of reputable Unionists like future governors Edmund Jackson Davis and Elisha Marshall Pease, and Henry Clay Pedigo, a prominent judge in Texas. On average, the tenure for the men appointed by Gregory was 8.4 months, higher than the overall average of the Bureau in Texas (7.8). (See Table 2-1.) Civilians made up more than 31 percent (11 of 35, or 31.4 percent) of the agents Gregory appointed. They remained with the agency slightly less than their military counterparts. At the time of Gregory's removal in March 1866, ten remained in the field with the organization.

Their efficacy ranged from superb to criminal and incompetent, with the latter two being the rule. In fact, with the exceptions of John F. Brown and J. Orville Shelby, both of whom did adequate jobs, and Philip Howard, considered industrious, hard working, and dedicated, the rest of Gregory's civilian agents were apathetic, incompetent, controversial, or criminal. Of the seven men dismissed by headquarters, some of whom were dismissed because of economizing efforts or past Confederate service, all but one were civilians, with most of them dismissed for actions considered contrary to the agency's goal and values. Table 2-2 lists reasons Gregory's military and civilian agents left the Bureau. Bureau historian William L. Richter concludes that Texas Bureau

Table 2-1   Length of Service for Agents Appointed by Gregory

Type of Bureau Agent	Number	Avg. Length of Service (Months)
Civilian	11	8.4
Military	24	8.5

Note: Dates came from Freedmen's Bureau Roster of Officers and Civilians.

Table 2-2   Reasons Agents Appointed by Gregory Left Bureau Service

Reason	Military Agents Total and Percentages		Civilian Agents Total and Percentages		Total and Percentages	
Bureau Operations: Bureau ended, consolidation, and transferal or reassignment w/i the agency	1	4.2	1	9.1	2	5.7
Military Operations: Mustered out or ordered to new assignment	16	66.7	0	0	16	45.8
Dropped on Request: Agent resigned appointment	4	16.6	2	18.2	6	17.1
Terminated: Dismissed for criminality, cruelty, Confederate service, or appointment revoked	1	4.2	6	54.5	7	20
N/A: Reason for leaving undetermined	2	8.3	2	18.2	4	11.4
Died: disease or accident	0	0	0	0	0	0
Died: murdered	0	0	0	0	0	0
Total: All Gregory's Agents	n=24	100	n=11	100	n=35	100

Note: The information in this table came from various sources, but much of it came from the U.S. Census and the Freedmen's Bureau's Special Orders and Correspondences.

"scalawags" were hardly worth the trouble, concerned with political patronage and revenge, and too often unqualified or malfeasant. Although the political patronage claim is debatable, Richter's sweeping indictment, despite harshness in its delivery, is accurate.[32]

Selecting civilian agents was more art than science. One case best illustrates this difficulty. After leaving the organization, George C. Abbott got mixed up with unscrupulous men and was killed. J. B. Kiddoo, Gregory's successor as Bureau chief of Texas, described Abbott as "a very bad man who was killed by an accomplice in rascality in a personal difficulty." That statement was unquestioned at that time, but Abbott's tenure with the agency suggests otherwise. Perhaps malfeasant at the time of his death, he showed no tendencies of the sort while serving the Bureau. Officials at headquarters never questioned Abbott's commitment to the freedpeople, and no one claimed he ever did anything other than what his duties called for.[33]

The Bureau's initial months in Texas can best be described as a work in progress. Officials and subassistant commissioners alike attempted to work out the bureaucratic kinks, but were not always successful. As the initial men entered their posts, full of zeal and pride, they too often lacked the necessary accoutrements. Pervasive ignorance about their authority and their underestimation of the workload only compounded the problem. Beyond the broad goal of implementing free labor and protecting the freed community's rights as citizens, much remained murky, as they were left to "use their best judgment." Such a situation caused unnecessary frustration and, at times, outright bickering. With agents "using their best judgment," the desired consistency was impossible. Rectifying this situation, however, would no longer fall to Gregory. White Texans were angered at his zeal for the freedpeople's welfare and many, including high-ranking military officials in Texas, believed his "zest and energy" for the emancipated came at the expense of their former masters as well as the Bureau's effectiveness. In late March 1866, in response, Howard reassigned Gregory to Washington, replacing him with Brevet Major General Joseph B. Kiddoo. It would be up to Kiddoo to fix not only some of the problems that bedeviled his predecessor, but also to extend the power and influence of the Freedmen's Bureau.[34]

3

Conservative Phoenix

The J. B. Kiddoo Era,
May 1866–Summer 1866

White Texans saw Gregory's removal as a victory, albeit limited. Encouraged to greater resistance, they believed they could alter their condition through "restrained belligerence." In the spring of 1866 whites increased opposition to federal attempts at Reconstruction in ways not seen since war's end. Their resistance moved from verbal criticism in the spring to acts of violence by the summer's end. Their struggle was set against the backdrop of restoration, for as whites defied the Bureau, they also busied themselves with readmission under President Andrew Johnson's Reconstruction plan. As state politicians met certain benchmarks for readmission, their constituents desired greater control over their civil affairs and less federal oversight. Embodying this sentiment was Governor James Webb Throckmorton, who was the torchbearer for his "defeated" countrymen. Amidst atmosphere, a new assistant commissioner attempted to succeed where his predecessor had failed.

Brevet Major General Joseph Barr Kiddoo brought much experience and commitment to his new position. Born in Pittsburgh in either 1837 or 1840, he entered military service in 1861. He served with the 63rd and 137th Pennsylvania Volunteer Regiments (units in the Army of the Potomac), rising through the ranks for his "meritorious" actions in the Peninsular and Chancellorsville Campaigns in 1862 and 1863. In late 1863 he transferred to the newly created all-black infantry service. An officer in both the 6th and 22nd United States Colored Infantry Regiments, Kiddoo participated in the siege of Petersburg throughout late 1864 and early 1865. While leading his men in an unsuccessful attack against the city's defenses, Kiddoo received a "lacerated wound of the back by a minié ball," a wound that never fully healed. For the rest of his life, it discharged "half an ounce to an ounce of pus" daily. This wound, which surely prematurely ended his life, was extremely painful and often incapacitating. For his actions before Petersburg, despite accusations of a "whiskey-crazed brain," Kiddoo was honored in September 1865 with a promotion to brigadier general.

After leaving Texas, he was reassigned to the Department of the Lakes and then to New York City as superintendent for recruiting. In that time, he became a lawyer and was admitted to the Bar of Allegheny County, Pennsylvania, in 1867. Kiddo left the military in 1870. Even with his wound, he remained active, joining the National Rifle Association and serving as a pallbearer to General George A. Custer's coffin after his death at the Battle of the Little Big Horn. Kiddoo later died in New York City in 1880. The army ordered his internment at the United States Military Cemetery at West Point.[1]

In the meantime, Kiddoo arrived in Texas in May 1866 and discussed conditions in the state with the outgoing Gregory. In a letter informing Howard about the situation in Texas, Kiddoo called it "very agreeable." "I am agreeably disappointed," he said, "in all I have heard or seen thus far." His glowing report, however, masked significant problems with the labor situation in Texas, most notably enticements (luring one to break a labor contract with another). Field agents reported numerous instances of enticement in early 1866, which "openly set at defiance the authority of the Bureau." For example, in Robertson County, Virginian native Champ Carter, speaking for more than a few, pleaded with superiors for redress. "I tell you frankly General," he declared, ". . . if the demoralization is not stopped—if the contracts are not enforced . . . if the freedmen are not required to return & comply with their contracts when they leave without cause—if the planter is not punished who hires a freedmen with another planter the whole planting interest & every interest [will suffer]." He continued with a warning that all "hangs on a balance as fickle as the wind." A *New York Herald* correspondent, who had toured Texas and witnessed these problems, compared the agency's attempt to regulate labor to tickling a rhinoceros with a straw. Doubtless, it was going to be as difficult.[2]

Within a few weeks of writing to Commissioner Howard about his agreeable disappointment, Kiddoo wrote a less sanguine letter detailing problems reported by his field personnel. A flawed policy and the difficulties inherent in transitioning from one labor system to another, according to Kiddoo, caused these problems. Gregory had shown sympathy for the freedpeople, realizing they, recently emancipated, had yet to learn "responsible citizenship." He justifiably dealt with them quite leniently. Such leniency, according to the more conservative Kiddoo, caused preventable problems. Both planters and their hands had to be held accountable, by a "vigorous system of labor." Kiddoo sounded this change in policy through Circular No. 14, a measure he deemed "simple justice." The new standard would throw "moral influence about the Freedmen in their transition state." With the order, he wanted to "induce them to maintain inviolate the provisions of so solemn a legal document as a written contract."[3]

Leniency resulted in "flagrant violation of the laws of Contracts," according to Kiddoo. He viewed enticement as "dishonorable . . . [and] destructive to the energetic system of labor the bureau desires to establish." The practice, in fact, had become so prevalent it threatened the state's agricultural interests. As one disgruntled employer put it, "High wages offered by asses has turned [the freedmen's] heads." Kiddoo hoped his circular would dissuade such "asses" by prohibiting "any employer, planter, or other person [to] tamper with, or entice laborers to leave their employers with whom they have contracted in good faith," with the amount of fines at the discretion of the Bureau agents. According to historian James D. Schmidt, Kiddoo had revived labor law not used in the North since the eighteenth century. In reality, the new policy was not much stricter than Gregory's, since officials still prohibited SACs from using physical coercion against freedpeople who refused to sign or had broken their contracts ("compel the negro to work without resorting to physical punishment"). As "their friend and guardian," they were to inform hands of the consequences of breaking their contracts. If persuasion did not work, the freedperson was to be fined (up to fifty dollars). The new regulations held the employer (fines up to five hundred dollars) and employee equally responsible for their actions.[4]

Of course, much of the labor system's success depended on the SACs. In another circular, Kiddoo required them to tour their subdistricts to explain the new regulations. Officials in Galveston had previously never explicitly mandated field trips. Kiddoo, on the other hand, now ordered such tours mandatory, greatly increasing their already sizable workload. Two examples will suffice. J. Ernest Goodman, the agent at Columbus, disclosed to his superiors that his wartime injuries allowed "but a partial tour" of his district. Livingston agent and wealthy planter, James A. Hogue, also wanted no part of this expansive duty, and after completing a tour of his district and finding the "crops of this section very bacward [sic]" and "the Blackman . . . not getting justice," he resigned his commission. During the spring and summer of 1866, many fellow agents reported satisfactory labor conditions in their districts, with labor and capital finally being married. For example, Massachusetts native and postal worker Alex B. Coggeshall stated that the "planters of this county seem to be disposed to treat the freedmen fairly and the freedmen have exceeded the expectations. . . ." But this, like so many other rules, had exceptions. A number thought these expressions of amity and fairness from planters fleeting.[5]

Problems still existed. There were still complaints planters had yet to settle with their hands for the previous year's work (a problem not experienced by all agents in the same degree). Plus, some professed confusion about the kind of payment that should be paid. Planters also expressed continued discontent with idle freedpeople. Despite claims to the contrary, misunderstanding about the meaning of Kiddoo's circular was another problem. Bureau officials in Galveston frequently referred subordinates to Circular No. 14 in answer to their questions: some misunderstood it, and others applied it in an ex post facto manner, something Kiddoo strictly prohibited. The SAC at Liberty, the local doctor J. Orville Shelby, for example, was a little confused. According to Shelby, the order allowed him to punish those who broke their contract with only a fine. He did not believe he could force them to return to the original employer they had contracted with. Richard Cole, already angry that many of his hands had left, disagreed and claimed Shelby misunderstood the circular. Cole thought it forced hands back to the employer they had contracted with. He wrote Kiddoo to inform him about Shelby. Shelby, however, stood firm, and Kiddoo concurred with him, for it was discovered that Cole had abused some of his hands, causing the contract to be annulled. Although Shelby was vindicated, the job took its toll on him, and he discovered that justice for the freedpeople came with a price. Before he could find redress, Kiddoo relieved him. A frustrated Shelby blamed his removal on a conspiracy by local citizens. But information had surfaced that he had been a surgeon in the Confederacy, precluding him from taking the required oath. In the spring of 1867 Shelby claimed that the Bureau owed him pay for his service. Superiors, however, reminded him that he served as a civilian with no pay.[6]

In the meantime, as agents dealt with Circular No. 14, a more pressing problem attracted their attention: uncertainty about the details of contracts. Questions about payment (specie or paper), work hours (sun-up to sundown or a ten-hour system), and other specifics to be listed in each contract flooded their offices throughout the spring and summer of 1866. This stemmed primarily from vagueness and ambiguity in Gregory's policy. This situation led A. H. Mayer to ask, "If any form of contract has been decided upon at your Hd Qrts please send me a copy immediately that I may be able to answer some of the ten thousand questions asked of me in the reference to contracts." In a series of circulars (Nos. 19, 21, 23, and 25) partly based on the recommendations of Bureau inspector William H. Sinclair, Kiddoo attempted to replace the uncertainty with more definite guidelines. Upon a complaint, SACs could place a lien on the crop. It constituted a claim for first payment of wages owed to hands "regardless . . . [of] any claims whatsoever." Monthly payment was in specie, with paper money not acceptable. Employers were required to pay their hands before shipping their crops. Although freedpeople could contract for monthly wages, Kiddoo preferred that agents dissuade them from doing so and instead urge contracts for a portion of the crop. Contracts considered fair were to be approved (only by an agent). When time came to sell the crops, field agents were to issue certificates that indicated hands had already received their share of the crop, guaranteeing its safe passage. Despite greater oversight and protection, Kiddoo, nevertheless, prohibited agents from interfering with the freedpeople's disposal of their crops, for they had the right to dispose of crops as they wished.[7]

The new regulations helped, but confusion still remained. A number miscon-strued Circular No. 23, which not only required planters to pay their hands before the crops were shipped, but also allowed Bureau agents to halt the ship-ment of products. Seizure was to happen only upon complaint, not otherwise. But some overlooked this feature and detained shipments anyway. Equally det-rimental to the flow of commerce were idleness and destitution. Kiddoo partly created his labor system to reduce what he saw as an increase of the two. In the spring and summer of 1866 men in the field described scenes of idle freedpeople not mentioned since immediately following emancipation. Vagrants and insol-vents made up a small fraction, with a majority having yet to contract or too sick or young to work. In a market economy, these dependents had little value. Car-ing for workers' needs affected planters' profits, and few wanted to invest in the well-being of these people. Planters, now absolved from the responsibility to look after slaves' welfare, thought more like businessmen and less like "authoritarian fathers."[8]

Agents reminded county officials that state law held them accountable for their poor regardless of color. In some cases, the county officials did. This, how-ever, was definitely the exception. Local officials resisted, citing either insuffi-cient funds or arguing that such destitution fell to the Freedmen's Bureau. Kiddoo, wanting to clarify who exactly was responsible for the poor, issued Circular No. 16. In it, he reiterated that state law vested responsibility for "all paupers and indigent freedmen to . . . the respective counties." As the Bureau steeled its resolve, local officials did as well. This tug-of-war would last through-out the agency's existence in Texas, and caught in the middle were agents and the freed community. The feud at Marshall, Harrison County, in early 1867 was fairly typical. A doctor and New Yorker, Charles F. Rand persistently informed county judge Obadiah Hendrick about his responsibilities for black indigents. An annoyed Hendrick claimed the county lacked the means to support them.

He also turned to Governor James Webb Throckmorton for help. "I forward you this [Rand's letter] to show in what esteem he holds the civil authorities," stated Hendrick. The governor appealed to Charles Griffin, commander of the District of Texas, for redress. Throckmorton claimed that state and local officials were doing all that could be done. He even questioned the need for relief and called on Bureau officials to use congressional appropriation to care for the poor. As officials at headquarters and state authorities dueled about jurisdiction, agents took matters into their own hands. For them, there were few options but to act.[9]

Little did Bureau agents realize their problems with state officials had only just begun. As the legislature "met" benchmarks set down by President Andrew Johnson, he declared Reconstruction complete, prompting whites to reassert greater domestic autonomy. The recently elected governor, Throckmorton, a Unionist during the war but a man imbued with racial beliefs of an ardent fire-eating Democrat, opposed federal intervention in civil affairs after the war. An adherent of Johnson's view of Reconstruction and critic of the Radical Republicans, Throckmorton, who one Union general called a disrupting force, interpreted the president's proclamation to mean the military had to relinquish domestic control to local and state officials. The governor believed that Texas's completion of Johnson's Reconstruction plan subordinated federal organizations to state control in civil matters. Of particular concern was the resented Bureau, which he sarcastically called "one of the grand Institutions of the country." Throckmorton announced that he would not "countenance any wrong or outrage" by it. He construed such "wrongs" to be any actions by agents other than caring for destitute freepeople. His belligerence not only caused conflict, but also emboldened local officials to resist.[10]

With the governor's backing, local officials insisted on greater control over county matters, which placed them at odds with agents, who believed their authority beyond state interference. Superiors reminded subordinates "you must not pay any attention to any action they [local officials] may take to interfere with you and in the discharge of your duties." These words had meaning at headquarters, but for field agents they were of little consolation. When written appeals for redress (both to state executives and Bureau officials) proved ineffective, local officials resorted to more forceful maneuvers, i.e., attempted arrest of SACs. Crockett officials indicted Stanton Weaver for interfering with a freedman's arrest. Bryon Porter similarly informed the Harris County sheriff issued a warrant for his arrest. Backed by the local post commander, however, Porter ignored the writ. Because of his actions in preventing the re-arrest of a freedman who had escaped local custody, Jacob C. DeGress also feared arrest if not for the local garrison's presence in Harris County. A few unlucky men did not have troops nearby, thus making it easier for local authorities to detain them when they "interfered." Generally, a simple "reminder" that an agent's power rested in federal authority and subjected to no state oversight defused the situation. But on rare occasions, that reminder had to come armed with bayonets.[11]

State officials caused most of the confrontations with the Bureau, by refusing to fulfill their obligations under law. In a few instances, however, disputes arose not from obtuse civil officers, but rather belligerent SACs. The cases of William Longworth and Samuel A. Craig are instructive. These two agents had great difficulties—for differing reasons—with local officials. Although born in New York, Longworth was called by white Texans a "scalawag," since he lived in the state for many years prior to the war. He experienced much animosity and abuse for his Unionism during the war. In fact, behind "[John] Hancock and [Andrew Jackson] Hamilton," he claimed to be the most persecuted man in west Texas. His Unionism and persecution at the hands of Rebels probably helped secure appointments as chief justice of Wilson County in Governor Hamilton's administration and as an agent under Gregory. Despite his travails during the war and his subdistrict's size, Longworth exuded confidence, bordering on hubris. "I think I am equal to the extent of the whole territory asked for," he boldly wrote, "and am in the bosom of almost every individual within the same."[12]

Longworth did not wait to test the people's love for him. He immediately conflicted over apprenticeship. As local officials used it to procure labor for employers, the practice could easily transition into "legalized kidnapping" or "cruel injustice." As chief justice as well as agent, Longworth heard many complaints by freed parents that their children had been apprenticed out to former masters. Moved by these pleas, he believed the system's negatives far outweighed any benefits, since the "unity of families must be maintained." As a result, he refused to apprentice freed children and returned all apprenticed to their parents or guardians. For example, Longworth ordered James L. Dial to return two freed children apprenticed to him. Longworth wanted to make a point. Rather than simply order the two children returned, the agent held a hearing with all parties present and fined Dial ninety dollars. He further charged Dial with kidnapping and false imprisonment and had him detained. The incensed defendant believed Longworth had disgraced "and continues to disgrace" his position and petitioned Kiddoo against this "tyrannical and oppressive course." Dial, however, found little sympathy from Kiddoo.[13]

The story might have ended there if not for Longworth's confrontation with William C. Wiseman, judge of Guadalupe County. Believing the SAC had violated state law, Wiseman demanded (and received) Dial's release. Judge Wiseman wrote to Longworth asking him to cease interfering with the county court's operations regarding apprenticeship, threatening a charge of kidnapping if there were any more problems. Wiseman continued by stating that any further difficulties between the court and the agent would be solely the fault of Longworth. The judge ended with a terse warning: "A word to the wise is sufficient." Not one to be cowed, Longworth responded in kind. "[I will not] tamper with the majesty of the laws of the United States, or the office I fill as to comply with your preemptory command." Although he thought his course to be sound, superiors began to wonder. Longworth received a letter from headquarters enumerating the many complaints about his conduct. Regretting only timidity in fining whites to the maximum and "doing a fraction of what might be done . . . for which the Bureau was established," Longworth dismissed such charges as unfounded attempts to besmirch him, calling the indictments "false, absolutely and unqualifiedly false" and "transparent." For having to answer them, he even chided Kiddoo and his staff for wasting the Bureau's already scarce paper. If there ever was any doubt to the justness of his cause, he continued, these critics, particularly Judge Wiseman, were the very men "I was sent here to counteract and keep in check." Longworth even asked for a court martial to clear his name.[14]

Kiddoo assured his subordinate a court martial was unnecessary. Longworth, nevertheless, lectured the AC that such an inquiry would embarrass those, both in and out of the agency, who doubted his sincerity. Wanting certainty, Kiddoo dispatched William H. Sinclair, the agency's inspector in the state, to investigate. In a surprise move Kiddoo decided not to wait for the inspector's report. Whether because of his "unnecessary" actions against the white citizens or his generally abrasive manner toward superiors, Longworth was relieved and replaced by James B. Moore, an officer in a colored regiment. (The official explanation was Kiddoo's desire to replace civilian agents with army officers.) What Sinclair found confirmed headquarters' suspicions: Longworth caused unnecessary strife. The report concluded he exceeded his authority, engaged in arbitrary justice, and threatened the free labor interests in his subdistrict. Sinclair, in fact, recommended his delivery to civil authorities to answer for his actions.[15]

Agent Samuel A. Craig had a similar yet different experience. Appointed in early spring 1866, Craig got into a dispute a few months later with the pro-Southern editor of the *Southern Banner*, Daniel Leonidas McGary. A former Confederate and ardent Democrat, McGary hated the Freedmen's Bureau and

used his newspaper as a sounding board against it. Within his "Red Hot Democratic Journal," he mocked the organization's name, questioned its reason for
being in Brenham, and editorialized that Bureau teachers instructed their
pupils to spell the state's name "Taxes" for the federal government's insistence
on collecting back taxes from the war. He also personally attacked Craig, claiming he looked "like a half way cross between a peacock and a jay bird." Officials
in Galveston told Craig to warn the editor his words had consequences and, if
"untrue and calculated to do injury, will subject [him] to official action."[16]

Craig brushed off the editor's remarks as nothing more than a mere nuisance.
But McGary persisted, accusing the agency of misleading the freed community.
When Craig showed him Kiddoo's letter, McGary responded defiantly with,
"Well, what are you going to do about it?" Kiddoo, believing the Bureau's integrity impugned, ordered Craig to arrest and fine McGary for "persistent abuse
[and] libelous and false" assertions "calculated to do injury." Craig fined the man
two hundred dollars. The editor offered to pay one hundred dollars, which was
refused. He then asked if he could have a little more time to get all the money,
which Craig granted. Instead of raising the money, McGary used the time to
appeal to the post commander at Seguin, Captain George W. Smith, who was
swayed by his appeal. Captain Smith informed the Bureau agent that he was
taking charge. Craig adamantly refused to yield jurisdiction. In kind, Captain
Smith refused any assistance in arresting the editor. Emboldened by this dispute,
McGary refused to pay the fine. Craig referred the matter to the military and
Bureau superiors, and military officials sent the Bureau man a detail of soldiers.
Kiddoo also warned his subordinate not to back down. Reading between the
lines, Craig arrested the delinquent editor and placed him in the county jail. For
his action, the *Galveston Tri Weekly News* anointed the agent as "perhaps the
most . . . atrocious and unmitigated [despot]" in the Lone Star State.[17]

McGary's stance made him a hero. White locals daily visited the new celeb-
rity in jail. On several occasions, guards even allowed him brief stints out of his
cell to parade defiantly outside the jailhouse. All the while, McGary continued
to write editorials from jail. "Captain Craig, the 'Booro man' hath an itching
palm," he wrote, "he refused to take greenbacks, but demands gold coin in payment of fines." Incensed, Craig again appealed to superiors for guidance. Once
again he was pushed toward stern action. By this time, Craig feared possible
violence, with many threats against his life. Despite this, he arrested the jailer
and deputy and decided to guard the three prisoners personally.[18]

Meanwhile, Governor Throckmorton, after many white citizens appealed to
him for help, involved himself in the matter. "I intend to demand Craig for

[this] matter and have him turned over," he wrote to a friend. The governor protested to Washington officials, including the president, who then pressured Commissioner Howard. After a myriad of letters and telegraphs, in which the president informed Kiddoo that Craig (and also Kiddoo) had overstepped their jurisdiction, Kiddoo ordered the release of McGary in early September 1866. Throckmorton had already called for Craig to be punished as "he deserves." But Kiddoo defended his subordinate's actions by stating if a SAC cannot protect himself against such "virulent and vulgar abuse as was heaped upon" him, then he has "*no* clearly defined powers." It soon became obvious the affair had irreparably damaged Craig's relationship with the white community, only encouraging more vitriol. Upon his release, the editor relished the opportunity to get in the last word. "The Bureau's jurisdiction is confined to refugees, freedmen, and abandoned lands," McGary pointed out. "Under which one of these headings, we wonder, do we come? We are not a refugee—we are not a freedman; perhaps we may be abandoned lands." With this, Kiddoo replaced Craig and reassigned him to Seguin, a place not any more welcoming than Brenham.[19]

At Seguin, Craig entered an already tense situation as the problems created by Longworth were still unfolding. Longworth, now a private citizen and smarting from his removal, told Bureau officials he fully expected ("it is inevitable") to have to answer to a "rebel jury." Never one to miss an opportunity for self-congratulation, however, he notified Kiddoo that the freedpeople "can scarcely realize the fact that I am out of office" and "will never give confidence to any one again, not even Capt. Craig." Despite belittling Craig, Longworth soon appealed to him for protection, especially after Guadalupe County (Seguin) officials arrested him for "illegal" acts committed during his time with the Bureau. Kiddoo ordered Craig to secure Longworth's release and seize all papers relating to his arrest. Although some at headquarters believed he deserved his current fate, Longworth still had acted in service of the U.S. government and his arrest was an affront to its authority. Such actions could not be allowed to stand, for the ramifications would be detrimental to all other Bureau agents.[20]

Craig, accompanied by some soldiers, freed Longworth from jail and secured all papers relating to his arrest. According to the county clerk, Craig forcefully "rifled" through the office looking for all papers dealing with Longworth, some of which happened to be locked away in the clerk's desk. At that moment, another local official arrived and threatened the clerk with arrest if he assisted by unlocking the desk. Craig, not taking this lightly, threatened the clerk with a military trial in San Antonio unless he unlocked the desk. The clerk immediately produced the keys, and Craig "abstracted" the desired records. Craig later comically compared the whole event to a child resisting medicine, noting how the "children" had "succumbed," but only after he had administered it with "a wholesome dash of brown sugar [the military force]." He laughingly emphasized by adding, "Chuck a cha lunk a cha lunk. . . ."[21]

His stern course drew praise from Kiddoo and enmity from civil officials. The district judge for the area, John Ireland, a former Confederate, wanted to "make short work of the Bureau." Described as "notoriously disloyal," Ireland issued a warrant for Craig's arrest, but the sheriff, who the agent had a "semi-friendly" relationship with, feared the soldiers still in the county and refused to arrest him. In fact, Craig informed the law enforcer that "I had ten men each armed with a 16 shot rifle [and] with plenty of provisions to withstand a siege," warning he "did not propose to be arrested, and would fight and kill, if any attempt were made." By early 1867, however, the soldiers had left the county and Ireland again moved against Craig. It was rumored that Ireland saw the agent on the street and yelled out, "What, isn't that God damn yankee-thief arrested yet!" Craig recalled later that the sheriff shortly thereafter arrived at a pool hall where he was playing. "I slowly with my cue in hand, backed toward the door and found it locked," the agent later wrote. "The sheriff came over near as tho[ugh] watching the game . . . Soon he took out the warrant and commenced to read it to me." Resistance was futile once six men had arrived to help the sheriff with the arrest, "all . . . loaded [with] six, six shooters to my one, it was no use to resist." Military officials ordered the recently departed detail back to Guadalupe County to affect his release. Although freed, the whole affair (and that which previously occurred at Seguin) weighed on Craig. He also lamented perceived Rebel victories throughout the state and yearned for the peace and quiet of home back in Pennsylvania. "Like a little boy who stands to one side with a finger in his mouth and a tear in his eye—Oh, say, fellers, I want to go home," he stated to superiors. He was discharged and returned north.[22]

The experiences of Charles F. Rand, William Longworth, and Samuel A. Craig underscore the general conflicts between civil officers and SACs. Rand's problems stemmed from derelict officials, not from any aggressive actions on his part. His insistence on holding them accountable for the county's poor was justified and proper. His case typifies many other similar frays with local officials: agent insists local authorities treat freedpeople the same as whites; local authorities will not; both agent and officials dig in their heels; and dispute intensifies. The point, however, is that the dispute developed for no reason other than Rand's insistence that local authorities uphold state and federal law. Longworth's experience shows how a zealous, committed man can blur the line between sound and unsound. It also shows how one could go too far, much to the chagrin of his superiors, his successors, and his charges. Certainly Longworth desired justice, but his vengeful approach not only reverberated back on him but also his successors. Longworth could not see—or maybe he could and did not care—that his actions had unintended consequences. His commitment to the freedpeople did not deter him from his controversial actions. Nor did it excuse him from any unwise, unsound, and generally hostile manner. Being a Bureau agent demanded patience, tact, and common sense, reinforced with fortitude and presence. It also demanded the ability to know when to act and, most important, when not to. Enough instances exist of agents being able to differentiate between benign slights by the white community and those actions and words meant to undermine their authority and credibility. Few, no matter how committed to the Union cause, used their positions for vengeful purposes. Bureau officials deemed it "desirable to have a discreet [agent] . . . who can do justice to both parties [because] any other will only make mischief." Unable to distinguish between the two, Longworth's unwise course unfortunately hurt the freedpeople, unnecessarily antagonized an already on edge white community, and needlessly made his successor's task more difficult.[23]

Craig took a more prudent course, a characteristic that prompted Kiddoo to call him "a good and efficient officer." He still experienced resistance. In his dealings with McGary, Craig did not want to act. He realized the editorials were nothing more than the words of frustration and mere annoyances. He thus ignored McGary, not because of any lack of fortitude, but because it was really not worth it. Craig decided his mandate was to protect the freedpeople, not to censor newspapers, and he moved against the editor only when forced to. Later that summer, after Commissioner Howard and President Johnson heard about the editor's arrest and punishment, Kiddoo was personally ordered by his superiors to "settle the difficulty." This resulted in Craig becoming an object of abuse, first by superiors and then by local officials.[24]

As civil officers recovered from the shock of defeat, so too did the citizens. Realizing the Radical Republicans' desires, white defiance increased. In the spring and summer of 1866 white Texans elected the Throckmorton administration to state office. Inspector for Texas William H. Sinclair attributed such behavior to "ignorance and ill-breeding." Although the vast majority of these insults amounted to little more than annoyances, a few whites went further. As Bureau historian George R. Bentley concluded decades ago, "planters did not think of the Bureau in its best [interest and] they resented its very existence, regardless of what it might do, for it had power over them and was beyond their control." Resistance increased throughout the spring and summer of 1866, especially as the agency's expected demise neared in July. (In March 1865 Congress had authorized it to operate for one year after the war's end.) In Falls County, A. P. Delano, who suffered maltreatment by several locals, described an incident in which a white man entered his store with "cocked pistol in his hand." "[He] attempted to get to me," he recalled, "which caused me to flee from my store to my office (in the rear part of the store) and place myself under lock and key." Samuel C. Sloan at Richmond heard many rumors about his possible assassination. "I have since seen enough," he wrote, "to convince me that such action of the Mil. authorities was absolutely necessary in order to enable me to discharge the duties of my office. . . ." Unless he received soldiers, Sloan wanted to be relieved. Philip Howard, while touring his subdistrict in the spring of 1866, had "some of the worst of mankind" accost him. New Yorker Charles C. Hardenbrook experienced a change with the white community after a detail of soldiers at Beaumont was reassigned. "I heard today," he wrote, "that I was soon to receive a dose that would silence me now that the Yankees had gone away." Hardenbrook requested the troops be returned or at least he be allowed to move his office closer to federal troops. When some whites signed a petition pledging their support for him, Hardenbrook admitted he "would rather have them before my face than behind my back." His suspicions were warranted. Only a month after prematurely writing superiors he did "not anticipate problems," Hardenbrook was forced to flee for his safety. Headquarters reassigned him to Houston. Perhaps influenced by his desire to live, his constant discomfort from wartime injuries, or his wife's failing health, he asked to be relieved. Kiddoo honored the request. In a parting shot, *Flake's Daily Bulletin*, a Houston newspaper, sarcastically remarked "What a pity."[25]

Events in Washington, D.C., only exacerbated problems. In early 1866 Bureau officials in Washington and Galveston warned personnel to expect trouble as Congress moved to renew the Freedmen's Bureau. President Andrew Johnson's actions proved these officials quite prescient. Through proclamations and vetoes, including the second Bureau bill and Civil Rights Act, the president resisted congressional influence in Reconstruction. With "a friend in Washington," white Texans were emboldened to resist. A planter from southeast Texas spoke for many white Texans when he applauded the veto of "that most rascally Freedmen's Bureau Bill." "[I]t was a great misfortune that President Johnson vetoed the Bureau Bill at this time," a dismayed Philip Howard stated. "I believe this year would have nearly or quite haved [sic] settled the hostility of the white man against the Black man and each would have been much better off than they are. . . ." But now, Howard lamented, whites were optimistic that "slavery will be returned in some shape. . . ." Champ Carter listed the "many vague notions" held by whites after the president's vetoes and proclamations. William Longworth, in the middle of his problems in Seguin, likewise witnessed the effect Johnson had on the local citizenry. "Between vetoes, proclamations, and writs," he noticed, "I have had rather a sweet time of it, in maintaining the jurisdiction of the Bureau." Hoping to steel the resolve of superiors, Longworth encouraged them "not [to] let the president's policy cow you." If they wavered, he predicted, "Johnson . . . will split the Union, you can safely note that down as a fact." Longworth strongly believed the "Bureau must be continued, on it rests the Unity of the states, do not let the humble source from which those assertions come make you doubt or disbelieve them." Never one to miss an opportunity at self-aggrandizement, he yearned for a showdown with the president and believed himself up to the task to check Johnson's ways. "Were I present in Congress, and could I get myself listened to," he boasted, "I could carry the Bureau Bill against forty vetoes."[26]

Since the Bureau never eliminated the president's influence, according to Reconstruction historian Donald J. Nieman, "it failed to go to the root of the problem." Many Bureau men in Texas disliked Johnson, not out of love for the Radical Republicans, but because he made their jobs more difficult. Even amidst the increased hostilities, reports of violence could be misleading, especially when based on hearsay and second-hand knowledge. "In reference to murders of union men and Freedmen, and outrages committed within this District," wrote F. B. Sturgis at La Grange in late 1866, "any Report I may make will be but from Hearsay and no evidence of facts." Unable to tour subdistricts effectively, some agents took shortcuts in their reports. Rumors, suggestions, and speculations were passed off as facts to meet superiors' need for information and timely monthly reports. John William De Forest, a Bureau agent in western South Carolina who later penned a memorable work about his experiences with the organization, admitted to judging in some of his reports. A few Bureau agents in Texas also exaggerated or embellished the violence in their subdistricts. William L. Richter, in his article on the Bureau in Paris, Texas, also found one agent's "accounts of a bloodbath seem exaggerated."[27]

The state's reputation affected those appointed to Texas. A mental picture of murder and mayhem already existed. Before even assuming their positions, they "expected" the worst. For some, it was worse than they could imagine. For others, it was as bad as they thought. But for a few, it was not. At Lockhart,

Thomas H. Baker arrived at his post in May 1868 and immediately requested troops, claiming white people's feeling "is any thing else but good either by words or actions," with the "freed people [receiving] no protection outside" his office. Within two months at his post, however, Baker notified superiors that "for the present the free people can manage to get along without them [troops]." For the rest of the year, he reported the same, even remarking in October, "I get along with my business to use a common saying as lasy [sic] as an old Shoe." Louis W. Stevenson at Columbus reported that local law enforcement was to carry out the execution of a freedman and requested a detachment of soldiers, worrying that "certain bad white men may take advantage of the event to cause a disturbance which is evidently desired." The next month, after the execution "passed off quietly," Stevenson admitted "I see no real necessity for troops." For the first half of 1868, James P. Butler at Huntsville expected trouble. "There are no troops stationed at this post," he wrote to superiors in March 1868, and "the necessity for their presence is very obvious to you and it would be almost super- fluous for me to report that I have so often embraced in my former reports in regard to their necessity. One thing very evident they give tone and force to the existence of a Bureau." By late spring of 1868, however, he reiterated his lack of troops, but "they are not much needed" and he was "under no difficulties in the performance of my duties, everything is progressing peaceably and amicably." Pennsylvanian James C. Devine expected trouble in Huntsville and frantically telegrammed for a "strong" guard, underscoring he believed the guard "actually necessary." He made those requests on October 22. Two days later, Devine, per- haps realizing he had misjudged the situation, relayed to superiors the situation in his district was "all quiet [I] am able to get along without troops."[28]

Later claims of hiding their misdeeds or collusion appear unsubstantiated. To suggest violence did not exist would be equally false. Reconstruction was an emotionally charged time and not all claims of violence were trustworthy. For instance, the "scalawag" Bureau agent Philip Howard at Meridian believed his life threatened throughout the spring and summer of 1866. Howard thanked "the Supreme ruler for my preservation in my laborious and arderous [sic] duties I have done with no force to protect me, things but few men would [have] attempted and has won general esteem for my firm and mild course with these people." Months later, he again commented on his impending assassination: "I have run great risk of my life in holding this office. I am old and they cannot cheat me out of many years if the[y] kill me, I have done what I considered was my duty under the surrounding circumstances." Howard heard about a fray in Waco between white citizens and soldiers and believed the incident would result in an assault against him. He confided he simply awaited his turn ("I do not know when they may attack me"). Before his anticipated demise, however, Howard, "tired of the risk," asked to be relieved of duty in late 1866. He was personally thanked for his service, no small gesture considering Kiddoo's opinion of civilian agents. Having "escaped" death, Howard was doubtless thankful to be free of the job. So thankful, in fact, he returned to Bureau service in 1867, accepting once again the position at Meridian and remaining there until early the next year. After his tenure, Howard even thought so much of those same people who wanted him "dead" he married a local girl and lived in the same county until at least 1880 when he disappeared from the census.[29]

Every agent could appreciate Howard's fears. His pleas reflected an underlying anxiety held by nearly every subassistant commissioner at one time or another in Texas: the feeling of being alone, in a foreign land among different and, at times, hostile people. Whether a particular agent's tenure was tranquil or violent, he desired protection and assistance. Even in less chaotic districts, the workload was immense. Believing his predecessor too lenient, Kiddoo instituted policies aimed at greater oversight. As a result, tours, settlements, and endless paperwork could last from "sun up to sun down" and on many occasions from "sun up to sun up." And, of course, some had more work than others. Depending on the number of freedpeople, the hostility of the white community, and the size of the subdistrict, the workload proved too much for some. They realized that far more agents were needed, and many hoped that legislation currently before Congress in the summer of 1866 would remedy their protection and manpower problems.

4

Bureau Expansion, Bureau Courts, and the Black Code

The J. B. Kiddoo Era,
Summer 1866–November 1866

By the summer of 1866, the Freedmen's Bureau extended throughout Texas. Congress renewed the Bureau for another two years. Its renewal seemed necessary when the state's legislature passed measures to control the emancipated. These laws greatly increased the pressure to prevent white Texans from completely subordinating the freedpeople. In July 1866, after multiple presidential vetoes, Congress renewed the agency until July 1868. The second bill appropriated funds for agents' salaries, ranging from five to twelve hundred dollars a year. In time, salaries increased to a low of seventy-five and a high of one hundred and fifty dollars a month. With the carrot came the stick. Officials could now use the threat of nonpayment to punish malfeasance or neglect. Veteran Reserve Corps officers already in Bureau service could also remain after their muster out. Finally, the act specifically sanctioned Bureau courts.[1]

The new law could not have come at a better moment. Mid-summer 1866 marked the height of white resistance up to that time. In some areas, agents described conditions for the freedpeople "worse than slavery." In Hallettsville, for instance, a place believed ruled by "the revolver and bowie knife," William H. Heistand reported that whites "are very hostile toward the 'Bureau' and . . . any supporter of the Government." He detailed an incident within his office:

> Yesterday a number of men all wearing revolvers entered my office [and] the one who appeared to be the leader . . . cursed and abused me and the 'Bureau' in a most shameful manner telling me to leave the country that it was not safe for me and that my life was forfeited. In the evening an attempt was made to assassinate me . . . I was however compelled to hide in my room and to remain there till morning.[2]

To protect subordinates, Kiddoo could draw from several sources. One was civilians. Kiddoo shied from them much more than any AC in Texas. Of the 44

Table 4-1   Length of Service for Agents Appointed by Kiddoo

Type of Bureau Agent	Number	Average Length of Service (Months)
Civilian	5	7
Military	39	10.6

Note: Dates came from Freedmen's Bureau Roster of Officers and Civilians.

men appointed from May 1866 to January 1867, only 5 (11.4 percent) were civilians. Compared to the 31.4 and 28.6 percent civilian-appointee rate by Gregory
and Charles Griffin (Kiddoo's immediate successor) and the more than
29-percent rate for J. J. Reynolds (Griffin's successor), Kiddoo clearly preferred
military men. On average, Kiddoo's appointees served for 10.6 months, nearly
two and a half months higher than the overall average (7.8). Unlike his predecessor, Kiddoo's civilian appointees served 34 percent less than their military
counterparts.

Despite a higher percentage of military appointments, tenures ending due to
military operations of Kiddoo's appointees, compared to Gregory's, were significantly lower: 45.7 to 13.6 percent. (Table 4-2 lists the reasons agents appointed
by Kiddoo left the Bureau.) Where those terminated for malfeasance or whose
reason was not available was comparable (20.5 to 20 percent and 11.4 to 13.6) to
his predecessor's, Kiddoo's left at a higher rate due to Bureau operations: 5.7 to
18.2 percent. He appointed the first to die in service.

Table 4-2   Reasons Agents Appointed by Kiddoo Left Bureau Service

Reason	Number	Percentage
Bureau Operations: Bureau ended, consolidation, and transferal or reassignment within the agency	8	18.2
Military Operations: Mustered out or ordered to new assignment	6	13.6
Dropped on Request: Agent resigned appointment	12	27.3
Terminated: Dismissed for criminality, cruelty, Confederate service, or appointment revoked	9	20.5
N/A: Reason for leaving undetermined	6	13.6
Died: Disease or accidents	3	6.8
Died: Murdered	0	0
Total: All Kiddoo's Agents	n=44	100

Note: The information in this table came from various sources, but much of it came from the
U.S. Census and the Freedmen's Bureau Special Orders and Correspondences.

The regular army and volunteer corps remained the main source for manpower, but there existed another: the Veteran Reserve Corps (VRC) or Invalid Corps. Formed in 1863, the VRC comprised men "who were in some way disabled but were still fit for rear echelon duty." In all, eleven VRC officers served, a number considerably lower than the twenty-three who served in Georgia and the nearly one in three appointed as agents throughout the South. Despite wounds, they acquitted themselves as well as might be expected and, at times, better, with few complaints their wounds limited their performances. Officials considered Charles F. Rand to be one of the best agents to have served in Texas. Superiors liked Edward Miller enough they recommended reappointment after his muster out. At Marshall, Isaac M. Beebe, one of the few VRC officers not appointed by Kiddoo, adequately did his job, considering the circumstances of northeast Texas. Kiddoo wrote to Commissioner Howard about Beebe's bravery, moral character, and, most important, competence. "I consider" him, wrote Kiddoo, "one [of] the best officers of his rank in the service." Beebe left few critics before his abrupt death in early 1866. Samuel A. Craig, dealing with the consequences of William Longworth's course, hardly let his disability hinder his performance. N. H. Randlett served the agency for thirty months. He was thought enough of that in late 1867, as he neared muster out, superiors recommended reappointment. Of all those who served in Texas, only four had such an honor.[3]

These men soon discovered their injuries would not shield them from criticism. For example, freedpeople directed repeated complaints against VRC officer James F. Hutchison. Accusations surfaced he had not "yet tried to make [his] position otherwise remunerative than [his] authorized pay." Officials wrote Hutchison "these people stated their case and the evidence of their sincerity" convinced Kiddoo "almost against his own will that you have been neglecting the interests of the freedpeople . . . in other words that the planters have got control over you." Already frustrated by accusations of intemperance, which he vigorously denied, Hutchison accused the former slaves of being "influenced and controled [sic]" by their former masters. Hutchison frustratingly reminded superiors he performed his duties at great expense to his finances and health, and besides, freedpeople were not above lying or mischaracterization. A perplexed and greatly annoyed Hutchison admitted,

> If watching their interests and guarding them when at stake, listening to all their complaints and differences between themselves and complaints against their employers; investigating every case brought under my observation and awarding justice when in my judgment justice was due; doing for them at all

hours of the day and late in the night, sick or well; [and] counseling with and advising them. If efforts of this kind can be called neglecting their interest then I must frankly admit that they have been grossly neglected . . . In what way does it appear that I am controled [sic] by the planters[?] Is gold . . . offered in order to bias my judgment; yes, thrust into my face it has been, & into my pockets and hands more than once, but never in any instance have I accepted it or taken it from their presence. There is one positive fact to be observed, however, and that is, money has never been offered to me after a settlement was made or a case adjudicated, but always previous to [the] action.[4]

Speaking for all fellow agents frustrated with superiors, Hutchison reminded officials the "bait" was enticing, considering he had a family to care for and had "to pay out of my salary thirty five dollars per month . . . for board in this miserable town." But he reiterated he had "nothing to regret or to condemn myself for." He admitted his attitude "may be deemed unmilitary and, perhaps, undignified, but [it is] the best and most candid defense I am able to mount." By summer, Hutchison asked to be relieved, but he changed his mind and remained in service until his muster out in June 1867.[5]

VRC officers' performances, like their more able-bodied counterparts, ranged from competent to incompetent. J. Ernest Goodman lost his leg at the Battle of Ringgold Gap in late 1863. With endorsements from high-ranking Bureau officers, Goodman received an appointment. Freedpeople claimed he countenanced pro-Confederate displays and asked the Bureau teacher to refrain from singing Union songs because of their inflammatory content. With controversy swirling, Goodman asked for and received his release. Bureau officials in Galveston later received information he had illegally sold military supplies (food stuffs) and pocketed the money. Confronted at his home in Pennsylvania, Goodman claimed Kiddoo ordered him to trash the "musty and full of weevils" food. Goodman sold the better stuff and claimed his "intention was to turn it over to the Commissary." Albert A. Metzner, Henry H. Eddleson, and William H. Horton, all VRC officers, also left the Bureau under a cloud.[6]

Disabled or not, their Bureau uniform was the "great equalizer." Those who donned it, despite their best intentions or prudent course, could easily conflict with the white community. For example, Alfred T. Manning experienced one difficulty after another in Waco. Having lost a leg at Chancellorsville in 1863 and being "inconvenienced from a defect in his artificial limb," he still toured his district regularly. Manning discovered things progressing well, with some employers paying hands twice the state's going rate. His problem, however, was white treatment of the freedpeople. He recounted stories that "make your flesh creep." One involved a young freedman, who was castrated after being accused of raping a white girl. Manning arrested the perpetrators of this "most atrocious [deed] in the annals of barbarity."[7]

Governor Throckmorton soon involved himself. After corresponding with the district commander of Texas General Charles Griffin about the incident, the governor and general allowed the matter to go to civil authorities. Superiors instructed Manning to oversee the process for irregularities. This angered and insulted him. Fearing he might unnecessarily interfere in the case, superiors transferred Manning to Cotton Gin, approximately fifty miles from Waco. Perhaps frustrated with how things developed at Waco or his love for a local woman, Manning appeared to have lost his zeal for service. His "inattention," however, did not shield him from white attacks. An unknown person shot him in his good leg as he traveled one night to a friend's house. Manning literally crawled back to town. Officials granted his request to recover in Galveston, where superiors questioned him about accusations of bribery and financial misdoings, all of which he denied. His undoing came with intemperance and a massive bar bill, which he tried to shirk. Tired of his shenanigans, superiors relieved Manning in late summer 1867.[8]

As the organization expanded into the interior, SACs experienced greater resistance. Some looked to troops for assistance. Kiddoo could do little for subordinates than pass their requests on to military officials. Entering the state with more than fifty thousand soldiers in June 1865, within a year the army's numbers had dwindled to around five thousand and continued to fall. Of those, most served on the frontier and border with Mexico. Louis W. Stevenson at Columbus best expressed the sentiments of many who needed troops but never received them. "Orders without troops," he told superiors, "are [not] better than troops without orders." Starting with Gregory and continuing with Kiddoo, ACs in Texas requested help from the military only to be victims of circumstance and bureaucracy. Even those who received troops soon discovered their limitations. Most soldiers in the interior came from infantry units. Cavalry were necessary to chase down the outlaws, many of whom were on horseback. Agents for the entire time the agency operated in the state frequently requested cavalry, only to hear they were unavailable, he "must do the best he can with the troops [infantry] he has," or cavalry "cannot be broken up into small detachments without special detriment to . . . the service." Cavalry proved a rare commodity away from the frontier. Field agents thus often had to do without military support.[9]

At times, U.S. soldiers could be more a hindrance than a panacea (although this was the exception rather than the rule). Few examples better underscore the unnecessary problems troops caused for agents than the "Brenham Fire" in early September 1866. Only days after a dispute between Daniel Leonidas McGary and agent Samuel A. Craig had been "resolved," one of the most famous (or infamous) incidents during Reconstruction occurred in Brenham. Details remain sketchy, but whatever transpired left a U.S. soldier shot and portions of Brenham in ashes. Although three different inquiries found different versions, the general story went that several soldiers got into a fracas with white citizens, who fired shots that wounded one of the soldiers. Later that night, his fellow soldiers exacted revenge on the alleged perpetrator and his business by burning it, with the fire spreading to other buildings in the city. One historian called the soldiers' actions "among the worst cases of misconduct by troops during Reconstruction. . . ." Federal inquiries, nonetheless, cleared of wrongdoing the post commander and future Bureau agent, George W. Smith. The state legislature's inquiry disagreed. State and local officials for months fruitlessly tried to bring him to "justice." Samuel A. Craig had an insufferable situation on his hands after the incident. The situation in Brenham, coupled with Craig's reputation as "the Brenham burner," undermined his ability to perform his duties effectively. Headquarters thus reassigned Craig to Seguin where, as earlier noted, the problems created by William Longworth awaited him. Such problems caused by soldiers continued throughout the Bureau's time in Texas. Then Bureau chief J. J. Reynolds, in spring 1868, even lamented to Commissioner Howard that some soldiers detached to agents had done "more harm than good."[10]

Of course, agents preferred troops to no troops. But there existed other means to protect the freedpeople: placing alleged offenders on trial. Through Bureau courts, as they came to be called, these men protected black equality and legal rights. Bureau officials believed in the "centrality" of such color-blind proceedings. They thus considered leaving "the Negro in the hands of Southern courts . . . impossible." These courts operated under Gregory, but it was not until the second Freedmen's Bureau bill that they were specifically authorized. Varied according to the individual agent and circumstances, they normally comprised a SAC and the freedperson's and planter's representatives (but planters often refused to appoint a representative). When this happened, agents simply rendered decisions, dispensing with the representatives. The procedures most resembled that of a justice of the peace court, with defendants appearing to answer charges and with the right to call witnesses and use lawyers. Punishment was discretionary, resulting in an array of decisions: from dismissal to promises from and advice to the parties, from leniency with paying the fines (according to the defendant's age, ability to pay, and attitude during the hearing) to threats to the accused about consequences of nonpayment. Discretion also affected sentences. Some agents preferred fines (generally not exceeding five hundred dollars, and later one thousand), while others leaned toward jail sentences. For example, Samuel C. Sloan, unlike many others, preferred to sentence guilty parties (black or white) to jail sentences and hard labor. Bureau men certainly had "all the different powers of legislature and court . . . in one person, who was also the judge."[11]

Since Bureau headquarters at Washington and Galveston did not set down specific fines for offenses, agents had much discretion in setting amounts. In one case, Stanton Weaver fined a white man in Crockett two dollars for slapping a freedwoman, believing she was partly at fault. He fined another white man twenty dollars for striking and throwing down a freedwoman. Weaver thought the fine should not be too excessive, since the woman had a reputation for being quite quarrelsome. In another case, Weaver believed the limits set by superiors on fines to be too lenient. One man, known to be a "hard master," was angered when a former slave left his plantation to find a "better home." The former master found the freedman and "tied him and took him back to his farm where he gave him 150 lashes." Appalled, Weaver questioned headquarters judgment: "What shall I fine him? Would $5000 or $1000 be more than just?"[12]

Bureau agents could not charge for adjudication. All decisions could be appealed to headquarters. Despite an agent's authority to "try" individuals, Commissioner Howard, prompted by the president's wishes, circumscribed the Bureau's judicial activities in 1866. Understanding the agency to be temporary, he realized the freedpeople "would have to live under a system administered by local whites" and "preferred" litigants to work through civil courts. He wanted subordinates to "only interfere when injustice is done or . . . the civil authorities refuse to recognize the right [specifically, black testimony, something specifically granted by congressional statute and later Constitutional amendment] of the freedmen." Texas civil officials generally refused to acknowledge such testimony because it presaged freedmen jurors, freedmen enfranchisement, and freedmen "to be made socially and politically equal to whites."[13]

According to the subassistant commissioner records,[14] there are 6,794 extant court cases. Most subdistricts ranged between one and five hundred cases, with some numbering in the dozens and others like Houston close to a thousand. Austin exceeded a thousand. From the exceptional to the mundane, any dispute could arrive before an agent. They adjudicated everything from the standard

contract dispute to the extraordinary accusation of bestiality, from the dangerous assault to the more political gun rights argument (see Table 4-3). Of these,
the Bureau agent ruled in the plaintiff's favor 41.6 percent (n=2,826) of the time.
Defendant prevailed in only 7.5 percent of the cases (n=510). That disparity does
not necessarily suggest impartiality. The records suggest they arrived at the
decision supported by the evidence. A more credible explanation could be the
simple fact that people tend to seek judicial redress, then as well as now, when
truly wronged. In more than half (50.9 percent; n=3,458), however, a definitive
winner or loser was not recorded. The SAC simply noted the case settled (by the
two parties, with no other details to outcome), continued (no notation to resolution), dismissed (either resolved or frivolous), referred (to civil authorities or
military for resolution), or compromised (both in and out of the Bureau office,
without details to resolution).[15]

Not surprisingly, the overwhelming majority involved a black plaintiff against
a white defendant. Of the 6,794 cases, 4,689 were of this nature (see Appendix B).
That exceeds 69 percent. More than eleven hundred cases (n=1,109) involved
black plaintiffs and defendants. Only 648 cases arose from a white plaintiff—a
paltry 9.6 percent. Including those in which the plaintiff or defendant's race
could not be determined (348 cases, or 5.1 percent), cases involving a black plaintiff accounted for more than 85 percent (n=85.3) of the Bureau court trials for
Texas. Such evidence highlights the freed community's positive attitudes and
white Confederates' negative feelings toward these proceedings. Civil courts,
freedpeople believed, favored the old order. Bureau courts were "theirs." Intent
on protecting the emancipated, agents meted out justice according to facts and
not skin color—evidence that only further undermines the incredulous claims
these proceedings did more to harm freedpeople than help.

Bureau courts were normally quite informal proceedings. Otto F. Steinberg,
for example, adjudicated a case in Gonzales between the brother of a deceased
woman and her former husband. The brother accused Primus Dickes, the
deceased woman's husband and children's father, of domestic abuse and a relationship with his eldest daughter "in an unlawful and criminal manner." Steinberg sent a letter to Dickes to appear in his office to answer the charges. After
Dickes denied the charges, Steinberg ordered a hearing. Dickes, his accusers
(including the deceased's mother) and the children, along with all the parties'
lawyers and witnesses were present. Steinberg allowed witnesses for the accused
and accuser (on the alleged acts of cruelty and carnality and as character witnesses). After their testimony, he cleared the room to personally interview the
children and examine their physical demeanor. Analyzing all the testimony

Table 4-3   Types of Cases Adjudicated in Texas Freedmen's Bureau Courts

Type of Case	Number of Cases	Percentage of Cases
Settlement of Crop or Contract	640	9.4
Money Owed, Wages, or Debt	3,324	49
Assault, Threats, Fighting, Shooting, Murder, or Robbery	948	13.9
Contract Violation/Contract Interference	475	6.9
Apprenticeship	184	2.7
Possession of Property, Destruction of Property, or Theft	615	9.1
Domestic Issue	246	3.6
Slander or Defamation	11	.2
Abduction of Person or Retention	4	.1
Fraud, Blackmail, Embezzlement, Bribery, or Swindling	36	.5
Combination of Types	93	1.4
Other: Nothing, False Imprisonment, Disorderly Conduct, Unjust Fine, etc.	218	3.2
Total	n=6,794	100

Note: Cases came from the Register of Complaints in each subdistrict.

and evidence, Steinberg brought all the parties back and rendered his decision in favor of the husband. "I reminded them this office could not be considered a court of law," he stated,

> . . . that their services in cases brought before me . . . were not essentially necessary. . . . That judicial cases brought before me would be transacted in such a way as to *bring the complaint and accused to mutual and satisfactory understanding* between the parties and that I would be guided in my decision principally by plain common sense and impartiality. [italics added][16]

Many dispensed with the proceedings, hoping to "bring the complainant and accused to mutual and satisfactory understanding" and to prevent disputes from escalating. They realized their limitations and allowed common sense and fairness to guide them, or as agent George C. Abbott wrote, "Do as [I] would have be done." William H. Sinclair admitted being moved by a "sense of justice and equity between man and man." Mortimer H. Goddin divulged that he "must use considerable tact . . . [to keep] both black and white confined to justice and equity in getting along. . . ." William Garretson at Matagorda followed a course "in accordance with equity. . . ." Because many complaints were for small amounts and minor infractions, field personnel routinely "advised" or "talked to the parties" with no further action. As counselor, they hoped to educate the parties, preventing subsequent disputes. "I have endeavored to collect the debts by getting the parties together and advising them," wrote Abner Doubleday of baseball fame and the honor of firing the first shot in defense of Fort Sumter, "if necessary, to compromise in preference to going to the law." Whenever possible, they dismissed charges after promises to act better. Samuel C. Sloan settled "by force of personality alone, never assessing a fine" with apparent satisfaction to all. As historian Sara Rapport stated, agents mattered, not issues.[17]

At times, Bureau men cast a skeptical eye toward claims by employers against their hands. Suspicion sometimes guided their policy toward whites. "It is not to be expected," thought F. D. Inge at Leona, "that the slave owner (who is now the employer of the freedmen) who from time 'immemorial' has used the whip[,] lash[,] and stick will give it up at once, unless in the presence of a power that is capable of enforcing." Guided by their experience with the two groups, agents took the former slave's word more seriously. Even when they were at fault, they tempered their punishment, or as one agent put it, punished them "mild but firm." Agents had jurisdiction in any case involving a freedperson. Cases, however, were to be limited to minor disagreements, or what one historian calls "small quarrels and petty disputes." Superiors worried subordinates lacked the legal expertise to try felonies like grand larceny, rape, or murder. On a few rare occasions, though, Bureau men did punish whites for attempted rape and murder. In later years, they could arrest offenders accused of felonies, but they then had to release them to military officials or civil authorities. (Bureau officials in Texas subsequently acknowledged the benefit of legal training and pushed for men who were state judges.) Further inhibiting was the Supreme Court. In *Ex parte Milligan* (1866) the court ruled the application of military tribunals to citizens unconstitutional where civil courts were in operation. This not only cast continuing doubt on the Bureau's court operations but also insured the continuation and, at times, predominance of local judicial proceedings for the citizenry's redress. All the same, most cases comprised these categories: contract violations (on the part of whites or blacks), wages, or settlement resolution; denial of parental rights (either apprenticeship or custody); property disputes; and minor threats and assaults (see Table 4-4). Such approximated 91 percent of all proceedings. This breakdown continued until early 1867. Then

Table 4-4   Black Plaintiffs Economic and Nonviolent Criminal Complaints

Type of Case	Number of Cases	Percentage of All Cases (n=6,794)	Won by Plaintiff	Lost by Plaintiff	Neither Won nor Lost
Settlement of Crop/Contract	640	9.4	236	39	365
Wages/Money Owed/Debts	3,324	49	1,541	193	1,590
Contract Violation/Interference	475	6.9	175	35	265
All Economic Disputes	**4,439**	**65.3**	**1,952**	**267**	**2,220**
Possession/Destruction of Property/Theft	615	9.1	262	66	287
Fraud/Blackmail/Bribery	36	.5	13	2	21
Slander/Defamation	11	.2	1	2	8
All Nonviolent Criminal Issues	**6629**	**.8**	**276**	**604**	**2,536**

Note: Cases came from the Register of Complaints in each subdistrict.

Assistant Commissioner Charles Griffin limited proceedings to labor contract disputes, with all others transferred to the civil courts.[18]

Of the cases tried, an overwhelming majority dealt with settlement disputes (disputes about crop division), monetary and wage disputes (disputes concerning money/wages owed), and contract violations/interference (disputes about contract stipulations): collectively equaling 4,439 cases, or 65.3 percent of all cases: settlement (n=640), monetary and wages (n=3,324), and contract violation/interference (n=475). Less than three-quarters (74.9 percent) involved a black plaintiff and white defendant. Slightly more than one in ten (10.8 percent) comprised the inverse, while 13 percent were all freedpeople affairs. Fifty-six cases did not fit these categories (1.3 percent). One would suspect the high percentage involving black complaints against whites would correspond to a similar percentage of cases where the plaintiff wins. This does not appear to be the case. Collectively, the plaintiff won 1,952 of the 4,439, or approximately 44 percent.[19]

As Table 4-5 shows, the number of economic and nonviolent cases brought before agents increased each year, peaking in 1867. (Table 4-6 shows the number of such cases by region.) Congressional Reconstruction's ascendancy and Charles Griffin's tenure, who distrusted hostile civil courts, explains the zenith in 1867. Nearly 50 percent or more of the cases of an economic or nonviolent criminal nature occurred in 1867 alone: settlement of crop/contract (45 percent),

Table 4-5   Number of Economic and Nonviolent Criminal Cases Year by Year

Type of Case	1865	1866	1867	1868
Settlement of Crop/Contract	0	41	288	311
Wages/Money Owed/Debts	1	433	1,668	1,222
Contract Violation/Interference	0	64	280	131
All Economic Disputes	1	538	2,236	1,664
Possession/Destruction of Property/Theft	5	84	265	261
Fraud/Blackmail/Bribery	0	6	20	10
Slander/Defamation	0	3	7	1
All Nonviolent Criminal Issues by Year	5	93	292	272
Total Number	6	631	2,528	1,936

Note: Cases came from the Register of Complaints in each subdistrict.

wages/debts/money owed (50.2 percent), contract violation/interference (58.9 percent), possession/destruction of property (43.1 percent), fraud/blackmail/ bribery (55.6), and slander/defamation (63.6). With congressional Reconstruction waning and Griffin's successor readying for the not-so-distant day when the Bureau ceased operations, numbers in every case except settlement of crop and contract began tapering-off the following year. One would expect with the winding-down in late 1867 complaints not concerning contracts would effectively disappear. That was not the case. Where white Texans began to see it as a dead letter in 1868, the freedpeople continued to bring complaints of all types for redress to the organization.

Table 4-6   Number of Economic and Nonviolent Criminal Cases by Region

Type of Case	North Texas	South Texas	East Texas	Gulf Coast	Central Texas
Settlement of Crop/Contract	1	3	216	129	291
Wages/Money Owed/Debts	52	45	978	1,250	999
Contract Violation/Interference	0	6	100	77	292
All Economic Disputes	53	54	1,294	1,456	1,582
Possession/Destruction of Property/Theft	2	4	137	202	270
Fraud/Blackmail/Bribery	0	2	12	6	16
Slander/Defamation	0	0	0	6	5
All Nonviolent Criminal Issues by Region	2	6	149	214	291
Total Number	55	60	1,443	1,670	1,873

Note: Cases came from the Register of Complaints in each subdistrict. For counties of each Region, see Appendix B.

If he found an employer guilty of nonpayment, an agent generally ordered him to pay his laborers. To increase the likelihood of payment, he sometimes placed a lien against the crop. On occasion, agents confiscated personal property for sale to pay the owed wages. Even this did not always guarantee payment. Both uncooperative local officials and the lack of troops in the immediate vicinity to help enforce decisions contributed to white noncompliance. "Give me Military backing and I can get along well," Charles Haughn declared. "Without troops I can only settle claims referred to me by both parties. Those who wish to cheat the [freedmen] will not come before me . . . ." Nesbit B. Jenkins at Wharton stated that "the apathy of the civil authorities and the want of power to enforce any order or decision I may give constitute my chief difficulty." Because of the proceeding's nature, compliance rested a great deal on the offending party's faith, desire, and capability to "do the right thing." Field agents often used practical arguments to increase compliance. "I do not wish to interfere if you can make any satisfactory arrangement with" the plaintiff, the SAC at Austin informed one defendant. "A failure to comply with the above [decision]," wrote John F. Stokes, "will cause more inconvenience than so simple a matter would warrant." Patrick F. Duggan warned one that failure "on your part to return the property may cause you more trouble than the [property] would be worth."[20]

Even when civil courts settled cases involving freedpeople, agents still offered protection. Superiors authorized subordinates to oversee civil proceedings to ensure impartiality, and so long as civil authorities were, they were not to interfere. If a freedperson did not receive justice, agents could abrogate the decision and retry the individual. Since Bureau courts operated under martial law, constitutional questions of double jeopardy did not apply. In response to such moves, however, civil officers criticized Bureau courts, calling them unconstitutional, a travesty of justice, and discriminatory. Even with a hostile state judiciary, Bureau officials were rather ambivalent about circumventing civil courts. They hoped to secure "the co-operation of the civil authorities" and preferred not to interfere until local authorities forced their hands. When that happened, agents were to intervene and retry the individual. If local authorities protested, they were not to "pay any attention [to anything from them] that interferes with your job." Agents determined whether local officials had been unbiased. Such a policy founded on "one's best judgment" only caused many more letters to headquarters for concurrence and guidance. "I therefore feel a delicacy in acting on these complaints," admitted Jacob C. DeGress, expressing the sentiments of many a field agent, "unless I will be sustained by you in my action."[21]

Although a few local administrators tolerated this federal intervention, such instances proved the exception. Throughout the state, local authorities resisted Bureau interference. "It [was] generally understood that it was my intention to release (by force if necessary) all [controversial] cases from duress and examine into the facts myself," wrote Samuel C. Sloan at Richmond. "The counsel for the defense shrewdly took advantage of it as an argument before the jury & the consequence was that no freedman was sentenced to imprisonment . . . I have every reason to believe that such action on the part of the officers of the Bureau is absolutely necessary to insure the freedmen any justice before the civil authorities." J. Ernest Goodman disputed with Colorado County authorities, who continuously arrested one freedman only to have Goodman intervene each time to have him released. They rewarded Goodman's "good deed" with an indictment of his own, which Bureau officials simply ignored. "In all their actions concerning the Bureau," Stanton Weaver at Crockett assured superiors, "they illustrate perfectly the fable of the 'mountain which . . . shook like an earthquake, and produced a mouse.'"[22]

Two possible remedies came with General Ulysses S. Grant's General Orders No. 44 and the recently passed Civil Rights Act of 1866. The former authorized the military to arrest civilians accused of violence against United States government personnel when civil authorities neglected to bring such individuals to trial. Once in custody, the military could hold them until civil authorities were willing or capable to try them. The Civil Rights Act of 1866 guaranteed the former slaves equality before the law. Those violating the bill's provisions would be tried in federal, not state, courts. Enforcement was left to federal officials, including Bureau agents, to arrest anyone suspected of violating the act. These measures were hardly a panacea. Grant's order allowed Bureau agents to make arrests, but that was possible only with troops, which by 1866 were in short supply in the interior. Also, so long as General Orders No. 26, which required the military to transfer all citizens they arrested to the civil authorities for trial if the civil tribunals were functioning, was believed to apply to Texas, Grant's G. O. No. 44 was only a "stopgap" measure. Jacob C. DeGress, for example, complained whites in southeastern Texas thought G. O. No. 44 had been revoked. They became "defiant or something to that effect [and are] refusing to acknowledge the authority or power of this Bureau to arrest parties for abusing negroes," he remarked. "There seems to be a general system of whipping and abusing freedmen as the Planters say 'because they can,' that the Military are now subordinate to the civil authorities, and that the Freedmen's Bureau nuisance is done away with." According to historian Donald G. Nieman, the Civil Rights

Act of 1866 had limitations. Bureau and military officials, aware of the president's desire to transfer cases to the civil authorities, failed to coordinate a uniform policy. Individual agents ultimately determined if the bill was violated, which created an inconsistent and tempered policy. Indifference and hostility from certain politicians in Washington and the difficulty in obtaining convictions against state officials in federal court further undermined the bill's effective use to enforce civil rights for the freed community.[23]

Despite limitations, G. O. No. 44 and the Civil Rights Act of 1866 were still "extraordinary assertions of national power" for their time. The Bureau still assumed that states eventually would "resume principal responsibility for civil rights protection," even though state courts were generally unfavorable toward the emancipated. The agency's judicial actions drew much criticism from state and federal officials, most notably Governor Throckmorton and the president. Since the first Bureau bill never specifically authorized Bureau courts, officials had to depend on President Andrew Johnson's authority to try cases. He placed great limitations, pressuring for transferal to civil courts as quickly as possible. Federal officials in Texas, however, had greater "leeway" than in other states. The state legislature still had not completed the president's Reconstruction plan. "[I]nadequacy was due primarily to the virtually insurmountable practical obstacles to civil rights enforcement," noted legal historian Robert J. Kaczorowski, and "political considerations rather than the inadequacy of legal authority prevented more effective civil rights enforcement by the Bureau."[24]

With so many orders and proclamations that seemed to conflict from above, naturally, confusion existed. The main cause stemmed from the uncertainty whether General Orders No. 26 applied to Texas (since the state legislature had yet to complete the president's Reconstruction plan). As noted, if it did, SACs would have to transfer cases to civil courts. Kiddoo asked the military headquarters at New Orleans for the answer. The Texas district commander, Brevet Major General Horatio G. Wright, believed the order did, since the president had declared the rebellion over earlier that spring and civil courts were in operation. He therefore informed Kiddoo Bureau courts would no longer be permitted. A worried Kiddoo, who believed "civil courts worse than a farce," disagreed, noting the Texas legislature had not fully complied with the president's Reconstruction plan. With conflicting answers, Kiddoo wrote to Commissioner Howard about G. O. No. 26, wanting to know if Wright had made a mistake. Much to Kiddoo's chagrin, Howard notified him it did apply to Texas "as well as anywhere else, if the Civil tribunals are in operation." Meanwhile, Wright, showing doubt to whether the order applied, contacted his superiors at the War Department. From his conversation with them, he issued a new order that repealed No. 26 within Texas, but only until the state legislature completed the president's Reconstruction program. Until then, Bureau courts could operate.[25]

In late summer 1866 the Texas legislature "completed" the requirements of Johnson's Reconstruction Plan and elected a new state government. The freedpeople would now have to find redress in the unfavorable civil courts. Agents reported numerous instances of civil authorities who "punished [freedmen] by their law but do not protect them." When all appeared lost for the agency's ability to protect the freed community, Commissioner Howard sent Kiddoo a confidential letter. Ordered not to publish it, he was to use the letter's contents as a framework to reestablish Bureau courts if necessary and to send a copy to each field agent. Where Bureau courts had been abolished, the instructions were to be disregarded; but where they still operated, agents were to use this framework as an outline for their judicial operations. To Kiddoo, the commissioner's instructions were not as important as his intent: for the time being, the agents' judicial responsibilities would remain in effect in Texas.[26]

The situation created by congressional statutes, presidential proclamations, and military general orders created much confusion and uncertainty. Those in the field flooded headquarters with points of clarification. Superiors tried to remedy the confusion. But for men with little legal training, confusion, of course, remained. At times, even Kiddoo and military officials were confused at what applied and what did not. So, too, were the men in the field. Therefore, they had to rely upon their own "judgement [sic] according to what [they] conceive to be right." With room for interpretation, there never existed uniformity in the Bureau's legal procedures in Texas. Agents could only hope to create a "mutual and satisfactory understanding between the parties." Whites, however, saw almost any decision favorable to the freedpeople as outrageous. According to Nesbit B. Jenkins at Wharton, he "never in any case gives Judgment in favor of a Plaintiff until the Defendant has been cited to appear and has had ample means and time allowed him in which to prove his non-indebtedness or Justify his proceedings." Samuel A. Craig remembered, "I had a hard time convincing the white employers that even if the negro did not work, it was no cause for his beating and assaulting him, and a fine of ten or twenty dollars could make them hot and felt that my judgment was 'prejudiced,' 'outrageous' etc." Freedpeople, on the contrary, greatly valued what agents did for them, evidenced by the numerous cases brought before them for adjudication, understanding these proceedings "challenged the racial beliefs in the South and imparted some sense

[that] the black person now was a citizen." Bureau men helped establish the freedpeople as the newest citizens. Jacob C. DeGress and George C. Abbott, for example, referred to them as "citizens" long before Congress defined them as such. Oliver H. Swingley implied the same with the "negro is free and entitled to the same protection . . . as the white man." Despite what agents did for the freed community, some historians have criticized them and their judicial pro-ceedings for being too conservative and ephemeral, concluding "the tragic failure of the Freedmen's Bureau [was its] . . . futile efforts to establish equal justice in the South." According to critics, their attempts to ensure equality turned out to be a "conservative solution to a complex problem."[27]

These criticisms, although valid in some limited circumstances, miss the main point. These men, as "judge and jury," achieved the best that could be expected at the time. They walked a thin line, balancing the wishes of their superiors (in Galveston, New Orleans, and Washington), the country's uneas-iness with actions threatening federalism, and the nation's hesitancy to try civilians in military courts. Moreover, these critics discount the ability of civil authorities to impede justice in ways not so readily apparent. Civil authorities could easily create the "illusion" of justice by admitting black testimony and then disregarding it or delaying the case until the plaintiff ran out of money or no longer wanted to pursue the matter. Local officials could "investigate" freed-people's claims but not indict, or they could investigate, indict, try, and convict white individuals, but "punish" them leniently. All limited the effectiveness to protect the former slaves' legal rights. To be sure, the presence of Bureau courts had a salutary effect. They provided a forum to people who had little money for legal fees and knowledge about the law. Plus, agents attempted to use their legal authority to force white Southerners to recognize the freedpeople as exactly that—free people. Even critics grudgingly admit these courts, despite their "problems," benefited the emancipated as a "benevolent midwife," who demanded "from the southern states legal recognition of the freedmen's right to be heard in court. . . ."[28]

Subassistant commissioners' judicial responsibilities became all the more important in late 1866. Under Johnson's Reconstruction plan, former Confeder-ate states had benchmarks to meet. Desirous to retain as much of the old system as possible, these state legislatures passed controversial laws in late 1865 and early 1866, collectively called the Black Code. On the surface (and only after passage of the Civil Rights Act of 1866), lawmakers touted these laws as racially neutral. But in practice, they aimed to circumscribe the freedoms of recently emancipated. In 1866 the Eleventh Legislature passed statutes that regulated everything from apprenticing minors to punishing vagrancy, from regulating labor to establishing schools. The Code granted to freedpeople some never before held rights, including the right to be secure in person and property, to sue and be sued, to contract, and to marry. Not nearly as punitive as other former Confederate states' codes, the Texas Black Code still had the same intent: reestablishing control of the former slaves.[29]

Kiddoo instructed subordinates either to apply the state laws in a way fair to both parties or to ensure that local officials did the same. He wanted to ensure that local officials did not use it in a way that violated the recently passed civil rights bill. Of those portions abrogated by the Bureau, most important was the labor law. According to Bureau authorities, its intent was to bring back slavery in a new form. One measure stipulated any unauthorized termination on the laborer's part, "without *cause* or *permission*," resulted in lost wages. The labor law also outlined stringent codes of conduct for workers. This allowed employers to deduct wages or simply dismiss him/her for "gross misconduct."[30]

With the Code's adoption, field agents now took a greater interest in apprenticeship (see Table 4-7). In the nineteenth century, apprenticeship was an accepted and recognized measure to deal with indigent or orphaned children. A practice mostly confined to the North, yet "almost nonexistent" by the beginning of the war, apprenticeship occurred when a local magistrate determined that a child was parentless or poor and bound him/her out. Those who received the child (after placing a bond) were required to provide proper housing, medical care, and education or to teach "a specified trade or occupation." All contracts had a release age: all minors under fourteen could be bound with the consent of their parents or legal guardian until married or upon reaching the age of twenty one, and anyone fourteen and older could be apprenticed only with parental consent.

Table 4-7   Apprenticeship Cases Brought Before Bureau Agents in Texas, 1866–1868

Plaintiff	Number of Cases	Number Won by Plaintiff	Percentage Won by Plaintiff
Freedman/men	90	27	30
Freedwoman/women	76	30	39.5
Freedpeople	1	0	0
White Person	12	8	66.7
U.S./Texas Government	5	1	20
Total	n=184	n=66	

Note: Cases came from the Register of Complaints in each subdistrict.

Under no circumstances were Bureau agents to bind out those old enough to enter labor contracts. In the North, race played little part in the system. In the South, especially with slavery's end, apprenticing became not only a way to care for indigent black minors, but also a way for whites to procure labor. The Bureau, in fact, "sought to mediate in these cases . . . as was the pattern with the negotiation of labor contracts for field hands and tenant farmers. . . ."[31]

Prior to the state's apprentice law, headquarters ordered agents not to bind out children or allow civil authorities to do the same. Instead, they had to "make the best temporary disposition you can for them." This meant either act as the minor's guardian or find a "good home for them [and] give the parties permission to keep them until further orders. . . ." In most cases agents became the primary caretaker in the child's "moral and physical health." This policy not to bind out children until the state passed an apprentice law, however, had ramifications. Although agents refused to apprentice children, state judges went ahead and bound out freed children to whites anyway. The Bureau's "wait and see" policy actually led to a more proactive policy against apprenticeship abuse. The policy (not binding out children until the state passed an apprentice law) threatened to increase the number of indigent minor and orphaned children, since planters initially refused to enter apprentice contracts fearing they would not be upheld. With their favored options blocked (like compensation for slaves), these same planters soon warmed to the practice. Further increasing indigent black children were mothers who could no longer care for their children and began leaving them to the care of subassistant commissioners.[32]

Although Bureau officials in Galveston refused to allow children to be bound out until the state passed an apprenticeship law, field personnel still requested instructions on exactly what to do. According to Kiddoo, he confessed "the matter of guardianship" gave the agency the most trouble under his command in Texas. It appears that a number did not know or understand the policy. "I have been somewhat at a loss to know what to do with orphan minors," wrote Austin agent Oliver H. Swingley, "there being no apprenticeship law in the State." Superiors either ignored him or he did not understand their response, for a month later he again requested "instructions in regard the appointing Guardians for Orphan minor." Ira P. Pedigo at Woodville asked if "I have the right to bind them out as poor children are bound out in many of the states." At Marshall, Hiram Seymour Hall also requested guidance on the organization's apprentice policy. Before agents could be educated to the policy, however, superiors shifted direction and instructed them to recognize and to enforce the recently passed state apprentice law. Contracts were to be approved only if made with no distinction to color, made in good faith by all parties, and made according to the state's law. Headquarters ordered agents not to bind out "children who have parents [but] to give them to their parents." The mother was to have primary control, a policy very similar to the ones followed in Georgia and Virginia. This policy, however, applied only if the mother, and in a few instances the father, could financially provide for the child(ren) or to "families that have competent heads." If an agent determined a mother unable to care for her child (such as being on federal relief) or the child lacked a "competent" family member, he could allow that child bound out. John T. Raper, for instance, had a case in which an unmarried freed mother had contracted for room and board with a white man. She had six children but could care for only three, with "the other three running wild over the country." According to Raper, she was "improvident" and "weak-minded." He informed superiors he could get those three children "employment" with good white families. Raper asked if he could consider the children orphans "when they cannot, or will not provide for themselves . . . always keeping in view their best interests." This meant apprenticing them to "a permanent home" instead of changing "homes every year, picking up the vice of every plantation as they go."[33]

Even after passage of the state's law and subsequent policy change, some still needed direction. As late as August 1868, ignorance about the Bureau's apprentice policy remained. William J. Neely in Victoria bluntly asked, "Is it my duty to apprentice orphan children?" Even F. P. Wood at Brenham, who concurrently performed as a justice of the peace, admitted confusion. "[S]ometimes the employer and often the minor and I am at a loss to decide these cases," he admitted, "as I find some conflict of Military orders on the subject." He asked whether apprentice contracts issued by civil authorities under the state's old statute (the one passed prior to the war) were recognized or were contracts made under the statute passed by the Eleventh Legislature (the one passed with the Black Code) the only legitimate ones? Wood wanted further clarification: "Have [I] the right to annul these letters—except for failure on the part of the employer or contracting party to fulfill his obligations?" Confusion aside, it appears Wood recognized that many apprentice contracts, although in compliance with state law, were made under less-than-equitable circumstances.[34]

Bureau agents' responsibilities did not end once a child was bound out. They soon discovered some white Texans attempted every way possible to violate apprentice contracts. David S. Beath voided one, ordering the children returned after the white man left Texas for Mississippi "without complying with the law." A woman known as Mrs. Roberts beat her apprentice. The agent in consequence fined her twenty dollars, and threatened to void the apprentice contract. With a promise from a white man to pay her flour and wages in the future, freedwoman Rachel Hunter agreed to apprentice her daughter Mary to him. He agreed that if he did not make the promised compensation, the girl would be returned "anytime [she] was dissatisfied." Despite reneging on the flour and the girl's desire to return to her mother, the white man refused to release her. She complained to the agent who secured her release. After a child had been apprenticed, a Bureau agent's role then became "supervisory, except when flagrant cases of injustice occur when it becomes his duty to act."[35]

Of course, they did not uphold apprentice contracts under all circumstances. They rarely hesitated to break them if unfair, even if drafted according to state law or even with the mother's approval. In fact, a mother's parental rights were not absolute. If a freedwoman bound her child(ren) out in a way they deemed unjust, Bureau men voided them and returned the child(ren) to parent(s) or allowed them to earn a living on their own. "No mother has any right to make such a contract," stated William H. Sinclair about one unfair apprentice contract, and if she agreed to such a contract, "she is a fool to have done it even [if she] had the right." To be sure, agents had the final word, with superiors generally supporting their actions. Until satisfied the child's welfare was secured, Bureau agents would not approve the contract.[36]

When infractions occurred, SACs did their best to address them according to the law or what they saw as equitable. This approach meant releasing freed children bound out "without the consent of their parents or the children." On numerous occasions, the freed community brought such cases to the attention of local agents: 168 of the 184 cases had a black plaintiff, or more than 91 percent (91.3). Such instances are frequent enough to contradict later historical claims that freedwomen (and men for that matter) rarely turned to the agency for assistance or only did so as a means of last resort. "In several cases where minor children were bound out without consent of parents," wrote Samuel C. Sloan from Richmond, "I have upon proper complaint had them delivered up to their parents . . . [because they] are the legal guardians of and have a right to the services of their children." Charles E. Culver, witnessing parents and siblings of illegally bound children pleading with planters for their release, reported that these "new time Slave Holders" often times responded to the parent's pleas with "go to Hell or the Bureau." Although Culver intervened, he admitted his impotence without troops, since they were "the most influential and at the same time some of the worst men" in his district. Gregory Barrett admitted "very few of the freedpeople can read [and] those interested immediately have no

Knowledge of the Apprentice[ships] until 'after' its consummation by the Court." When he found such situations, he "revoke[d] all such acts of indenture, unless otherwise ordered." William G. Kirkman at Boston returned a freed boy to his grandfather once the "evidence [was] considered." On a different occasion, he annulled a contract when the white defendant refused to appear at his office. Parental rights even extended to fathers. His personal philosophy and outlook about nineteenth-century domesticity, child welfare, and free labor, of course, greatly influenced a Bureau man's decision than any mandated policy. Walter B. Pease at Houston, for example, returned a child to his father, deeming him "a hard working industrious man" with the ability "to support him." If they deemed the contract illegal or not properly fulfilled, Bureau men did not hesitate to return children to parents, grandparents, and even siblings.[37]

These men held not just whites to the contract and law but also the apprenticed and their parents. Of those cases where a definite winner and loser could be determined, whites (both women and men) won 41 times out of 184, or approximating 22 percent. A local judge came to Louis W. Stevenson with a complaint that the child bound to him had run away. Stevenson found "no question [the child] was treated well" and returned the child. Anytime parents of bound children complained about illegality or mistreatment, agents rarely hesitated to investigate a claim, void a contract, or fine the guilty if they found the accusations valid. If they found the claims baseless, of course, they upheld the apprentice contract. J. D. Vernay at Goliad investigated a black grandmother's complaint about abuse against her apprenticed granddaughter. What Vernay discovered was every time a new Bureau agent arrived, the old woman solicited him for help. Not only did the girl want to stay with the white man, but Vernay thought "the girl is much better treated than if she was with her grandma." P. Johnson, a white man, brought a complaint against Guy Johnson, an apprenticed freed boy. After his son had been apprenticed, with "his consent" at the time, Robert Johnson changed his mind and took his boy back. P. Johnson turned to the Bureau for recourse. William G. Kirkman investigated. He determined the apprenticeship valid and P. Johnson to be fulfilling its stipulations. Guy Johnson was ordered returned.[38]

To a great extent, SACs believed their problems would be greatly lessened if only freedmen fulfilled their paternal responsibilities. As historian Mary Farmer-Kaiser stated, they had to be taught their "manly responsibilities." This included caring for his children and their mother. For example, N. H. Randlett at Bryan heard a claim by one freedwoman that a freedman named Frank had promised marriage, and she was pregnant with his child. Although "the evidence is not sufficient neither are appearances sufficient" to prove the pregnancy, Randlett ordered Frank to support the woman "in event of its birth by the time . . . it will be born." In the city of Austin, Elisa Morgan, a freedwoman of "indifferent character" with "several children by different men," approached agent Henry Young for help. Young found that for the last two years she had lived with a white man named Presser Hopkins, who had a bad reputation. According to Morgan, she "got him in the family way" as recently as two weeks ago and was apparently pregnant by him, despite the relationship being less than amicable. To complicate matters, Hopkins had already agreed to marry another. Young, who believed Hopkins was "dating" both women simultaneously, inquired to superiors about bastard laws, which Texas did not have at the time. Informing his subdistrict had many bastard children, Young suggested "a precedent [be] given" so that "many of their mothers would bring actions against the fathers." Agents even held white men responsible for their children with freedwomen. By holding fathers accountable, they hoped to ensure not just that dependency would remain a private rather than public matter, but that far fewer freedpeople would become wards of the state.[39]

A few men defined the child's best interest very broadly, believing mothers "should not be deprived of such guardianship even at [their] request." Anthony M. Bryant at Sherman boasted that the state's apprenticeship law "in my District [is] a dead letter" and "the men who made [this law should] be ashamed of [it] or at least I think they ought to be." In Corpus Christi, John Dix likened the practice to slavery. He refused to allow "colored children [to be] apprenticed to white people, for . . . most people would treat them as slaves. . . ." As we have seen, William Longworth also believed its negatives far outweighed any positives. At La Grange, Isaac Johnson likewise had nothing but contempt for apprenticing. "[A]ny Law," he sermonized, "that will place any considerable number of freed children under the control and power of the white people of this County with their present feeling and disposition towards the black race" is egregious. Charles Haughn concurred: it "only makes slaves of the children."[40]

Bryant, Dix, Johnson, and Haughn, however, were not the norm. Most sub-assistant commissioners realized its need or, in the words of one historian, countenanced it as "an unavoidable evil in the immediacy of emancipation." Therefore, they had a less antagonistic approach to the system. To guard against dependency, apprenticeship would exist. According to recent scholarship, Bureau men were "undeniably shaped" by their notions of free labor and when whites abused the apprenticeship system, these men, offended at the "denial of the principles of free labor," backed freed parents "who worked to release [their children] from such unjust bonds. . . ." To preclude dependency and protect the freed children, parental rights of freedpeople occasionally were set aside for those of their children and the common good. Agents found themselves in a bit of a pickle, pulled in opposing (and often incompatible) directions: the emotion of aggrieved parents, the interests of the children, and the interests of the state and public. Attempting to square this circle, they had to "use their best judgment" or "do as was right and proper." They tried to account for the child's wishes, white's intentions, and the parent's moral state and financial ability. With so much information to "process," agents relied heavily upon common sense and their sense of fairness. Such an approach precluded uniformity, resulting in varying actions from the excesses of William Longworth, to the one-sided courses of Anthony M. Bryant and John Dix, to the case-by-case approach by the vast majority of others. Not all parties, of course, were satisfied. On occasion, perhaps, they probably erred. More often than not, they made what they believed to be the best, most just, and fairest decision according to the facts, the law, and, most important, what they saw as the child's interest.[41]

If the apprentice contract was shown to be illegal, these men did not hesitate to break it. They realized apprenticing, although an imperfect solution to an unacceptable societal problem, was open to abuse. Bureau men in Texas consequently did not attack the institution of apprenticeship. They did not attack apprenticeships as vigorously as did agents in Maryland, where local officials ultimately abandoned the practice altogether. Texas Bureau men did not "strongly advocate" or, at times, "demand" binding out as many agents did in Tennessee. Nor did they always uphold contracts "at the expense of the view of the primacy of parental rights" as many did in North Carolina. Those in Texas followed a course similar to the one in Georgia and Virginia. They decided apprentice cases generally in favor of parental (freedpeople) rights. This occurred only in conjunction with what they believed to be in the child's best interest not necessarily, in the words of one historian's claim, because they believed the practice "a legalized form of child slavery and forced labor."[42]

This juggling act, however, has been a source of criticism, especially when agents did anything other than return freed children to their mothers or relatives. As historians have begun to focus more attention on gender in Reconstruction, some have criticized Bureau men's relationship with apprenticeship. According to this view, these men, at best, displayed insensitivity and chauvinism. At the worst, their misogynistic ways wrecked homes, circumscribed parental rights, and helped to destroy the freedpeople's familial integrity. Historian Laura Edwards, for example, concludes they overlooked "the blatant inequities of the system if not for the freedmen themselves, who kept agents' attention riveted on the issue, whether they liked it or not." Lynda J. Morgan likened their actions to the "interstate slave trade." She concludes "occasionally" SACs broke apprenticeship contracts, but in general they "colluded with planters in the apprenticeship system." Leslie A. Schwalm, another gender historian, is critical of their "ignorance of extended families and the cultural significance of a community's sense of mutual duty and obligation among extended and fictive kin [and] the reconstitution and defense of black family life. . . ." Even historians rather sympathetic to agents' relations with the black family unit are quite critical of its use and defense of apprenticeship. "Bureau policy makers may have objected to the use of apprenticeship as a method of racial control," concluded Mary Farmer-Kaiser, "but the same simply could not be said when it came to using the practice as a way to limit the rights of mothers." Charges of racism and sexism, of course, lie beneath the surface of all these criticisms as these white men (as well as most other nineteenth-century white Americans) placed more importance on the white family and male masculinity, since they believed freedmen (and in some cases, freedwomen) "lacked the independence and responsibility necessary for parenthood."[43]

Later indictments notwithstanding, apprenticeship was an accepted way to help the improvident and orphaned. It was also a way to combat dependency, something viewed by nineteenth-century Americans as unqualified for citizenship. Later claims that the freed community would have cared for every one of these children defy credulity. The very thing that necessitated the Freedmen's Bureau's existence also necessitated the apprentice system: many former slaves were in need of care. Whether these men were culturally knowledgeable of the freed community matters little. For sure, some freed parents proved capable of caring for these children. When that was determined, agents returned the child to a parent, relative, or guardian; but only if he deemed it in the child's best interest. The undeniable fact remains that many former slaves could not care for their children, let alone the noticeable number of orphans in Texas following the Civil War, regardless of any history of "extended families" or prevalence of "fictive kin" relationship. Would these children have benefited by remaining with parents or guardians unable or unwilling to care for them properly and living a life marred by homelessness, hunger, and abject poverty? Bureau agents did not think so. Apprenticeship proved a viable and acceptable option (for the times and for federal policy makers) for agents to remedy destitution. These men believed that they were doing what was best for the apprenticed. For some children, that meant being bound out, but agents made sure the apprentice contract was "not enforced in the spirit in which [it was] passed by the legislature." For others, that meant remaining with their parent(s) or relatives. The simple fact was, for the time being, the freedpeople were dependents of the government, subject to its regulations and desires, with little recourse but to accept that inevitability.[44]

In the summer and fall of 1866, as Congress renewed the agency for another two years, the Bureau had greatly expanded, both in the territory it covered and personnel. This expansion could not have come at a better time, especially as white resistance reached its most intense since the close of the war. In addition to protecting the freed community from violence, Bureau agents had to protect them against the excesses within the Black Code. SACs, through Bureau courts, attempted to secure the former slaves' legal rights and to "educate" white Texans that they had rights that must be respected. Furthermore, they urged freedpeople to obey the law and to learn what their civil responsibilities were. During Kiddoo's administration, this education extended beyond the courtroom and into the classroom. In fact, he would place emphasis on freedmen's schools to such an extent that it would be one of his most important legacies. They were to be taught how to read and write, but also educated on proper Victorian behavior and their responsibilities as men, women, and citizens.

5

The Bureau's
Highwater Mark

*The J. B. Kiddoo Era,
November 1866–January 1867*

In conjunction with teaching the freed community to abide by the law, sub-assistant commissioners tried to educate them to contemporary societal behavior. They believed much of their social behavior, especially sexual relations, were those of slavery, not freedom. They had to learn that society had expectations. Although Bureau men led by example and, at times, through punishment with fines, they mostly educated the freedpeople about their social duties through freedmen's schools. These schools were to teach reading and writing as well as proper Victorian behavior. Kiddoo placed great emphasis on such education.

This emphasis further expanded agents' duties and the agency's bureaucratization. By the end of 1866, the Freedmen's Bureau in Texas had reached its zenith, overseeing all aspects of the freedpeople's lives free from interference. From then, however, Bureau and military officers slowly transferred authority to civil authorities. In the meantime, agents' responsibilities with Bureau courts, labor contracts, marriages, and the Black Code all contributed to the agency's bureaucratization. During Kiddoo's administration, in fact, a good portion of an agent's work was little different from the clerks' back at headquarters. Kiddoo would also order many inspection tours, which, in conjunction with the increased paperwork, served to apprise superiors of any malfeasant subordinates. At the same time all this occurred, a new labor practice developed in Texas. Sharecropping would alter the relationship between the planter and field hand and affect the South far into the future. More important for this study, however, it would have lasting consequences for the image of the subassistant commissioner.

With slavery's demise, the Bureau struggled to educate the freedpeople of their familial responsibilities, particularly matrimonial and domestic issues. In all, Bureau agents arbitrated 246 cases involving domestic issues, with the plaintiff winning 33.7 percent (n=83). Those dealing with domestic issues were the most racially homogenous, with 87.8 percent having both parties black. Considering the character of domestic issues, conflicts developing between married or sexual partners, helps explain the homogeneity. The defendant came out victorious only 18 times—the rest being referred, settled without specificity, dismissed, or continued. As Table 5-1 shows, agents dealt with the spectrum of domestic problems.

Table 5-1   Cases Brought Before Texas SACs with Black Plaintiffs and Black Defendants

Issue	Number of Female Plaintiffs	Number of Male Plaintiffs	Total Number of Domestic Cases (n=246)	Percentage of All Domestic Cases
Desertion/Abandonment	30	12	42	17.1
Abuse/Assault/Ill-treatment	33	3	36	14.6
Domestic/Marital Issue	20	12	32	13
Polygamy/Adultery/Fornication/ Infidelity/Cohabitation	10	11	21	8.5
Alimony/Care/Support (w/o specifying child)	12	3	15	6.1
Divorce/Separation	4	8	12	5
Interference w/Wife or Relationship/Impudent Behavior w/ Wife/Decoying Wife Away/Insulting Wife	1	5	6	2.4
Combination of Issues	4	2	6	2.4
Retains/Abduction of Wife	1	2	3	1.2
Promise to Marry/Breach of Promise	3	0	3	1.2
Other	1	2	3	1.2
All Cases Involving Adult Relationships (Above) Only	**n=119n**	**=60n**	**=179**	**72.7**
Child Custody/Possession of Child	20	18	38	15.5
Child Support/Desertion of Child/Bastardy	20	2	22	9
Child Abuse	2	1	3	1.2
Custody of Wife and Child/ Reunion of Family	0	2	2	.8
Other	1	1	2	.8
All Cases Involving Children Only	**n=43**	**n=24n**	**=67**	**27. 3**

Note: Cases came from the Register of Complaints in each subdistrict.

Prior to 1865, Texas did not recognize slave marriages. After the war, the United States government deemed relationships that existed during slavery ("Persons cohabitating together or associating as man and wife") as marriages. SACs proactively moved to promote the sanctity of these relationships. The word "sanctity," of course, embodied something. To the agency, it meant the marriage contract. Commissioner Howard reminded subordinates that ideally their marriage policies should conform to state law. Although Howard recommended subordinates to instruct "all Freedpeople what the law demands of them in regard to marriage," assistant commissioners in each state were essentially left free to create their own marriage policies.[1]

E. M. Gregory instituted marriage regulations in early 1866. His successors continued it relatively unchanged: no male under eighteen or female under fifteen could marry, and each marriage required parental or guardian consent for boys under twenty-one and girls under eighteen. Although authorized to decide on behalf if a parent or guardian was not available, superiors refused to grant such authority to agents regarding divorces. They wanted to curb sinful behavior among the former slaves—illegitimacy, promiscuity, and infidelity. Superiors reiterated to agents their responsibilities to rectify "the existing evils on this subject." In essence, according to law historian Katherine M. Franke, they "operationalized the normative expectations of citizenship by regulating African American families and testing their ability to 'manage dependency.'" As historian Michael Grossberg has shown, "Without such legitimacy, a sexual union was considered only a casual connection between a man and a woman."[2]

Since these "existing evils" were quite prevalent, SACs had a difficult task. At Marlin Falls in 1866, A. P. Delano was "mindful of their [the freedmen] morals" and had corrected "many evils." He admitted being troubled by "an inclination on the part of man and wife to sepperate [sic]" and "have now become fully convinced of the real necicity [sic] of making a support for themselves and families, and in many instances resort to separation to rid themselves of such incumbunces [sic]." Later that year, he continued to struggle "to keep them together as they have been accustomed thru life to a change of pastures it is now pretty hard to confine an old Buck . . . and more particular when the young fawns are of different stripes."[3]

Although headquarters forbade divorces, this did not always translate into official policy in the field—agents officially could not grant divorces, but rather counsel the parties to seek a divorce in the civil courts. Twelve cases involved divorce or separation (separation meant cohabitation, but not officially married by the state). Headquarters' response, despite its policy, was never uniform.

Superiors sometimes countermanded the decision or responded with a letter expressing their wishes (this, of course, was more an order than suggestion). At other times, they did nothing, apparently allowing the decision to stand. Why would headquarters countenance such apparent acts of insubordination? What appears to be toleration actually could be a simple oversight. With the enormous amount of information coming into headquarters, officials were bound to overlook, miss, or ignore business. As every field agent could attest, letters often went unanswered. Perhaps a more accurate explanation is the course superiors often took when solicited for guidance by Bureau men: use your best judgment. They realized that circumstances might dictate the need for a divorce, and the agent on the scene, privy to information and nuances not easily expressed in writing, was in the better position to determine this.

The proceedings for "divorce" were similar to all others. The agent summoned the parties, took testimony (of parties and any witnesses), received evidence (if any), and either offered guidance or, if necessary, a binding verdict. The reasons for wanting the dissolution ranged from ill-treatment to "dissatisfaction" and "interference." In three cases the plaintiff was a freedman. A freedwoman's complaint, though, represented the typical case. One example from the SAC at Brenham should suffice. In December 1868 F. P. Wood heard Sally King's complaint against Bob King. She accused him of "cruel treatment." Wood believed the facts sustained the charge and "ordered that the woman be permitted to live separate from her husband." He noted that she had to apply to the civil courts for it to be legal. In addition to granting the separation, Wood ordered Bob King to divide equally their communal property.[4]

Field agents constantly battled behavior contrary to Victorian societal norms. Although each passing year instances dwindled, personnel never completely ended it. As late as September 1868, David S. Beath at Cotton Gin reported "cohabitation." Henry Gouldsy, a freedman, had been living with one woman, but "promised another if she [would do] right he would marry her." Obviously jilted, the first woman reported Henry's actions to Beath, who, after a thorough investigation, fined him almost two hundred dollars. It remains uncertain whether Beath's moral beliefs influenced such a high fine or whether he simply wanted to make a point, but it definitely "had a great effect on the Freedpeople as not one case of adultery has been reported since this case was tried." In place of fines, John Dix gave "moral lectures." Harris County agent J. D. O'Connell investigated a group of freedwomen, accusing them of acts in "utter violation of common decency." Instead of trying them, he referred the case to the Houston civil authorities "with a request that the full penalty of the law be visited upon them." Regardless, most approached the problem with understanding, not condemnation. "[N]inety-nine of the Negroes in a hundred might be found guilty of" adultery, wrote B. J. Arnold, "as they do not realize that it is a crime since they have never been taught the contrary."[5]

Personal preference and philosophy greatly influenced each agent's course. Their "best judgment" *was* policy. Later historians would criticize this: within marriage, women essentially lost their "being" to their husbands. In return for his protection and support, as well as dispelling any suspicion concerning her "moral compass," the wife owed her subordination and, in many ways, her self-identity to her husband. Samuel C. Sloan, for example, adhered to the old common law maxim: the "husband controls the wife" (something E. M. Gregory codified as early as 1865). By doing so, they followed contemporary ideas concerning domestic gender roles as well as "absolve [the government] of responsibility for the costs of care of needy women and children." Nonetheless, freedmen were not free from government oversight, as Bureau men ensured they provided for dependents. When a freedman failed in his "manly duties," they did not hesitate to punish him. In most cases, however, they preferred to give "good advice." Consider the case of Sheania Crawford who complained that her husband, Allec, refused to care for her. Byron Porter ordered Allec to care for his wife, including medical care. When freedmen did not "realize the solemnaty [sic] of their marriage relations," wrote agent James P. Butler at Huntsville, "I counsel and advise with them and tell them the best mode to pursue."[6]

With their entry into the private sphere, agents often decided cases of custody. Freedwomen who made complaints, if seen to be "virtuous women, dutiful wives, and devoted mothers," were more likely to receive redress. Those who offended contemporary norms, whether man or woman, discovered agents could be a "condescending intermediary" or "foe." Consider the case of Henry Roark. Roark (freedman) set up a claim to get custody of his son, who, at the time, lived with his mother (Matilda) and had been apprenticed to the man she worked for. Henry fathered other illegitimate children and had two other "wives." One he abandoned; the other he lived with. The mother claimed "he has never done anything for him [the boy] nor pretended to set up any claim to him until recently." The boy wished to remain with his mother. Thus, the agent ruled the boy should be with her. Despite the decision he had "no shadow of legal claim to the boy as against his mother," Henry persisted in winning custody of his son. Superiors supported the agent's ruling. One of the more unique complaints, one that today would probably not reach the level of judicial review, was brought by freedwoman Emma Ha(r)tfield. She lived (she stated he "induced" her) with Lacy McKenzie, a white man who promised a house and a lot. For more than a year, she lived with him and was pregnant with his child. McKenzie wanted her to have an abortion, but she refused. As a result, he went back on his promise of a house and a lot. Ha(r)tfield complained to Byron Porter. Rather than dismiss the case as a "lover's quarrel," Porter instead pursued the route of "breech of promise" by enforcing the verbal contract the pair entered into. He found the claim credible. Porter realized his limitations to force McKenzie to fulfill his promise—"I am to try & frighten [him] into a settlement." The threat apparently worked, because McKenzie "executed a deed to her." She, in turn, "signed an agreement releasing him from all claims."[7]

Emma Ha(r)tfield's experience was not unique for freedwomen. There are hundreds of such "quarrels." Freedwomen rarely hesitated to file complaints against freedmen—or white for that matter. There are numerous expressions by agents about what they deemed irresponsible behavior by freedmen. Those transgressed, as evidenced, did not shy from seeking redress. This raises doubts, at least for Texas, about accusations they "had internalized the nineteenth century cultural stereotype of the promiscuous black female, and thus did not take seriously many reports of sexual assault." Bureau agents often (and honestly) protected freedwomen against such violation. Freedwomen won more than 63 percent (n=64) of the cases with a documented winner (n=101). Of the 246 domestic issues cases, 162 involved a black female plaintiff(s). Of those, 154 involved a female plaintiff(s) against a male defendant: 140 black defendants and 14 whites (the remaining eight involved female plaintiffs). That comes to slightly more than 62 percent from a freedwoman's complaint. One of the more common complaints was of an economic nature. Accusations of desertion and abandonment and pleadings for child support equaled 64 cases, or more than 26 percent of the domestic issues cases—that number probably is higher when considering many cases listed as "domestic" or "marital" dispute probably involved dividing assets. A typical case was the one brought by freedwoman Mariah Random against her "husband" Lorenzo Random. Lorenzo, the father of her six grown children, abandoned her at the time of freedom. Scorned by having "worked for him & all the family" and by his abandonment "to get a young wife," Mariah sought compensation at the office of William H. Rock. After investigating, he decided Lorenzo had abandoned his wife and awarded Mariah damages after the defendant refused reconciliation. Rock ordered their present crop equitably divided, awarded damages of one year's wages for "cooking & washing," and assessed alimony in the form of "1/3 portion of the crop as long as she is able of working herself, then 1/2 of Defendant's wages or portion of the crop from year to year until Divorced or death."[8]

Despite any nineteenth-century gender predispositions, freedwomen saw agents as protectors. Thirty-six cases involved what the SAC listed as domestic assault, abuse, or ill-treatment (14.6 percent of domestic issues cases), with outcomes ranging from fines, to referral to civil authorities, from permission to separate, to arrest or dismissal. In the words of one historian, Bureau men denoted freedwomen "worthy of protection under the law, of bodily integrity, and of voice." William H. Rock, moved by the "Golden Rule" and his notions of womanhood and chastity, arrested a freedman, Jack Wiggins, for running away from his wife and absconding with a young black girl. When Rock found them, he discovered she had been battered and bruised by Wiggins. "[S]he is one of the most distressing girls & [an] object of pity," he observed. Believing she had been "seduced and ruined," Rock clothed and placed her in the care of a trustworthy freedwoman. Wanting the "great rascal" punished, Rock arrested Wiggins for vagrancy, "not being able to substantiate any other charges against him." Freedwoman Toney Hubert accused her husband John P. Cox of raping two women. J. H. Bradford investigated the accusation, concluding no rape had occurred. Instead, Bradford discovered the couple had a tumultuous relationship, with the accusation made out of spite. The agent advised the couple about their future behavior, condemned them on their past actions, and dismissed the case. Byron Porter likewise investigated a complaint by Dr. Jonathan Donaldson, a black doctor, who wanted the agent to "bring his wife back to him." He discovered the woman left because of abuse. Porter informed the doctor that she was justified in leaving and did "nothing for him."[9]

Protecting womanhood came with strings. According to the cultural idea (both men and women held this idea) of what it was to be a woman in the nineteenth century, some women "forfeited" any right to Bureau (societal for that matter) protection against degradation. At Galveston, Abner Doubleday heard a complaint from Jennette Le Claire. She accused another freedwoman of threatening her life and calling "her a bitch." Upon investigation, he discovered both were prostitutes. "Being women of the town," he decided, "no action was taken." Evidence suggests freedwomen understood such gender predispositions when bringing forth a complaint. Consider one case at Hallettsville in late 1867. Arica Ward, a freedwoman, charged freedman Dick Grey of "not do[ing] any thing for me and that he will leave the state" before his child is born. Her concern about being considered a prostitute, something detrimental to her reputation and possibly case, shows when she further adds a small yet important disclaimer to her disposition. "He did not pay me any thing [sic] for the intercourse," she stated. "We did it in a friendly manner." She willingly admitted to premarital sex; yet felt more concerned about reiterating it was in a "familial" way. Thus she maintained some semblance to being a lady. Nineteenth-century society never considered a prostitute a lady. Women of "ill-repute" forfeited such status. Anything other than a lady apparently risked more than just her reputation.[10]

Moral persuasion came not only from encouraging marriage, but also with agents' educational efforts. These efforts focused on the three Rs and moral uplift. Although a complete delineation of the agency's educational work is beyond this study, a quick summary is warranted. Without organizing schools per se, the Bureau financed and procured facilities for organizations committed to freedmen education. Based on Northern educational institutions, "Bureau schools," as they were called, had been established since the agency's arrival in the state. Not until the Kiddoo administration in 1866 did education become a paramount concern. His labor policy notwithstanding, Kiddoo promised to make education a "specialty" in Texas. Considering Washington officials believed Texas the "darkest field educationally in the United States," the work accomplished was astounding. Enrollment under Kiddoo reached its apex in 1866, making it "the year the whole race went to school."[11]

Where freedpeople showed interest in education, most Bureau men's responsibilities greatly increased. Where they lacked zeal, ironically, agent's attention to the subject was not any less. Superiors wanted subordinates "to make a special report . . . pertaining to schools." In each, they were to specify schools already in operation in their districts and "the character[,] prospects[,] and wants of each school." At first, these reports were simply letters; by the organization's end, headquarters had issued a printed form with nearly two dozen questions (Kiddoo's successor, Charles Griffin, continued this expansion and oversight of field agents' responsibilities with education in early 1867). What was delegated was quite broad, ranging from finding adequate teachers to protecting the schools. Each agent was now a "Superintendent of Freedmen's Schools for his District." "I doubt whether he [teacher] can be again secured to teach freedmens [sic] school," Patrick F. Duggan lectured superiors about teacher's low pay, "as he expressed himself dissatisfied with the treatment he has received and now looks upon the government officers with suspicion." William H. Rock at Richmond encouraged students through prizes, while Edward Miller at Millican disciplined in order to keep them attentive. "I have therefore made it my business to visit the school 2 or 3 times every week," Miller wrote, "and by a system of bestowing praise and little presents upon the best behaved, honest, and most improved." Louis W. Stevenson, rather than dealing with students, had to deal with an abusive teacher. Alex Coggeshall, like so many others, spent his own money; while O. E. Pratt dealt with castigations of "odium upon the Bureau schools." Showing necessity is the mother of invention, James P. Butler at Brownsville "devoted the most of my time" preparing black soldiers to be teachers. Mortimer H. Goddin at Livingston, donated land for a school. To him, schools were to be places where freedpeople could learn about their true friends. James C. Devine at Huntsville, a zealous education supporter, got personally involved in each student's efforts. Others instructed teachers "to be more particular with elementary lessons, imparting to the children a clear and distinct knowledge and mind to each letter before advancement."[12]

These men influenced the educational efforts with their zeal or apathy and their knowledge or ignorance about the white citizens and freedpeople. Men such as Isaac M. Beebe, Ira H. Evans, David L. Montgomery, Charles F. Rand, George T. Ruby, John M. Morrison, and E. M. Wheelock, who eventually was appointed superintendent of schools, took great interest in the emancipated's education. Making multiple visits to their schools and extensive surveys for possible school sites, these, as well as others, considered education the "only and lone hope of attaining [their] elevation. . . ." While these men displayed interest in education, others did not. Whether apathy, racial predispositions, neglect, or the simple fact that certain duties, like contracting, took precedence, some gave only passing interest. Developing freedmen education was an easier task for some in Texas, especially those who had assistance by the white community. The task proved more difficult for some. The sight of "[l]ittle niggers as well as grown ones" going to school offended white sensibilities. For those lacking white assistance, Texas truly was the "darkest field educationally." Agent Hardin Hart at Greenville was frustrated by whites "not willing to give State[,] county[,] or individual assistance. . . ." L. S. Barnes had the same problem in his district. At Bastrop, Alex B. Coggeshall informed superiors the white owner of a building that had been chosen as the school had changed his mind. He declared, "he will not give up the building." Coggeshall threatened to remove the freedpeople (i.e., the labor pool) from the area. "The whites of my Dist appear to quietly acquiesce on the effort made to educate the freedpeople," reported John H. Archer at Beaumont, "but most certainly . . . [believe] the 'nigger' should educate themselves." Mahlon E. Davis predicted without "the Assistance of the Bureau very little would be Accomplished in the way of Education." He noted whites believed the concept "quite repugnant to the feeling of the Texas Chivalry."[13]

White Texans, however, threw up only some of the obstacles. Some freedpeople appeared uninterested in education, not "making present sacrifice for a far off good." Consider two examples. In Round Top, H. S. Howe reported "both white and black are indifferent in regard to . . . education." In late 1866 John H. Archer frustratingly relayed "I came here to get the Freedpeople to subscribe sufficient energy to make the [school] building comfortable . . . [and] getting it done by them as it seems impossible to get them to understand the importance of education & I confess I am almost tired of lecturing them upon the subject. . . ."[14]

Besides reporting on the educational efforts, an agent's time was greatly consumed with protecting both the students and teachers. As freedmen's school historian Sandra Eileen Small noted, SACs could win acceptance from the white community, but the teachers generally could not. Most white Southerners simply resented "Yankees" indoctrinating the freedpeople. Bureau men took great pains to recommend the "right" person as a teacher, partly for the students' sake and partly for their own. Besides someone who could teach, they needed someone who would not unnecessarily exacerbate white resistance, or in the words of one, not "give the rebels too good a chance to cry 'Scalawag'. . . ." Some preferred men, since they had a presence in the classroom unlike women. A few desired married men. They would "not only add to the morale, but would . . . elevate the manners and social habits of the colored people." Nesbit B. Jenkins at Wharton, frustrated because the "good and faithful" teachers have been driven off, needed someone not "sordid," "mean," "too low to be hurt by insult," or "indifferent to contempt." Still, others did not have the luxury to be so choosy. "I have not much confidence in him [the current teacher]," admitted Thomas Bayley at Marshall, "but he is the only one I can get here." Agents, whenever they could find qualified applicants, recommended freedpersons as teachers. Locals believed them less "dangerous" than Northern white ones.[15]

Some, no matter the drawbacks, preferred women. To them, they had a "beneficial effect" on students. "Some complaints [have] been made to me about the teacher being a man," wrote James Jay Emerson. "They seem to think a Lady teacher would give more satisfaction." Being "ladies" or "gentlemen" was paramount. Agents ultimately dealt with "indiscretions," actual or perceived. The teacher in Columbus unnecessarily offended white residents with all-night buggy rides with an army officer. When reported to agent J. Ernest Goodman, he quickly relayed her conduct to superiors, resulting in her dismissal. The agent at Brenham had problems when students paraded down the streets singing songs their teacher had taught them that belittled Confederate icons. Headquarters advised to refrain from the more "sectional" songs.[16]

Such close contact between agents and teachers sometimes caused friction. At San Antonio, John H. Morrison had a problem when the Bureau teacher "abused" him by claiming he did not have to answer to him. Morrison requested he be removed, for he "is not a good man[,] is very unpopular with the Freedmen [, and] has not a friend in them and I do not think many any where." In the summer of 1867 Patrick F. Duggan had many questions about the school in his district. A preacher affiliated with the Methodist Episcopal Church wanted to use the building for religious instead of educational purposes. He dismissed Duggan's advice during the building's construction, greatly adding to its cost. Duggan, desiring the building to be completed, approached the preacher to give "me a lien deed upon the house for school purposes [so] I could finish it." Instead of "meeting me in the same spirit," he reported, the preacher "held a religious meeting and collected [money] with which to pay for covering the house [and] determined it possible to defeat my plans."[17]

During Kiddoo's administration, the Bureau became a true bureaucracy: rigid chain of command, greater oversight, and, most important, an endless amount of paperwork. Kiddoo mandated subordinates report monthly to headquarters, documenting everything from the labor situation to white violence, from education to hardships experienced in the performance of their duty. This increased information into headquarters, and according to some, greatly altered the role of those in the field. This prompted Bureau historian William L. Richter to label agents "glorified clerks"; while another historian, Robert Harrison, likened the agency to "a giant intelligence office." A Bureau man in South Carolina, commenting on the paperwork, was certain the "Romans conquered the world because they had no paper." Commissioner Howard prided himself on such paperwork. Since military procedures governed the Bureau's record keeping, officials at Galveston expected all forms to be completed correctly and promptly. Such attention to detail created delays and general inefficiency. A perusal of the records shows nearly all, for one reason or another, had some paperwork returned for corrections. Since superiors issued few guidelines, some never mastered the art. They repeatedly had records returned or rejected, despite being shown the proper way again and again by headquarters.[18]

Headquarters' attention to detail helped "circumscribe" any "opportunity for official conduct contrary to directives." For example, Alex B. Coggeshall at Bastrop, at times, described his position as "a perfect sinecure." Charges soon surfaced that he and his brother-in-law, Julius Schultze, had provided workers to planters in return for kickbacks. Although Coggeshall was never specifically identified by name, his activities appeared in the *Galveston Daily News*, claiming "unless a man can get in with them he cannot get any hands." Coggeshall was reassigned and replaced by Byron Porter, who investigated the accusations. He "concluded" he had covered his tracks through shoddy record keeping. "His papers appear to be in a state of great confusion," Porter reported. "I would suggest . . . contracts approved by him be carefully examined." Coggeshall responded, saying he did nothing wrong, and apologized that "I was not born a clerk." By protecting the freed community, he noted, the planters referred to him as that "Damned Dutchman." Plus, Coggeshall's prominent brother-in-law was described as an "outspoken thoroughgoing Radical Union man," who, as chief justice of Bastrop County, had very "prominent loyal [friends] in Western Texas." Superiors exonerated him of the charges, reminding him of the importance of proper record keeping. Coggeshall remained in service until relieved in early 1867, but returned as a civilian agent in July 1868.[19]

Since many, particularly civilians, were ignorant to the ins and outs of military record keeping, problems persisted between those at headquarters and field personnel. William H. Sinclair, while on an inspection tour southwest of Houston, noticed the "records of the [agents'] offices are very incomplete." One responded to superiors' questions about his report: "All I could have done would have been to forward a blank, stating therein that I had nothing to insert." After succeeding J. Orville Shelby at Liberty, A. H. Mayer discovered his predecessor had kept no records. Each time Mayer tried to contact Shelby about "such & such case," he "forgets" or "guess[es] at it." This affected Mayer's ability to keep accurate and orderly records. Superiors accused Fred W. Reinhard of disregarding "every Circular order relating to his reports of Persons." They lectured Charles E. Culver on matters of more importance requiring their attention "than the making out of retain copies of Reports for Sub Asst Commrs." Culver was condescendingly reminded SACs do not "dispatch business in a hurried and careless manner." In response to accounts dealing with crimes during the war, superiors reminded John Dix those "have nothing to do with Freedpeople" and "the expense of arresting criminals for offenses committed either during, or since the war, [was not] a proper charge against the Bureau."[20]

For others, the problem was not ignorance of military protocol. It was the fact they were both subassistant commissioner and post commander. This increased their workload and hindered their ability to meet report deadlines. For example, Walter B. Pease, the post commander and agent at Harris County, informed headquarters he needed clerical assistance.

The pressure of business and lack of sufficient clerical force in some measure prevents a prompt attention to the settlement of cases, and to the correspondence from other Agents. The duties of Commander of the Post, and of my company, require a great deal of my time and owing to the want of a competent clerk at the Post (the last one I had, having been detailed away to Dist. Hd. Qrs.) all reports and returns for the Post . . . have to be made by the adjutant, who is also [quartermaster] and Asst S. A. C. thereby depriving me of his assistance in the Bureau. I would therefore respectfully suggest the employment of an additional clerk in my office.[21]

Field agents generally accepted responsibility for blank, missing, wrong, or late reports. Hardin Hart, a "scalawag" agent at Greenville and attorney, spoke for many when he reminded superiors to be patient, since he was a "civilian [and] unaccustomed to the routine of doing business with military precision." At one time or another, every Bureau man drew the attention of superiors about paperwork. William G. Kirkman, in particular, routinely drew attention. "When I tendered you the advice not to make a property return, on the ground that the trouble of doing so, would be more trouble than the property purchased was worth," informed Assistant Acting Quartermaster Charles Garretson, "I wrote as an experienced Quartermaster and I was aware from some of the documents transmitted by you, that you knew nothing whatever about property or other papers." He was further lectured about the "hurried and careless manner" of his communications, which "should be carefully and concisely written [and] so arraigned that the gist of them can be readily perceived." Most agents quickly corrected the error, providing whatever record or correction superiors wanted. A proud lot, they were very sensitive to each inquiry or even censure, fearful superiors might think them negligent or dilatory in their duties.[22]

Although a few agents never learned the proper way, Bureau and military officials bear part of the responsibility. After receiving communications about "gross neglect on my part that my papers are incorrect," A. H. Mayer at Liberty reminded superiors he was not an "automaton." Mayer blamed some at headquarters for his returned reports. "You are mistaken. I have been harassed by [your] subordinates unnecessarily," he wrote, about "papers returned for correction that could have received the correction without being returned. Communications of importance from me not answered, seemingly pigeon holed without being read, either great neglect, apathy, or inattention shown by subordinates at Hdquarters." A few months later, his frustration boiled over. "No man tries harder than I do," the frustrated man declared.

> No man has more pride in his position and desire that all things eminating [sic] from his office shall be a little better than any one else than I am [but] I cannot perform impossibilities. I notice that a reflection is implied in your communication . . . I have never purchased a single item without first making application in writing or verbally and receiving permission without one exception . . . I suppose I've used thirty pound[s] of candles the past month, now must I perform all the labor of [my] pay for the candles to do it by. For God Sake, send an Inspecting Officer here then I do know, that the a/c for oil and candles will be allowed.[23]

Mayer exemplified what many agents believed: first, that personnel at headquarters did not fully understand their day-to-day operations; and second, they were unnecessarily (and offensively) suspicious, highlighted by Mayer's request for an inspecting officer to visit his district.

The increased workload and frustration proved too much for some, who asked for short leaves or to be relieved from service altogether. When headquarters refused such requests, it was partly because of the time of year: the most demanding time was at the end and beginning of each year. As harvesting and contracting neared in late summer and fall of 1866, Bureau authorities could hardly be satisfied with the current labor situation in Texas as white violence, planter and worker ignorance, field personnel's confusion, and the overall inconsistency in the agency's labor policy all adversely affected free labor's success. Completely overhauling the South's economic system would also take time. Time the Bureau lacked, since during Reconstruction, patience was not a virtue. With a less-than-rigid system, SACs were free to experiment. Some encouraged profits to convince the planters to accept the free market philosophy. They hoped increased revenue would prevent violence and mistreatment against the emancipated. If the planters financially succeeded, so too might the freedpeople. "Human nature is much the same under given conditions—the plastic character of the mind soon adapts itself to circumstances [and] fortunately the high prices of Southern products will be the incentive for action," observed one Bureau official. "[A]s selfishness was the enslaver of the negro, it will now be one of the means of his elevation." Some planters had discovered free labor superior to slave labor, not from any philosophical change, but rather from the "pecuniary point of view." Bureau men hoped now to "enlighten" the rest.[24]

Hardly novel to Reconstruction, free labor proponents had descended on the antebellum slaveholding South in a "friendly invasion" to demonstrate its benefits. After the war, Bureau agents also wanted to demonstrate its benefits. In other words, increased profits came with "the Yankee way of doing business." They soon made a concerted effort to remind both planters and freedpeople of similar interests. Superiors informed William Longworth to educate the former slaves "it is as much to their interest as to [the planter's] that a good crop be raised." Alex B. Coggeshall saw "a very great change in public opinion [toward] the freedmen." A few months later, he reported how planters now realized they will "have much [more] money . . . at the end of the year [and if they] have treated their freedmen badly during the past year have found that it will not pay." From San Augustine County, Albert A. Metzner noted "the scarcity of laborers is the principal reason of this kindness." According to Arthur B. Homer, "the demand for labor compels the white people to treat [the freedmen] justly." As a result, he informed superiors he had no troops and none were required.[25]

Competition for labor aided their course for protection. Planters were never as cohesive a group as generally portrayed. Edward Miller in Victoria reported "very good terms" between the freedpeople and planters, "obviously for the purpose of securing their services." He gladly accepted the situation, because "the rights of the freedmen would be secured by the civil authorities [even] if all the troops were removed." Samuel A. Craig noticed improved race relations as the number of workers dwindled. Those who want workers for the next year, he added, had to treat the emancipated fairly. "There are some planters who are not only willing but anxious to secure the freedmen's share of the crop," Jacob C. DeGress witnessed, "and get the officers of the Bureau to procure for them the highest market price. I am doing all I can to assist them and encourage their feeling, for the planters so disposed, will be the gainer, by being enabled to secure his hands for next year without difficulty." DeGress advised "freedmen not to labor next year" for any planters of bad character.[26]

Some generally believed the freedpeople could be protected through the encouragement of shares (i.e., sharecropping), rather than wages, believing it easier to ensure their payments. James F. Hutchison at Columbus witnessed more diligent laborers "when they are interested in part of the crop," while Albert A. Metzner desired shares, since they "caused me little trouble." A month later, however, after incessant rains and the arrival of the armyworm, Metzner saw the inherent risk with sharecropping. Many hands broke their contracts and hired themselves out for wages to others. Nonetheless, he "tried . . . to make them understand the foolishness of such a proceeding [working for wages]." Joshua L. Randall argued "the more intelligent" contracted for shares. L. S. Barnes at Crockett reported those who contracted for shares "are doing a fine thing for themselves and their employers."[27]

Others encouraged monthly wages instead. In early 1867 A. H. Mayer observed hands working for a share of the crop, "although (from experience) I have tried to induce them to work for monthly wages." According to him, those contracting for wages "have done so at a fair rate and [I] am satisfied they will succeed better." Furthermore, if the crop failed, they would not be nearly as affected as those who had contracted for a share of the crop. Lemuel K. Morton found it was more difficult to secure the freedpeople's payment with shares. He recorded fewer complaints "about the planters failing to pay their hands where they are hired by the month, but some of them seame [sic] enclined [sic] to take the advantage where they are working for part of the crop." A. G. Malloy at Marshall likewise argued the "system of working for a portion of the crop is not advantageous" and "recommended them to work only for money wages." With little consensus about what system of payment to encourage, the Bureau's responsibility for the institution in Texas appears peripheral at best. It appears to have developed because of the planters' and freedpeople's preferences rather than from any specific policy handed down. By the time headquarters in Galveston ordered subordinates to "encourage the renting and working of land, for a share of the products" in early 1867, sharecropping was already by the planters and hands for some time.[28]

In Texas, agents were not the main reason for the development of sharecropping. They lacked unanimity as to which system was better for the freedpeople. Similar to the situations in Florida and Louisiana, an agent's personal preference dictated whether he pushed wages or shares. They neither developed nor imposed it, leaving it "to the option of the parties whether said contract be for a portion of the crops or stipulated wages per month or year." As it became the preferable system in Texas, only then did the Bureau begin to encourage sharecropping. Bureau officials believed sharecropping had several benefits: first, it was easier to ensure the crop portion compared to monthly wages; second, it was hoped hands would be more diligent and industrious, since their production now directly affected their portion of the crop; and finally, since parties shared the risk of crop failure, it was hoped contract violations would diminish.[29]

With the rise of sharecropping, some later historians asked how such a system that "economically retarded" the South and "circumscribed" the freedpeople's opportunities could develop. A number placed blame on the Freedmen's Bureau. These critics overlook the main aspect in sharecropping's development: neither employer nor employee were passive participants. Under instructions from superiors, agents were to instruct the freedpeople and planters to the benefits of the free-market system, but not to decide what they did with it. Headquarters, in fact, warned not to interfere in what they agreed to, but rather only to ensure that both parties understood their obligations and the proceedings were honest and fair. The criticism for implanting sharecropping accompanies the charge that subassistant commissioners also colluded with the planters to bind the former bondsmen to the land. In a few cases this charge is valid, but as a whole, it is not supported by the evidence. The debate between revisionists and post-revisionists, for many historians, has become history. But an examination using several tenets from the school of thought can be quite useful and relevant, if the post-revisionist theoretical framework is not. Criticism of agents for harm against the freepeople continues (simply from different angles and for different reasons). Highlighting the approach to claims of impropriety helps to undermine any such generalized indictments of the agency and its personnel. A. P. Delano, Albert A. Metzner, J. Albert Saylor, Mahlon E. Davis, James A. Hogue, Isaac Johnson, William H. Horton, Charles P. Russell, Alex B. Coggeshall, and a few others were all accused, at one time or another, of being tools of the planter elite. Some of these accusations proved accurate. Others did not. To be sure, most accusations proved false. Only five men were dismissed for abuse or collusion: 5 out of 195 agents whose departure could be determined, or 2.5 percent. White Unionists and freedpeople realized the agency's sensitivity to such claims and never hesitated to inform about collusion. Planters realized headquarters' attitude about such cooperation, even using the allegation in hopes of ridding themselves of effective, or what they called "troublesome," agents.[30]

For example, in late 1867 a few whites and several freedpersons accused Albert A. Metzner of collusion in San Augustine. Metzner denied the allegation, claiming it to be simply false and in a way "flattering." "I, almost a stranger, should in so short a time be enabled to exercise such an influence as therein stated," he wrote, "and I am sure it will be a matter of astonishment to you, it is simply ridiculous." He admitted "in one or more instances" that he had ruled against freedmen, "but it was because the fraud attempted to be practised [sic] against the white man, was palpable and apparent." He reminded superiors he never compromised principle or character in the discharge of his duties, and "I

flatter myself that I have by so doing, been [able] to accomplish more in execut-
ing the Orders of the Department than if I had held myself aloof from all
friendly and social intercourse with the [white] Community." Metzner's defense,
his job performance, several credible testimonials to the inaccuracy of the
charges, and the fact that the main accuser hoped to remove him in order to fill
his position all convinced superiors of the baseless charges. But months later, in
the summer of 1868, headquarters sent an inspector to investigate other charges,
like intemperance, which led to his removal from office.[31]

The drive to oust ineffective, inefficient, and detrimental agents frustrated
some. A few, in fact, were quite offended. Consider the case of Mahlon E. Davis,
Samuel A. Craig's successor at Brenham, who was accused of neglect in early
1867. William Howard, a freedman, asked the agent to protect his portion of the
cotton. Davis informed him he would do this, for it was his duty, but it would
only be done after the freedman fulfilled his contractual obligations. Rather
than do this, Howard took "the whole of it and sold it," which resulted in his
arrest by local authorities for theft of his employer's portion of the cotton. Upon
his arrest, Howard contacted Daniel Leonidas McGary, the "noted Rebel [edi-
tor] . . . who does not hesitate to denounce the action of the U.S. Government
and the Bureau especially." McGary, who Davis suspected to be the driving
force behind Howard's actions and words, instructed the freedman to "report
the case to the Asst. Commissioner" and accuse the agent of theft of some of his
belongings, including his pistol, cart, and oxen.[32]

Superiors wanted an explanation from Davis concerning accusations of
"neglecting his duties." He was quite offended by the rather insulting and accu-
satorial tone of the letter. After giving his side of the story, which included many
things Howard failed to mention, Davis pointed out that according to the plaintiff's "statement the Bureau seems to have taken but little part in his, and the
other Freedpeoples [sic] troubles." He continued:

> Allow me to inform you that this office is situated in one of the most wealthy
> counties in the state, that there are more Planters & more Freedpeople
> employed than in any other. Also that I have devoted all my time night and
> as well as day to the interest of the Freedpeople in my Dist. that I have worked
> faithfully and I believe acted justly and that I do not think proper Justice is
> done me, when a report like the one which called for this report—a report
> coming from a man who devoted all his time to making trouble for Capt.
> Craig when he was Agt. here & whom Capt. Craig was compelled to confine
> in Jail is given credence to.[33]

Davis was eventually exonerated. He remained at Brenham for a short while after the incident before being reassigned to Wharton County. There he had no further problems until he left the agency in April 1867. In early summer 1868, however, Davis returned to Bureau service in Harris County and remained there until the organization ceased operations in late 1868.[34]

Most certainly, accusations against some were clearly warranted. Consider the examples of James H. Hogue and A. P. Delano. "Scalawag" agent James H. Hogue shirked his responsibilities in Livingston. The commander at the post, Captain W. H. Redman, informed headquarters that he (Hogue) rarely called upon him for assistance. This the captain thought quite unusual. Captain Redman, who had doubts about civilian Bureau agents, further described how Hogue dealt with the freedpeople's complaints. Upon a complaint, he would allegedly write a note to the planter urging the necessity to settle with his hands and would state "to the employer that if the matter comes before him again that he will refer it to [Bureau headquarters] for settlement." This, according to the post commander, "answers the purpose intended." Through a ruse that involved the "employer[']s translation" of Hogue's note and the freedpeople who believed the agent had protected them, some "very persuaded" hands had entered "with a settlement at the terms of the employer." Captain Redman concluded that "an understanding" between the agent and the planters existed "to use every means" to keep the former masters in control. One white Unionist compared Hogue's collusion to a monster that had been slain. "Slavery is dead," the Unionist lamented, "but the tail of the dambed [sic] monster still moves." Within a few months, Hogue had been relieved.[35]

While at Falls County in November 1866, A. P. Delano made the "condition of the freedpeople worse than even slavery." To please the planters, he made the emancipated work "like dogs." If they resisted, he hanged them by their thumbs or threatened them with a loaded weapon. It was little wonder that planters in the county expressed in a letter to Bureau officials their satisfaction with "their" Bureau agent. To ensure that Delano was doing his job, superiors sent an inspector to Falls County. What he found he likened to a "hungry wolf" and "a lamb." "All the difference between the condition of the freedpeople of Falls now and in the time of slavery," he concluded, "is that the County has 3 Overseers [Delano had two co-conspirators] instead of one to each plantation." Defending his performance, Delano declared he had the "acknowledgement of the Freedmen as their true friend and adviser," and noted they "thought me rather hard," but with "intentions [of] good and meant them no harm." Regardless, Delano was relieved from service. Such actions show prompt investigation by superiors (and dismissal if substantiated) whenever serious complaints developed against personnel.[36]

The freedmen's education and moral uplift were all ancillary to the agency's primary mission: the transition from slavery to free labor. This mission, already underway for a year, still had to work out many of the initial kinks. White violence, the ignorance of free labor, idleness, and many other things still bedeviled those in the field. Agents apprized superiors about problems caused by freedwomen leaving the fields for housework, while others experienced difficulties with the crop's division, settlement of accounts, and idleness. Not all, though, had complaints, as they reported satisfactory labor conditions. Kiddoo was concerned about the state's labor situation, especially as harvest and contract time approached. Before he acted, he needed specificity, instead of a collection of anecdotes. He ordered William H. Sinclair, the agency's "eyes and ears" in Texas, on an inspection tour. A natural staff officer, Sinclair held nearly every Bureau position during his time in Texas. Perhaps historian William L. Richter overstates Sinclair's influence as the agency's "real head" in Texas. But his importance cannot be denied. In late 1866 Kiddoo sent him throughout Central Texas, the upper Brazos River Counties, and parts of south Texas. Greatly dismayed by what he found, Sinclair noticed many still ignorant about their responsibilities and authority. This, of course, was because of the lack of necessary orders and regulations from headquarters. "This is partly owing to the fact that agents . . . have very little to guide them in the performance of their duties," he believed. "It requires a man of no small amount of talent and a good supply of common sense to make a good agent." Sinclair criticized the agency's reliance on "scalawags." He suspected they shared the Rebels' racial attitudes. In addition, he noted how a few men had entered the cotton business at the same time they were Bureau agents, something "not at all advantageous to the public interest."[37]

After his tour, which gave him "a good insight into the workings of the Bureau," Sinclair recommended improvements. He suggested contracts no longer be drawn in a way that assumed all parties understood it. Sinclair noticed the "indefinite manner in which they are gotten up" and "too many things which should be in are left out or said to be understood." They often lacked specifics, like the number of workdays and hours, the amount of rations provided by employers, or the payment (specie or paper). Bureau agents, Sinclair warned, "cannot be too careful in having the contracts fully understood." Unnecessary disputes arose when planters attempted to sell the crop, only to have their hands complain about being swindled. "By far," he believed, "the best way is to give them [freedmen] their share of the crop and let them dispose of it as they choose." In short, printed contracts were needed with "the obligations of both parties." Sinclair further recommended, and officials agreed a short time later, agents send monthly reports detailing their work and the conditions in their subdistrict.[38]

With his recommendations, Sinclair placed responsibility for the problems on headquarters. Kiddoo, with the contracting season soon approaching, implemented all the recommendations: Circular No. 25 (and a subsequent circular letter) reiterated the need for diligence in observing contracts. Whether Kiddoo's policies worked would be another's concern. In late January 1867 Charles Griffin, commander of the District of Texas, relieved him as Bureau chief. Since Griffin's arrival in Texas, their relationship was anything but cordial. Griffin, Kiddoo's superior, made it policy to communicate through his headquarters staff, rather than personally himself. This greatly annoyed Kiddoo. "I have never had any such trouble, or rec[eived] such discourtesy before," Kiddoo complained to Commissioner Howard. Kiddoo also resented the way Griffin treated the Freedmen's Bureau. Although subordinate by law, the organization was allowed free rein by previous district commanders. Griffin, however, consolidated the positions of district commander and assistant commissioner under one man. This Kiddoo believed a "complete compromise of the dignity of the Bureau." The relationship became unsalvageable when Kiddoo sent a letter to Howard criticizing Griffin. This was the last straw for Griffin, who relieved him from command. Remembering his own previous censure of Kiddoo "about his drinking and profane language in public" while visiting Washington in late 1866, Commissioner Howard supported the decision.[39]

Kiddoo had left his mark on the Bureau and on Texas. He oversaw its expansion into the interior and greater focus on freedmen education. This would be his historical legacy for many. For white Texans, however, Kiddoo's legacy was his labor policy. They much appreciated Circular No. 14, which returned the freedpeople to the cotton fields. "When Gen. Kiddoo came among us the people received him kindly, and in parting with him we are glad the same spirit prevails," stated the *Galveston Daily News*. "Personally, our relations with him have been most agreeable . . . General Kiddoo has managed the Bureau rather satisfactorily which we think is more than can be said of any other of the heads of the . . . Bureau."[40]

The agency greatly expanded under Kiddoo, with order being (despite problems) brought to the labor situation in the state. Agents struggled with these problems. Planters and hands tried to find a satisfactory relationship after slavery's demise, as a new labor situation developed. As field personnel dealt with labor, they also struggled to educate the emancipated to the ways of Victorian societal norms. The freed community needed to learn the sanctity of marriage. Freedmen were lectured about their manly duties. Behavior countenanced during slavery, like promiscuity and "cohabitation," was no longer acceptable. Freedwomen, on the other hand, were reminded of their womanly duties. At the time of Kiddoo's departure, the Bureau had the look of a modern bureaucracy. In fact, those under Kiddoo had become not only protectors, but information gatherers for headquarters. They would continue this role under Kiddoo's successor, Charles Griffin, who, suspicious of his predecessor's decisions and appointments, would continue the use of inspection tours to dismiss anyone not meeting his standards. But those under Griffin would also spend a great deal of time on something that previous Bureau men had not, and something many in nineteenth-century white America believed would protect the freedmen: politics.

6

"They must vote with the party that shed their blood ... in giving them liberty"

Bureau Agents, Politics, and the Bureau's New Order: The Charles Griffin Era, January 1867–Summer 1867

When Charles Griffin assumed leadership in early 1867, the Bureau had reached its apex in power. At no other time would it be involved in more aspects of the freedpeople's lives with as little civil and state interference. Griffin, however, would reverse this by transferring much responsibility to civil authorities, believing Kiddoo's policies caused unnecessary "collisions." This delegation occurred at the very time Congress consolidated its own, wresting the Reconstruction process from the president and passing measures, making the governments created under Presidential Reconstruction provisional. The Reconstruction Act of 1867 called for voter registration of all white and black men who did not voluntarily aid the Confederacy. Griffin hoped to use the newly enfranchised to create a "new order" in Texas. With voter registration, the Bureau would enter the maelstrom of politics.

Reversing Kiddoo's policies, Griffin hoped his "new order" would further freedpeople's self-reliance with little interference (beyond protection of their wages) by subassistant commissioners. Griffin, however, was not going to leave them powerless. Through his "jury order," they became jurors to help ensure their own justice and protection. Nor was Griffin going to leave subordinates powerless. Although he transferred many responsibilities to civil authorities, he also consolidated the Bureau and the military under one central command in Texas. No longer were agents assigned to remote areas with little protection. This change in attitude would produce very suitable conditions in much of Texas.

Graduated from West Point, Charles Griffin served in an artillery regiment during the war. A native Ohioan, he participated in the First Battle of Bull Run in 1861. The next year, after marrying the daughter of an influential Maryland family, he transferred to an infantry regiment. With a "cool, quiet and precise" demeanor, Griffin quickly rose through the ranks, receiving command of the V Corps in the Army of the Potomac. He participated in every major battle with the Army of the Potomac and was present for Robert E. Lee's surrender at Appomattox in April 1865. After the war, he was placed in command of the

District of Texas by his friend and staunch opponent of Presidential Reconstruction, Major General Philip H. Sheridan. His "gentle and generous disposition" and "sense of humor" showed during the war. At the time of his
appointment in Texas, Griffin had a no nonsense reputation and was "quick to
resent insult, fancied or real."[1]

Griffin's rather volatile temperament was, on several occasions, directed at
Kiddoo. After Kiddoo's removal, Griffin let it be known what he thought of his
predecessor's policies. In General Orders No. 5, he wiped the slate clean, completely abrogating previous general and circular orders like the ban on enticement (Circular No. 14) and its enforcement (Circular No. 17), Kiddoo's contract
guidelines (Circular No. 25), and the order to agents to disregard the state's
labor law (General Orders No. 2). This policy simply conformed to the War
Department's General Orders No. 26. With consent from Commissioner Howard, Griffin also moved to cancel Kiddoo's order for fees approving labor contracts. Although in place for only a couple of months, the payment order had
already caused much confusion. Griffin finally clarified the boundaries for each
subdistrict (pinnacle of 57 in July 1867). Since Gregory's administration, subdistrict boundaries remained unspecified. Agents were simply informed their
jurisdiction extended to any case they could reach. Friction, naturally, occurred
when they investigated cases that another believed under his jurisdiction. Nevertheless, superiors still expected agents to act in "all cases occurring when it
may be more convenient for you to act than any other sub asst com upon whose
jurisdiction it may be possible you are encroaching on. . . ." Field personnel were
either to render assistance, if possible, regardless of subdistrict boundaries, or
inform the adjacent agent of the situation. Either way, they had to act.[2]

This new course was laid down in General Orders No. 4, issued to bring
about a "natural sense" believed to be lacking in Texas. Griffin delineated
changes closer to the essence of free labor, with as few constraints as possible on
the choice of employment and compensation. Beyond ensuring that no labor
contract lasted longer than one year, field agents were not to hinder the freedpeople's choice of employer and wage. Griffin allowed local officials, such as
county judges and clerks and justices of the peace, as well as subassistant commissioners, to approve contracts. This marked a departure from previous policy.
The AC wanted to end the constant collisions between local officials and the
agency about authority. He reiterated, however, the state's vagrancy and apprenticeship laws were to be enforced only if local officials impartially administered
them. Agents still retained the right to annul any contract or interfere with any
civil case they deemed illegal or discriminatory. "I now propose to make interference with the state [authorities] the exception and not the rule," Griffin

pledged, "but that every decision that the Bureau does make shall, if necessary, be instantly backed up by the Military force necessary to command obedience and respect."[3]

In early summer of 1867, Griffin issued a circular to all field personnel. He repeated his conviction that the path to success for the emancipated lay with contracting. "Whenever you may think it necessary," he wrote, "you will address the freedmen urging . . . the necessity of industry & of close adherent [sic] to their contracts." Acknowledging the former slaves' choice in the system, the Bureau chief believed that choice should be an informed one. Finally, although he wanted them to pursue moral persuasion, Griffin instructed subordinates, if necessary, not to refrain from more forceful remedies to change behavior.[4]

Simultaneous to altering the agency's direction, he also moved to restructure its field operations. Already joint commander in Texas, Griffin further married the army and the Bureau through his Circular Order No. 3. With it, the number of field personnel greatly increased. When Griffin assumed control, there were 29 men in the field, including 2 civilian agents (those who had no military experience during the war). At the time of his death in September 1867, the number had increased to 57 SACs, 10 ASACs, and 1 traveling agent, including 15 civilians. The circular order made all post commanders SACs (only if there was not already an assigned agent to the area), and greatly expanded the number of Bureau agents, peaking at 72 in July 1867 (61 SACs and 11 ASACs). Because most military posts ringed the extent of white settlement in the state, rarely was a civilian assigned to the frontier of Texas-Mexico border. Civilians were primarily, though not always, assigned to the interior and coastal regions.

Griffin also appointed the most agents with 70: that is slightly more than J. J. Reynolds's 62 (his successor); significantly higher than Kiddoo's 44; and double Gregory's 35. Twenty-nine percent were civilians, a number similar to Gregory and Reynolds. Despite his hostility toward civilian agents, Griffin, surprisingly, had the highest number of appointed civilians. Overall, Griffin's appointments served slightly higher than the overall average: 8.6 compared to 7.8 months. This average correlates with Gregory's 8.4 yet deviates from Kiddoo's 10.2. Table 6-1 shows the average length of service for agents appointed by Griffin.

Table 6-1   Length of Service for Agents Appointed by Griffin

Type of Bureau Agent	Number	Average Length of Service (Months)
Civilian	20	8.5
Military	50	8.7

Note: Dates came from Freedmen's Bureau Roster of Officers and Civilians.

As Table 6-2 shows, slightly more than 50 percent of Griffin's appointments left the agency for bureaucratic reasons (Bureau operations and military). This is similar to Gregory's, but nearly two-thirds above Kiddoo's. Despite having the highest number of civilians, Griffin had the lowest percentage (compared to his predecessors' 20 and 20.5 percent) terminated for criminality or unbecoming conduct. Of the Texas ACs, Griffin had the highest percentage who died in service.

Griffin's expansion placed an agent within reach of all citizens, something nearly one-half of Texans could not say under Kiddoo. General Orders No. 3 further increased the protection for agents through easier access to the full weight of the United States Army. No longer would they be unprotected. Each received an escort (five men), and, of course, those simultaneously performing Bureau and post commander duties had their companies for assistance. Upon request, all post commanders were to render assistance to agents. According to William L. Richter, a student of the Bureau in Texas, "it was not merely the numbers that were important, it was an attitude." Griffin hoped to create a "new order" in place of, what he considered, his predecessor's chaotic and misguided policies.[5]

A change in attitude also came from Congress. Angered by a lack of remorse from the former Confederates and frustrated by a stubborn president, Radical Republicans wrested control of Reconstruction from him in early 1867. Both houses of Congress passed the Reconstruction Act of 1867 over the president's veto. Under its provisions, all state governments in the former Confederate

Table 6-2   Reasons Agents Appointed by Griffin Left Bureau Service

Reason	Number	Percentage
Bureau Operations: Bureau ended, consolidation, and transferal or reassignment within the agency	16	22.9
Military Operations: Mustered out or ordered to new assignment	19	27.1
Dropped on Request: Agent resigned appointment	8	11.4
Terminated: Dismissed for criminality, cruelty, Confederate service, or appointment revoked	4	5.7
N/A: Reason for leaving undetermined	13	18.6
Died: Murdered, disease, or accidents	10	14.3
Total: All Griffin's Agents	n=70	100

Note: The information in this table came from various sources, but much of it came from the U.S. Census and the Freedmen's Bureau's Special Orders and Correspondences.

states (except Tennessee) established under Presidential Reconstruction were now provisional. Congress divided those states into five military districts, with a military officer heading each district. In early 1867 the former Confederacy was placed under martial law. Each district's commander would call for a constitutional convention to draft a new constitution and also supervise the election of a new governor and state government, which had to meet certain requirements before being readmitted to their seats in Congress. Texas and Louisiana constituted the Fifth Military District, with Philip H. Sheridan as its commander. With his appointment, Congressional Reconstruction had begun.[6]

Empowered with new political functions, Griffin's "new order" would come about through the ballot and the jury box. In a series of orders throughout the spring of 1867, Griffin implemented guidelines for agents to "coordinate the registration process." The Reconstruction Act of 1867, which made the Throckmorton government provisional, called for voter registration of all males, who were to elect delegates to create a new state constitution. Anyone disqualified by the Fourteenth Amendment (anyone who swore an oath to the U.S. then engaged in rebellion) could not vote for delegates. There was much room for interpretation in the Act. It allowed Sheridan and Griffin to interpret the restrictions for voting quite narrowly, ordering subordinates to "exclude from registration every person about whose right to vote there may be doubt." Griffin created fifteen registration districts (which comprised 11–15 counties each) throughout the state. Within these districts, he appointed white Unionists, freedmen, and some SACs to three-man boards of registrars. Located in every county, these boards were to make a list of those registered and disqualified (using their best judgment) in each county. They had broad authority to disfranchise anyone who they believed dishonest about past loyalty. Registration was to be completed by September 1, 1867.[7]

Field agents had authority to oversee the registration process to begin in early summer of 1867. They were to lend assistance and make out monthly reports to superiors on the progress of registration. Beyond protection, agents were not to "interfere in any way with the Registrars in [their] subdstricts." To aid in the process and fearing trouble from "unreconstructed" whites, Griffin ordered all boards to operate out of county courthouses. If need be, agents could recommend more suitable sites. Boards were ordered to create a list of men to replace those deemed as "impediments to Reconstruction." Griffin, biding his time before he sprung his trap, believed former Confederates incapable of rendering impartial justice. Only Unionists could be trusted to protect the freedpeople's "rights of person and property" and protect against "insurrection, disorder, and violence." "I should just as soon look to the English Crown to leave the establishment of peace in Ireland to the Fenians," he declared, "as to see our nation leave the reconstruction of the southern states to those that tried to destroy the government."[8]

With voter registration, the Bureau entered the "maelstrom of politics." Its agents were now the foot soldiers for a Republican political machine, despite Howard's attempts to resist being an "overt" political organization. But the very work it performed and the relationship its agents had with the freed community naturally brought it into politics. In their political role, they were to explain voter registration to the freedpeople and to protect them in their suffrage rights. No evidence exists that SACs in Texas publicly made partisan speeches against Democrats as in other states. Rather they preferred actions "under the noses" of white Texans. Nor did they advise, campaign, or help the Democratic party. Nor would agents in Texas consider themselves Radical Republicans. They suspected the president's policies, and Democrats by default, made their job more difficult. Since opposing the president's policies were the Radicals, agents at times sympathized with the Radicals and worked for their ascension to power in the state.[9]

One of the main duties of agents during the registration process was to protect registrars, who whites saw as tools to disfranchise the white community and enfranchise the emancipated. Since many registrars in Texas were black, that made the protection afforded all the more a necessity. William A. A. "Big Foot" Wallace, the famed former Texas Ranger, for example, attempted to register to vote, but was disqualified. He recalled the incident many years later:

> I don't think I ever felt less like giving quarter in my life but once, and that was when a big buck nigger, with a nose like [a] dormant window, and a pair of lips that looked like he had been sucking a bee gum and got badly stung in the operation, objected to my registering as a voter. He was one of the board of registrars at Clarksville, but he was not in a condition to object to any one else registering that day, and probably the next, for I took him a club over the head that would have stunned a beef, but he never winked; I changed my tactics and gave him twelve inches of solid shoe leather on the shins that brought him to his milk in short order. The buro fined me fifty dollars and costs, but the amount is not paid yet, and probably won't be until they can get a crowd that is good at traveling and fighting Indians to pilot the sheriff to my ranch.[10]

Besides recommending possible registrars (on a few occasions appointing them), Bureau agents had to compile lists of "undoubted" Union men capable of taking the ironclad oath in order to develop "national principles" in the state. This list would aid in finding replacements for those county officials deemed "impediments to Reconstruction." Although military officials removed some high-level state officeholders, most notably Governor Throckmorton, in the summer of 1867, they were hesitant to "wipe the slate clean." They still wanted subordinates to find men to replace local officials for possible future removals. With few qualified men who could take the oath, compiling a list at times proved difficult. With their removal now possible, some civil authorities have "show[ed] a disposition to do justice to all parties." A few agents need not worry about such judges, because they themselves were judges.[11]

Including those who served concurrently as judges (Albert Latimer, Hardin Hart, Thomas H. Baker, and F. P. Wood), 35 men out of the 239 (or 14.6 percent) held public office at one time or another. No man held political office and served as Bureau agent simultaneously. They either left Bureau service for public office or entered politics shortly after the organization ceased operations. Of those who held public office, 20 were civilian agents, having no military experience during the war. Tables 6-3 and 6-4 show, respectively, the military experience and birthplace of agents who entered politics. They were slightly older than thirty-four years

Table 6-3   Military Experience of Bureau Men Who Entered Politics

Military Experience	No Military Experience
n=15	n=20
42.9 percent	57.1 percent

Note: The information in this table came from various sources, but much of it came from the U.S. Census, biographical entries, and the agent's application to the Freedmen's Bureau.

Table 6-4: Origin of Birth of Bureau Men Who Entered Politics

(Place of Birth) Confederate South	North	Slaveholding North	Foreign	No Data
10	14	3	5	3
28.6 percent	40	8.6	14.2	8.6

Note: The information in this table came from various sources, but much of it came from the U.S. Census, biographical entries, and the agent's application to the Freedmen's Bureau.

old (34.4 years of age). They were nearly two years younger than their fellow agents as a whole (36.3). On average, they far exceeded the average wealth, nearly doubling their fellow agents in Texas: $7,032.4 to $3,967. Bureau service certainly helped with their future political careers, but it would be easy to overestimate its importance. The small number is surprising, considering there were so many opportunities and political vacancies during Reconstruction and there were thousands of newly enfranchised supporters, who had unquestioned faith and confidence in Bureau agents. To be sure, an agent would be elected if he chose to run. That so few did shows how committed to Bureau service they were.

Who were these men who entered politics? After a very eventful and indispensable Bureau career, William H. Sinclair received an appointment as clerk and county treasurer for Galveston County. In 1870 he won election to the state legislature from Galveston. A Republican, he soon became Speaker of the House during an intraparty feud that involved then Speaker and former Bureau agent Ira H. Evans. Sinclair later returned to Galveston as collector of internal revenue for the city and postmaster general as well as greatly contributed to the industrialization of the city. He died in Galveston in 1897. Prussian-born Jacob C. DeGress was the first Texas state superintendent of schools, an appointment he received from Radical Republican Governor Edmund Jackson Davis. He held it until 1873, when a Democratic governor removed him. To prevent the Democratic governor who had removed him from taking office, DeGress and others tried to load the cannon displayed on the capitol grounds but found it spiked. Despised as a "carpetbagger," DeGress remained active in the state's Republican party. He served as mayor and postmaster of Austin and a delegate to several state Republican conventions until his death in 1894.[12]

Some who left for political office were not missed. For every George T. Ruby, who from all accounts acquitted himself very ably, there was another like P. B. Johnson, who was derelict in his duties, or William Garretson, who fell to constantly complaining. Or, for instance, consider the case of Mortimer H. Goddin. Born in Virginia, Goddin immigrated to Texas in the 1850s. Although a slave owner, he opposed secession and resisted the Confederacy. Despite being a "scalawag," Griffin trusted him. On several occasions, he offered him a position in the agency (ironically, Goddin often warned officials against appointing "scalawags" because they could not be trusted). He initially refused the offer, but eventually accepted. He reminded headquarters he never saw the day where "I would have taken the oath to support Jeff Davis' Wheelbarrow concern." He considered himself a "white livered, sand gizzard, Dirt eating Unionists." Such a stance won an appointment as justice of the peace during the Andrew Jackson

Hamilton administration. When appointed to Livingston, Polk County, Goddin looked forward to giving the Rebels some of their own medicine: "How I do want a chance at them." His opportunity lasted but a few months and would end with him fleeing Livingston for his life.[13]

Upon assuming the position, Goddin performed zealously. His zeal, however, transitioned into belligerency. He described whites in his district as so disloyal as to make the "Devil blush." He was certain "[t]he Devil is in some of them as big as Hell itself." He unnecessarily clashed with locals, even with a fellow agent, and his abrasive tone and demeanor led to one assassination attempt. In late summer of 1867, Goddin informed the post commander at Woodville that his subdistrict was in "insurrection." Having sent soldiers to help Goddin three previous times, L. H. Sanger, the post commander, having personally investigated conditions in Livingston, informed superiors that the agent might be a little paranoid. Appreciating when Goddin "acts vigorously," Sanger nonetheless believed he had acted "too" vigorously, even bordering on recklessness. Sanger observed no rebellion, but for the "result of his [Goddin's] own fears and the tales of idle freedmen." If "any disturbance does take place it will be caused by [Goddin's] own injudicious course and lack of judgement [sic]." According to Sanger, the agent often had decided cases by his political leanings, without an investigation or "good reason."[14]

Sanger did not doubt Goddin had received threats to his life. "[B]ut these he magnifies," he surmised, since they arose from "his want of discretion." Goddin so irritated the white people several of them convinced a couple of U.S. soldiers to try to kill him. Sanger recommended his removal "at once" before he was murdered or caused any further damage. As Sanger wrote those words, Goddin was fleeing to Huntsville for his life. After resigning, Goddin was a delegate at the state's Constitutional Convention of 1868–1869, district clerk and justice of Walker County, mayor of Huntsville, and editor of a Radical Republican newspaper. His troubles, however, were not over. In addition to a brief dispute with William H. Howard, the agent at Huntsville, Goddin was confronted by four men, perhaps individuals angered by his tenure in Livingston, who forced him "to beg for his life."[15]

Goddin's case showed how a man no longer with the organization could still face the possibility of violence for "past transgressions." For the white community during Reconstruction, memories rarely faded and debts were always outstanding. Several men learned that their Bureau service, although distant in their own minds, still burned fresh in white Texans' minds. Consider the case of Charles Haughn. After serving as agent in various spots around the state, he entered politics as justice of the peace in Marion County. Considered a Republican leader in northeastern Texas, he continued defense of the emancipated. As a result, he faced the same persecution. "[F]or the last ten years of his life," reported one U.S. attorney, "Haughn, solely on account of his political convictions, was at no time safe from personal damage, so far from 'persecuting' people he was 'persecuted' to death himself, his faults consisted of his devotion to the principles of the Republican party which he sealed with his blood." After a day's work at his office in 1883, the former Bureau man left for home. While en route, he was ambushed by 50–75 men. Haughn immediately surmised their purpose. "Are you going to kill me?" he asked. "Yes I am going to kill you," the ringleader answered, "you God damned son of a bitch." Shots rang out and Haughn lay dead. The investigation into his death found his involvement as a witness in a pending election fraud case as the immediate motivating factor in his death. But it was not the only reason. "For years," reported the federal investigator, "Haughn has been surrounded by men who earnestly wished him in his grave, and they but awaited the opportune time."[16]

Although there are a few exceptions, most notably John A. Carpenter and Paul A. Cimbala, most historians agree the Bureau was active in politics. The question, however, is to what extent. Were subassistant commissioners tools of the Republican party, and did they use their positions for political aggrandizement? A noticeable number in Texas, although refraining from openly campaigning for the Republican ticket, influenced the freedpeople's vote and worked hard to ensure Republican victory. Alfred T. Manning, Charles E. Culver, and George T. Ruby joined or organized patriotic clubs, such as the Union League, which was a Radical Republican organization to "evangelize" and mobilize the newly enfranchised freedmen. Ruby even became the club's president in 1868.[17]

Mathew Young squelched a Democratic meeting at Belton, considering "it detrimental to the peaceness [sic] and quietness of the Government and this County in particular." He further added those "who are not Citizens of the US have no right to express their views in public . . . those that are Citizens are duty bound by their oath not to [allow] language incendiary to the acts of Congress or the Government of the United States [and] any violation of the above will be severely dealt with by this office." "I shall go tomorrow to Sabine County," reported agent and Union League member Albert A. Metzner, "in order to secure the vote of the colored for Mr. [William] Philips [Radical Republican in the county]. All the most influential colored men of Sabine Co. have already received instructions to that effect and I am confident that he will be elected."

Word spread in Cotton Gin that the SAC was to give a speech about politics. Both races turned out, each for different reasons. Dismayed at the crowd of whites, Charles E. Culver gave a speech filled with platitudes about free labor and fair play, but with a hidden message. Not wanting the freedpeople fooled by those claiming to be their friends, Culver told them to ignore all until they received a "sign" from him. His sign would come tomorrow, he informed superiors, and "I will defy any one to get it, or make [the freed community] vote [for them] without getting the sign." With a child's giddiness, Culver admitted, "The best of the joke is I done it right under the noses of those who came . . . As it is [the whites in attendance] went away fully satisfied that 'the Bureau' took no interest in politics." At Marlin Falls, F. B. Sturgis, with freedpeople coming for "advice," told them "they must vote with the party that shed their blood and spent their money in giving them liberty." He finally reminded them if they "voted with the south," they would be "legislatured [sic] back into slavery."[18]

Whenever agents discovered Democrats campaigning to win the freed community's vote, they often intervened. Planters in Sterling worried about being disfranchised by the Radical Republicans. "They propose to get enough Union men," Joshua L. Randall wrote, "to offset the Radicals." Randall, fearful the emancipated might be swayed to the Democrats, investigated the situation and reported "the Freedmen possess more intelligence that [sic] they are credited for having. The very fact that Planters want them to vote one way, they say is a sufficient reason why they should not vote that way." The freedpeople, he assured officials, "will vote as the Bureau Agent instructs [because they] believe in him [and] know what he is sent among them for and will obey him in every respect." Randall was so confident about their voting Republican he ran as a delegate to the state's Republican convention after his tenure.[19]

At Waco, Charles Haughn reported the "feeling has been very bitter though the hatred seems to have abated as the [freedmen] seem to have become reconciled to join the Democratic party." Griffin quickly passed this on to Commissioner Howard in Washington. The agent at Lockhart notified superiors about a similar situation in his district. "The disposition of the white people towards the freed people is not so bad as heretofore," wrote Thomas H. Baker. "The Rebels have come to the conclusion that their only alternative to get into power again is to influence the collored [sic] vote." Charles Schmidt likewise saw whites "forming democratic clubs among the freedmen." Although concerned, he resisted intervening too forcefully because the Democrats' attempts to win favor with the emancipated had "produced a better feeling between the races, as the whites are trying to induce the freemen to believe them their friends." In his monthly reports, John Dix often reported the "disposition of the Rebels, Copperheads, and Democrats appear to be to induce the Negroes to vote for them, and then Disfranchise them, if by the aid of their vote, they can get into power." During the 1868 presidential canvass, F. P. Wood informed not only superiors in Galveston, but also Commissioner Howard about freedpeople joining Democratic clubs. Agents in Texas never willingly did anything to help Democrats and rarely countenanced any attempts by the "opposition."[20]

These attitudes were encouraged and accepted by superiors. Even the most important agent in Texas openly admitted this active role in politics. William H. Sinclair, on one of his many inspection tours in April 1867, commented on the influence Bureau men had with freedmen voters and recommended ways to use it to help the Republican party. After inspecting Fred W. Reinhard and James C. Devine, the agents at Leon and Walker Counties respectively, Sinclair commented on the superior ability of these two men, especially Reinhard, who he called "one of the best agents we have." Part of their superior ability, according to the inspector, was their ability to "control nearly all the freedpeople in their counties when any move is made towards reorganizing the state." He continued:

> I respectfully suggest that it will be well to change as few agents as possible from this time until the vote shall be taken for an adoption of the Sherman bill [Reconstruction Act of 1867] for they can control more of the freedpeoples [sic] votes than any other class of persons. A word from the 'Bureau' or a ticket from him will be received with the most confidence and they will act as he suggests before that of any one else. Agents throughout the state understand the influence they will have in the coming reorganization and intend to use it, but where there are no agents the planters will generally control the votes of their laborers. Old long established agents can do much more than those newly appointed and who have not secured the confidence of the freedpeople. The state is so large and agents so scarce that it will be difficult to control a majority of the freedpeoples [sic] votes without the influence of agents in the localities where they are stationed but they need no instructions in regard to this matter. I mean that it will take the influence of agents in localities where they are stationed to control [and] influence the votes of the freedpeople in such a way as to give a majority against the side that will be most popular with the white population, which will be the secession side.[21]

From George T. Ruby encouraging the "Party of Lincoln" to Mathew Young preventing Democratic speeches, from William H. Sinclair influencing the freedmen's vote to Alex Ferguson investigating a Democratic candidate accused of buying freedmen's votes, Bureau agents winked at the idea of being nonpartisan. Considering their work, it was difficult to be anything but politically involved. Fearing white violence, officials cautioned about being too partisan publicly. Nonetheless, field agents understood a strong Republican party in Texas would not only aid their work, but also help protect the freedpeople. If the state's civil offices "were in the hands of original Union men," believed Anthony M. Bryant, "the country would be redeemed in a very short time." Philip Howard went so far as to declare "the Bureau might be done away with if we had loyal men in our county offices. But so long as a Rebel is in office . . . the Freedmen require protection." All they had to do was think about the source of many of their problems to help the freed community: the "Rebel community;" those who made war against the United States and resisted the Bureau at every turn. That community embodied the Democratic party. To that end, they worked for its defeat. Whether protecting a laborer's wages or ensuring a freedwoman's right to her children, an agent's work, at its foundation, was political. It benefited the freedpeople and helped to define them as new citizens. That which benefited the emancipated aided the Republican cause.[22]

As noted, one of the political responsibilities was to recommend civil officials for removal. Dismissal from office, however, was a double-edged sword. Suspicious of civilian agents, Griffin considered some not far removed from the state's Democratic officeholders. He preferred to fill his organization with military officers, but this was not always possible. His desires gave way to reality. Nearly half the SACs during Griffin's administration were civilians, even with greater "militarization" of the Bureau. Since the agency needed them, headquarters wanted to ensure their commitment, and those not meeting expectations (manpower needs or not) were dismissed. Griffin instituted a network of surveillance (inspectors, traveling agents, SACs, and, at times, even loyal citizens), hoping to remove troublesome and ineffective personnel.

Part of what Griffin wanted to do with this inspection system was to discover those with a Confederate past. Information surfaced that civilian agents Edwin Finch, James Burke, D. S. Hunsaker, A. P. Delano, H. S. Johnson, and a few others had supported the Stars and Bars. When the accusations were proven, most were dismissed, being unable to take the ironclad oath. For example, D. S. Hunsaker, a local doctor, was appointed as Bureau agent to his home county (Trinity). Soon loyal whites questioned his Unionism, calling him a "rabid secessionist" and revealing he disliked President Abraham Lincoln and fired a shot at the president's effigy in 1861. A former slaveholder, Hunsaker, according to the accusations, showed his "extreme pro-slavery proclivities" by "idioticly [sic] and barbarously without provocation" beating his $1,800 slave. Avoiding Confederate service by hiring a substitute, whom he never paid, Hunsaker moved to another county and eventually to Mexico, "not because he was prin-cipaled [sic] against secession . . . but because he was too big a coward and pol-troon to stand up to the principals [sic] he had time and again avowed." Another accusation appeared in the local paper alleging "grossly improper conduct" while in Bureau service. Wanting to defend himself and believing Griffin would dismiss any accusations appearing in a "Rebel" newspaper, Hunsaker sent copies to him. He misjudged Griffin, who, despite freedpeople expressing their support for Hunsaker, summarily dismissed the doctor from office.[23]

A single standard did not exist. Certain indiscretions could be overlooked. John Dix and Anthony M. Bryant, for example, were both "scalawag" agents appointed by Griffin. Many white loyalists attested to Dix's Unionist creden-tials. But the former Rebel community had no such love for him. They expressed their anger in a letter to Griffin, accusing Dix of oppression and giving "sub-stantial aid and comfort to the enemies of the Union—that [he] took the oath of allegiance to the confederate states." They additionally claimed he armed Con-federate gunboats. Such charges resulted in the dismissal of others, but not Dix. He had power and influence on his side. In addition to the endorsement of the leading Radical Republican in the state, Edmund Jackson Davis, Dix had the confidence of Griffin, who knew his patriotism and loyalty to be unquestioned. Griffin apparently dismissed the accusations, since no further mention of the charges exist in the records.[24]

Anthony M. Bryant, a long-time resident of Texas, wealthy farmer, former slaveholder, and county judge during Andrew Jackson Hamilton's adminis-tration, was appointed agent at Sherman, Texas, in March 1867. Information, however, soon surfaced he had run for a position (as a Unionist candidate) in the Rebel government in late 1861. Although Bryant lost to his Rebel oppo-nent, there was some doubt if he could take the ironclad oath. "I can take any other part of the oath," he stated. "I can swear that I did not run for the office to aid the Rebellion but to the very reverse." Because the oath also disqualified those who "sought" political office in the Confederacy, Bryant's appointment was in jeopardy. Griffin, nonetheless, intervened, retaining him in service. He concluded he "sought office not to aid but resist the rebellion. . . ." By the end of the year, after a commendable tenure, Bryant left the agency for political office.[25]

In April 1867 the AC followed his orders on registration with "the most celebrated act of military interference with civil courts during Reconstruction."
Griffin designed Circular Order No. 13 to bring about fairness and justice. Based
on the Civil Rights Act of 1866, it intended "solely to protect loyal residents in
their lives and property." The order precluded those disqualified by the "ironclad oath" from serving on juries and required all prospective jurors to take the
oath. Required of all federal employees since 1862, the oath disqualified any
person who voluntarily gave "aid, countenance, counsel or encouragement to
persons engaged in armed hostilities" against the U.S. Under the Reconstruction Act of 1867, General Orders No. 26, which required the military to transfer
all citizens arrested to the civil authorities for trial, was now nullified. Griffin
now had the option to try individuals by civil courts or military commissions.
Bureau officials, preferring to work through the civil courts if impartial,
banked the mere threat would prompt civil authorities to act fairly. In conjunction with the threat, Circular Order No. 13 allowed an influx of freedmen to the
jury box, to ensure justice and possibly remedy the problem of uncooperative
state courts.[26]

Along with confusion, field agents immediately met resistance to the order.
Most often, complaints were about conscious efforts to evade the order. In July
1867, one month after telling superiors troops were unnecessary in his district,
A. H. Mayer requested their presence. He did not need them to quell white violence, but to force judicial officials in Liberty to abide by the order. Charles E.
Culver experienced the same difficulty with those in Cotton Gin. "I find that
they did not even make as much as an inquiry as to whether there were or were
not men in the County [who] could take the prescribed Oath," reported Culver.
"They won't have Negroes & they just as [soon] leave [than] have a Negro as a
man that can take the Oath 'i.e.' they don't want & won't have either." To counter
local officials' moves, he issued an order releasing all prisoners who had been
held for more than three months in confinement or those who had bonds of less
than five hundred dollars. Gregory Barrett in Tyler had a case of a court clerk
refusing to impanel a jury with freedmen. J. U. Wright, the court clerk, who
"swore publicly that before he would swear a 'nigger' as a juryman he would leave
the Court," further warned Barrett if he continued to insist he would get "his
head shot off." Barrett desired to accommodate the incorrigible clerk's wish "to
leave the court," recommending J. K. P. Shelton be appointed in his place. Joshua
L. Randall in Robertson County was frustrated by one judge who "rendered it
[the order] impractical to empanel a jury" and simply ceased legal proceedings

for the remainder of 1867. Even Byron Porter, very optimistic about the prospects of the order in June, reported a month later Judge John Ireland, a staunch
Democrat, had blatantly violated the order by "preferring no doubt . . . a white
man."[27]

Not all expressed complete happiness with this new course. Some orders
from superiors, particularly those transferring responsibility to local officials,
worried a few. John H. Morrison suggested everything "pertaining to Freedmen
ought to be entirely in the jurisdiction of the Bureau," admitting "I have to be
. . . leniant [sic] on Rebellious people . . . [T]wo or three come to my office and
rase [sic] a row at a time and the crowd refuses to obey any summons of officers
to qell [sic] disturbances." J. P. Richardson predicted civil authorities would
shirk their responsibilities, while James Oakes, although noting "a disposition
to do justice to the freedperson in all cases . . . referred to them by this office,"
worried whites would believe "the Bureau has no authority except through the
civil courts." Oakes was not alone. Walter B. Pease at Houston noticed a "greater
difficulty in settling . . . claims" against planters for wages due, as they now
"seem to think that the <u>power</u> of the <u>Bureau</u> is gone, and have openly <u>defied</u> its
<u>agents</u>." Even Commissioner Howard expressed concern, until Griffin assuaged
his mind.[28]

When field personnel conflicted with local officials, they attributed it partly
to ignorance and confusion with the orders from headquarters. Local officials
believed Griffin's orders transferred *all* responsibility to them, abrogating the
agency's power. James C. Devine at Huntsville, for example, who a month earlier noted the whites' better disposition, had problems with local courts illegally
apprenticing freed children. He informed a justice of the peace that he could
bind out children only "under cover of vagrant laws and even then the stretch of
authority is so great that an investigation by your superiors would pronounce
your conduct not only false in the eyes of the laws, but reprehensible in morals."
Devine reminded him nothing had stripped "the agent of the Bureau of all powers" but simply redefined them "to be supervisory, except when flagrant cases of
injustice occur when it becomes his duty to act." Others had few complaints
with Griffin's orders. According to them, the new policy, along with the Reconstruction Act of 1867, greatly reduced problems in their subdistricts. Consider
two examples. Enon M. Harris admitted conditions "are good [and] very few
disturbances have occurred during the month." Later that summer, he again
reported the same, with a few "trifling civil cases." He attributed it to the "fear
of <u>removal</u>," which had "stricken almost <u>all</u> officials." In June 1867 Patrick F.
Duggan stated whites in Columbia had shown "a disposition to have as few

difficulties as possible, treating [the freedmen] in a manner best calculated to create a greater degree of harmony." That same month, after seeing conditions in another section in his subdistrict, he admitted the recent bill from Congress and the orders from headquarters seemed "to have a soothing effect upon the most turbulent spirits.[29]

After the order, those in the field throughout Texas reported race relations that ranged from "very bitter," "indifferent," and "apathetic" to "as good as could be expected," "honest," "well disposed," and "quiet," if not completely "amicable." In a few places, it was nothing short of "good." To be sure, it was so "good" in some places they admitted not needing troops. Those stationed along the Mexican border and the Texas frontier reported such occurrences (mainly due to so few freedpeople), but more than a few in the interior, especially coastal counties, reported the same. Seventeen counties were quiet enough that those stationed there reported no need for troops. Certainty is difficult, primarily because so many things, such as the effect of the Reconstruction Act of 1867 to the white community's need for labor to the ability of the Bureau man, influence the conditions. But a generalization can be made. Of the seventeen counties, all but four were located near or on the coast (Upshur, Kaufman, Leon, and Bosque were exceptions). These generally had either higher percentages of freedpeople or much lower percentages compared to noncoastal counties and the state as a whole. For example, in Wharton and Refugio Counties freedpeople represented 84 percent and 10 percent of the total population in these counties, respectively. Nearly two-thirds of the counties in which the agent reported not needing troops had freed populations either below 30 percent or above 50 percent.[30]

A former U.S.C.T. officer and one of the most respected and longest tenured agents in Texas, William H. Rock had no troops in his district. Throughout the spring and summer of 1867 and continuing into 1868, the Richmond agent claimed their presence was unnecessary as long as local officials were cooperative. An Ohioan and officer in the 35th Infantry Regiment, J. R. Fitch observed white attitudes toward the freedpeople that ranged from "indifferent" to "kindly disposed" and "friendly" in Refugio, a costal county north of Corpus Christi. Although he encountered little difficulty during registration, he believed the presence of troops necessary as a show of force. With voter registration's conclusion in the late summer of 1867, Fitch no longer thought them necessary: "I do not think there would be any difficulty." He now believed the only thing the county needed was a good magistrate. Should superiors appoint one, he suggested, the man "should also be the Sub Asst Comm." and that "would be all that is necessary and be much more efficacious than a military comdr." A. H. Mayer noticed "Slave on the brain." Thus, he did not need troops until perhaps when registration began.[31]

In mid-1867 Hiram Clark, a "carpetbagger" from Illinois, had little trouble in his coastal subdistrict. "I have no troops and think none are necessary," he reported that July. "The people seem to realize the condition they are in and promptly comply with all requests and obey all orders." This continued for the rest of the year. In La Grange, Isaac Johnson, a native Pennsylvanian and late captain in the 114th U.S.C.T., had no troops at his post. Despite acknowledging white's hostile disposition (words not actions) toward the freedpeople, Johnson could "get along without them until the settlement [time]." To Johnson, the situation was due to "the present system of procuring juries." Edward Miller, a man who impressed superiors enough to be reappointed after his muster out, credited the calm situation in Bryan City, Brazos County, to the Reconstruction Act of 1867. A "carpetbagger" from New York and VRC officer, he believed "there is no necessity" for troops in Bryan City, often repeating in subsequent reports that local officials "are always willing to assist me in the execution of my duties."[32]

At Huntsville, James P. Butler was surprised by the good race relations. Throughout the spring and early summer, he reported local officials doing their job. He believed his presence in the district was all that was required to keep the situation calm. Troops were needed only for the "unavoidable pleasure" of arresting those who refused to settle with their hands. A similar situation existed in Beaumont. John H. Archer, an Englishman, saw no need for troops in mid- to late 1867. When he applied to the Bureau, he confidentially informed Commissioner Howard he wished to "make my home in the South." Archer was adamant that he would go anywhere "except in the State of Texas." Apparently no longer fearful of the Lone Star State, he attributed the situation to cooperative civil officials and that most freedpeople in the area worked in the lumber business, not on plantations. "I can say they [would be better to] never have been freed than to remove the troops," reported Philip Howard at Meridian in June 1867. The "scalawag" agent was considered by one Texas AC one of the best civilian agents in the state. By year's end, after the troops left, Howard had changed his tune. With one exception in October (due to registration), he reported good race relations and few complaints by freedmen. So good were relations, he reported he did not "kneed [sic]" any troops.[33]

Instances of not needing troops continued until the agency's end in late 1868. Even as the Bureau wound down and violence increased throughout the state in

1868, there were districts that remained orderly enough not to necessitate troops. In the summer of 1868 A. K. Foster had a very effective sheriff in Hallettsville. Foster repeatedly informed superiors he had no troops, "nor can I say that there is a necessity for any." According to Fred W. Reinhard, no troops were desired because the "civil authorities in [the county] do their duty." In Columbus, New Yorker Louis W. Stevenson described white attitudes toward the emancipated "generally as expressed, the feelings [were] good." He thus did not need troops. At Lockhart, Thomas H. Baker, throughout the summer and fall of 1868, informed superiors he thought troops unnecessary in his district, while Hamilton C. Peterson, Baker's predecessor at Lockhart, also believed protection by soldiers was unnecessary: the "feeling between white & freedpeople is pretty good," he wrote. Thomas C. Griffin experienced some problems with rowdies in Kaufman in late summer 1868. By year's end, he had a competent sheriff and things had calmed down enough that he could do without troops. Hiram Clark had few troubles in 1868: "I have no troops" and "none are desired for the protection of the Freedpeople." Though he had no troops in late 1868, William Holt believed the freedpeople in La Grange were "as safe as other men." For much of 1868, the SACs at Victoria and Goliad admitted no troops were needed to perform their duties.[34]

Some historians would dismiss this as evidence of shirking: painting an overly optimistic picture to hide their misdeeds. For example, historian John A. Carpenter concluded "monthly reports provide the best way of sizing up the officer, what his prejudices and reactions were, what kind of job he was doing."

> But when the reports contain virtually no information or when the agent month after month wrote briefly that all was going very well, then it must be concluded either that the agent was careless in making out his reports, or, more likely, was not doing a conscientious job. It is always possible that their reports reflected the true situation, yet, with other agents reporting atrocities, unfair treatment, and other forms of hostility to the freedmen, the objective observer can only assume that some of these agents were lax in the performance of their duty.[35]

Not wanting to be accused of incompetence if conditions changed for the worse, these men also could have believed it better to report all was good. In his study of an agent in Virginia, William F. Mugelston found such discrepancies when he compared the man's monthly reports to his private diary. So it is possible that all who stated they did not need troops were "exaggerating" or "lying." But this does not hold up upon scrutiny. Just as historians have begun to discover that "the South," "Southerners," and "Confederates" are narrow definitions imply-ing consensus, with little difference and diversity, so too perhaps are the claims about violence within all subdistricts and experienced by all agents. Many fac-tors influenced violence: such as political events from Austin and Washington, D.C.; economic forces, like a bad crop; the number of freedpeople in the district; presence of U.S. troops; the planters' acceptance of the freedpeople's changed political status; and even the actions of the Bureau agent toward the citizens in his district. As reasons differed over time, it should be expected so too would the level of violence and resistance reported by agents during the Freedmen's Bureau's existence in Texas.

Furthermore, such claims do not consider the attitudes of many at head-quarters in Galveston: suspicion toward the former Rebel community and state's reputation. It would not make sense to report something different. A report contrasting what superiors believed or greatly differing from other agents, who reported chaotic conditions and repeatedly requested troops, would definitely have raised superiors' eyebrows. In the agency's voluminous records there exist no instances of superiors questioning these reports. Nor do dis-patches reminding of the importance of accurately reporting conditions exist. No inspectors were ever sent to confirm or refute claims of not needing troops. By all accounts, superiors unsuspiciously accepted these assertions. Agents were proud, taking offense at any suggestion of dereliction of duty. Shirking their responsibilities was not an option and very difficult to accept when com-pared to their reactions when their performance was, in their judgment, unfairly questioned. To claim such reports as false indicts the organization as a whole: it requires a leap to conclusion that the Bureau was a conspiracy against those under their protection—the freedpeople.[36]

In the first half of 1867, as Congressional Reconstruction commenced, SACs entered politics. The Reconstruction Act of 1867 made Throckmorton's govern-ment provisional and called for registration to elect delegates to draft a new state constitution. Agents had to ensure an orderly process and protect freed-men's suffrage rights. Further, they became Republican "foot soldiers," because a strong Republican party in Texas would ease their job and protect the freed-people. Griffin transferred much responsibility to local officials to reduce fric-tion so prevalent during Kiddoo's administration. Where some agents reported problems with local officials due to confusion and misunderstanding, others reported they were cooperative and willing to protect the emancipated. For some, conditions had improved to a point that made troops unnecessary. This "quiet," however, did not fool most agents. They likened it to the calm before the storm. Rather than permanent, some simply saw this as one round in a long fight. The orders from superiors, the admittance of freedmen to the jury box, and the passage of the Reconstruction Act had simply temporarily abated white resistance. "The disposition and feeling of the white people . . . towards the Freedpeople," DeWitt C. Brown wrote, "and in fact towards all that pertains to the Government of the United States, is vicious and vindictive," and "their apparently good acts are prompted by selfish motives . . . Hypocrisy is as prevalent among these people as it certainly could have been in the day of Charles II. Ignorance and the late war of the Rebellion . . . have unduly stimulated among them the baser passion of human nature." DeWitt as well as many of his fellow agents braced for a Rebel counterstrike.[37]

7

Violence, Frustration, and Yellow Fever

The Charles Griffin Era, Summer–Fall 1867

The latter half of 1867 would be a very violent and difficult time for many agents in Texas. General Griffin would institute a new labor policy. One he hoped would better protect the emancipated. While the agency developed the labor situation, its agents dealt with increased white resistance. The brief calm that followed the Reconstruction Act of 1867 and Griffin's "new order" would come to an end. These concerns steeled the agents' commitment to the freedpeople. Other obstacles also had to be overcome. Voter registration, the onset of a deadly epidemic of yellow fever, and the daily trials of service all weighed heavily on the agency's personnel. This would be a deadly year; nine of the fourteen agents who died while in service did so in 1867. That year really became the "year of crucifixion."[1]

As voter registration progressed, violence intensified throughout portions of the state. In certain areas, agents had little trouble. As if the problems with registration were not enough, now there was a more familiar problem: President Andrew Johnson. By mid-1867, Johnson and the Republican-held Congress were at irreconcilable odds. As the president and Congress wrangled over Reconstruction, SACs experienced the rippling effects. "Intense excitement exists at this place," wrote Jasper agent James Lowrie. "A rumor has reached here that Andrew Johnson has called in the army of the United States as commander-in-chief and annuls the registration law and all partisan measures of Congress." A few months later, he reported the white citizens believed the president had enfranchised every man North and South and "dispensed with Military Districts, Bureaus, and all other partisan measures of congress." According to Mortimer H. Goddin, the president's "course has ruined every thing." John Dix at Corpus Christi grappled with both white anger about registration and resistance inspired by the president's policies and actions. "The late Amnesty and Pardon proclamation has inspired the rebels with new hopes of being admitted to the ballot box," he wrote. These people "<u>are lost to all honor</u>,"

A. H. Mayer likewise declared about whites in Liberty in July 1867; "they cannot be trusted in any way. If they can beat the 'damned Bureau or the damned nigger' that is a feather in their [cap]."[2]

Whites turned their anger especially on what they believed was the force behind registration: the subassistant commissioners. From threats to physical assaults to murders, they personally experienced the aftershocks of freedmen's enfranchisement. The latter part of 1867 proved a difficult time. Albert Evans at Sherman was "fully satisfied" bushwhackers "plotted against" him, with operations paralyzed since he could hardly leave his office. This was also a problem for his successor, Thomas Murray Tolman. H. S. Johnson, who admitted he could only give "a good scare," worried after ordering the arrest of one suspect. "I think they will put him [the victim] through," he believed, "and perhaps when I return [from a tour] he will attempt to do me the same favor." Albert A. Metzner at San Augustine, describing chaotic conditions in Shelby County, "received three or four messages that I would be hung whenever I showed myself there, [and] I shall leave for Shelby tomorrow to try it."[3]

Ira H. Evans, future House Speaker in the Texas State Legislature, was confronted by George Quinan, a lawyer in Wharton County and local tough. As the two conversed, Quinan soon accused Evans of wanting to "injure him." He angrily berated the agent with "very offensive language." Evans stated he would not tolerate such talk, and "not wanting to become engaged in a quarrel I left him and proceeded to my office." Still agitated, Quinan and a companion arrived at the agent's office a short time later. He wanted some papers relating to a particular case. Evans told him he had no such papers, but agreed to look and give "him all the information I was able." At that moment, Evans noticed Quinan winking and "moving his lips in a very significant manner" to his companion. When confronted, Quinan launched into another verbal tirade. Evans had him escorted out of his office. Throughout the next day Quinan continually baited Evans, but the agent demurred. Frustrated, Quinan verbally lashed out, calling Evans a scoundrel within earshot of many pedestrians. For this slight, Evans asked Quinan to follow him to his office and, after disarming him, fined and jailed him. "I know of no other course which I could pursue without subjecting myself to constant abuse and insult from those infamous rebels," he argued. "It is unnecessary for me to say that if I am not allowed to protect myself from insults and abuse by summarily punishing the guilty parties, I shall be subject to insults and abuse every day and shall only be able to protect myself by shooting those who insult me." In the end, superiors approved of his course.[4]

Joshua L. Randall, unfortunately, stepped into the mess created by his predecessors in Sterling, Robertson County. E. H. Mitchell, a very prominent woman and local planter, was accused of nonpayment and abuse. As Randall investigated, several citizens warned him about her. "[I]f I had any actions against her," they said, "I should get more than I bargained for." Hoping to avoid "any difficulty with a woman of Mrs. Mitchell's antecedents and character," Randall was steeled by the sheer volume of complaints for justice. He called upon her at her plantation. Mrs. Mitchell denied accusations of nonpayment. But when he asked for her account books, she could not find them. In fact, while Randall talked with Mrs. Mitchell in one room waiting for the books, her husband was "franticly" doing something in a back room. After almost an hour, her husband "found" them, handing them over with the ink still wet.[5]

He informed she owed hundreds of dollars to her workers. She refused to pay and accused him "of wanting to be bribed." Randall further stated "she had no doubt I intended to divide the money with the nigger[s]," since she considered him "some great 'abolition[ist] nigger worshipper.'" Mrs. Mitchell contacted Bureau officials, wanting Randall "ousted from office, if it cost $1000." Her husband was willing to pay as much as "$10000." Recognized by one historian for doing "a magnificent job," Randall was unmoved in his determination for justice, despite numerous bribery offers, threats, and slights. All the same, Randall admitted that he feared for his life. Military officials dispatched soldiers for protection, and Bureau officials in Galveston ordered no further action in the Mitchell case until instructed. After the Mitchell case, Randall surprisingly reported a transformation in his subdistrict throughout 1868. For most of that year, even after the troops left, he performed his duties without the need for them.[6]

In Harris County, Byron Porter, a friend of William H. Sinclair and a man considered one of the "most efficient officers on duty in the Bureau in this state," fined a man for threatening the life of the president. The county sheriff thought the fine illegal and tried to arrest Porter, who sought protection with the post commander. Porter was soon reassigned to Austin, where he remained until being reassigned to Bastrop. Where the state capital was rather uneventful, in Bastrop he ran afoul of the Bell family. William J. A. Bell and his son were accused of shooting a freedman more than a year earlier. While Porter interrogated a witness to the shooting, the elder Bell burst into the proceeding, calling the witness a "God d-m liar." A few days later, Porter ordered Bell's arrest for the assault on the freedman. After a local court exonerated Bell, the Bureau agent believed the trial a farce and rearrested him. According to the SAC, Bell "said

... that I 'must' pay him back that fifty dollars, 'or one of us must die.'" Since his (Bell's) arrest and fine, Porter told superiors he was "perfectly furious with me and has endeavored in all possible ways to annoy me." Moreover, he reported Bell was capable of murder, attributing this to an anonymous letter "warning me that I had better leave." In the late summer of 1867, Porter also ordered the arrest of Bell's son; with aid from his father, he evaded capture. One day on the streets of Bastrop, Porter was approached by the elder Bell. He wanted to talk, but Porter brushed him off, and continued down the street. Feeling slighted, the elder Bell confronted Porter and "pointed a six-shooter at me and said, 'God d-m[,] you wouldn't stop to talk with me but by God you've got to now.'" Porter stood there and took it. "[If] I had made the slightest demonstration or had turned to leave him," he admitted, "he would have shot me down." Tiring of the standoff, Bell "moderated his tone," holstered his pistol, and rode off, warning the agent he would "call [him] to account" for his actions.[7]

Throughout the next week, a prostrated Porter endured Bell's death threats. "While I was lying very ill with the fever, and it was reported that I was dying," he informed, he "drove his carriage past my house several times making all the noise he could making faces and yelling." For this, Porter had Bell arrested and placed him under the military's protection to prevent any attempts at escape. Many Bastrop citizens, including former agent Alex B. Coggeshall, came to Bell's defense (Coggeshall might have wanted to even the score against his successor for his [Porter's] critical inspection report about his performance earlier in the year). At his trial, after Porter had testified about the initial confrontation, Bell had his lawyer change his plea to guilty of aggravated assault, but only if the case could go straight to the jury with no further evidence. The jury let him off. An infuriated Porter called the proceeding a farce. To make matters worse, Bell continued his threats and was sworn in as a deputy sheriff. Fearful their act might result in removal by military officials, Bastrop civil officials rescinded the appointment. Less fearful was Bell, who continued to harass Porter. For the rest of his time as an agent, Porter had to countenance his shenanigans. In fact, the local man sued Porter in civil court. "[This is a] series of annoyances," he noted, "which I shall have to undergo on account of my official acts." Although shielded by the military from the suit, Porter soon resigned and returned home.[8]

Some suffered physical assaults as well as verbal threats. Unknown whites in Jasper, who James Lowrie believed part of a serenading party, shot him in the thigh as he slept in his room. As he lay wounded, Lowrie dispatched his roommate, a freedmen's teacher, to get help. The post commander and agent at

Livingston, Louis Sanger, arrived with his men but found the attacking party had dispersed. With a few troops to protect him, things remained quiet for Lowrie. Yet he still feared another attempt on his life. The quiet ended when Lowrie arrested the sheriff for murder. According to Lowrie, he had to release him "owing to excitement and armed people threatening to rescue him." Although he promised to remain in the county, the sheriff quickly fled the area. Superiors ordered the SAC in Beaumont, John H. Archer, to Jasper to investigate the shooting of Lowrie. Archer suspected many had participated in the shooting, concluding the "only way to prove who are the guilty parties is to arrest the whole town. . . ."[9]

The attempt on his life greatly affected Lowrie. For the rest of his tenure at Jasper, he spent much time away from his post at Woodville in the company of the detachment of soldiers there. While accompanying them to the state capital (they had been ordered there to be reassigned), Lowrie received word that Inspector William H. Sinclair was due to arrive at Jasper, whereupon Lowrie quickly returned to his post. Confronted by Sinclair about his whereabouts, Lowrie said that he considered it too dangerous to remain in Jasper. The reason he did not go to Austin, he claimed, was his conscience had gotten to him. Sinclair doubted this since "he has transacted no business" since early 1868. Sinclair suspected Lowrie was en route because he thought the Bureau "would play out" soon, and he wanted to "get to Austin . . . and settle up and go home." On Sinclair's report, superiors relieved Lowrie in July 1868.[10]

Throughout the summer and fall of 1867, Charles E. Culver complained not about the actions of white citizens (not yet anyway) but those of the soldiers in Cotton Gin. A few months later in October, after problems with black soldiers threatening public safety, Culver again had troubles with troops. Considering the troops worthless, he recalled an incident when they were disarmed and "completely cowed down" by civilians. He worried "they have too much gas & not enough fight." Culver was informed that while attending a meeting the other day "a half dozen Revolvers were pointed at [him]," and all the perpetrators wanted was "an unguarded moment to put a bullet in me." Culver, describing his district's conditions, expressed an opinion held by more than a few agents. "You who are so far away from this scene," he reminded superiors, "cannot see the picture as it is, nor can I write so as to give you an adequate idea."[11]

Although as "good natured as the day is long" and not easily "aggravated into imposing" on the white locals, Culver had every reason to worry. A devout Congregationalist, he entered Bureau service to help the less fortunate. Refusing white amenities, he put himself in danger (both for the white and freed communities) by often traveling unprotected in his subdistrict. He even had to get his point across through the barrel of his gun on more than one occasion. His zeal and incorruptibility were intolerable to many whites in the area. As he returned from a trip, for instance, a white man stopped him on the road leading into Cotton Gin. The man, not recognizing the SAC, inquired if Culver was another sent to replace "that damned Culver." While at a July 4th celebration in Corsicana, which was in an adjacent county, one white referenced him a "damned Yankee Bureau man" in a speech. This only encouraged the rest of the crowd to join in on the verbal attacks. They further showed their "resiliency" in late 1867 when Culver, trying to enforce a local ordinance, was gunned downed and killed in the streets of town. Whites in other counties would use Culver's death for effect. Wanting to scare the agent in their area, whites in Dallas "publicly threatened" William H. Horton with "a fate similar to Capt. Culver." This was one of several death threats against Horton while in Dallas.[12]

The constant strain could be just as debilitating as physical violence. The case of Albert H. Latimer and his successor, Charles F. Rand, is revealing. An opponent of secession, state comptroller in Andrew Jackson Hamilton's administration in late 1865, a Unionist delegate to the Constitutional Convention of 1866, and later a prominent Republican politician and judge in Edmund Jackson Davis's gubernatorial administration, Latimer's loyalty was unchallenged. He came highly recommended, having been "tried and found pure." He received an appointment to his home county of Red River. It bordered the Indian Territory (Oklahoma) and was notoriously lawless. "The rowdy class . . . ride rough shod over [everybody]," observed one inspector about the area, and "are all enemies to reconstruction and everything tending to law and order." Latimer was heralded as the right man at the right place. The workload and county's conditions, however, soon weighed on the sixty-year-old. He constantly pleaded for troops and sent only one monthly report to superiors during his service as Bureau agent. Wanting to know what Latimer was doing (or not doing), officials ordered an inspector to Red River County. What William H. Sinclair found shocked him. "My God," he cried out, "how your heart would bleed for the union men of this county." It was simply "pandemonium." "I thought the war was over," Sinclair thought, "but since I've been here I find I was dreaming. It isn't." The calm, collected Sinclair, who prided himself on his accurate reporting, worried how he would be perceived by this account. "I have written so earnestly," he admitted, "that you will think me wild." When he visited Latimer, Sinclair noticed "the times and the condition of affairs here are killing him." He "looks ten years older than when I saw him a year ago." Latimer feared for his life and wished to be relieved. Concerned about the Union cause in the county, Sinclair recommended superiors replace the aged agent with a "young man with blood in his eyes," one "who is up to the times" and with "backbone." That man was Charles F. Rand. Sinclair believed him indispensable.[13]

A native New Yorker and VRC officer, Rand took great pride in his reputation and work. Whether assigned to Matagorda, Marshall, Wharton, or Gilmer (his previous posts), Rand was fair and prudent, which won him respect from fellow agents, superiors, the emancipated, and even some whites. Possessing "backbone," he often performed his duties without the aid of soldiers and, according to one, was not "a man inclined to be scar[ed]. . . ." Rand's ability and courage were greatly tested when superiors reassigned him to Clarksville, Red River County, in late 1867. In the first couple of months there, he busied himself with contract disputes.[14]

The county's conditions tested Rand's effectiveness. He faced "the most bitter, prejudicial, vindictive, malicious and unreliable" whites in Texas. He hoped to calm the situation by prohibiting firearms within the city's limits, an order that one local tough, John Henderson, brazenly disregarded. When Rand confronted Henderson in the courthouse, Henderson refused to relinquish his gun. Rand then ordered the sheriff, who the agent was talking with at the time, to arrest the man. Henderson immediately lunged at Rand with a club. The Bureau man, with the use of only one arm from an injury in the war, deflected the blow, only then to stare down the barrel of a revolver. Defying "invalid status," Rand quickly dived into an empty room, while Henderson fled. Adding insult to injury, superiors reprimanded Rand that "agents . . . are not the proper authority to issue" a ban on firearms. It would "place the law abiding citizens who would obey the order at the mercy of the outlaws who would not." Thus, they countermanded the order. Already frustrated after his request for a leave of absence due to ill health was declined, Rand thought their treatment disrespectful, further frustrating him.[15]

Rand's troubles were far from over, however. Throughout the summer of 1868, desperadoes routinely entered Clarksville. They threatened Unionists (white and black), even firing into Rand's room in hopes of killing him. Rand did not take these offenses lying down. He invoked General U. S. Grant's statement during the Overland Campaign during the war and promised to "fight it out on that line." That fight came immediate, because Ben Griffith, a notorious former Confederate cavalryman and the agency's scourge in Clarksville, arrived in the city. Having recently escaped from federal officials, Griffith returned with hopes of exacting revenge. After bragging to a crowd of local whites about his exploits, Griffith, while leaving the town, robbed a freedman. The victim, luckily escaping death, returned to town and reported the incident to Rand. Rand quickly gathered a posse and found the desperado a mile outside of town. When the agent yelled halt, Griffith tried to escape. He did not get far, before the posse riddled the outlaw with bullets. The outlaw's death only worsened the situation for Rand, however, as white locals focused their anger against him. For protection, he slept in a different place each night. The intrepid agent was at a loss what to do. To stay in town, he noted, with no troops for sixty miles "and [Confederate] sympathizers all around, is to say the least very unpleasant." "I am worn out . . . by constant anxiety both day and night," Rand confided. Military officials sent troops to Clarksville, and under cover of night sneaked Rand out of the "blood-thirsty hole." The military sent a detachment to replace the departed Bureau agent.[16]

Helpless at times, agents were rarely passive observers. They often made "practical and judicious suggestions" to make the "Bureau more efficient." In 1867 headquarters, realizing their ignorance about conditions in the interior, inserted a question on the pre-printed report forms each agent completed and sent in monthly ("Make such practical and judicious suggestions as will, in your opinion, render the operations of the Bureau more efficient, etc., etc."). Many seized upon the opportunity to make suggestions. They suggested appointing more clerks, reducing subdistricts to no more than one county, assigning a detachment of cavalry to every agent, or providing mounts for infantry. Whenever possible, military officials sent cavalry, but they never provided horses for infantry.[17]

Their personalities or particular problems influenced suggestions. They included calls to increase their authority, to increase inspection tours, and to limit their focus to only labor or education. For some perspective, two examples will suffice. Patrick F. Duggan relished this opportunity. Besides suggesting a clerk be appointed to each subdistrict, he thought headquarters should "pay a little more attention" to "the communications I send him in regard to forage for my horse." Since his appointment "there has been a constant drain on my purse to pay expenses caused by the performance of my duties which would otherwise have been neglected." If the forage situation would not or could not be remedied, Duggan suggested immediate pay upon assuming the position and "thereby save [him] from being under pecuniary obligations to a class of people that look upon him as an instrument of oppression." Although critical of the chain-of-command system regarding the use of troops, Anthony M. Bryant thought the Bureau ran rather smoothly and needed little improvement. "I have no suggestions to make as enunciated," he wrote, the "wise policy adopted by the department if carried out will secure the Freed people in all their rights." Such suggestions to improve the effectiveness in protecting the emancipated continued to the agency's end.[18]

Of all the problems, the labor system topped their list. Even with Griffin's policy changes earlier in the year, some difficulties remained. Griffin's new order was to change the labor regulations set down by his predecessor and bring back some kind of "natural and nominal conditions of capital and of free labor" in Texas. Agents were to allow "all labor . . . to offer itself in the market upon the best terms it can obtain." Contracts could not exceed one year. Local officials, such as justices of the peace or county clerks, and SACs had the authority to approve labor contracts. Despite this delegation, Griffin reminded civil officials that agents still retained the authority to abrogate any contract they deemed "manifestly unjust."[19]

Griffin further mandated a delegation to the civil courts. This included all freedpeople's cases except those "arising from contracts for labor," something he "thought . . . the Bureau . . . [should] control." Agents were to continue to act as adjunct county judges. In the end, Griffin wanted justice based more on law, rather than agents' personal opinions, and reduce "collision[s] with the civil authorities and contempt . . . upon the National Government . . . [for] the want of tact and judgment on [agent's] part . . . with their own peculiar judgment and experience without any uniform guiding principles." He understood the limitations on the military to provide protection and justice for field agents. Labor contracts notwithstanding, Griffin wanted subordinates to act as observers to civil proceedings. If an agent believed civil authorities rendered biased justice, he could overrule the decision or refer it to superiors for review. The agency's role was diminishing. Each day, agents intervened less and less to resolve disputes.[20]

Problems that plagued labor policies under Kiddoo remained under Griffin's plan. Phineas Stevens relayed that planters in Hallettsville refused to work another year with freedpeople because of their inefficiency and irresponsible ways. Copies of contracts were not made and filed as required, and some agents unnecessarily seized cotton, even without a complaint by a freedperson. William Garretson reported the emancipated in his district disrupted the labor situation by organizing a paramilitary unit. This worried whites in his district. "I advised [the hands] to attend to the requirements of their contracts," he wrote, "and that if any military demonstrations were necessary, they would be made by the U.S. authorities and that they should not be led away from their duties by any foolish representations. . . ." Byron Porter witnessed "knavery and corruption" toward freedpeople. "It is not an uncommon thing for merchants to give planters a large percent on all the trade they send them," he admitted. "This percent ranges from 10 to 25 and of course a corresponding increase of price is put on the goods. Some planters get the things for their hands themselves and then charge them 25 to 100 percent more than the merchants charged them saying all the time that they are charging just the store prices. The negro feels that he is cheated in some manner but can not tell how. He knows that he made a good crop sold it at a fair price [and] has not been extravagant, but come out in debt."[21]

At the same time he delegated to local authorities, Griffin further centralized a part of the labor process. To reduce the "knavery and corruption" described by Porter, the AC proposed a way to ensure freedpeople's wages. Griffin blamed his predecessors for the problems going back to 1865. Under his tenure, hands would be dealt with fairly. This would happen through a two-part plan. First and foremost, the issuance of General Orders No. 11. In it, the "accounts against freemen will not be allowed to constitute a lien upon" their portion of the crop (this, however, did not apply if the hand agreed in the contract to a lien on his share and a Bureau agent approved it). This, Griffin hoped, would remedy planters charging workers for everything, leaving them in debt by year's end. Agents were also to "urge . . . the freedmen" to settle all their debts upon the sale of their crop. Second, Griffin proposed a single merchant house, A. Ruttkey & Co., to handle all the crops for the freedpeople in Texas. He wanted subordinates "for the pecuniary security of the Freedmen[,] to recommend in all cases that they consign their crops." The house would set a minimum and fair price. The assistant commissioner wanted to force all other merchants into fair practice toward the freedmen or risk going out of business.[22]

Some believed General Orders No. 11, the no-lien policy, necessary. "Many accounts of last year are brought in by the planters themselves & squaring up their accounts & balancing their books occupies a good deal of my time," reported Charles E. Culver. "I am alone called upon to [go] over to plantations to see the cotton and corn is equally divided." Culver also noted the uncertainty whether an attachment constituted a lien. As a result, civil authorities could evade Griffin's order. Some observed "much discontent concerning Genl. Order No. 11 & as I rigidly enforce it, I am not much esteemed." Others described confusion for all, including the agents. Superiors received "numerous applications" from subordinates for clarification. Planters and merchants now refused credit to the freedpeople, hoping they would "take advantage of [the order] to the full." Edward Collins believed the policy furthered dependency. "The main object of the Bureau in my opinion [is] to enable the Freedmen to take care of themselves as soon as possible," he wrote. Informing superiors the "whole system of contract labor" and the lien policy instituted by Griffin was "a complete failure," Collins wanted G. O. No. 11 revoked due to the many instances of "breach of contract." Collins considered the lien policy a "positive injury" to them. "They depend upon the Government for protection where they ought to protect themselves," he wrote, "and are perfectly willing to remain in this state of dependence so long as it eases the exercise of brain or muscle." A few field personnel as well as Commissioner Howard were concerned with granting a monopoly to A. Ruttkey & Co. Some may never have received the general orders. Although explicitly addressed in the order, Edward W. Whittemore still wanted to know if hands could voluntarily bind their crops as a lien. Superiors replied so long as they would not be taken advantage of they could sign a contract "binding their crops [as] payment for their debts, or for advance." J. H. Bradford at Centreville also expressed confusion about how to enforce Griffin's lien order.[23]

Realizing their own limitations, headquarters wanted subordinates to help "police" the agency. Bureau men rarely shied from exposing those whom, through their actions, failed the freedpeople. In fact, they had a vested interest in purging troublesome or derelict men: they insulted those who took their duties seriously. J. H. Bradford warned about H. S. Johnson, as "there are many reports that he is corrupt in his official action." Bradford's report prompted an investigation that discovered Johnson's corruption (see Chapter 6). Anthony M. Bryant helped expose William H. Horton at Dallas. Although suspicious of accusations by whites, Bryant was "fully satisfied . . . [about] the source from which the charge originated." A few months earlier, he raised concerns about Hardin Hart, a "scalawag" judge and SAC at Greenville, who he believed derelict. "Hart is a truly loyal citizen," he declared, "but I fear that he is not giving the attention to the interest of the freed people that their interest[s] demand." An investigation confirmed Hart, due to his advanced age, derelict and led to his dismissal.[24]

Of course, not all indictments were substantiated. Accusers sometimes based their claims on hearsay. Agents like J. H. Bradford, Mortimer H. Goddin, who could hardly be called a planter tool, and Fred W. Reinhard, who superiors considered one of the best SACs in Texas, were all accused of misdeeds. The charges, after an investigation or use of common sense by officials, were all dismissed. As Bureau men became "whistleblowers," quite naturally, disputes and squabbles developed. For example, Liberty Bureau agent A. H. Mayer feuded for many months with his predecessor, former agent J. Orville Shelby.

Upon entering the post at Liberty in the summer of 1866, Mayer found conditions he "deemed and styled a perfect chaos; order and discipline had left its Throne. Freedmen were running wild, Contracts of all kinds without intent or purpose afloat, Employers dissatisfied, all wrong, all wrong, and I was called upon & expected to make all wrong, Right." Through a frantic work schedule, comprising tours and crop seizures, Mayer restored order where chaos once existed. His problems with Shelby were far from over. Mayer soon discovered his predecessor was still "acting" like a Bureau agent "making contacts for himself and others." Moreover, continued Mayer, Shelby tried "to convince the freedmen that he is the man to whom [they] must look up to, and that I am only subordinate to him." He further stated Shelby had threatened his workers that he would "drive them off" if they "went near the office of the Bureau."[25]

When complaints that Shelby refused to settle with his hands reached his office, Mayer issued a special order. Shelby ignored it. This infuriated Mayer. "Now what am I to do?" he cried out, "make it a personal matter, go out & slap Shelby's face, then shoot him [in order to] accomplish the object in view." Mayer wanted to fine and arrest the delinquent former agent. After that, he would make him pay his workers, fine him again for violating their contracts, and send him to prison for a year. Mayer's troubles soon increased as voter registration commenced. When Mayer recommended their removal, one of the registrars who was removed, Ira P. Pedigo, a friend of Shelby and a former SAC in Texas, wrote a letter to military officials. He claimed Mayer was angry he "was not consulted in regard to the formation of the Board." With information provided by Shelby, Pedigo further claimed the agent had received "a large amount of money as bribes. . . ." Superiors wanted Mayer's explanation. The "accusations are false in every particular," he responded. "I am respected throughout my District (and out of it) by both Black & white from the fact that no man has it in his power to say that he ever paid or gave me money or anything else directly or indirectly." To underscore his point, he requested a military commission to clear his name. Officials must have been satisfied since no further mention of the incident can be found in the records. Mayer remained in service until early 1868. Upon leaving, superiors personally thanked him "for [the way] he has discharged his duties."[26]

The usual relationship between Bureau men was much better than Shelby's and Mayer's. Far more examples exist of cooperation than to the contrary. They had a commonality, a shared experience. Their experience differentiated them from headquarters personnel. Agents never hesitated to call on a fellow agent, whether in searching for freedpeople's family members separated during slavery or in finding whites who fled to another county to evade justice. Cooperation even extended beyond state boundaries. Those stationed along the Louisiana and Arkansas borders cooperated to bring to justice the many outlaws in the area. "I returned from [Arkansas] last evening," wrote William G. Kirkman at Boston, "when I went to . . . consult with Lt. [Hiram F.] Willis the Bureau Agent at Rocky Comfort . . . to secure his co-operation in endeavors to arrest the desperadoes that infest [this region]."[27]

In 1867 one of the trials that bonded those in the field was "Yellow Jack." Throughout the nineteenth century, yellow fever routinely ravaged Texas coastal communities. A particularly bad epidemic occurred in late 1867 that greatly disrupted Bureau operations. In the summer and fall of 1867, Bureau schools had to close for fear of spreading the epidemic. The disease also disrupted field operations. George Lancaster in Hempstead had to cease operations from September through November of 1867, while Edward Miller reported disruption of everything in Bryan City, Brazos County. Things got so bad that Miller had to send his wife out of the county, fearing for her safety. With dozens dying, Miller dubbed it the village of the dead. Field agents in Walker, Anderson, and Galveston counties also reported chaotic conditions because of the epidemic. In all, one in twenty residents of Galveston would die from the disease. The SAC at Columbus wrote the disease had left Galveston a virtual ghost town. William M. Van Horn in Harris County reported that citizens refused to leave their homes. "I have considerable difficulty in performing my duty on account of the prevailing epidemic," he reported. "In most instances the parties who have been ordered to appear before me have refused to do so, unless compelled by force." In his report for September 1867, Isaac Johnson stated his only difficulty was the epidemic. During the scourge, field agents discovered how it paralyzed military operations, as post commanders often declined to send any troops fearful of transmitting the disease. Because of the disease, Bureau men incurred great personal expense. They had to pay for their own medical treatment when army doctors contracted the illness. On several occasions they even had to pay for the medical treatment of civilians, including the burial expenses of freedpeople. Regardless of the circumstances, agents had to protect those in their districts from all threats.[28]

In the chaos of late 1867, however, some shirked this responsibility. Enon M. Harris, the agent at Columbus, for example, left a trail of corruption and neglect in his wake not uncovered until late 1868. His undoing involved the death of a freedmen's teacher. While on an inspection tour in southeast Texas, William H. Sinclair interviewed the widow of James J. Jameson, a freedmen's teacher who had died of yellow fever. Mrs. Jameson, also a former freedmen's teacher who now lived in Galveston on public charity, claimed Harris had murdered her husband. She wanted him brought to justice. She told Sinclair that Harris refused them medical assistance or to call for a doctor when they contracted yellow fever. According to Mrs. Jameson, her husband died a slow, agonizing death because of his neglect. But for the actions of a few freedpeople, the widow further recounted, she too would have died. Still "delirious" with the disease, Mrs. Jameson claimed her caretakers had loaded her in a wagon and took her to see Harris, who, she retold, took her to his house and put her in a room with a pillow and blanket. Thinking she was almost dead, she claimed, he removed the pillow. Sinclair was moved to the point of anger. "I have not written one half [of what] she told me," he fumed, and if "one half [of the accusations] were true he would be a disgrace to mankind."[29]

Harris, who frequently clashed with Bureau teachers during his eighteen-month tenure with the organization, vehemently denied the story. He claimed he did all he could for the couple. Short of calling her a liar, he insinuated Mrs. Jameson was an unstable and crazy woman. This infuriated Sinclair, who, in fact, came away from the conversation doubting the agent's honesty and stunned at how he had "traduced the [couple's] character." "I know them both [the Jamesons]," he reported, "I would as unhesitatingly vouch for their chastity as I would for my own sister." Superiors ordered Sinclair to investigate. He discovered a slew of problems. According to the inspector, Harris, instead of being a "friend and defender," was "the reverse." He also stole Bureau school money and was submitted false medical bills to defraud the government. Sinclair recommended his immediate removal, which headquarters officials did.[30]

After his removal, Harris vowed revenge. Blaming Sinclair for his removal, Harris began to spread rumors against him. In an article in the *Galveston Republican*, he accused Sinclair and his brother-in-law, E. C. Bartholomew, a headquarters clerk, of being "part of a cabal of evil men who . . . had worked to destroy the Bureau's image." He basically accused the two of trying to undermine the Reconstruction process in Texas. According to the accusations, Griffin had discovered what Sinclair was doing, and but for his death from yellow fever, he would have dismissed him from service. These accusations soon came to the attention of Commissioner Howard, who wrote to Griffin's successor, J. J. Reynolds, for a report. After an investigation, Reynolds dispelled "any rumors that Sinclair is trying to defeat Reconstruction in the state."[31]

The Bureau did not escape the epidemic unscathed. Agents paid with their money; a few with their lives. The disease prostrated many, killing six. J. D.

O'Connell and L. H. Warren at Houston, Sam W. Black at Hempstead, Augustus B. Bonnaffon at Indianola, Patrick F. Duggan at Columbia, and James C. Devine at Huntsville all died from the disease while on duty (the disease even claimed William Garretson, although after his time with the agency). Some moved to assist those who "shared the line of fire with them." For instance, James P. Butler bonded with the supervising voter registrar in his district. When the man died from yellow fever, Butler lobbied his salary be paid to his widow. He "deserves credit for the fidelity manifested by him in remaining to complete the report, after the balance of the [registration] board [had] deserted," Butler wrote. "He leaves a wife in poor pecuniary circumstances and it would be a great favor for her to receive the amount due him for his services."[32]

To ward off an even worse epidemic, certain agents sought to battle the disease directly. Officials wanted subordinates to "render any assistance in your power to prevent the entrance or spread of this disease." The agency had engaged in health and sanitation measures before. During this epidemic, its attention to disease prevention and sanitation greatly increased (at the time no one knew that mosquitoes spread the disease). Field personnel, nonetheless, advised about proper sanitary living and instituted measures to prevent unhealthy and dangerous living situations, like overcrowding. Local officials were more willing to cooperate in support of sanitary and health measures than with any other Bureau operations; but of course only to a point. For example, T. J. Krutz dealt with unsanitary conditions in Galveston throughout August 1867. He buried destitute freedpeople who died of yellow fever. This was not only inhumane, according to Krutz, but also a health hazard. He emphatically told local officials that funds needed to be provided to care for these people, and when they died, it was "absolutely necessary that [their bodies] be removed." Krutz reported people burying the refuse of yellow fever victims anywhere they could. Locals had deposited bedding from fever victims in a prairie near his office, and "he has full benefit of the infected air." Besides being unsanitary, this caused a "putrid and disagreeable" atmosphere. Krutz recommended that such persons, who endangered public health, be punished. Unwilling to wait for superiors to act, he sent out "a search for [the] parties guilty of such [coarse] conduct detrimental to the laws of humanity." Meanwhile, he asked for "chloride of lime" as a disinfectant.[33]

The onset of winter finally ended yellow fever's "reign of terror." Included in the September death toll was Assistant Commissioner Charles Griffin. He remained at his post in Galveston despite being warned to leave. For his commitment, he paid with his life. His body was returned to Washington, D.C., and buried in historic Oak Hill Cemetery. At Griffin's death there remained much work uncompleted. Many of the same problems that had plagued his predecessors were still unresolved. The transition from slave to free labor was still an ongoing process with many kinks yet unresolved. Although Griffin's labor measures, such as the no-lien policy, were to protect the freedpeople's wages, whites still found ways to evade payment. Evasion of payment coupled with the confusion agents had with the no-lien policy helped to limit the effectiveness of Griffin's policies. Further hindrance was increased violence. In the first half of 1867 white violence had abated in much of the state, attributed to the "new attitude" from headquarters and Congress. In the latter half of 1867, however, this respite ended. Violence increased to levels not seen since late 1866, especially as registration commenced. Failure to win political favor with the freedmen caused white Texans to focus their frustration on field agents. Several were assaulted and others murdered. Increasing the organization's death toll in the latter half of 1867 was the yellow fever epidemic. Brevet Major General (and former Bureau agent in Brownsville) Joseph J. Reynolds would replace Griffin. He not only would have his opportunity to solve these problems that bedeviled his predecessors, but he would also oversee the Bureau's end in the Lone Star State.[34]

8

General Orders No. 40 and the Freedmen's Bureau's End

The J. J. Reynolds Era,
September 1867–December 1868

Shortly before Griffin's death, the Freedmen's Bureau had the highest number of agents and subdistricts it would have in its more than three years in the state. From then on, however, it gradually lessened operations, transferring authority to civil authorities until it ceased operations (except for educational programs) at the end of 1868. While SACs wound down their operations, preparing the emancipated for life "after the Bureau," events beyond their control affected the process. Some military officials, particularly the commander of the Fifth Military District, Winfield Scott Hancock, preferred civil control with little interference. In General Orders No. 40, he transferred the main responsibility for protecting the freedpeople to local officials. Nearing the agency's end, whites resisted in intensity not seen since the Bureau entered the state in 1865. Most whites saw a final opportunity to strike at this most despised symbol of defeat. In the Bureau's last year, Reynolds still held subordinates to high standards, not hesitating to dismiss any for dereliction. Reynolds worked diligently to ensure the agency and its personnel remained professional. If the Bureau was to "be crushed down by the weight of public opinion," it would at least go out dignified and honorable.

Born in Kentucky in 1822, Brevet Major General Joseph Jones Reynolds was graduated from West Point in 1843. He served in Texas prior to the Mexican War. After the war, he was an instructor at West Point, before returning to duty in Indian Territory. Reynolds resigned from the military to accept a teaching position at a university in St. Louis in 1857. When the Civil War started, he was appointed colonel of an Indiana militia unit. Within months, he reached brigadier general of U.S. Volunteers. He participated in the major battles of Chickamauga and Chattanooga in 1863 before being appointed commander of the New Orleans defenses in early 1864 and later that year to the command of the Department of Arkansas. He remained there until the army's reorganization in July 1866, when he took command of the 26th Infantry Regiment. The following year, Reynolds was brevetted brigadier and then major general in the U.S. Army. He served for a short time as U.S. senator from Texas. He lost the seat after the election was challenged. Following his tenure as AC in Texas, Reynolds was reassigned to frontier duty in Montana, commanding forces against the Arapaho and Northern Cheyenne. Having captured Crazy Horse's "winter hideout and pony herd," Reynolds prematurely retreated without engaging the warriors. His oversight contributed to General George A. Custer's defeat months later. Superiors, in fact, offered him command of Custer's ill-fated expedition. He declined because of poor health. Reynolds was court-martialed for actions during another Indian campaign (subsequently found guilty, receiving a suspended sentence) and retired shortly afterward in 1877. He died in 1899 and is buried in Arlington National Cemetery.[1]

Meanwhile, Reynolds immediately made his mark on Bureau operations. He relocated agency headquarters from Galveston, where it had been since September 1865, to Austin. Better climate dictated the move. He also appointed men of his own choosing as his headquarters staff, even as Griffin's staff remained in Galveston and still functioned as a headquarters staff. He also began appointing his own field personnel. At the time of Reynolds's appointment in Texas in September 1867, there were 57 SACs, 15 ASACs, and 1 traveling agent. In all, the new assistant commissioner appointed 62 agents, with more than 70 percent with military service. Table 8-1 shows the length of service for agents appointed by Reynolds.

Like Kiddoo, Reynolds had few terminated for malfeasance, as shown in Table 8-2. Surprisingly, none of Reynolds's appointees voluntarily quit their positions. Even with the problems ceasing operation, the number and percentage who died in service was lower than all, except Gregory's.

Military officials in Washington wanted to muster out all remaining military men, especially those VRC officers still in Bureau service. By late 1867, only four served in Texas. They, according to Reynolds, were superb agents. He greatly desired their retention since they "proved themselves able and efficient." Commissioner Howard agreed and offered each a civilian appointment after

Table 8-1   Length of Service for Agents Appointed by Reynolds

Type of Bureau Agent	Number	Average Length of Service (Months)
Civilian	18	6.8
Military	44	4.6

Note: Dates came from the Freedmen's Bureau Roster of Officers and Civilians.

Table 8-2   Reasons Agents Appointed by Reynolds Left Bureau Service

Reason	Number	Percentage
Bureau Operations: Bureau ended, consolidation, and transferal or reassignment within the agency	32	51.6
Military Operations: Mustered out or ordered to new assignment	16	25.8
Dropped on Request: Agent resigned appointment	0	0
Terminated: Dismissed for criminality, cruelty, Confederate service, or appointment revoked	5	8.1
N/A: Reason for leaving undetermined	8	12.9
Died: murdered, disease, or accidents	1	1.6
Total: All Reynolds's Agents	n=62	100

Note: The information came from various sources, but much of it came from the U.S. Census and the Freedmen's Bureau's Special Orders and Correspondences.

their muster out. Of these (Edward Miller, Charles F. Rand, N. H. Randlett, and Albert A. Metzner), all but Miller accepted. Although overseeing the agency's contraction, Reynolds still needed men for an orderly delegation of its control. When it ceased operations, fifty-seven men were still in the field. Only twenty-one were officers in the military.[2]

Many of Reynolds's policies were to prepare the freedpeople for the day without the agency. In General Orders No. 17 he ordered subordinates to allow the freedpeople to "dispose of their crops as other people dispose of their own property—without restraint from anyone." Reynolds thought they had come to rely too heavily on the government (because of Griffin's orders) and less "on themselves." Agents could advise but "are not directed to recommend certain commission houses for purchase to the exclusion of others." Reynolds also canceled the no-lien policy, believing it unfair to planters and quite confusing. Liens now could be placed on the worker's shares but only with the approval of a SAC, who was to enforce all fair debts.[3]

Reynolds realized the agency's temporariness and proposed a plan to Commissioner Howard to "replace Sub Asst throughout the state" with "county officers." This plan, he argued, would ease the transfer of responsibilities and help to "secure a more harmonious and satisfactory administration of the Bureau than can be attained under the present system." Reynolds sent a copy for Howard's approval. As he waited, the military command made Reynolds's plan unnecessary. In New Orleans Winfield Scott Hancock, the new commander of the Fifth Military District, "reconfirmed" his preference for civil rather than federal control of state matters. He did this by revoking Griffin's Circular Order No. 13 (jury order) and removing Reynolds's ability to make political appointments, a power Hancock believed Bureau officials had abused. Going even further, Hancock issued General Orders No. 40 in late 1867. This greatly circumscribed military interference with civic duties. In other words, the "right of trial by jury, *habeas corpus* . . . [and] freedom of speech . . . must be preserved." Hancock believed the "maintenance of the civil authorities in the faithful execution of the laws as the most efficient [approach] under existing circumstances." He based the order on the powers as district commander in the Reconstruction Act of 1867, which "exempt[ed] no class of persons" from civil tribunals and required him to protect "all persons in their rights of person and property."[4]

According to Hancock, the Bureau was too meddlesome and abusive. His idea of the proper relationship between SACs and state officials matched that of the society at large: the government's recent actions threatened federalism. Hancock wanted that "proper" relationship reestablished, intended "to confine Agents . . . [to] their legitimate authority," and determined to lessen the unnecessary disputes between agents and civil authorities about jurisdiction, disputes he believed contrary to the military's role to preserve the peace. Although Hancock appeared to make jarring changes, much of what he implemented was already in place. He, in fact, did not "make any extraordinary change in policy," but simply "spell[ed] out the conditions that [had already] legally existed" under his predecessors. To be sure, he "instituted a change in attitude."[5]

This "change in attitude" was not well received by field personnel. They believed it contradicted the Reconstruction Act's intent and inhibited their performance. Of particular concern was G. O. No. 40, which they reported greatly hindered their attempts to protect the freedpeople. Their letters expressed their frustration. Some whites now believed the Bureau "played out." There was an impression "the officers of the Bureau have no power to take action in any case wherein the parties litigating are White & Black that all such cases must be referred to the Civil Courts," reported A. H. Mayer from Austin. "The only power vested in the S.A. Comm. is to arbitrate cases wherein both parties litigating are freedmen." Mayer further described "a bitter feeling" between white employers and their employees. Whites now viewed the agency as "a thing that was" and dared agents to sue in the civil courts and "be d-d." James P. Butler at Huntsville complained civil officers have "become . . . elated with the idea of 'Civil law in Texas.'" From Richmond, William H. Rock informed whites were "being influenced" by the recent order. They even threatened to arrest him. It "is beginning to become adverse," he continued, "and in every way very unfair [for] the [freed] people under Genl. Hancock's orders," for the whites "refuse to them (the f. m.) their wages & tell them to 'sue in court.'" A frustrated Rock wanted advice about how to proceed if "I meet with the reply that [the Bureau agent] must now sue me at the Civil Courts [because] General Hancock orders you to refer all cases to the civil authorities except cases between the <u>niggers</u> and you have no authority over me." One local white C. C. Clark wrote to D. F. Stiles, the agent at McLennan County. "Allow me Sir to remind you," he mockingly stated, "one Bell Co. has civil officers and if you will get some competent man to read the order of Gen Hancock you will find out that you have no business with me."[6]

Hancock's general order also made it more difficult to regulate labor. A freedman complained to John H. Morrison that his employer had won a judgment against him in civil court. He discovered the two had a verbal contract for fifteen dollars a month, and the planter had actually broken the contract. Morrison thought a "great injustice" had occurred and nullified the judgment. The planter appealed to Bureau headquarters. Superiors contacted Morrison for a report. "I hope you [sustain] my action in the case," he responded. In the end, superiors ordered Morrison to allow a new trial in civil courts, but he was to "supervise it." And "if they [civil authorities] fail to render a decision according to law and evidence," Morrison was to "report . . . the case . . . to this office for action." Another had similar problems with civil authorities in Huntsville, as they had "the idea that General Hancock has taken away all authority and power from the Bureau and its officers." James P. Butler reiterated his displeasure with Hancock's course when he wrote that "every civil officer in the Town & County is a rampant, notorious rebel, and they adhere to the old principles of Democracy and Slavery with a tenacity that would shame Napoleon." Butler asked, "Now upon what grounds were such men elected to office?"[7]

Although agents were no longer to adjudicate disputes, numerous letters from white Texans detailing agents adjudicating and punishing them still arrived at Fifth Military District headquarters in New Orleans. They claimed SACs had "been in the habit of sitting as Judges, holding Court, and adjudicating upon complaints and cases brought before them. . . ." Hancock asked Reynolds for an explanation since such actions violated General Orders No. 40. "Such being the fact, many . . . seem not to be aware of it," he told his subordinate in Texas. "In Texas some are yet holding Courts, trying cases, imposing fines, taking fees for services and arresting citizens for offenses over which the Bureau is not intended by law to have jurisdiction." Reynolds responded that Hancock had been misled. Agents were not "'judges' in the legal sense." He stated white Texans adopted the term "Bureau Court" and "Freedmen's Court" to mean any agent who a white person had to appear before. Reynolds further reminded that numerous congressional statutes and several circulars and general orders had granted his men the power to adjudicate cases involving freedmen.[8]

Hancock, however, responded those "may have been in force under previous District Commanders but nothing therein contained inconsistent with the orders and instructions of the present commander will be sanctioned or practical in this command." He reminded Reynolds the civil tribunals were operational and all cases had to go through them. Wanting to underscore his point, Hancock told Reynolds that his argument might have worked with others but no longer. Hancock ended with "the authority of the District Commander cannot be interfered with in any manner by" the head of the Freedmen's Bureau in Texas. The very Reconstruction Act of 1867 referenced granted him the sole power to deal with all legal matters in his district.[9]

To Hancock, Bureau courts conflicted with his policy and would not be tolerated. Reynolds, not meaning to meddle or disobey, simply wanted to protect the integrity of his personnel and protect the freedpeople. Believing his predecessors' policies confusing with "unsatisfactory results," Reynolds desired uniformity in his command in Texas. He reiterated his desire to transfer power to civil authorities. This paralleled Hancock's wishes. Wanting to secure his agency's authority, he nonetheless, reminded Hancock that so long as the Bureau existed "the freedpeople cannot be properly prevented from appealing to the Agents for advice and action." Reynolds even appeared to question his superior's judgment in issuing an order for a state that he knew little about. "The condition of affairs generally in Texas," he stated, "is not comprehended by people out of the State, and to fully appreciate [it] must be experienced."[10]

As it appeared the Bureau's authority had been all but eliminated, Hancock resigned as commander of the Fifth Military District in early spring 1868. He resigned after superiors reversed some of his decisions to remove individuals from office in Louisiana. According to David M. Jordan, General Hancock's biographer, "It was clear to Hancock that the reversal . . . had fatally compromised his effectiveness in the district. . . ." Seeing an opportunity, Reynolds moved quickly to reestablish his agency's authority and to "insure greater uniformity of action" within Texas. In General Orders No. 4, which was very similar to his previous proposal to Howard countermanded by Hancock, Reynolds outlined his plan to establish uniformity, to correct the many "unauthorized things" agents had done, and to sustain field personnel "in the exercise of their legitimate authority." Admitting that a few agents had exceeded their authority and realizing their limited legal knowledge, Reynolds limited subordinates to minor cases involving freedpeople. Although all major cases were to be decided in civil courts, Bureau agents' "jurisdiction will not be limited by the amount in [question]." When a freedperson's case went before a civil magistrate, Reynolds wanted to "give advice and if necessary personal supervision in important cases" and to ensure the proceeding's impartiality. G. O. No. 4 did not "restrict the power already exercised by Agents of the Bureau," but authorized them "to order the Civil Officers to execute their orders." Local law enforcement had to honor all writs and warrants issued, and any civil official deemed derelict could be replaced. Reynolds, to ensure honesty, had inspectors who would routinely measure their performance.[11]

Reynolds's order reestablished field agents' authority to handle certain cases. By limiting agents to minor cases, Reynolds hoped to solve the problems that plagued his predecessors. The same difficulties experienced in judicial matters during Gregory's, Kiddoo's, and Griffin's tenures, in fact, continued during Reynolds's administration. Many were still uncertain about their authority and what was to be left to the civil authorities. To a large extent, this confusion stemmed from the ever changing policies from above. T. M. K. Smith at Marshall wanted to know if he had the authority "under recent orders" to fine individuals for breach of contract and assault. William G. Kirkman likewise confessed he did not know the state's laws concerning the jurisdiction of a justice of the peace. William H. Rock not only requested a copy of "Sayle's Treatise" (contains the proceedings for justice of peace), but also inquired whether his jurisdiction extended to criminal cases. F. P. Wood at Brenham inquired if he could "set aside" decisions by "Civil Tribunals such as Mayors and Justices" if the decisions were "unjust and onerous." Because of the many changing orders, Charles Schmidt was hesitant to "assume authority." With such uncertainty and in some cases unwillingness to "assume authority," whites were emboldened to "defy . . . authority" with words as well as violent actions.[12]

With so much confusion among field personnel and resistance from whites against the Bureau's judicial proceedings, Reynolds ordered Sinclair to investigate further the efficacy of Bureau men settling disputes. After his tour, he proposed that General Orders No. 4 be revoked, and for agents "hereafter to turn over to the civil authorities all cases . . . and act as advisor and council for the freedpeople." (A policy very similar to Hancock's.) When there are "civil officers who fail to execute the criminal laws of the state" the inspector wrote, they "generally [are] so plain that any violation or disregard of the laws governing them can be easily detected by an agent watching the course of the proceedings." Sinclair understood "the freedpeople must soon look for redress in all cases to the civil law and it is better that the change be gradual and while they have some one to advise them, than [wait] up to the last moment [when] agents . . . suddenly leave them as it were in the dark." He wanted Reynolds to focus on the "greater good . . . agents do" instead of their mediation. The "real business they do does not by any means represent the actual value they are to the freed-people." They work in a "silent manner," with a "presence" to prevent innumer-able outrages against freedpeople.[13]

Sinclair also investigated the labor situation, specifically any adverse effects from Hancock's orders. He discovered planters, believing the Bureau irrelevant, had been using the old labor laws passed in the state's Black Code to deprive workers of their wages. Reminding superiors of the Bureau's past policy to "set aside and disregard" these laws, Sinclair advised Reynolds to guarantee "that the first lien upon the crop should be for those [freedpeople] who made it." If they did not "guarantee . . . wages as the first lien," he believed, it would greatly hinder the ability to "secure to the freedpeople the fruits of their labor." Sinclair wanted to convey the "helpless condition the freedpeople are left in when they have no recourse but through the laws of the state to recover . . . the fruits of their labor."[14]

In conjunction with the labor problems was increased violence. Unlike prior administrations, Reynolds's time, for the most part, witnessed unabated resis-tance, numerous instances of outrages against freedpeople, and constant verbal and physical attacks against subordinates. As Figure 8–1 shows,[15] field agents reported a constant level of "bad" or "worsening" white sentiment toward union-ist forces throughout 1868.

More conspicuous was the precipitous drop in "good," "improving," or "indifferent" feeling. The intensity of resistance against reconstruction efforts perhaps may not have increased at all. It appears the level of support or apathy from the white community instead decreased. According to the monthly reports from October 1867 through December 1868, agents collectively reported "bad" or "worsening" opinion from the white community in ten of the fifteen months. The worse months for rebellious attitudes were April and June 1868, with hostile sentiments reported in 67 percent of the reports (April=16/24 and June=20/30). It would be too simplistic to indicate this trend to any one event, with that year having several divisive affairs. More than likely, the political col-lisions throughout the year synthesized a constant level of hostility. Whether caused by President Andrew Johnson's impeachment in the spring and early summer of 1868 or the increased political activity of the freedpeople and agents,

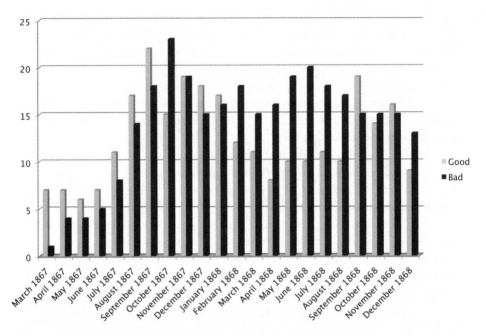

Figure 8–1. Monthly Reports of White Attitudes Toward Freedpeople.

white Texans resisted federal authority at every turn. At Marlin, Charles F. Rand, who routinely stated he had no troops and required none, finally admitted the situation required soldiers. In Seguin in summer 1868, C. C. Raymond, who also routinely stated not needing troops, likewise reported that "white men in disguise" were a disruptive force. The situation in Charles Haughn's district was bad enough for him to state that slavery, at least, offered some protection to the freedpeople. "In time of slavery," he wrote, "they had to bear only the abuse of their masters. Now they bear the abuse of every drunken, worthless, murdering villain in the country." In Tyler, Gregory Barrett admitted the "disposition of the whites toward the freedpeople, is as bad as can be."[16]

Many attributed the resistance to the impeachment trial of President Andrew Johnson and the upcoming presidential and state elections. T. M. K. Smith noticed prominent businessmen refusing to hire any freedman "who does not produce a certificate membership of the Democratic club and who does not pledge himself to vote as his employer shall dictate." In Corpus Christi, a place that generally had good race relations, John Dix detected "a strong disposition to break down Negro sufferage [sic]." He predicted whites would now bring "all the means that can be brought to bear upon the subject, except violence, and many rebels would use violence, if not restrained by fear of military authority." According to Dix, planters threatened not to hire any former slave who voted Republican. They ridiculed the thought of black political participation. Following the canvass, Dix reported good relations between the races. Meanwhile, the deteriorating conditions soon spread to quiet districts; or so it was reported by at least a few who thought it would spread. Consider the case of Arthur B. Homer, who reported all was quiet in Columbia in August 1868, "but I fear trouble during the election." When no trouble occurred, he later admitted race relations were "improving [and] outside of [the] political, there is no trouble—and only talk of that." Improving to the point, indeed, he needed no troops.[17]

Deteriorating conditions raised a new concern for some: the emancipated arming (or rumors of arming) themselves for protection. This problem was not widespread, and only a few actually had to deal with it. Consider the case of F. P. Wood in Brenham. According to Wood, freedpeople armed themselves after they heard about Ku Klux Klan terror. They even carried weapons to the fields for protection. The trouble began when the Austin County sheriff arrested two freedmen. Many considered this an excuse by the Klan to detain them until they could be "dealt" with later. Hearing of the arrests, the freed community immediately organized and set out to find the sheriff. When confronted, he released the two. The sheriff, who was not part of any Klan conspiracy, actually arrested the two for killing several oxen. For unknown reasons, however, he did not inform the two the reason of their arrest or to the others who witnessed it, causing them to think the worst. Wood believed the whole situation was caused by "rumors and vague statements" and "distempered imaginations" in the freed community, usually from past "evil designs" by whites. Wood had soldiers patrol the town and disarm any who tried to enter armed. A later inspection, nonetheless, placed much of the blame for the problems in the county on the action (and in this case, nonaction) by Wood. "[I]nstead of attending to their cases [claims by freedpeople against whites] and seeing that they had a speedy examination or were released," the inspector concluded, Wood went "to his plantation." Although Wood was not relieved from duty, probably because the harvest season was near, Reynolds instead removed Austin County (Hempstead) from his district. Alex B. Coggeshall was appointed to the new district. Conditions quickly improved and Coggeshall informed he neither had troops, nor needed them.[18]

VRC officer N. H. Randlett had to deal with more than just rumors. Appointed in early 1866, Randlett served at Navasota, Courtney, and Palestine before going to Bryan, Brazos County. Reynolds thought very highly of Randlett, reappointing him as a civilian agent in early 1868 after his muster out. He experienced few problems at Bryan. But that changed in the early summer of 1868, when "the Ku Klux attempted to frighten the freedmen by marching through their village." Not easily cowed, the freedpeople took pot shots at the disguised men. They beat a hasty retreat. The Klan vowed revenge. The emancipated mobilized for protection. With former slaves drilling and "forming a military organization," whites in Brazos County appealed to Randlett to "stop the carrying of arms by the freedmen." The agent, however, told them he would disarm them only after "the whites put a stop to . . . the K Ks." The whites agreed, and he ordered the blacks to disarm and to disband. Military officials dispatched troops to ensure compliance. The soldiers did not remain long, leaving Randlett alone. All was quiet until mid-July when rumors surfaced Miles Brown (freedman) had been hanged. Black leaders organized a party to search for Brown and marched out of town in military style, creating "uneasiness with the whites." They received information that Andrew Halliday, a white man who previously disputed with the victim, was responsible for the hanging. Halliday fearfully called on civil authorities for protection. They quickly raised a posse and marched to his aid. In the meantime, the freedpeople, perhaps having second thoughts, left Halliday's residence and headed for town. Approaching town, as fate would have it, the two posses met. They did not immediately fire on one another. As leaders of the two groups conversed, however, a shot rang out and caused "a general firing . . . from the whites." The freedpeople scattered. Randlett, at best, could only speculate which party fired first, evidenced by several changes to his reports.[19]

Later that night, after the groups had returned to their respective neighborhoods, local officials met with one of the leaders of the freed community in Millican and a participant in the earlier incident, George E. Brooks. Brooks declared "he would not agree to any terms of peace," which "caused intense excitement in town." With so much "excitement," things were bound to escalate. For several days in Millican, a group of whites attacked prominent freedpeople. Randlett, however, quickly intervened to stop the assaults, but not before five freedmen had been killed, including Brooks, whose body was never recovered. Although lives were lost, federal officials realized it could have been far worse if not for the "prompt and efficient" actions of Randlett. His problems, however, had only begun. After the "Millican riot," Randlett reported he had been "assaulted, insulted and my life threatened." He normally paid "little notice of this," dismissing such slights as mere nuisances. But with increased frequency, he believed them credible and requested protection. Without it, he wrote, "no business can be transacted." He asked superiors not to publish his communication "as it would render my stay very unpleasant if not dangerous." Randlett remained in Millican until October, when he tendered his resignation.[20]

As the Bureau's end neared, the Rebel element needed little to get parting shots on the soon to be departed symbol of what had been lost. A few examples should suffice. DeWitt C. Brown described Paris as "the most demoralized community that I have ever had the misfortune to live in." An unknown assailant even made two attempts on his life in one day. He attributed it to Cullen Baker and his gang, who "have a particular spite at me." He further suspected they did the work for others. "The citizens of this place are in confederation with them," he declared. "The program . . . is to get rid of me and force the negroes into the Democratic ranks for protection." Leading Democrats offered protection to any freedperson supporting the Democratic party. Two months after requesting assistance (which headquarters declined), Brown "was compelled to flee from my station" as a "band of desperadoes hover[ed] about the city." The "Bureau is a dead letter in this country," he declared from "exile," and "is like the grass that grows beneath a plant—it is crushed down by the weight of public opinion supported by the revolver, the bowie knife and the shot gun." In early 1868 Alex Ferguson had his office broken into, and "all my papers, Records, Contracts . . . carried into the streets." He also received four anonymous notes warning him that he would have to leave once the troops had left. Ferguson was confused and a little ignorant about Southern attitudes, because he had performed his duty impartially and ably with little reason for such criticism. He penned a letter to Nacogdoches citizens to ask them "if I had not done my duty as an agent . . . they inform me of the fact to my face and not in such a manner." Superiors offered a reward for information that would lead to the arrest of the vandals, but no one came forward with information.[21]

Agent Nesbit B. Jenkins predicted once troops left Wharton County, he "would be subjected to every kind of abuse and indignity if indeed his life was not sacrificed." He even asked to be relieved if he could not be protected from such outrages. Reynolds denied his request. After the soldiers left, Jenkins's concern was justified. His time was "marked by continual disturbance and attempts [by] the disloyal element to bring on a conflict." In that hostile community, one man stood out. It all began when George Quinan, a lawyer, disrupted a deposition to a "most foully and brutally" murder. The freedman was "mutilated by cutting off his penis." Quinan verbally abused court officials in a "shameful and disgraceful manner" and threatened Jenkins with death if he tried to arrest him.[22]

Lacking troops, Jenkins was powerless to arrest Quinan. Such fecklessness encouraged others to resist. For example, whites held a Democratic party rally at the courthouse "for no other purpose than to abuse or hear the abuse of the military appointees." Jenkins was listening to the speeches when some white men entered. One began criticizing the Radical party and then "turned his attention to" Jenkins, calling him a "God damned Son of a Bitch[,] a G-d d-d liar and other such terms. . . ." Not wanting to escalate the situation, the agent simply ignored the rant and left for his room. The speaker followed and asked permission from the agent's roommate to enter. "Very soon however," Jenkins recounted, "he began to talk politics . . . and turned to me and asked me what my politics were." Jenkins politely refused: "I never discuss politics and that I did not wish to do so now." This refusal only further angered the unwelcomed guest, who began "making many insulting insinuations." Jenkins, annoyed by this affront, told him he had no right to talk to him in that manner and that he "did not feel warranted to engage" him.[23]

At that moment, the man lunged at Jenkins. He believed he would have struck him if not for the action of his roommate, who "half pushed, half persuaded" the attacker from the room. The verbal berating continued from the street, with Jenkins called "every opprobrious term" and threatened with physical harm. Ignoring the insults, Jenkins could not ignore the threats because of witnesses. He arrested the man, charging him with "personally insulting and using the most abusive language." Jenkins fined him twenty-five dollars and jailed him until payment. The man's attorney, Wells Thompson, wrote Reynolds for a writ of habeas corpus. Superiors wrote Jenkins for a report on the incident. While not excusing the incident in his room, he did attribute it to "the outrageous conduct of George Quinan," which Jenkins had to endure "in silence." He further reminded superiors about the difficulty to perform his duties in a fair and honest manner minus protection. Self-preservation explained his actions. These people "imagine or pretend to imagine that they have a perfect right to insult and abuse me as soon as my foot has left the office," he wrote. "If their view . . . is right and sustained, I could not stay in Wharton a day." Jenkins, despite the problems in his district, remained in service until the Bureau's last days.[24]

In early October one of the most celebrated acts of Reconstruction violence in Texas involved the SAC at Jefferson, Marion County. It all started when former Union officer and "carpetbagger" George Washington Smith relocated from New York. Smith, a local merchant, angered many white Jeffersonians with his insistence on payment of debts and especially his political beliefs and activism. An ardent Radical, he preached racial equality, allegedly socializing with freedpeople in ways offensive to white sensibilities. With freedpeople's help, he was elected as a delegate to the Constitutional Convention of 1868–1869. Returning from that convention, Smith had a bag stolen by members of a local vigilante group, the Knights of the Rising Sun. Occurrences over the next twenty-four hours would result in Smith and some freedmen being arrested by local authorities and held in an enclosure in the middle of town.[25]

The town's agent and post commander, James Curtis, was responsible for guarding the prisoners. Although he ordered a detail of soldiers to the enclosure, Curtis worried it was insufficient. His intuition was correct. Later that night some Knights approached the enclosure where the prisoners were held. Through deception, they were able to enter the enclosure. Hearing the commotion, Curtis rushed to the scene. He immediately began to plead with the Knights, even placing himself between them and Smith (Smith was being held in an iron structure located within the enclosure and separated from the freedmen). Each time he placed himself in front of the iron door, however, the Knights removed him, the last time with a warning not to interfere again or else. The attackers eventually gained entry and killed Smith. Simultaneously, others took the freedmen from the enclosure and killed two of them. For the next six months, Jefferson was under martial law, with federal authorities arresting and trying the perpetrators in what became known to Texans as the Stockade Trial. Curtis, criticized for his actions that night, was transferred out of Jefferson and removed from further Bureau service.[26]

In 1868, as conditions worsened, two SACs were murdered performing their duties. On his way to Dallas to replace William H. Horton, George Eber was robbed and murdered. His murderer(s) remained at large. While at Boston, near the border with Indian Territory, William G. Kirkman constantly battled the unreconstructed element. He received death threats and an indictment for murder in September 1868 for shooting a prisoner trying to escape. While at Boston, Kirkman simply survived, living day to day. But his luck ran out. With the situation deteriorating in northeast Texas in late 1868, Reynolds recalled subordinates from the area, including Kirkman. He delayed his departure to collect his records. As he busied himself, Cullen Baker and his gang arrived in town. Kirkman noticed them and tried to make it to a nearby house for better protection. Before he could make it, he was shot down in the street. As his body lay in the street, white Bostonians took it upon themselves to insult Kirkman one last time by stealing the money out of his pockets, the watch from his hand, and his horse.[27]

Even with the increased resistance in 1868, the vast majority departed the Freedmen's Bureau alive. To be sure, 92.8 percent (181 out of 195) of agents in Texas, whose departure could be determined, survived their tenure in the Lone Star State (the reason for departure for 44 agents could not be definitively determined). Fourteen men died in service (7.2 percent), seven of those because of yellow fever. Outlaws or ruffians murdered four. The rest fell from disease, natural causes, or accidents. Table 8-3 shows the reasons why terms ended in Texas.

As can be seen, nearly two-thirds (n=127; or 65.1 percent) of the men left the agency for bureaucratic reasons, either policy of the Bureau or military exigencies; with the overwhelming majority of those departing at the agency's end or when the military reassigned or reappointed men from its service. The number of men who asked to be relieved or were dismissed because of their actions was surprisingly low, with the latter equaling 27 and the former 27 (approximating slightly more than 27 percent collectively). Of those who voluntarily resigned, their reasons varied. Some left for political opportunities (n=5; or 2.6 percent), others for business (n=5; or 2.6 percent). A few could no longer continue because of health reasons (n=2; or 1 percent). Still others simply tired of the stress and frustration (n=12; or 6.2 percent). Reasons for dismissal also varied. Most removed (n=20; or 10.3 percent) were for abuse, incompetence, criminality, neglect, or "conduct unbecoming an agent," such as intemperance and promiscuity. Officials relieved A. P. Delano, William H. Farner, Hiram Johnson,

Table 8-3   Reasons All Subassistant Commissioners Left the Freedmen's Bureau

Reason	Number	Percentage
Bureau Operations: Bureau ended, consolidation, and transferal or reassignment within the agency	61	31.3
Military Operations: Mustered out or ordered to new assignment	66	33.8
Dropped on Request: Agent resigned appointment	27	13.85
Terminated: Dismissed for criminality, cruelty, Confederate service, or appointment revoked	27	13.85
Died: murdered, disease, or accidents	14	7.2
	n=195	100

Charles Russell, Robert McClermont, and J. W. McConaughey for abuse of freedmen, with the remainder going because of neglect, criminality, or "conduct unbecoming an agent." A further four agents (2.1 percent) were dismissed for Confederate service, although such a past did not necessarily result in automatic dismissal. The dismissals of three men could not be determined, other than their dismissal.

Never passive participants, although at times it seemed, field agents considered desperate measures to combat resistance. While some suggested removing freedpeople from those areas wracked with violence, others sought solutions a little more logistically plausible. A noticeable number believed they could manage if Reynolds's policies were not so restrictive. Unable to protect their charges, they could now do little more than document outrages. A few examples will suffice. "I respectfully ask" Charles Haughn pleaded, "that if you consider me competent to use the Authority without abusing it and it is intended . . . that the sheriff shall obey my orders when I am acting in my official capacity that you give me some written instructions that I can present to the sheriff of this county if it shall become necessary." He wanted the authority because every time he had previously ordered the local authorities to act, "I am obliged to fight all the Lawyers" who "discuss my right to act in their case." If he can "beat them in arguing," Haughn wrote, "they will obey me." Within a month, though, superiors transferred Haughn to Cotton Gin, a place that he did not "fear to go," but was "considered by almost every one to be very unsafe." At Tyler, Gregory Barrett, a bit annoyed by an accidental shot to his leg, complained local officials were "determined that no more arrests shall be made by the military" and desired to "nullify the laws of Congress" so as to make "it . . . impossible for me to maintain my position." Not relying on them, he employed soldiers to make arrests. Smith County residents informed Bureau officials about his allegedly "arbitrary oppressive & despotic" ways. Reynolds reminded Barrett that civil authorities were to make all arrests whenever practical, and that "military aid [would be] given whenever requested." He further noted Barrett should bear "in mind that troops are stationed at Tyler to assist the civil authorities in maintaining order as well as protect you in the discharge of your duties." Reynolds's key words, of course, were to assist the civil authorities. "The tenor of the foregoing paragraph . . . is uncalled for," answered Barrett. "I have often stated . . . that the civil authorities will not make arrests of criminals and that no one has yet been arrested by them in this Sub District . . . I have issued writ[s] time and again and directed them to the civil officers, but in no criminal case have they been executed, and in my opinion no such writs will be executed . . . until the people are taught a severer lesson than they have yet received." Although field personnel thought some headquarters' policies too weak and confusing, and impotent regarding situations on the ground, this opinion, by no means, was universal. One of the best to serve in Texas, William H. Rock at Richmond, in fact, found General Orders No. 4 provided "ample protection."[28]

As the Bureau's end neared, officials in Austin still expected professionalism from subordinates. One requirement in Reynolds's General Orders No. 4 was vigorous inspection tours to measure their performances. Reynolds refused to countenance ineffectiveness and corruption. Subordinates would remain professional, in no way disparaging the Bureau in its waning days. In Huntsville, William H. Stewart failed to meet such standards. Stewart, although committed and zealous, was considered by one inspector to be "mentally incompetent," with "no education hardly" and barely able to read or write. He kept little record of his duties, and what "he has is perfectly shocking to look at." Moreover, the inspector noted, he was profligate and unprofessional. "I think it very unfortunate that he was appointed," the inspector lamented, "as he is in no way fitted for the office and is so sadly lacking in education that I am ashamed that he has ever written and sent a line out of the office." Stewart, realizing his limitations, issued a terse letter of resignation. Reynolds quickly accepted.[29]

White Unionists accused A. F. N. Rolfe at Columbia of being "continually intoxicated" and associating with the "bitterest of rebels." Reynolds investigated the charges. "His associates have been the vilest of rebels and the vilest of men—barroom loafers and common drunkards," inspector William H. Sinclair concluded, and he had performed his duties "from the barroom . . . to the disgrace of the government he represents." He forged a signature to run up a thirteen-dollar whiskey bill. Rolfe also "had not the least conception" of his duties, with not a single contract approved for 1868. Sinclair dismissed him from service immediately, a move Reynolds wholly supported. A. H. M. Taylor, the acting assistant adjutant general at district headquarters who recommended Rolfe for service, apologized for his brother-in-law's behavior. "I am sorry he ever came to Texas," he wrote Reynolds, "for I feel he has disgraced himself and everyone connected with him." Otto F. Steinberg, the SAC at Gonzales, had previously served the agency in Alabama. A veteran of the war, Steinberg had been dismissed from service in Alabama for embezzlement and later court martialed. He was convicted and detained until the two-thousand-dollar fine was paid. F. Otto Steinberg (the name he went by in Alabama), however, was mistakenly mustered out and relieved "before the findings of the court and the sentence were promulgated." After being apprised of Steinberg's past, Reynolds immediately dismissed him.[30]

As the Bureau wound down its operations, SACs were ordered to headquarters with all their papers and to transfer all copies of contracts on file to the county clerks. But a number of men implored superiors to reconsider. They wanted to continue their work and feared for the emancipated under civilian "protection." Nesbit Jenkins at Wharton feared leaving "the helpless and ignorant colored race to the cold pity of a hostile world." He urged superiors to have "greater caution . . . in appointing of all civil officers and the greatest watchfulness exercised over them. . . ." At Bastrop, David S. Beath concurred with Jenkins's sentiment. "I believe if the civil officers were removed and others appointed," he proposed, it "would be a great consolation to the Freedmen and the Loyal people throughout the County." According to James Gillette, the Bureau's influence "should at once be directed towards inducing such changes in the civil laws of the state as will render the decision of labor claims and collection of debts an easy matter in the office of Justice of the Peace or ordinary courts." He wanted a "thorough and rigid examination or inspection" of all justices of the peace to determine their competency and loyalty. Once achieved, Gillette believed, then and only then should the agency redirect its operations. "It is true that by turning over all the complaints and cases for trial . . . to the civil authority much labor would be saved," Edward C. Henshaw admitted from Marshall, "but in so doing much injustice and great expenses would attach to these poor creatures . . . I would be defeating the very object for which this Bureau was instituted."[31]

Their pleas for reconsideration were all for naught. On the last day of December, the Freedmen's Bureau ceased operations. Its educational responsibilities continued for another year, when the agency left the state altogether. For those who served under Reynolds, their time as Bureau agents was marked by the knowledge their work would end soon, and their remaining time was to prepare the freedpeople for that day. Whether caused by Hancock's General Orders No. 40, the increased white resistance, the perplexing and persistent problems with the labor system, or the agents' suspicion toward civil authorities, the transfer of authority and winding down of operations was, at times, anything but smooth. Many difficulties occurred in 1868, some of which existed prior to late 1865. Although Hancock's order was reversed, Bureau officials in Texas noticed the winds of change. His attitude toward federalism coincided with most Americans. For most nineteenth-century Americans, what needed to be accomplished already had been: the Union was preserved, slavery abolished, stability returned

to the former Confederacy so that they could not wage war again, and citizenship and a modicum of rights granted to the freedpeople. Further measures were
unnecessary and potentially even dangerous. By late 1868, Americans believed
that the agency had served its purpose, doing all that could (or should) be done.
The freedpeople's hopes and subassistant commissioners' desires were ultimately
"all crushed down by the weight of public opinion. . . ."[32]

Conclusion

*The Subassistant
Commissioners in Texas*

In March 1865, in the war's waning days, Congress created the first social-welfare organization in American history. The Freedmen's Bureau, established to help former slaves make the transition to freedom, had an enormous task. Criticized for one reason or another, the nation still entrusted it to reverse nearly three centuries of black (and for that matter, white) Southern degradation. Although criticized for achieving only "a modicum" of what "was owed," agents, considering the condition of the emancipated at war's end, achieved what one historian called "near miracles." By the time the agency ceased operations, its personnel had established some order where only chaos had existed, discouraged the South from resuming hostilities against the Union, protected freedpeople against white violence as well as helped them begin their education, and helped to establish them as self-reliant citizens with legal and civil rights. They established the emancipated as something they had never been in the slaveholding South: citizens.[1]

The average agent in Texas was generally mature and of Northern birth, from the middle and upper middle class and with some military service during the war. Officials in Texas shied from appointing Southerners and those from the Old South planter class. Some served because of patriotism. Others desired the opportunity for revenge against former Confederate enemies. Still others simply needed employment. Those in the Veteran Reserve Corps wanted to prove their worth and make their personal sacrifice mean something more than the status quo antebellum.

Although they entered service for varied reasons, and their abilities differed from the superb to the abysmal, from the upstanding to the corrupt, most shared one characteristic: their commitment to the freedpeople. They understood the freedpeople were their prime responsibility. William H. Heistand certainly spoke for many when he defined his "duties [to] consist [of looking] over the interest of the Freedpeople . . . as their adviser and protector." They

understood that between the two parties—freedpersons and whites—the former were the weaker. As a result, agents showed a slight bias in freedpeople's
favor, guided "by equity—paying little attention to the technical violations of
contracts, as . . . the employer has a decided advantage over the employee, and
can with little difficulty get an abundance of evidence to prove his point." In the
words of agent George C. Abbott, they believed "it only fair play . . . to look out
for the Negroe [sic], for . . . the white men [were] fully competent to look out for
themselves." Whites, angered by this, were aware agents were "friend[s] to the
freedmen." Freedpeople, however, appreciated and, despite any later misgiv-
ings to the contrary, showed confidence in them. "Where a [SAC] does his
duty," announced A. H. Cox, "the freedmen have confidence in him and they
will obey all that he may say to them and they think it all wright [sic]. . . ."
Despite the occasional "bad apple" agent, the emancipated's confidence still
remained strong toward them.[2]

One important responsibility was protecting freedpeople from white violence. The "unreconstructed" could not accept the war's outcome or the former
slaves' new status. Agents, representing a painful reminder of what was lost,
were to ensure the emancipated were treated as free people. Violence was more
a problem for some than others. At certain times, particularly after the Reconstruction Act of 1867 and before voter registration, those in the interior even
reported not needing soldiers. Some of the ablest and most respected agents in
the state made such reports. Charles F. Rand, Edward Miller, William H. Rock,
A. H. Mayer, and N. H. Randlett, among others, all served in districts that, at
one time or another, required no soldiers.

Other districts did require troops when white violence paralyzed operations.
In places where white Texans refused to accept the war's outcome, their best
efforts fell well short of perfection. Agents could do little more than document
outrages or hope the violence would abate. Evading punishment for crimes
because agents' power was limited was frequent. Nineteenth-century Americans' hesitancy to use the military to solve what they believed a civil matter
constrained at times field personnel's efficacy. Even if headquarters had been
able to blanket Texas with SACs, equipped with all the troop protection some
later critics believed necessary, the freedpeople's plight probably would not have
been significantly different. Simply put, "bayonets cannot reform hearts and
minds." Americans' preference for federalism and pecuniary concerns certainly
restricted the use of military power. The inability of the former Confederates to
accept the emancipated as individuals, guaranteeing "life, liberty, and the pursuit of happiness," was the major factor in what some historians call the "failure

of Reconstruction"—a failure remedied only by another century of time, new generations, and historical events.[3]

With few troops available, SACs relied heavily on Bureau courts. With little legal training, and with confusion about their authority, agents were guided by common sense and a sense of fair play. They wanted to bring about a "mutual and satisfactory understanding." Although achieved with a fine or confinement, most preferred to resolve disputes with a warning, advice, or lecture. The courts' effectiveness relied heavily on the plaintiff's willingness to appear or to abide by the ruling. They had to use persuasion and threats to increase the chances of white compliance. They also had to be willing to compromise to obtain justice. Agents, in the end, knew their judicial powers were limited in protecting the freedpeople.[4]

Beyond courts and troops, field personnel had other means to protect their charges. One was to educate the planters to the benefits of fair treatment. Prior to Reconstruction, free labor proponents had tried to show Southerners the "Yankee way of doing business." SACs continued this idea that planters' and workers' interests coincided. Their hopes focused on the employer's "pecuniary point of view." "[F]reedmen are treated kindly by their employers," concluded DeWitt C. Brown, "not from feelings of kindliness or interest but . . . otherwise their hands would give up in weeks." Planters who were fair and honest had no problem procuring labor, while those who were not experienced difficulties procuring labor.[5]

Not all planters, however, understood (or even cared) to deal honestly with their hands. They often did things contrary to their financial interests. In some counties SACs noticed a greater proclivity for honesty toward the freedpeople. In others, however, they witnessed an unwillingness to do so. Thus, Bureau men searched for ways to help the freed community. Some encouraged shares (i.e., sharecropping), believing hands worked "harder when they are interested in part of the crop," and this made it easier to ensure their portion of the crop. Others preferred monthly wages, realizing the dangers inherent with sharecropping (bad weather, etc.). To them, wages limited violence against freedpeople. The role agents had in the rise of sharecropping in Texas appears, at best, peripheral, for there was little consensus on which system of contract to encourage. A particular agent's preference dictated which system he promoted. By the time superiors issued orders to encourage contracting for a share of the crop, the system had already been in practice for some time. Only after it started to become the preferred way of payment did Bureau officials begin to encourage it. In Texas, sharecropping developed more out of the

push and pull between workers and planters and very little from any governmental policy.[6]

They knew the day would come when the agency would no longer exist.
Freedpeople would have to "stand on their own." This, it was thought, could be
achieved through the ballot box. Agents not only protected their right to register and vote, but actively worked for Republican victory. They encouraged (a few
even joined) the freedmen to organize Loyal Leagues, recommended the
removal of Rebel officeholders to be replaced by loyal men (who were generally
Republicans), and influenced the freedmen to vote "for their friends" (i.e., the
Republican party). Field agents fully understood their influence with the freedmen, and rarely hesitated to use it. They worked (on a few occasions campaigned)
hard "in order to secure the vote of the colored" for the Republican party. Their
political work, however, was often done covertly. Superiors warned subordinates about public, partisan acts and prohibited them from actively seeking
political office while serving the agency. They understood a strong Republican
party in Texas was a way to protect the emancipated post-Freedmen's Bureau.
Subassistant commissioners in Texas were politically active and assisted the
Republicans because it benefited the emancipated, helped them, and assisted
the organization's overall mission in the state.[7]

With the passage of the Texas Black Code, the protection afforded became all
the more important. With this code, state lawmakers hoped to circumscribe the
former slave's freedom, especially through restrictive labor and apprentice laws.
SACs were ordered to disregard the labor law but enforce apprentice contracts if
local officials applied it impartially. So long as counties refused to care for their
black indigents, so long as indigent and orphaned freed children existed, and so
long as some freed parents remained unable or unwilling to care for their children, apprenticing would be necessary. Historians would later indict apprenticeship. For the time, it was an accepted alternative to starvation and dependency
for nineteenth-century America. Alex B. Coggeshall was "fully satisfied that in
some cases [apprenticing] would be for the interest of the minor." Agents in
Texas did not uphold the institution under all circumstances. They never hesitated to break the contract if they determined it illegal, unjust, or not in the
child's best interests. In order to determine this, they used their "best judgment" regarding the "child's best interest." A few, of course, were excessive.
They abrogated all regardless of legality. Still even fewer abused their authority to help former masters obtain labor. Not all parties were satisfied, and on
occasion Bureau agents certainly erred. Nonetheless, they acted in what they
believed to be in the child's best interest. In some cases that meant upholding a

legal apprentice contract and in others it meant voiding it. In the words of historian Mary Farmer-Kaiser, Bureau men could be "both freedwomen's ally and adversary." They enforced some apprentice contracts, but Bureau agents did not enforce apprentice contracts "in the spirit in which" the planters desired. Since it relied so heavily on an agent's judgment, the agency's apprentice policy was never uniform. It was determined by field personnel on a case-by-case basis.[8]

In protecting the sanctity of marriage, these men, the foot soldiers in a "bureaucratic juridical apparatus," regulated and taught the freedpeople about what it meant to be husband and wife. Each understood their responsibility to educate and tried to approach infidelity and "cohabitation" with sympathy, offering counsel and advice instead of indifference. Their personal preference and philosophy greatly influenced their approach. Similar to apprenticeship, an agent's judgment was the Bureau's policy. Through compassion and advice and, at times, punishment, they attempted to correct generations of ignorance and behavior contrary to societal values and help the former slaves learn the ways of citizens.[9]

Moved by prevailing social attitudes, Bureau men made the freedman head of his family, bestowing upon him the mantle of provider and protector of his family. Freedwomen were relegated to a subordinate position, since the "husband controls the wife." Nevertheless, agents generally protected women within their marriages. Guided by their judgment, they based decisions, once again, on common sense or their sense of fairness. Freedwomen were neither allowed to be cheated out of their property by their husbands nor left defenseless against an abusive or neglectful man. By establishing freedmen as heads of households, agents held them to a higher standard. Rarely did they hesitate to intervene when freedmen abandoned their "manly duties." According to legal historian Katherine M. Franke, freedpeople "in the immediate postbellum period were not born, but could become, citizens." Whether adjudicating apprentice contracts, custody battles, or marital disputes, agents, in the words of John Dix, "I did only what I thought was right and just in the matter."[10]

Most Bureau agents' time was consumed by their mandated duties. A good portion also dealt with trivial matters, mere annoyances, strange happenings, or comical events. Since the office work for the Bureau agent at Galveston required clerical assistance, William H. Sinclair hired a clerk to assist. Quickly, however, the relationship soured and Sinclair fired him. Samuel Dodge, the clerk, complained to headquarters. He claimed Sinclair had unjustly fired him to hire his (Sinclair's) brother-in-law, an accusation Sinclair vehemently denied.

"I concluded," wrote Sinclair, "that he was not a fit man for the place. . . ." He continued:

> I did not think him competent to perform the work in the manner I required it done. Moreover, he was a prolific spitter of Tobacco juice over the floor and made my office look more like a Barroom than anything else, a habit I could not correct even after a spittoon was procured. [When asked why he fired and replaced Dodge, Sinclair stated that] I employed [John] Scott, an ex-Military officer, because he was a good penman, is thoroughly conversant with the duties of the office having been for a long [time] a Sub Asst Coms, understands the Reports thoroughly, and does not chew Tobacco.[11]

Samuel A. Craig recalled in his "Memoirs" a "day I had a call to come . . . some 15 miles away to address [them] upon their duties as citizens. . . ." Craig further stated:

> The way seemed to be very lonely, so I watched loosely the thick patches of woods and the sharp turn of the road. Soon I heard a loud racket, so unaccountable that I became quite nervous. There was swearing, loud scolding tones, loud talk noises like striking. It sounded very strange in the dense forest, usually so quiet. As I rode on it grew louder and louder, until at a turn I discovered a poor old raw boned mule and a horse team, a little old man, rather ragged, with shaggy long hair and beard, sitting among a few bundles in the bottom of an old wagon. He was yelling at the top of his voice at that old horse and mule and pounding vigorously with a stick, [yelling] "You Bill; Jim, glang; Geland (bang) hep; hep; there (bang) you lazy good for nothing critters, you git up, git up there, (bang) damn you, don't you hear? (bang) Get away; damn [you] (bang)." He sat still, swung his arms vigorously and jerked the lines with the other, spitting over his shoulder at times, but keeping up his yelling and pounding . . . I watched him for a few minutes wondering at such energy, whether drunk or merely his usual habit.[12]

The day-to-day operations of field personnel were never-ending: they traveled many miles, adjudicated many disputes, approved many contracts, and met many who needed their assistance. They had set office hours. In reality, they were never off duty. They performed duties all throughout the day. Superiors mandated work be documented, which created an immense amount of paperwork and longer work hours. Although a product of the nineteenth century, the

Freedmen's Bureau had all the trappings of a modern-day bureaucracy, with nearly everything being documented for, reported to, or approved by head-quarters. The position was anything but a sinecure, for these men were "always on duty."

Their duties consumed a great deal of time and required endless paperwork. This paperwork probably created more frustration and conflict between superi-ors and subordinates than any other aspect. If it was late or incorrect, many, particularly the civilians who were usually ignorant about military record keeping, received what they deemed offensive reprimands and condescending letters from superiors. Men like A. H. Mayer, William H. Rock, Anthony M. Bryant, Fred W. Reinhard, David L. Montgomery, Charles E. Culver, and John Dix, among others, most of whom were among the most respected agents to serve in Texas, drew the ire of headquarters for improper, incomplete, or "hur-ried and careless" paperwork. Superiors' demand to detail was understandable since it was used to develop policy, to weed out corruption, and to account for expenditures. Many, however, believed the insistence on perfect paperwork was, at best, impractical and, at worst, obsessive and insulting. Or it was "calcu-lated to cut." Bureau men in Texas acknowledged their faults and ignorance. Yet many believed headquarters' approach was condescending and petty. Such beliefs contributed to the frustration and suspicion of field personnel toward those at headquarters. It only reinforced their belief that those at headquarters were ignorant to the rigors and demands of their duties in Texas.[13]

Many performed their duties without the necessary equipment. They often lacked tables, chairs, pens, ink, and forage for their horses, among many other things. Superiors did not provide the basic office furniture and office supplies. To obtain them, field agents routinely personally purchased them. Superiors further failed to provide the mandated tools "for the proper and regular dis-charge of their duties." They were supposed to provide copies of all pertinent orders, including congressional statutes and military and Bureau regulations to guide subordinates in their duties. Of course, the deficiency had an adverse effect, placing agents "in a very unpleasant situation so far as their duties and jurisdiction are concerned." With four assistant commissioners in as many years, all with different policies and emphases, and many orders, some of which conflicted and were vague, disseminating from Galveston, New Orleans, and Washington, even the most capable man could become confused to agency policy. Further contributing to the problem was the fear of reprimand. Through-out its operation in Texas, Bureau agents' duties were too poorly defined and their authority not fully understood.[14]

Even when in possession of the required guidance, confusion remained. Each new AC in the state issued orders outlining their policies. Some were designed as corollaries to already existing Bureau or military policy, but much of it was to countermand what they believed to be the "flawed" and "misguided" policies of their predecessors. This stream of new guidelines, when many of the previous guidelines had yet to be fully understood, created a situation that left field agents swamped with information, much of it confusing and contradictory. Thomas H. Baker expressed the sentiments of many fellow agents by admitting "I have about one hundred and eighty Circulars and Genl. Orders on my table. My time has been so occupied in the performance of my official duties that I could not inform myself relative to their contents."[15]

Much of the confusion stemmed from the decentralized manner of the agency. Commissioner Howard believed most of the policy in each state "must be left to the discretion of those engaged in [the footwork], as all such things are." He resisted "one minute system of rules." This allowed for a decentralization, where SACs had latitude to use their best judgment or "to do as was right and proper" when interpreting, implementing, and enforcing orders. Ironically, the very thing that helped to cause confusion brought about a situation that allowed for leeway and greater authority for those in the field. What was a liberating aspect, in the end, helped to inhibit some of its operations, as uncertainty sometimes paralyzed agents from acting.[16]

The Bureau agents in Texas neither desired "social acceptance" from the white community nor colluded with the planters. There definitely were a few men who betrayed their oath to protect the freedpeople. In all cases, however, once superiors discovered such improprieties, they promptly dismissed the man. Men who were discovered to be "planter tools" were the exception, not the rule. Most understood their responsibility to help, not hinder, the emancipated. Any suggestions, slights, or accusations they had been derelict, corrupt, or ineffective was often answered with a vehement denial. Many learned to countenance the criticisms and epithets from whites, dismissing them as mere annoyances. Yet they rarely brushed aside any allegations that impugned their character or reputations, particularly of collusion. They reacted in an even more forceful manner when the accusations (or at times, insinuations) came from superiors. This frustrated and irritated them. They expected such sentiment from former Rebels, not from superiors. They incurred great hardships to honor their responsibilities, not only to the freedpeople but to the U.S. government. Each man took an oath. Thus, their word and reputations were at stake, something very important in the Victorian period.

The four men (there was a fifth, but he oversaw only the educational responsibilities in 1869) who served as assistant commissioner in Texas brought abilities that affected, sometimes hindered, their performance and their subordinates' performance. Edgar M. Gregory, the agency's first chief, was "the most upright in his own conduct" and "the strongest in his feelings of sympathy" toward freedpeople. He was the least realistic in his outlook toward white and black citizens in Texas. His desire for justice for the freedpeople was greater than the size, influence, and scope of the Bureau. Furthermore, he held contempt for the former masters and admiration for the freedpeople (each to a fault). It thus hindered his ability to lead the Bureau effectively. According to Gregory, the emancipated were "docile, industrious, orderly, free from serious crime, and with all the substance that goes to make the good citizen." He was incapable of seeing whites as anything but masters ("not one of whom has ever been punished, or even tried") and the emancipated as anything but victims lacking agency. Gregory's adversarial approach, influenced by his "abolitionist" leanings, made him very unpopular with whites in the state. He lacked the "nature, education, or prejudice for getting along harmoniously."[17]

Gregory had the difficult task of introducing the Bureau to Texas. Upon entering the state, he faced a situation that required someone with organizational skills. Skills he lacked. For the eight months he served, he failed to expand the agency much beyond his headquarters in Galveston. When he did extend its influence into the interior, he had to rely on civilians, many of whom proved rather troublesome. His subordinates were plagued with supply shortages and confusion about their most basic authority. Certainly some of this was due to bureaucratic delays, the dislocation of war, and the problems inherent in any organization's beginning. But Gregory shoulders some of the responsibility.

His successor, Joseph B. Kiddoo, believed conditions in Texas were little different from those that existed when the Bureau entered the state in late summer of 1865. Major problems, some caused by his predecessor, plagued the labor system in Texas, especially enticement. Kiddoo, a strong free labor proponent, viewed the agency as the "guardian of the freedman. . . ." Contrary to Gregory, he believed the agency should also consider the interests of the planters, holding workers to their contracts. This approach, naturally, endeared him to white Texans in a way Gregory could not have been. Besides labor, Kiddoo focused a great deal of subordinates' attention on the freedpeoples' moral and educational uplift. No other AC in Texas took such an interest in their education as Kiddoo. He understood their need for guidance. His view was doubtless paternalistic and quite different from Gregory's in that Kiddoo's opinion of the freedpeople was more pragmatic and realistic. For the foreseeable future, the freedpeople's future would be in the fields and open to governmental intrusion.[18]

Kiddoo's policies caused problems for his field personnel. Whites saw in Kiddoo, mistakenly of course, someone who shared their aspirations for the freed community. As they moved to circumscribe the freedpeople's freedom in mid-1866, the power struggle and conflict between the Bureau, planters, and state officials began. At the very time this struggle commenced, the military was decreasing its numbers. This made it difficult for Kiddoo to protect the freedmen and his subordinates. All this spelled doom for him. Superiors blamed him for the problems throughout the state. Whether because of his attitude, his drinking, or his pragmatism (which many thought a little too favorable to the president's Reconstruction plan), Kiddoo was removed as the agency's head in Texas. He was an able leader and was more a victim of circumstance than his personal shortcomings and faults might suggest.

Succeeding Kiddoo was Charles Griffin. A proponent of the Radical plan of Reconstruction, Griffin revamped the Bureau to an organizational level not matched during any other's. He specified subdistrict boundaries, attempted to strike a proper balance by transferring some responsibilities to civil authorities at the same time strengthening subordinate's authority, streamlined the commands of the military and Bureau in the state, and extended the agency's influence throughout the state. "[M]y force is not large enough to spread over the state, and by overawing the people, compel the enforcement of the laws," Griffin admitted. "I merely lessened the power of the Sub Asst Commrs [to protect] the freedmen in the most effective manner. . . ." During his tenure, the agency reached its zenith in personnel and subdistricts. Similar to Kiddoo, Griffin focused much attention on the labor system, particularly securing the freedpeople's wages. But his policies, such as the no-lien law and "monopoly order," although with good intentions, created problems for planters, hands, and subassistant commissioners, who complained about the confusion it caused and the problems of enforcement.[19]

Griffin not only protected the freedpeople's economic interests but their rights as voters. He judged that the best protection for them would be their political power. He used agents as foot soldiers for the Republican cause and, throughout his joint command in Texas, helped with the removal of "Rebel" officeholders. This more forceful approach created, for a brief time in early 1867, rather quiet conditions around the state. The future looked promising and possible "success" within reach. It was fleeting, however, because Griffin misjudged whites' resistance to freedmen voting and to the Freedmen's Bureau's political activities in general.

The last head of the agency in Texas was Joseph J. Reynolds. He was to wind down the agency, delegating to civil authorities and making the new citizens as self-sufficient as possible. During Reynolds's term, field agents' main objective was still to protect their charges. But as they provided "all the protection possible with the means at [their] disposal," they were also to "leave them free to act for themselves in all things pertaining to their material welfare." Under Reynolds, subassistant commissioners served more as advisors than protectors.[20]

Unlike his predecessors, particularly Kiddoo and Griffin, Reynolds appeared to waver in his support to protect subordinates as the date neared to cease operations. On several occasions, he refused (or was very dilatory) to involve himself on their behalf. Many of their letters went unanswered. Fred W. Reinhard at Crockett, for example, who served almost thirty months, faced many accusations by whites in his district. Upon discovering the sheriff had accepted bribes from freedpeople, Reinhard fined him and requested his removal for a more capable and honest man. Reynolds ordered the fine to be repaid and did not replace the sheriff until the spring of 1869. In other cases, like that of William H. Howard, who had problems with a former SAC, Reynolds refused to get involved, ignoring his pleas for help. Perhaps his time was preoccupied with politics, or perhaps with General Winfield Scott Hancock and his G. O. No. 40, or on the business of closing down the agency. Whatever the case, Reynolds seemed more willing to "ride out" the remaining days than zealously fulfill his obligations to those under him.[21]

With such a monumental task assigned to the Bureau, its agents certainly did not achieve perfection, leaving much incomplete. When the agency ended in Texas, the former slaves did not entirely enjoy the fruits of emancipation, and throughout the next generation, their freedom would be even more circumscribed. By late 1868, though, they enjoyed unprecedented freedom for a people only recently emancipated: they could choose their employer, were compensated for their labor, were enfranchised, and for the first time in Texas (and the South for that matter) they became (with the aid of SACs) a political force. Bureau men, despite some complaints about their racial beliefs, their antiquated views by today's standards, and the organization's "bureaucratic mismanagement," worked hard to achieve this progress for the freedpeople.[22]

The Bureau was temporary, its demise being "preordained at its conception." Developed to deal with emancipation's and the war's effects, it did not have specific long-range goals. Its effort in Texas was founded on faith, faith that whites had learned their lesson, faith that they were contrite, and faith that they would cooperate to help the freedpeople. Bureau officials, guided by a strong belief in states' rights, misjudged the willingness to aid in this process. Agents, after their experiences with civil officers, were frustrated they had to rely so heavily upon them. Leaders failed to anticipate the extent of white resistance to Reconstruction. "It is impossible for me to [support] any measure which makes the negro the equal of the white man," wrote Robert W. Loughery, the fire-eating editor of the *Marshall Texas Republican*, who expressed the beliefs of many white Texans "that the negro can never become the political equal of the white man. . . ." The *Dallas Herald* editor believed God intended blacks to be subordinate to whites and defiantly stated whites "should forbid that the negro should ever be entrusted with the exercise of any political rights, or . . . make him politically and socially equal of the whites." Bureau officials, ignorant of the depths of these beliefs, failed to understand whites would never "voluntarily participate" in their "own degradation."[23]

If superiors misjudged white intransigence, many SACs were soon privy to it. They quickly understood all Confederate army surrenders, all the constitutional amendments, and all Congressional reform could not erase two hundred years of social beliefs and attitudes, attitudes that moved white Texans to attempt to destroy the Union. Confederates agreed to surrender their arms, not their beliefs. By the agency's end in 1868, many agents realized their limitations and understood what was really needed for the freedpeople to fully enjoy their freedom and for the whites to be reconstructed. "I am of the opinion," William G. Kirkman concluded, "that reconstruction that will be lasting will have to begin at the Heart of those who are now so biased and warped in their views . . . [since] I know of no practicable suggestions . . . to overcome the feelings the southern people have against northern citizens. The feeling they have and always have had I think it has got to be forever done away with before there will be peace."[24]

Some students of Reconstruction have claimed that a greater show of force could have brought about the peace referenced by Kirkman. If the U.S. government had only supported its activities with tens of thousands of additional soldiers, these critics claim, Reconstruction might have succeeded. For example, according to historian William L. Richter, officials had the necessary troops, particularly cavalry, to keep violence in check. He indicts the federal government's efforts in Texas, criticizing its inflexible and inefficient command structure as well as its lack of commitment to counter violence. Federal officials,

Richter concludes, finally employed the correct policy in October 1868, two months before Bureau operations ceased in the state. Reynolds, apparently tired of the chaos in certain portions of Texas, ordered a squadron from the 6th Cavalry to northeast Texas, arguably the most notorious region in the state. This unit was under the command of former Bureau agents Thomas M. Tolman and Adna R. Chaffee and was charged with neutralizing the "unreconstructed" in the area. As they swept through, they worried little about civility and less about taking prisoners. Adna and Chaffee euphemistically reported outlaws "lost in the swamp" or "shot while trying to escape." Those not reported "missing" were sometimes abused (hanged by the thumbs), including any citizen who misled the soldiers with false information. These methods were doubtless quite unsavory and were criticized by many whites as despotic. Nonetheless, the column cleansed the area of much of the outlaw element that had threatened and killed Bureau agents and terrorized the freedpeople. Richter sees this as evidence of what might have been.[25]

"Chaffee's Guerrillas" (its nickname by locals) worked in isolation, especially toward outlaws who respected no authority. But, in reality, it would have been unsustainable or impracticable as a long-range policy at the time. The public would not have tolerated placing thousands of troops for decades in Texas, let alone the entire former Confederacy. Not only would this mean immense expenditures, contradict Americans' dislike of martial solutions to civil problems, expand the size of the federal government at a time when Americans preferred the opposite, and require a large peacetime army (an anathema to nineteenth-century Americans), but the course's overall effectiveness and practicality are doubtful. Such tactics worked in the short term, but for the long term would have probably proved counterproductive in achieving Reconstruction's main goals: to reform former Confederates to be loyal citizens, to respect the federal government and its laws, and to accord equality to the freedpeople.

William Blair, a student of the military's role during Reconstruction, proposed such an alternative. He asked: "What could have been done to ensure the black people enjoyed a better chance at receiving long-term justice and the protection due them as citizens?" He examined the possibility of a greater "military posture . . . for a longer duration." Blair offered a counterfactual that included maintaining current troop levels at twenty thousand for the rest of the century. For that duration, they would take on the role of law enforcers, ensuring freedpeople's rights and privileges. The "military intervention through the turn of the century had virtually no chance for implementation," Blair ultimately concludes. "Committing 10,000 to 20,000 troops to long-term occupation of the South was unthinkable for practical, economic, and political-ideological reasons." A litany of examples exists in history of populations being forced to accept another's authority. And in each case, the occupier's desired effect failed to take root. Little evidence exists to suggest white Texans would have been any different. Reform rarely comes at the point of a bayonet.[26]

In 2005, *Civil War History* had an entire issue examining the "what ifs" of Reconstruction. In a series of short articles, historians proposed counterfactuals on how a different course would have finally fulfilled the nation's promissory note, to pirate a famous ancestor of the freedmen's resonating words, to freedpeople. In this attempt to "reconstruct Reconstruction," these authors put forth a myriad of alternatives. They proposed land redistribution to the emancipated, a "Marshal Plan" for the South, less vague and expansive 13th, 14th, and 15th Amendments, a greater use of military in the former Confederacy, the construction of a bureaucracy "to enforce obedience to the law," or a more savvy and astute black leadership. Had such things only happened, the North might have continued Reconstruction efforts until the South really was reconstructed. Thousands of words later, each author ultimately admits Reconstruction's outcome, the one so criticized by the academy for its conservatism, shortsightedness, and oppression, was really the only outcome. Even before Reconstruction commenced, there existed forces that already determined its outcome. An outcome that left the white Southerner, imbued with ideas of racial superiority, still in control of the South's political and economic apparatuses as well as the freedpeople. "These historians who are critical of the performance [of the country] for not achieving more for black Americans," historian Brooks Simpson writes, "find it rather difficult to offer a historically viable alternative that improves markedly on what happened, even with the immense advantages offered by hindsight."[27]

All the bayonets, soldiers, congressional measures, and Bureau men in the North could not change what white Texans felt in their hearts and believed in their minds. Only time could transform their attitudes about the freedpeople and allow for a situation conducive to "peace." Subassistant commissioners in Texas realized their (and the nation's) expectations far exceeded their capabilities. The true reconstruction of Texas, the one that aimed at the hearts and minds, would have to be left for future generations and a different federal government. As historian Joe M. Richardson states, "what the freedmen needed after their emancipation was something that no federal agency could secure for them, a change in the attitude of the white South."[28]

Bureau men protected the freed workers as independent laborers, secure in their rights to receive just wages and to choose an employer. With the help of federal and state law, they established their right to set up a household (and to be protected within in it), they worked to recognize their marriages, and, despite the practice of apprenticeship, they tried to establish their parental rights. These men further ensured freedpeople had the right to an education and their day in court. And finally, they protected their right of mobility, something they never had while in bondage. Certainly the emancipated's condition in late 1868 was far from what Americans in the late twentieth and early twenty-first centuries would consider ideal. It nonetheless was also far from "chattel slavery." "[T]he differences between slavery and freedom," wrote historian Willie Lee Rose, "is about the greatest difference in status we can imagine, no matter how kindly a view some historians want to make slavery, no matter how limited and curtailed freedom may have turned out to be." Their freedom was neither curtailed nor circumscribed by the efforts (or lack thereof) of Bureau agents. Their freedom instead was limited by circumstances at the time, which were well beyond any institution's or person's control. Critics must remember not all things were possible after the Civil War. Those so-called failed promises, in other words, were incapable of being fulfilled. That any were ever promised (whether due to the optimism of the war's outcome or the naïveté that all things were possible with slavery's demise) is the real tragedy of Reconstruction.[29]

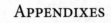

APPENDIXES

Appendix A

If the reader has reached this point in the work, I thank you for reading. If not for at least glancing the work. To be sure, this work includes large amounts of numbers. It is based on extensive and expansive accumulation of data. The data are from a myriad of sources. Personal information, such as ages, origins, wealth, comes primarily from census sources. When that proved insufficient, other sources were used. Unlike the numbers for wealth, which fluctuates over time and thus had to come from a single source (1870 census) and at a single time, the other personal information could be gleamed from applications for employment, obituaries, newspaper articles, service records, pension records, official/personal correspondences as well as any census within the subassistant commissioner's lifespan. Birthplace would be the same for the agent whether listed in the census as a dependent in 1850 or head-of-household in 1900. Furthermore, one's age is obtainable with relative accuracy with a simple arithmetic. For example, an agent may not be found in the 1860 or even 1870 censuses. He, however, was found in 1880 and 1900. If he was 50 years of age in 1880 and 71 in 1900, it is safe to assume he would be 35-ish in 1865. I would simply add an additional year until the agent's appointment say in 1867. I listed that man in the data as 37 years old.

Information on an agent's tenure and reason for dismissal came specifically from Bureau records. Tenures came from Special Orders and the Freedmen's Bureau Roster of Officers and Civilians. Special Orders were specific actions by headquarters, such as an appointment to the agency. Headquarters officials issued a roster of personnel on a monthly basis for informational purposes for the civilian population in Texas. Listed were the SACs and the counties that comprised their subdistricts. In order to determine an agent's tenure I calculated the time from his appointment to departure. When a specific date was unavailable, I referred to the roster and placed that agent's starting date as the first of that month. If an agent appeared for the first time on the July 1868 roster, his starting date would be July 1.

I determined the reason for departure from the agency through different Bureau records. Sometimes it came from a letter from the departing agent, listing his reason for leaving. Other times it came from headquarters that agent so-and-so had been dismissed due to criminality or incompetence. Still others would be a notification of death. Additional information came from the numerous inspection tours dispatched by headquarters. Such tours and subsequent reports not only apprised superiors to conditions in the state, but also of the actions of their subordinates.

Other records determine whether someone left the Freedmen's Bureau due to military service. On occasion, headquarters issued a special order releasing an officer from Bureau service. Most of the time, however, there rarely existed an order relieving an officer simultaneously serving as post commander and sub-assistant commissioner in the subdistrict. To find that man's reason for leaving, I looked in future censuses to see if he was still serving in the military. I considered his reason for leaving a military one if found in any census after 1860.

The most voluminous, and time-consuming I might add, of the data came from the agency's Register of Complaints. For each subdistrict, the agent compiled a list of complaints for redress. As noted, these complaints overwhelmingly involved a black plaintiff against a white defendant and concerned generally minor incidents. Rather than use the list of complaints located in the Assistant Commissioner Records, I instead used those from the Records of the Field Offices. Despite being the same data, the number at the subdistrict level exceeds those at headquarters. Records were lost in transit, destroyed by looters, or simply not sent in by those in the field. Thus, the total of cases from the field offices equals 6,794 cases, far surpassing the total at headquarters.

I enumerate the cases according to criminal offense, race of plaintiff and defendant, and outcome. This study has twelve categories of offenses. The first, second, and fourth consist of complaints concerning settlement of crop, money owed, or contract violations. These three combined represented the vast majority of complaints, with 640, 3,324, and 475 cases respectively. Rounding out those cases of an economic nature was the sixth category. Numbering 615, these were disputes about possession of property, destruction of property, requests for damages, and theft.

Economic issues were not the only issues brought by aggrieved parties. The third category consisted of assaults, threats, and fighting and equaled 948. Superiors preferred SACs to settle assaults of a minor nature only, but some were of the serious kind. The ninth category involved accusations of abduction and retention. This represented the smallest number of complaints with only four cases.

Some of the cases involved a familial element. The fifth and seventh categories included apprenticeship and domestic issues. Complaints about apprenticed children numbered 184, while those of a domestic nature, generally involving disputes arising between sexual partners and husband and wife, equaled 246.

The remaining complaints consist of the eighth, tenth, eleventh, and twelfth categories. This included slander and defamation, cases categorized under other, offenses combining two or more of the above complaints, and fraud, embezzlement, and blackmail. Eleven cases of slander and defamation were arbitrated. I designated complaints that did not fit into any of the above categories as other: such as an agent listing the offense as "violation" or no offense at all. Added to these included cases of drunkenness, disorderly conduct, false imprisonment, but to name a few. Collectively, these equaled 218 cases. A combination of any of the aforementioned categories, such as fraud and assault or contract violation and abduction, totaled 93. Accusations of fraud, blackmail, and embezzlement came before agents in the field 36 times.

Of the 6,794 cases, there was a definite winner in 3,336: 2,826 in favor of the plaintiff and 510 in favor of the defendant. The rest of the 3,458 cases subassistant commissioners described as settled (772), continued (245), dismissed (311), referred (531), compromised (30), transferred (8), adjourned (11), or disposed (1). Included in those were the cases in which the agent listed no outcome at all—there were 1,549 such instances.

Appendix B

The breakdown of complaints within each subdistrict and region of Texas are as follows.

Gulf Coast

Houston, Harris County, had 850 cases: settlement of crop/contract (18), money owed, wages, or debt (625), assault, threats, fighting, or shooting (48), contract violation/interference (15), apprenticeship (11), possession of property, destruction of property, or theft (92), domestic issue (20), slander or defamation (1), abduction of person (1), other (10), combination of above (5), and fraud, blackmail, embezzlement, or swindling (4)

Richmond, Fort Bend County, had 319 cases: settlement of crop/contract (20), money owed, wages, or debt (172), assault, threats, fighting, or shooting (37), contract violation/interference (7), apprenticeship (8), possession of property, destruction of property, or theft (11), domestic issue (14), slander or defamation (0), abduction of person (0), other (49), combination of above (1) and fraud, blackmail, embezzlement, or swindling (0)

Beaumont, Jefferson County, had 31 cases: settlement of crop/contract (1), money owed, wages, and debt (5), assault, threats, fighting, or shooting (16), contract violation/interference (0), apprenticeship (0), possession of property, destruction of property, or theft (6), domestic issue (0), slander or defamation (0), abduction of people (0), other (3), combination of above (0), and fraud, blackmail, embezzlement, or swindling (0)

Wharton, Wharton County, had 87 cases: settlement of crop/contract (19), money owed, wages, or debt (22), assault, threats, fighting, or shooting (16), contract violation/interference (5), apprenticeship (4), possession of property, destruction of property, or theft (9), domestic issue (3), slander or defamation (0), abduction of person (0), other (6), combination of above (3), and fraud, blackmail, embezzlement, or swindling (0)

Hallettsville, Lavaca County, had 58 cases: settlement of crop/contract (6), money owed, wages, or debt (18), assault, threats, fighting, or shooting (14), contract violation/interference (8), apprenticeship (4), possession of property, destruction of property, or theft (5), domestic issue (2), slander or defamation

(0), abduction of person (0), other (1), combination of above (0), and fraud, blackmail, embezzlement, or swindling (0)

Liberty, Liberty County, had 106 cases: settlement of crop/contract (12), money owed, wages, or debt (46), assault, threats, fighting, or shooting (14), contract violation/interference (10), apprenticeship (4), possession of property, destruction of property, or theft (10), domestic issue (3), slander or defamation (1), abduction of person (1), other (2), combination of above (2), and fraud, blackmail, embezzlement, or swindling (1)

Columbia, Brazoria County, had 93 cases: settlement of crop/contract (11), money owed, wages, or debt (27), assault, threats, fighting, or shooting (16), contract violation/interference (14), apprenticeship (2), possession of property, destruction of property, or theft (15), domestic issue (3), slander or defamation (0), abduction of person (0), other (1), combination of above (3), and fraud, blackmail, embezzlement, or swindling (1)

Galveston, Galveston County, had 337 cases: settlement of crop/contract (2), money owed, wages, or debt (204), assault, threats, fighting, or shooting (50), contract violation/interference (7), apprenticeship (11), possession of property, destruction of property, or theft (24), domestic issue (27), slander or defamation (4), abduction of person (0), other (8), combination of above (0), and fraud, blackmail, embezzlement, or swindling (0)

Columbus, Colorado County, had 291 cases: settlement of crop/contract (40), money owed, wages, or debt (131), assault, threats, fighting, or shooting (56), contract violation/interference (11), apprenticeship (8), possession of property, destruction of property, or theft (30), domestic issue (5), slander or defamation (0), abduction of person (0), other (10), combination of above (0), and fraud, blackmail, embezzlement, or swindling (0)

North Texas

Meridian, Bosque County, had 70 cases: settlement of crop/contract (1), money owed, wages, or debt (52), assault, threats, fighting, or shooting (10), contract violation/interference (0), apprenticeship (3), possession of property, destruction of property, or theft (2), domestic issue (0), slander or defamation (0), abduction of person (0), other (2), combination of above (0), and fraud, blackmail, embezzlement, or swindling (0)

South Texas

Gonzales, Gonzales County, had 8 cases: settlement of crop/contract (1), money owed, wages, or debt (1), assault, threats, fighting, or shooting (1), contract violation/interference (0), apprenticeship (1), possession of property, destruction of property, or theft (0), domestic issue (4), slander or defamation (0), abduction of person (0), other (0), combination of above (0), and fraud, blackmail, embezzlement, or swindling (0)

Clinton, DeWitt County, had 5 cases: settlement of crop/contract (0), money owed, wages, or debt (0), assault, threats, fighting, or shooting (1), contract violation/interference (2), apprenticeship (0), possession of property, destruction of property, or theft (1), domestic issue (0), slander or defamation (0), abduction of person (0), other (1), combination of above (0), and fraud, blackmail, embezzlement, or swindling (0)

San Antonio, Bexar County, had 67 cases: settlement of crop/contract (2), money owed, wages, or debt (44), assault, threats, fighting, or shooting (5), contract violation/interference (4), apprenticeship (3), possession of property, destruction of property, or theft (3), domestic issue (0), slander and defamation (0), abduction of person (0), other (4), combination of above (0), and fraud, blackmail, embezzlement, or swindling (2)

Central Texas

LaGrange, Fayette County, had 26 cases: settlement of crop/contract (6), money owed, wages, or debt (11), assault, threats, fighting, or shooting (1), contract violation/interference (4), apprenticeship (0), possession of property, destruction of property, or theft (1), domestic issue (2), slander or defamation (0), abduction of person (0), other (1), combination of above (0), and fraud, blackmail, embezzlement, or swindling (0)

Bryan, Brazos County, had 16 cases: settlement of crop/contract (0), money owed, wages, or debt (3), assault, threats, fighting, or shooting (7), contract violation/interference (4), apprenticeship (0), possession of property, destruction of property, or theft (1), domestic issue (0), slander or defamation (0), abduction of people (0), other (0), combination of above (1), and fraud, blackmail, embezzlement, or swindling (0)

Lockhart, Caldwell County, had 84 cases: settlement of crop/settlement (6), money owed, wages, or debt (52), assault, threats, fighting, or shooting (5), contract violation/interference (2), apprenticeship (0), possession of property, destruction of property, or theft (15), domestic issue (0), slander or defamation (0), abduction of people (0), other (4), combination of above (0), and fraud, blackmail, embezzlement, or swindling (0)

Brenham, Washington County, had 92 cases: settlement of crop/contract (28), money owed, wages, or debt (16), assault, threats, fighting, or shooting (6), contract violation/interference (15), apprenticeship (1), possession of property, destruction of property, or theft (17), domestic issue (5), slander or defamation (0), abduction of person (0), other (4), combination of above (0), and fraud, blackmail, embezzlement, or swindling (0)

Seguin, Guadalupe County, had 183 cases: settlement of crop/contract (24), money owed, wages, or debt (46), assault, threats, fighting, or shooting (49), contract violation/interference (10), apprenticeship (18), possession of property, destruction of property, or theft (23), domestic issue (7), slander or defamation (1), abduction of person (0), other (4), combination of above (1), and fraud, blackmail, embezzlement, or swindling (0)

Austin, Travis County, had 1,248 cases: settlement of crop/contract (123), money owed, wages, or debt (554), assault, threats, fighting, or shooting (158), contract violation/interference (88), apprenticeship (33), possession of property, destruction of property, or theft (128), domestic issue (103), slander or defamation (3), abduction of person (2), other (17), combination of above (28), and fraud, blackmail, embezzlement, or swindling (11)

Belton, Bell County, had 160 cases: settlement of crop/contract (28), money, wages, or debt (59), assault, threats, fighting, or shooting (32), contract violation/interference (3), apprenticeship (9), possession of property, destruction of property, or theft (21), domestic issue (1), slander or defamation (0), abduction of person (0), other (4), combination of above (3), and fraud, blackmail, embezzlement, or swindling (0)

Marlin, Falls County, had 269 cases: settlement of crop/contract (23), money owed, wages, or debt (60), assault, threats, fighting, or shooting (34), contract violation/interference (110), apprenticeship (1), possession of property, destruction of property, or theft (24), domestic issue (5), slander or defamation (0), abduction of person (0), other (9), combination of above (1), and fraud, blackmail, embezzlement, or swindling (2)

Waco, McLennan County, had 339 cases: settlement of crop/contract (49), money owed, wages, or debt (181), assault, threats, fighting, or shooting (38), contract violation/interference (14), apprenticeship (4), possession of property, destruction of property, or theft (37), domestic issue (7), slander or defamation (0), abduction of person (0), other (6), combination of above (1), and fraud, blackmail, embezzlement, or swindling (2)

Millican, Brazos County, had 132 cases: settlement of crop/contract (4), money owed, wages, or debt (17), assault, threats, fighting, or shooting (47), contract violation/interference (42), apprenticeship (2), possession of property, destruction of property, theft (3), domestic issue (4), slander or defamation (1), abduction of person (0), other (6), combination of above (5), fraud, blackmail, embezzlement, or swindling (1)

East Texas

Marshall, Harrison County, had 140 cases: settlement of crop/contract (11), money owed, wages, or debt (43), assault, threats, fighting, or shooting (42), contract violation/interference (13), apprenticeship (0), possession of property, destruction of property, or theft (14, domestic issue (4), slander or defamation (0), abduction of person (0), other (12), combination of above (1), and fraud, blackmail, embezzlement, of swindling (0)

Boston, Bowie County, had 80 cases: settlement of crop/contract (3), money owed, wages, or debt (20), assault, threats, fighting, or shooting (19), contract violation/interference (9), apprenticeship (8), possession of property, destruction of property, or theft (2), domestic issue (1), slander or defamation (0), abduction of person (0), other (15), combination of above (3), and fraud, blackmail, embezzlement, or swindling (0)

Crockett, Houston County, had 89 cases: settlement of crop/contract (11), money owed, wages, or debt (62), assault, threats, fighting, or shooting (7), contract violation/interference (4), apprenticeship (0), possession of property, destruction of property, or theft (0), domestic issue (2), slander or defamation (0), abduction of person (0), other (3), combination of above (0), and fraud, blackmail, embezzlement, or swindling (0)

Huntsville, Walker County, had 117 cases: settlement of crop/contract (58), money owed, wages, or debt (31), assault, threats, fighting, or shooting (9), contract violation/interference (2), apprenticeship (0), possession of property, destruction of property, or theft (5), domestic issue (5), slander or defamation (0), abduction of person (0), other (5), combination of above (1), or fraud, blackmail, embezzlement, or swindling (1)

Centreville, Leon County, had 13 cases: settlement of crop/contract (1), money owed, wages, or debt (1), assault, threats, fighting, or shooting (6), contract violation/interference (5), apprenticeship (0), possession of property, destruction of property, or theft (0), domestic issue (0), slander or defamation (0), abduction of person (0), other (0), combination of above (0), and fraud, blackmail, embezzlement, or swindling (0)

San Augustine, San Augustine County, had 7 cases: settlement of crop/contract (0), money owed, wages, or debt (1), assault, threats, fighting, or shooting (5), contract violation/interference (0), apprenticeship (0), possession of property, destruction of property, theft (0), domestic issue (0), slander or defamation (0), abducting of person (0), other (0), combination of above (1), and fraud, blackmail, embezzlement, or swindling (0)

Sterling/Sumpter, Trinity County, had 244 cases: settlement of crop/contract (19), money owed, wages, or debt (133), assault, threats, fighting, or shooting (29), contract violation/interference (20), apprenticeship (7), possession of property, destruction of property, or theft (18), domestic issue (5), slander or defamation (0), abduction of person (0), other (6), combination of above (4), and fraud, blackmail, embezzlement, or swindling (3)

Cotton Gin, Freestone County, had 33 cases: settlement of crop/contract (5), money owed, wages, or debt (8), assault, threats, fighting, or shooting (2), contract violation/interference (4), apprenticeship (2), possession of property, destruction of property, or theft (6), domestic issue (4), slander or defamation (0), abduction of person (0), other (1), combination of above (1), and fraud, blackmail, embezzlement, or swindling (0)

Nacogdoches, Nacogdoches County, had 207 cases: settlement of crop/contract (38), money owed, wages, or debt (84), assault, threats, fighting, or shooting (36), contract violations/interference (3), apprenticeship (4), possession of property, destruction of property, or theft (27), domestic issue (3), slander or defamation (0), abduction of person (0), other (6), combination of above (0), and fraud, blackmail, embezzlement, or swindling (6)

Palestine, Anderson County, had 303 cases: settlement of crop/contract (31), money owed, wages, or debt (204), assault, threats, fighting, or shooting (31), contract violation/interference (6), apprenticeship (6), possession of property, destruction of property, or theft (14), domestic issue (1), slander or defamation (0), abduction of person (0), other (10), combination of above (0), and fraud, blackmail, embezzlement, or swindling (0)

Tyler, Smith County, had 690 cases: settlement of crop/contract (39), money owed, wages, or debt (391), assault, threats, fighting, or shooting (101), contract violation/interference (34), apprenticeship (30), possession of property, destruction of property, or theft (51), domestic issue (6), slander or defamation (0), abduction of person (0), other (7), combination of above (28), and fraud, blackmail, embezzlement, or swindling (3)

Notes

Introduction

1. John A. Carpenter, "Agents of the Freedmen's Bureau," John A. Carpenter Papers, New York Public Library, New York, New York, 3–4.

2. *Congressional Globe*, 38th Congress, 2nd Session (Washington, D.C.: Blair and Rives, 1866), 692, 689–691, 959–960, 1308; Ira C. Colby, "The Freedmen's Bureau: From Social Welfare to Segregation," *Phylon* 46 (3rd Qtr., 1985): 220–221; George R. Bentley, *A History of the Freedmen's Bureau* (Philadelphia: University of Pennsylvania, 1959), 35–38. For a complete examination of the Freedmen's Bureau creation, see John M. Bickers, "The Power to Do What Manifestly Must Be Done: Congress, the Freedmen's Bureau, and Constitutional Legislation," *Rogers Williams Law Review* 70 (2007): 1–58.

3. Ibid.

4. O. O. Howard, *Autobiography of Oliver Otis Howard*, 2 vols. (New York: The Baker and Taylor Company, 1908), 2:363; Eileen Boris and Peter Bardaglio, "The Transformation of Patriarchy: The Historical Role of the State," in *Families, Politics, and Public Policy: A Feminist Dialogue on Women and the State*, ed. Irene Diamond (New York: Longman, 1983), 71–72; William A. Dunning, *Reconstruction, Political and Economic, 1865–1877* (New York: Harper and Row Publishers, 1907), 33; Michael W. Fitzgerald, *Splendid Failure: Postwar Reconstruction in the American South* (Chicago: Ivan. R. Dee Publishers, 2007), 30–31; William S. McFeely, *Yankee Stepfather: General O. O. Howard and the Freedmen* (New York: W. W. Norton and Company, 1968), 84; Paul A. Cimbala and Randall M. Miller, eds., *The Freedmen's Bureau and Reconstruction: Reconsiderations* (New York: Fordham University Press, 1999), xvi; Victoria Olds, "The Freedmen's Bureau as a Social Agency" (Ph.D. diss., Columbia University, 1966), 82–83, 219; Louis Henry Bronson, "The Freedmen's Bureau: A Public Policy Analysis" (D.S.W. diss., University of Southern California, 1970), 282–283.

5. Barry A. Crouch, "Guardian of the Freedpeople: Texas Freedmen Bureau Agents and the Black Community," *Southern Studies: An Interdisciplinary Journal of the South* 3 (Fall 1992): 185. Studies focusing on the SACs are Ted Tunnell, ed., *Carpetbagger from Vermont: The Autobiography of Marshall Harvey Twitchell* (Baton Rouge: Louisiana State University Press, 1989); Ted Tunnell, *Edge of the Sword: The Ordeal of Carpetbagger Marshall H. Twitchell in the Civil War and Reconstruction* (Baton Rouge: Louisiana State University Press, 2001); William A. Campbell, ed., "A Freedmen's Bureau Diary by George Wagner," *Georgia Historical Quarterly* 48 (June 1964): 196–214; William A. Campbell, ed., "A Freedmen's Bureau Diary by George Wagner," *Georgia Historical Quarterly* 48 (September 1964): 333–359; Ruth Currie-McDaniel, *Carpetbagger of Conscience: A Biography of John Emory Bryant* (New York: Fordham University Press, 1999); Cecil Harper, Jr., "Freedmen's Bureau Agents in Texas: A Profile" (unpublished

manuscript, Texas State Historical Association, 1987); Russell Duncan, *Tunis Campbell, Freedom's Shore: Tunis Campbell and the Georgia Freedmen* (Athens: University of Georgia Press, 1986); James M. Smallwood, "Charles E. Culver, A Reconstruction Agent in Texas: The Work of Local Freedmen's Bureau Agents and the Black Community," *Civil War History* 27 (December 1981): 350–361; James M. Smallwood, "G. T. Ruby: Galveston's Black Carpetbagger in Reconstruction Texas," *Houston Review* 5 (Winter 1983): 24–33; Thomas H. Smith, "Conflict and Corruption: The Dallas Establishment vs. the Freedmen's Bureau Agent," *Legacies: A History Journal for Dallas and North Central Texas* 1 (Fall 1989): 24–30; William L. Richter, "'The Revolver Rules the Day!': Colonel DeWitt C. Brown and the Freedmen's Bureau in Paris, Texas, 1867–1868," *Southwestern Historical Quarterly* 93 (January 1990): 303–332; William L. Richter, "'This Blood-Thirsty Hole': The Freedmen's Bureau Agency at Clarksville, Texas, 1867–1868," *Civil War History* 38 (March 1992): 51–77; William L. Richter, "'A Dear Little Job': Second Lieutenant Hiram F. Willis, Freedmen's Bureau Agent in Southwestern Arkansas, 1866–1868," *Arkansas Historical Quarterly* 50 (Summer 1991): 158–200; John Edmund Stealey, "Reports of Freedmen's Bureau Operations in West Virginia: Agents in The Eastern Panhandle," *West Virginia History* 42 (Fall/Winter 1981): 94–129; Paul D. Escott, "Clinton A. Cilley, Yankee War Hero in the Postwar South: A Study in the Compatibility of Regional Values," *The North Carolina Historical Review* 68 (October 1991): 404–426; Charles L. Price, "John C. Barnett, Freedmen's Bureau Agent in North Carolina," *Of Tar Heel Towns, Shipbuilders, Reconstructionists, and Alliancemen: Papers in North Carolina History* 5 (Autumn 1981): 51–74; Barry A. Crouch, *The Freedmen's Bureau and Black Texans* (Austin: University of Texas Press, 1992); Barry A. Crouch, "View from Within: Letters of Gregory Barrett, Freedmen's Bureau Agent," *Chronicles of Smith County, Texas* 12 (Winter 1973): 13–26; Paul A. Cimbala, "On the Front Line of Freedom: Freedmen's Bureau Officers and Agents in Reconstruction Georgia, 1865–1866," *Georgia Historical Quarterly* 76 (Fall 1992): 577–611; Paul A. Cimbala, "Making Good Yankees: The Freedmen's Bureau and Education in Reconstruction Georgia, 1865–1868," *Atlanta Historical Journal* 29 (Fall 1985): 5–18; and J. Thomas May, "The Freedmen's Bureau at the Local Level: A Study of a Louisiana Agent," *Louisiana History* 9 (Winter 1968): 5–19.

6. For an overview of Reconstruction historiography, excluding recent works, see Eric Foner, "Reconstruction Revisited," *Reviews in American History* 10 (December 1982): 82–100; and John David Smith, "'The Work It Did Not Do Because It Could Not': Georgia and the 'New' Freedmen's Bureau Historiography," *Georgia Historical Quarterly* 82 (Summer 1998): 331–349. Recent works can be found in Robert Harrison, "New Representations of a 'Misrepresented Bureau': Reflections on Recent Scholarship on the Freedmen's Bureau," *American Nineteenth Century History* 8 (June 2007): 205–229 and Thomas J. Brown, ed., *Reconstructions: New Perspectives on the Postbellum United States* (New York: Oxford University Press, 2006). Brown's work posits the "traditional," "revisionist," and "post-revisionist" historiography no longer is necessary. According to Brown, Foner dismantled the "post-revisionist" argument. I believe that premature. Recent critics of the Bureau use the same approach as the "post-revisionists," particularly when indicting the agency regarding care for families, gender, and marriage. The battlefield might have changed, but not the tactics. For early

criticisms, see John Rose Ficklen, *History of Reconstruction in Louisiana Through 1868* (Baltimore: The Johns Hopkins Press, 1910); John S. Reynolds, *Reconstruction in South Carolina, 1865–1877* (Columbia: The State Company Publishers, 1905); James W. Garner, *Reconstruction in Mississippi* (New York: Macmillan Company, 1901); William B. Hesseltine, *A History of the South, 1607–1936* (New York: Prentice Hall Inc., 1936); Honorine Anne Sherman, "The Freedmen's Bureau in Louisiana" (Master's Thesis, Tulane University, 1936); C. Mildred Thompson, *Reconstruction in Georgia: Economic, Social, Political, 1865–1872* (Savannah: The Beehive Press, 1972); Laura Josephine Webster, *The Operation of the Freedmen's Bureau in South Carolina* (New York: Russell and Russell, 1970); C. Mildred Thompson, "The Freedmen's Bureau in Georgia in 1865–1866: An Instrument of Reconstruction," *Georgia Historical Quarterly* 5 (March 1921): 40–49; and E. Merton Coulter, *The South During Reconstruction, 1865–1877* (Baton Rouge: Louisiana State University, 1947).

7. "Revisionist" works, not noted above, are Edward Longacre, "Brave, Radical, Wild: The Contentious Career of Brigadier General Edward A. Wild," *Civil War Times Illustrated* 19 (June 1980): 8–19; Ross Nathaniel Dudley, "Texas Reconstruction: The Role of the Bureau of Refugees, Freedmen and Abandoned Lands, 1865–1870, Smith County, (Tyler) Texas" (Master's Thesis, Texas A&I University, 1986); Steven E. Nash, "Aiding the Southern Mountain Republicans: The Freedmen's Bureau in Buncombe County," *North Carolina Historical Review* 83 (January 2006): 1–30; Ross A. Webb, "'The Past Is Never Dead, It's Not Even Past': Benjamin P. Runkle and the Freedmen's Bureau in Kentucky, 1866–1870," *Register of the Kentucky Historical Society* 84 (Autumn 1986): 343–360; Patricia A. Haskins, "The Freedmen's Bureau in the Jackson Purchase Region of Kentucky, 1866–1868," *The Register of the Kentucky Historical Society* 110 (Summer/Autumn 2012): 503–531; and John A. Carpenter, *The Sword and the Olive Branch: Oliver Otis Howard* (Pittsburgh: Pittsburgh University Press, 1964).

8. "Post-revisionist" interpretations are Leon Litwack, *Been in the Storm So Long: The Aftermath of Slavery* (New York: Alfred K. Knopf, 1979); Louis Gerteis, *From Contraband to Freedman: Federal Policy Toward Southern Blacks, 1861–1865* (Westport: Greenwood Press, 1973); McFeely, *Yankee Stepfather*; Michael Perman, *Emancipation and Reconstruction, 1862–1877* (New York: Harper & Row, 1988); George D. Humphrey, "The Failure of the Mississippi Freedmen's Bureau in Black Labor Relations, 1865–1867," *Journal of Mississippi History* 45 (February, 1983): 23–37; Patrick Groff, "The Freedmen's Bureau in High School History Texts," *Journal of Negro Education* 51 (Autumn 1982): 425–433; Edmund L. Drago, "Black Georgia During Reconstruction" (Ph.D. diss., University of California-Berkeley, 1975); James L. Owens, "The Negro in Georgia During Reconstruction, 1864–1872" (Ph.D. diss., University of Georgia, 1975); Daniel Novak, *The Wheel of Servitude: Black Forced Labor After Slavery* (Lexington, Ky.: University of Kentucky Press, 1979); Donna L. Franklin, *Ensuring Inequality: The Structural Transformation of the African-American Family* (New York: Oxford University Press, 1997); Robert Cruden, *Negro in Reconstruction* (Englewood Cliffs, N.J.: Prentice-Hall, 1969); Arvarh E. Strickland and Jerome R. Reich, *The Black American Experience: From Slavery Through Reconstruction* (New York: Harcourt Brace Jovanovich, 1974); and Robert F. Engs, *Freedom's First Generation: Black Hampton, Virginia, 1861–1890* (Philadelphia: University of Pennsylvania Press, 1979).

9. Mary Kaiser-Farmer, *Freedwomen and the Freedmen's Bureau: Race, Gender, and Public Policy in the Age of Emancipation* (New York: Fordham University Press, 2010), 3. For works within this "new" historiography, see Richard G. Lowe, "The Freedmen's Bureau and Local White Leaders in Virginia," *Journal of Southern History* 64 (August 1998): 455–472; William H. Burks, "The Freedmen's Bureau, Politics, and Stability Operations During Reconstruction in the South" (Master's Thesis, U.S. Air Force Academy, 2009); and William L. Richter, "Who Was the Real Head of the Texas Freedmen's Bureau? The Role of Brevet Colonel William H. Sinclair as Acting Assistant Inspector General," *Military History of the Southwest* 20 (Fall 1990): 121–156.

10. Paul A. Cimbala, *Under the Guardianship of the Nation: The Freedmen's Bureau and the Reconstruction of Georgia, 1865–1870* (Athens: University of Georgia Press, 1997), xv.

1. "A *Stranger* Amongst *Strangers*": Who Were the Subassistant Commissioners?

1. For the historiography of subassistant commissioners, see Introduction, notes 6–8. For the connection between the Bureau's failure and its legacy during Hurricane Katrina, see Pamela Denise Reed, "From the Freedmen's Bureau to FEMA: A Post-Katrina Historical, Journalistic, and Literary Analysis," 37 *Journal of Black Studies* (March 2007): 555–567.

2. Circular letter from [O. O. Howard], April 1867, Box 401–860, Texas Adjutant General's Office, Texas Adjutant Generals Department, Archives and Information Division, Texas State Archives and Commission, Austin, Texas (hereafter cited TxAGO); Byron Porter, Bastrop, to J. T. Kirkman, A.A.A.G., April 2, 1867, Reports of Operations and Conditions, December 1866–May 1867, Records of the Assistant Commissioner for the State of Texas, Bureau of Refugees, Freedmen, and Abandoned Lands, 1865–1869, Record Group 105, National Archives and Records Administration, Washington, D.C. (Microfilm M821, reel 20), hereafter cited AC; John William De Forest, *A Union Officer in the Reconstruction*, ed. James H. Croushore and David M. Potter (New Haven: Yale University Press, 1948), 41; Eric Foner, *Reconstruction: America's Unfinished Revolution, 1863–1877* (New York: Harper & Row Publishers, 1988), 143.

3. Randy Finley, *From Slavery to Uncertain Freedom: The Freedmen's Bureau in Arkansas, 1865–1869* (Fayetteville: University of Arkansas Press, 1996), 11; Cimbala, *Under the Guardianship of the Nation*, 256. For studies citing 202 agents in Texas, see Crouch, *Freedmen's Bureau and Black Texans*, 9; and Harper, "Freedmen's Bureau Agents in Texas," 2. For those mislabeled Bureau agents, see Ron Tyler, ed., *New Handbook of Texas*, 6 vols. (Austin: Texas State Historical Association, 1996), 1:112–113, 795, 383. For an unsanctioned appointment by a field agent, see Steven Hahn et al., eds., *Freedom: A Documentary History of Emancipation, 1861–1867, Series 3, Volume 1: Land and Labor, 1865* (Chapel Hill: University of North Carolina Press, 2008), 975–977.

4. The months examined in Figure 1–1 are: October 1865, January 1866, April 1866, July 1866, October 1866, January 1867, April 1867, July 1867, October 1867, January 1868, April 1868, July 1868, and October 1868. The men for each month are taken from the monthly "Roster of Officers and Civilians." For October 1865, April 1866, and April

1867, due to no extant roster, the number of agents was determined by examining tenures. I counted all assigned to the district on the first day of the month. Any agent
assigned later in the month was not. For example, if agent A was the agent for district
B, but replaced later in the month by another agent, agent A would appear in the sample. The number of Bureau agents for each of the months, starting with October 1865,
is as follows: 12, 20, 29, 31, 33, 30, 40, 75, 63, 55, 45, 46, and 55. Those agents with military
experience (either serving during the war or serving after the war as well as serving as
Bureau agent) are included in the numbers for "Military." Those agents with no military experience during the Civil War and Reconstruction are included in the numbers
for "No Military." "Northern" includes all agents born outside of the Confederate
states, including slaveholding states, such as Kentucky, that did not secede. "Southern"
includes all agents born in one of the eleven Confederate states. "N/A" includes those
whose birth state could not be definitively determined. The information comes from
the monthly Roster of Officers and Civilians.

5. Barry A. Crouch and William L. Richter both understate the number in the field
at any one time. Crouch claims the high to be 69, while Richter, in two different works,
cites 70 and 69. According to the Bureau's Roster of Civilians and Agents, the actual
high was 61 SACs and 11 ASACs. The two extra are attributed to the Huntsville subdistrict having two and another SAC not yet assigned a district. See Crouch, *Freedmen's
Bureau and Black Texans*, 28; William L. Richter, *Overreached on All Sides: Freedmen's
Bureau Administrators in Texas, 1865–1868* (College Station: Texas A&M University
Press, 1991), 157; Richter, "Who Was the Real Head of the Texas Freedmen's Bureau?"
122, 124; and Roster of Civilians and Agents, July 1867, AC, Issuances and Rosters of
Bureau Personnel and Special Orders Received, reel 19); Foner, *Reconstruction*, 143;
Finley, *From Slavery to Uncertain Freedom*, 11; Kenneth B. White, "Black Lives, Red
Tape: The Alabama Freedmen's Bureau," *Alabama Historical Quarterly* 43 (Winter
1981): 244–245; and Solomon K. Smith, "The Freedmen's Bureau in Shreveport: The
Struggle for Control of the Red River District," *Louisiana History* 41 (Fall 2000): 436.
Rather than examine a sample, this study identified all. Because of the vague and
imprecise way Reconstruction records were collected and the rather generic information within the 1870 federal census, not all of the agents could be located and identified
precisely. For consistency, I used only those found in the 1870 census (for wealth 110 of
239, or 46 percent; for occupation 139 of 239, or 58 percent; for head-of-household 105 of
239, or 44 percent; and for marital status 105 of 239, or 44 percent) to obtain the data
for wealth, occupation, head-of-household, and marital status. For other categories,
such as age, birthplace, and military status, additional sources, such as military
records, encyclopedias, and dictionaries were used. This can be done without jeopar-
dizing consistency or skewing the results. Of course, such an assumption could not be
made with wealth, occupation, or marital status, all of which can easily and significantly change through the years. Thus, the denominator for age (n=154), place of origin
(n=185), and military service (n=182) will be higher than the aforementioned indices.
Furthermore, all agents, whose tenure as agent could be definitively determined (with
specific starting and ending dates), were examined in this study, including those who
might have served a short period of time. A population that consisted of a large number of men who had very short tenures with the Bureau could easily skew the findings.

For example, if Texas had a significant number who served only a few days or a couple of months, they would definitely not represent the "typical" agents. But that is not the case. Of those whose tenure could be definitively established (n=213), approximately 15 percent served less than three months, and only 27 percent served for less than four months (n=58). The data for occupation, age, wealth, marital status, and head of household are from the 1870 federal census. I realize the imperfect compilation of that particular census, but deemed it necessary for this study. Since a good portion of the agents before the war lived with their parents, thus rendering it very difficult to locate them, the 1860 census would not have been as helpful. Due to the inherent problems in data collection in the nineteenth century and the condition of the country following the war, approximately half (105, 110, and 139) of the individuals who served as Bureau agents in Texas were located. Other such studies found a comparable percentage of their target individuals (see Maris A. Vinovskis, "Have Social Historians Lost the Civil War? Some Preliminary Demographic Speculations," in *Toward a Social History of the American Civil War: Exploratory Essays* [Cambridge, England and other cities, 1990]: 1–30; W. J. Rorabaugh, "Who Fought for the North in the Civil War? Concord, Massachusetts, Enlistments," *Journal of American History* 73 [December 1986]: 695–701; Thomas R. Kemp, "Community and War: The Civil War Experience of Two New Hampshire Towns," in *Toward a Social History of the American Civil War: Exploratory Essays*, ed. Vinovskis, [Cambridge, England and other cities, 1990]: 31–77; and Lowe, "Freedmen's Bureau and Local White Leaders in Virginia," 455–472). Vinovskis located 55 percent, Rorabaugh 48 percent, Kemp 47 percent, and Lowe 52.4 percent, respectively.

6. Carpenter, *Sword and Olive Branch*, 101–102.

7. Paul A. Cimbala, "The 'Talisman Power': Davis Tillson, the Freedmen's Bureau, and Free Labor in Reconstruction Georgia, 1865–1868," *Civil War History* 28 (June 1982): 157; Lowe, "Freedmen's Bureau and Local White Leaders," 459–460; Bell Irvin Wiley, *The Life of Billy Yank: The Common Soldier of the Union* (Baton Rouge: Louisiana State University Press, 1971), 307.

8. According to U.S. Census Records, the population for the United States in 1870 was 38,558,371, with 5,567,229 of those born abroad. The Middle Atlantic had a population of 8,810,806; the Upper South had 4,079,915; New England had 3,487,924; the Great Lakes had 10,318,537, and the states of the former Confederacy had 9,487,386. These numbers came from Campbell J. Gibson and Emily Lennon, comp., "Historical Census Statistics on the Foreign-Born Population of the United States: 1850 to 1990" (unpublished Working Paper No. 29, U.S. Bureau of the Census, February 1999).

9. Richter, *Overreached on All Sides*, 322; E. M. Gregory to O. O. Howard, September 21, 1865, Letters Received, October 1865–February 1866, Registers and Letters Received by the Commissioner of the Bureau of Refugees, Freedmen, and Abandoned Lands, 1865–1872, Record Group 105, National Archives Records Administration, Washington, D.C. (Microfilm M752, reel 24) hereafter cited M752C. For studies in other states showing hesitancy to appoint civilian agents, see William T. Alderson, "The Influence of Military Rule and the Freedmen's Bureau on Reconstruction Virginia, 1865–1870" (Ph.D. diss., Vanderbilt University, 1952), 35–36. The definition of "carpetbagger" and "scalawag" comes from James A. Baggett, Allen W. Trelease, and

Richard N. Current (see James A. Baggett, *The Scalawags: Southern Dissenters in the Civil War and Reconstruction* [Baton Rouge: Louisiana State University Press, 2003]; Allen W. Trelease "Who Were the Scalawags," in *Reconstruction: An Anthology of Revisionist Writings*, ed. Kenneth M. Stampp and Leon F. Litwack [Baton Rouge: Louisiana State University Press, 1969], 299–322; and Current, "Carpetbaggers Reconsidered," 223–240).

10. Tyler, ed., *New Handbook of Texas*, 4:102.

11. Tyler, ed., New *Handbook of Texas*, 5:706. For the biography of George T. Ruby, see Barry A. Crouch, "Black Education in Civil War and Reconstruction Louisiana: George T. Ruby, the Army, and the Freedmen's Bureau," *Louisiana History* 38 (Summer 1997): 287–308; Randall B. Woods, "George T. Ruby: A Black Militant in the White Business Community," *Red River Valley Historical Review* 1 (August 1974): 269–280; Smallwood, "G. T. Ruby," 24–33; Merline Pitre, *Through Many Dangers, Toils, and Snares: The Black Leadership of Texas, 1868–1900* (Austin: Eakin Press, 1985). For doubt concerning Ruby's lineage, see Carl H. Moneyhon, "George T. Ruby and the Politics of Expediency in Texas," in *Southern Black Leaders of Reconstruction Era*, ed. Howard N. Rabinowitz (Urbana: University of Illinois Press, 1982), 363, 389–390; and Crouch, "Black Education," 287.

12. Ira Hobart Evans, Vertical File, Center for America History, University of Texas at Austin, Austin, Texas; Tyler, ed., *New Handbook of Texas*, 2:904–905; *Members of the Texas Congress, 1846–2004* (Austin: Senate Publications, 2005), 2:131. There exists an extensive collection of Evans papers at the University of Tulsa, but this material focuses primarily on his business dealings after Bureau service.

13. George Lang, Raymond L. Collins, and Gerard F. White, comps., *Medal of Honor Recipients 1863–1994*, 2 vols. (New York: Facts on File, Inc., 1995), 1:1087; Charles F. Rand File, Pension Record, Bureau of Veterans Affairs, National Archives and Records Administration, Washington, D.C., Record Group 15 (hereafter cited Pension Record); George A. Otis, ed., *Medical and Surgical History of the War of the Rebellion*, 12 vols. (Washington, D.C.: Government Printing Office, 1876): 10:529; *Washington Post*, October 13, 1907.

14. For occupation numbers in Texas, see *Ninth Census, Wealth and Industry*, 3:808–823. The percentage for those in the Union army listing farming as their occupation is in Wiley, *Billy Yank*, 304. All subsequent numbers and percentages for the state or country come from the *Ninth Census, Wealth and Industry* source unless specified otherwise. The exact percentage for the state is 70.4 percent.

15. Martin Abbott, *The Freedmen's Bureau in South Carolina, 1865–1872* (Chapel Hill: University of North Carolina Press, 1967), 23; Finley, *From Slavery to Uncertain Freedom*, 11; Cimbala, "On the Front Line of Freedom," 583–588; John Cornelius Engelsman, "The Freedmen's Bureau in Louisiana," *Louisiana Historical Quarterly* 32 (January 1949): 162.

16. J. B. Kiddoo to [O. O.] Howard, May 28, 1866, M752C, Letters Received, May–August 1866, reel 36 (hereafter LR); Charles Haughn, Waco, to C. S. Roberts, A.A.A.G, September 5, 1868, AC, LR, 1867–1868, reel 12; E. R. S. Canby to O. O. Howard, February 9, 1869, AC, LR, 1867–1869, reel 16; William Sinclair, Inspector, to C. S. Roberts, A.A.A.G, September 8, 1868, AC, LR, 1867–1869, reel 15; H. K. Taylor to William H.

Sinclair, Inspector, April 23, 1868, AC, LR, 1867–1869, reel 16; L. H. Sanger, Commanding Post of Livingston, to A. H. M. Taylor, A.A.A.G, August 5, 1867, AC, LR, 1866–1867,
reel 8.

17. John Cox and LaWanda Cox, "General O. O. Howard and the 'Misrepresented
Bureau,'" *Journal of Southern History* 19 (November 1953): 440–441; Carpenter, *Sword
and Olive Branch*, 100.

18. E. M. Wheelock to J. B. Kiddoo, September 23, 1866, Letters Received, 1866–
1867, AC, reel 9. John W. Sprague, assistant commissioner of Arkansas, also favored
those who served in all-black regiments (see Thomas S. Staples, *Reconstruction in
Arkansas, 1862–1874* [New York: Columbia University Press, 1923]).

19. J. Orville Shelby to [J. B.] Kiddoo, July 26, 1866, AC, LR, 1866–1867, reel 8; A.
Willis to J. J. Reynolds, May 8, 1868, AC, LR, 1867–1869, reel 16; J. B. Kiddoo to O. O.
Howard, August 8, 1866, AC, Letters Sent, September 1865–March 1867, reel 1 (hereaf-
ter LS); Circular letter from O. O. Howard, December 22, 1865, AC, Unregistered Let-
ters Received, 1865–1866, reel 17 (hereafter ULR); Olds, "Freedmen's Bureau as a Social
Agency," 120.

20. Texas agents awarded the Congressional Medal of Honor are Ira Hobart Evans,
Charles F. Rand, William Rufus Shafter, and Hiram Seymour Hall.

21. Lang, et al., comps., Medal of Honor Recipients, 1863–1894 , 1:198; Tyler, ed.,
New Handbook of Texas, 1:987–988; *New York Times*, November 13, 1906; Paul H. Carl-
son, "Pecos Bill": A Military Biography of William R. Shafter (College Station: Texas
A&M University Press, 1989), 160–188; Charles D. Rhodes, "William Rufus Shafter,"
Michigan History Magazine 16 (Fall 1932): 375–377; Tyler, ed., *New Handbook of Texas*,
1:556–557; Joseph Jones Reynolds File, Pension Record; Ezra J. Warner, *Generals in
Blue: Lives of the Union Commanders* (Baton Rouge: Louisiana State University Press,
1964), 397–398. Another notable Bureau agent was Ranald S. Mackenzie (see Ernest
Wallace, *Ranald S. Mackenzie on the Texas Frontier* [College Station: Texas A&M University Press, 1993], 60–168; Charles M. Robinson, III, *Bad Hand: A Biography of General Ranald S. Mackenzie* [Austin: State House Press, 1993], 323–329; Michael D. Pierce,
The Most Promising Young Officer: A Life of Ranald Slidell Mackenzie [Norman: University of Oklahoma Press, 1993], 223–233; and Warner, *Generals in Blue*, 302–303). For
criticisms of Shafter during the Spanish-American War, see Warren Zimmerman, *First
Great Triumph: How Five Americans Made Their Country a World Power* (New York:
Farrar, Straus, and Giroux, 2002).

22. Portrait and biographical album of Washtenaw County, Michigan, contains
biographical sketches of prominent and representative citizens, together with biogra-
phies of all the governors of the state, and of the presidents of the United States (Chicago: Biographical Publishing Company, 1891), 525–527; Gregory Barrett File, Pension
Record; Tyler, ed., *New Handbook of Texas*, 2:565–566; Austin American Statesman,
March 4, 1954; Houston Post, November 24, 1968.

23. Hiram Seymour Hall File, Pension Record; Barry Crouch, "The Freedmen's
Bureau in Beaumont," *Texas Gulf Historical and Biographical Record* (Part One) 28
(1992): 11; William H. Horton File, Pension Record; Frank Holsinger File, Pension
Record; Ninth Census of the United States, 1870, Schedule I (Inhabitants), National

Archives and Records Administration, Washington, D.C. (hereafter cited Ninth
Census).

24. J. B. Kiddoo to [O. O.] Howard, May 28, 1866, M752C, LR, May–August 1866,
reel 36; United States Bureau of the Census, *The Statistics of Wealth and Industry . . .
Compiled from the Original Returns of the Ninth Census,* 4 vols. (Washington, D.C.:
Government Printing Office, 1872), 3:812 (hereafter cited *Ninth Census,* and specific
volume title); Lowe, "Freedmen's Bureau and Local White Leaders in Virginia," 461,
464; Cimbala, *Under the Guardianship of the Nation,* 256; J. B. Kiddoo to O. O. Howard, May 14, 1866, AC, LS, September 1865–March 1867, reel 1.

25. The agents' ages, as shown in Figure 1–4, are from various sources, with most
found in one of the U.S. Census.

26. Wiley, *Billy Yank,* 303. The breakdown of the 154 men whose age could be determined is as follows: 40 in their 20s; 67 in their 30s; 30 in their 40s; 11 in their 50s; and 6
more than 60 or older.

27. Lowe, "Freedmen's Bureau and Local White Leaders in Virginia," 463.

28. This bracket, $1,000 to $4,999 was taken from Randolph B. Campbell and
Richard G. Lowe, *Wealth and Power in Antebellum Texas* (College Station: Texas
A&M University Press, 1977), chapter 3. The amount of wealth between $1,000 and
$4,999 is a good indicator of the middle class. Campbell and Lowe found that a plu-
rality (35.1 percent) of white Texans had a total wealth within this bracket. With that
many people, it can be claimed, they were the middle class in mid-nineteenth-century
Texas (see Campbell and Lowe, *Wealth and Power,* 46).

29. The total wealth in this study came by using the total assessed wealth from
the country (14,178,986,732) divided by white heads-of-households (6,621,957). Black
men and women household heads were not included, because their total wealth was
inconsequential. According to his study of Harrison County, Randolph B. Campbell
found the average black head-of-household to possess only $29 in total wealth. In
1870 there were 956,096 black heads-of-households. Using Campbell's total for black
heads-of-households' total wealth ($29) multiplied by the number of black heads-of-
households in the country in 1870 (956,096) equals $27,726,784 in total wealth. It
would not be a stretch to conclude the total wealth of black household heads approximated this number. When this number is divided by 6,621,957 (white heads-of-
households only) it equals a little more than $4 per head. As a result, the average
black head-of-household's wealth was not excised from the total wealth in the
United States for it would have changed the overall average very little (see Ninth
Census, *Statistics of Wealth and Industry,* 3:10; Randolph B. Campbell, *A Southern
Community in Crisis: Harrison County, Texas, 1850–1880* [Austin: Texas State Histor-
ical Association, 1983], 301; and Susan B. Carter, et al., *Historical Statistics of the
United States: Earliest Times to the Present,* 6 vols. [New York: Cambridge University
Press, 2006], 1:679–681).

30. Ninth Census, *Statistics of Wealth and Industry,* 3:10; Carter, et al., *Historical
Statistics,* 1:680.

31. Lee Soltow, *Men and Wealth in the United States, 1850–1870* (New Haven: Yale
University Press, 1975), 23–24, 33.

32. Cimbala does not specifically state the average wealth (personal and real estate) of the 71 agents he found in Georgia's tax records. Nor does he list their specific taxable property. Instead, he simply states those above a specified amount. For example, 15 agents had taxable property worth $1,000 to $4,999. The average for Georgia's agents is approximate, but still greatly exceeds the average wealth held by those agents in Texas (See Cimbala, *Guardianship of a Nation*, 256).

33. Lowe, "Freedmen's Bureau and Local White Leaders in Virginia," 460, 458; Cimbala, *Under the Guardianship of the Nation*, 256. For works showing the generally greater wealth of officeholders, see Randolph B. Campbell and Richard G. Lowe, "Wealthholding and Political Power in Antebellum Texas," *Southwestern Historical Texas* 75 (July 1978): 21–30; and Lee Soltow, *Patterns in Wealthholding in Wisconsin Since 1850* (Madison: University of Wisconsin Press, 1971).

34. A. P. Ketchum, A.A.A.G., to J. B. Kiddoo, October 5, 1866, AC, LR, 1866–1867, reel 6.

35. Examples of "scalawag" Bureau agents being persecuted during the war for their Union beliefs are Johnathan T. Whiteside, Courtney, to E. M. Gregory, December 1, 1865, AC, ULR, 1865–1866, reel 17; John H. Morrison to [E. M.] Gregory, [Spring 1866], AC, LR, 1866–1867, reel 7; and Henry C. Pedigo to [E. M.] Gregory, January 27, 1866, AC, ULR, 1865–1866, reel 17.

36. Eli W. Green, Columbus, to Chauncey C. Morse, A.A.A.G., October 24, 1865, AC, ULR, 1865–1866, reel 17; A. H. Mayer, Liberty, to J. P. Richardson, A.A.A.G., February 18, 1868, AC, LR, 1867–1869, reel 13; George C. Abbott, Hempstead, to [E. M.] Gregory, October 31, 1865, AC, ULR, 1865–1866, reel 17; A. H. Mayer, Liberty, to William Garretson, A.A.A.G., September 25, 1867, AC, LR, 1867–1869, reel 13.

37. George C. Abbott, Hempstead, to [E. M.] Gregory, October 31, 1865, AC, ULR, 1865–1866, reel 17; George C. Abbott, Hempstead, to E. M. Gregory, November 23, 1865, AC, ULR, 1865–1866, reel 17; William H. Farner to [E. M.] Gregory, November 25, 1865, AC, ULR, 1865–1866, reel 17; Albert Evans, Sherman, to J. T. Kirkman, A.A.A.G., February 17, 1867, AC, LR, 1866–1867, reel 5.

38. Philip Howard, Meridian, to E. M. Gregory, March 22, 1866, AC, LR, 1866–1867, reel 6; Philip Howard, Meridian, to [E. M.] Gregory, April 30, 1866, AC, LR, 1866–1867, reel 6; Henry C. Pedigo to [E. M.] Gregory, January 25, 1866, AC, ULR, 1865–1866, reel 17.

39. William H. Sinclair, Inspector, to J. T. Kirkman, A.A.A.G., March 19, 1867, AC, LR, 1866–1867, reel 8; John H. Morrison to [E. M.] Gregory, [Spring 1866], AC, LR, 1866–1867, reel 7; L. S. Barnes, Crockett, to William H. Sinclair, A.A.G., July 9, 1866, LR, 1866–1867, reel 4; Special Orders No. 96, July 28, 1866, AC, IRB, October 1865–April 1869, reel 19; Thomas J. Mortimer to J. B. Kiddoo, January, 1867, AC, LR, 1866–1867, reel 7.

40. J. R. S. Van Vleet to [E. M.] Gregory, March 12, 1866, AC, ULR, 1865–1866, reel 17; William D. Price to [E. M.] Gregory, February 22, 1866, AC, LR, 1866–1867, reel 7; Tyler, ed., *New Handbook of Texas*, 2:196–197. For information on Edwin Miller Wheelock, who was a Unitarian minister and was moved to join the Union with the issuance of the Emancipation Proclamation, see Charles Kassel, "Edwin Miller Wheelock," *The Open Court* 34 (September 1920): 564–569; Charles Kassel, "Edwin Miller Wheelock: A

Prophet of Civil War Times," *The Open Court* 36 (February 1922): 116–124; and Edwin Miller Wheelock, Vertical File, Center for America History, University of Texas at Austin, Austin, Texas.

41. W. A. Howard to O. O. Howard, April 25, 1866, AC, LR, 1866–1867, reel 6; Henry C. Pedigo to [E. M.] Gregory, January 27, 1866, AC, ULR, 1865–1866, reel 17; Tyler, ed., *New Handbook of Texas*, 2:657.

42. Edward Miller, Millican, to Brvt. Maj. Gen. L. Thomas, Adjutant General, June 23, 1867, AC, LR, 1866–1867, reel 7; William H. Horton, Bastrop, to J. P. Richardson, A.A.A.G., April 25, 1868, AC, LR, 1867–1869, reel 12.

43. Michael Butler to J. P. Richardson, A.A.A.G., April 20, 1868, AC, LR, 1867–1868, reel 16; George Eber to C. S. Roberts, A.A.Q.M., March 7, 1868, AC, LR, 1867–1869, reel 11; Robert McClermont to J. B. Kiddoo, August 30, 1866, AC, LR, 1866–1867, reel 7; Charles Schmidt to J. J. Reynolds, March 12, 1868, AC, LR, 1867–1869, reel 15; C. S. Roberts, Austin, to O. O. Howard, September 19, 1868, AC, LR, 1867–1869, reel 12.

44. Eugene Smith, Indianola, to Chauncey C. Morse, A.A.A.G., January 1, 1866, AC, ULR, 1865–1866, reel 17.

45. William Longworth, Sutherland Springs, to [E. M. Gregory], January 15, 1866, ULR, 1865–1866, reel 17; William H. Sinclair, Galveston, to Henry A. Ellis, A.A.A.G., October 7, 1866, AC, LR, 1866–1867, reel 5; William Longworth, Sutherland Springs, to J. B. Kiddoo, November 12, 1866, AC, LR, 1866–1867, reel 6.

46. William Longworth, Sutherland Springs, to [E. M. Gregory], March 9, 1866, AC, LR, 1866–1867, reel 6; William H. Sinclair, Galveston, to Henry A. Ellis, A.A.A.G., October 7, 1866, AC, LR, 1866–1867, reel 5; William Longworth to [E. M.] Gregory, October 28, 1865, AC, ULR, 1865–1866, reel 17.

47. John H. Morrison, Palestine, to [J. B. Kiddoo], June 7, 1866, AC, LR, 1865–1866, reel 7; John H. Morrison to [E. M.] Gregory, [Spring 1866], AC, LR, 1866–1867, reel 6; Mahlon E. Davis to William H. Sinclair, A.A.G., September 4, 1866, AC, LR, 1866–1867, reel 5; David S. Beath to J. J. Reynolds, July 9, 1868, AC, LR, 1867–1869, reel 16.

48. Patrick F. Duggan to J. T. Kirkman, May 29, 1867, LR, 1866–1867, reel 5; George Johnson to Charles A. Vernou, A.A.A.G., August 4, 1868, AC, LR, 1867–1869, reel 16; J. J. Reynolds to O. O. Howard, August 30, 1868, AC, LR, 1867–1869; Brvt. Maj. W. Harper, Jr., to C. S. Roberts, A.A.G.M., August 21, 1868, AC, LR, 1867–1869, reel 16; N. H. Randlett, Palestine, to C. S. Roberts, A.A.A.G., December 30, 1867, AC, LR, 1867–1869, reel 14.

49. Philip Howard, Meridian, to E. M. Gregory, March 22, 1866, AC, LR, 1866–1867, reel 6; A. H. M. Taylor to General, August 29, 1867, AC, LR, 1867–1869, reel 16; A. H. M. Taylor, A.A.A.G., to O. O. Howard, August 29, 1867, AC, LR, 1867–1869, reel 16; A. F. N. Rolfe to J. J. Reynolds, November 13, 1867, AC, LR, 1866–1867, reel 7; Edwin Finch to Gen. Charles Griffin, June 20, 1867, AC, LR, 1867–1869, reel 11; Albert Evans, Sherman, to J. T. Kirkman, A.A.G., February 17, 1867, LR, 1866–1867, reel 5.

50. James Burke to O. O. Howard, May 1, 1868, AC, LR, 1867–1869, reel 10; James Burke to Charles A. Venou, A.A.A.G., May 29, 1868, AC, LR, 1867–1869, reel 10; James Burke to J. J. Reynolds, June 2, 1868, AC, LR, 1867–1869, reel 10; Lowe, "Freedmen's Bureau and Local White Leaders in Virginia," 465–472; Lawrence Powell, "The Politics of Livelihood: Carpetbaggers in the Deep South," in *Region, Race, and Reconstruction:*

Essays in Honor of C. Vann Woodward, ed. J. Morgan Kousser and James S. McPherson (New York: Oxford University Press, 1982): 315–347.

51. William H. Heistand, Hallettsville, to A. H. Lathrop, A.A.A.G., December 31, 1866, SAC, LS, May–June 1866 and October 1866–March 1868, reel 21; John T. Scott, Victoria, to Captain, January 18, 1866, AC, ULR, 1865–1866, reel 17; Patrick F. Duggan, Columbia, to Mr. Ship, September 25, 1867, SAC, LSR, April 1867–November 1868, reel 15.

2. "The Post of Greatest Peril": The E. M. Gregory Era, September 1865–April 1866

1. W. E. B. DuBois, "The Freedmen's Bureau," *Atlantic Monthly* 87 (March 1901): 254; Statutes at Large, Treaties, and Proclamations of the United States of America from December, 1863 to December 1865, 119 vols. (Boston: Little, Brown and Company, 1866), 13:507–509 (hereafter cited as Statutes at Large).

2. Carpenter, *Sword and Olive Branch*, 91; Howard, *Autobiography*, 2:216, 208; Warner, *Generals in Blue*, 237–239.

3. There is dispute about Gregory's age. One source has him 61, another aged 69 in 1865 and still another 63 (see *Philadelphia Inquirer*, November 8, 1871; Eighth Census of the United States, 1860, Schedule I [Inhabitants], National Archives and Records Administration, Washington, D.C.; and Seventh Census of the United States, 1850, Schedule I [Inhabitants], National Archives and Records Administration, Washington, D.C.).

4. Augustus Buell, *The Cannoneer: Recollections of Service in the Army of the Potomac* (Washington, D.C.: The National Tribune, 1890), 320–321; Howard, *Autobiography*, 2:218; Charles F. McKenna, comp., *Under the Maltese Cross, Antietam to Appomattox: The Loyal Uprising in Western Pennsylvania, 1861–1865* (Pittsburgh: The 155th Regimental Association, 1910), 220; Tyler, ed., *New Handbook of Texas*, 3:330–331; *Flake's Daily Bulletin*, July 1, 1866; *New York Times*, November 8, 1871; *Philadelphia Inquirer*, February 5 and November 8, 1862; *The Sandusky Clarion* (OH), December 28, 1844; Mark M. Boatner, III, *The Civil War Dictionary* (New York: David McKay Company, Inc., 1959), 358. McFeely calls Gregory a "radical Abolitionist." Richter considers him a "committed abolitionist." Crouch, however, doubts Gregory's abolitionism. Nor did Commissioner Howard ever mention his subordinate being an abolitionist (see McFeely, *Yankee Stepfather*, 68; Richter, *Overreached on All Sides*, 7; Crouch, *Freedmen's Bureau and Black Texans*, 15; and Howard, *Autobiography*, 2:217–218).

5. Letter of Advice to Assistant Commissioners from O. O. Howard, June 14, 1865, LS, May 16–December 30, 1865, Selected Series of Records Issued by the Commissioner of the Bureau of Refugees, Freedmen, and Abandoned Lands 1865–1872, Record Group 105, National Archives and Records Administration, Washington, D.C. (Microfilm M742, reel 1), hereafter cited M742C; E. M. Gregory to O. O. Howard, September 21, 1865, AC, LS, September 1865–March 1867, reel 1; O. O. Howard to Bvt. Gen. Gordon Granger, July 17, 1865, M742, LS, May 16–December 1865, reel 1; Bvt. Maj. Gen. Christopher Columbus Andrews, "Speech at Brenham, Texas, July 20, 1865," in *Early Steps in Reconstruction: Speeches by General C. C. Andrews of Minnesota in Texas and Arkan-*

sas (Washington, D.C.: Union Republican Congressional Committee, 1865): 2–3; F. W. Emery, A.A.G, District of Texas, to Col. John Kelly, June 28, 1865, *The War of the Rebellion: The Official Records of the Union and Confederate Armies*, 128 vols. (Washington, D.C.: Government Printing Office, Office, 1889–1903), series 1, vol. 48, pt. 2, pp. 1017–1018. For initial trips into Texas, see E. M. Gregory to O. O. Howard, September 21, October 31, and December 9, 1865, and January 31, 1866, AC, LS, September 1865–March 1867, reel 1; Allan Ashcraft, "Texas, 1860–1866: The Lone Star State in the Civil War" (Ph.D. diss., Columbia University, 1960), 255–259; Brad R. Clampitt, "The Breakup: The Collapse of the Confederate Trans-Mississippi Army in Texas , 1865," *Southwestern Historical Quarterly* 108 (April 2005): 499–536; Thomas North, *Five Years in Texas* (Cincinnati: Elm Street Publishing Company, 1871), 183–184; and Charles W. Ramsdell, "Texas from the Fall of the Confederacy to the Beginning of Reconstruction," *Quarterly of the Texas State Historical Association* 11 (July 1907–April 1908): 199–219.

6. Olds, "Freedmen's Bureau as a Social Agency," 120, 246. For E. M. Gregory's requests for particular officers and returns, see E. M. Gregory to C. H. Whittelsey, A.A.G. for October through December 1865 in AC reel 17. Military problems experienced transitioning to peace are in Clayton R. Newell and Charles R. Shrader, "The U.S. Army's Transition to Peace, 1865–1866," *The Journal of Military History* 77 (July 2012): 867–894.

7. William E. Strong, Inspector, to O. O. Howard, January 1, 1866, *House Executive Documents*, 39th Congress, 1st Session, No. 70, 313; E. M. Gregory to O. O. Howard, September 21, 1865, AC, Letters Sent, September 1865–March 1867, reel 1; Richter, *Overreached on All Sides*, 37. Hiram Seymour Hall, Jacob C. DeGress, and John Scott made their posts at Marshall, Galveston, and Victoria, respectively. Others had assignments at the main hubs for shipments of crops to market from the interior, such as George C. Abbott at Hempstead, William H. Farner at Millican, Ira P. Pedigo at Woodville (Tyler County), and F. D. Inge in Leon County. Oliver H. Swingley went to Austin, the state capital. The remainder received appointments to regions with large black populations: B. J. Arnold at Brenham, John T. Raper at Columbus, John F. Brown at Grimes, and Johnathan T. Whiteside at Courtney (Grimes County) all fit this description.

8. Circular No. 2, December 5, 1865, AC, IRB, October 1865–April 1869, reel 19; O. O. Howard to E. M. Gregory, September 6, 1865, AC, Unregistered Letters Received, 1865–1866, reel 17; Carpenter, "Agents of the Freedmen's Bureau," 15. All occupations came from the Manuscript Ninth Census and slave-owning status in the Manuscript Eighth Census of the United States, 1860, Schedule II (Slave Population), Record Group 29, National Archives and Records Administration, Washington, D.C. (Microcopy No. 653).

9. James Speed, Attorney General, to E. M. Stanton, Secretary of War, June 22, 1865, AC, ULR, 1865–1866, reel 17; Circular No. 1, October 12, 1865, AC, IRB, October 1865–April 1869, reel 19; Endorsement of letters by Samuel C. Sloan, Brenham, to William H. Sinclair, A.A.G., May 26, 1866, AC, ES, April 1866–September 1867, reel 2; O. O. Howard to E. M. Gregory, November 3, 1865, M742C, LS, May 16–December 30, 1865, reel 1; Crouch, *Freedmen's Bureau and Black Texans*, 15; Paul Moreno, "Racial Classifications and Reconstruction Legislation," *Journal of Southern History* 61 (May

1995): 271–304; Herman Belz, *A New Birth of Freedom: The Republican Party and Freedmen's Rights, 1861 to 1866* (New York: Fordham University Press, 2000), 92–112; Herman Belz, "The Freedmen's Bureau Act of 1865 and the Principle of No Discrimination According to Color," *Civil War History* 21 (September 1975): 197–217; Circular No. 22, December 22, 1865, AC, ULR, 1865–1866, reel 17.

10. Circular No. 11, July 12, 1865, TxAGO, Box 401–861, Folder 861–821.

11. Charles E. Culver, Cotton Gin, to J. T. Kirkman, [A.A.A.G], June 26, 1867, AC, LR, 1866–1867, reel 4; H. W. Allen, Hempstead, to William Sinclair, A.A.G., June 5, 1866, AC, LR, 1866–1867, reel 4; Endorsement of letter from H. W. Allen, Hempstead, to William H. Sinclair, A.A.G., June 7, 1866, AC, ES, April 1866–September 1867, reel 2; Christopher B. Bean, "Freedmen's Bureau and Logistical Problems in Texas, 1865–1868," *Military History of the West* 39 (2009): 5. For other examples of conflicts, see William H. Sinclair, Inspector, Galveston, to Henry A. Ellis, A.A.A.G., November 30, 1866, AC, ULR, 1865–1866, reel 17; Gregory Barrett, Tyler, to Charles A. Vernou, A.A.A.G, June 24, 1868, AC, LR, 1867–1869, reel 10; L. J. Warner, Inspector, to Henry A. Ellis, A.A.A.G., December 6, 1866, AC, LR, 1866–1867, reel 9; Samuel A. Craig, "Memoirs of Civil War and Reconstruction," *Civil War Times Illustrated Collection of Civil War Papers*, U.S. Army Military History Institute, Carlisle Barracks, Pennsylvania, p. 79; and Johnathan M. Wiener, *Social Origins of the New South: Alabama, 1865–1885* (Baton Rouge: Louisiana State University Press, 1978), 55–56.

12. P. B. Johnson, Woodville, to J. T. Kirkman, A.A.A.G., June 1, 1867, AC, LR, 1866–1867, reel 6; Samuel I. Wright, A.Q.M, to General, December 12, 1865, Press Copies of Letters Sent, December 1865–October 1866, Records of the Field Offices for the State of Texas, Bureau of Refugees, Freedmen, and Abandoned Lands, 1865–1870, Record Group 105, National Archives and Records Administration, Washington, D.C. (Microfilm M1912, reel 1) hereafter cited SAC; William Longworth, Sutherland Springs, to Captain, January 29, 1866, AC, Unregistered Letters Received, 1865–1866, reel 17. For other cases of logistical problems, see George C. Abbott, Hempstead, to Chauncey C. Morse, A.A.A.G., November 2, 1865, AC, ULR, 1865–1866, reel 17; Charles P. Russell, Gonzales, to Colonel, July 24, 1866, AC, LR, 1866–1867, reel 7; John T. Raper, Columbus, to E. M. Gregory, November 29, 1865, Unregistered Letters Received, 1865–1866, reel 17; B. J. Arnold, Brenham to Chauncey C. Morse, A.A.A.G., December 2, 1865, AC, ULR, 1865–1866, reel 17; Johnathan T. Whiteside, Courtney, to [E. M. Gregory], December 8, 1865, AC, ULR, 1865–1866, reel 17. For similar problems procuring supplies from the military, see J. Thomas May, "A 19th Century Medical Care Program for Blacks: The Case of the Freedmen's Bureau," *Anthropological Quarterly* 46 (July 1973): 160–171.

13. Edward Miller, Bryan, to J. P. Richardson, A.A.A.G., November 27, 1867, AC, LR, 1867–1869, reel 13; John Dix, Corpus Christi, to J. J. Reynolds, December 5, 1867, AC, LR, 1866–1867, reel 5. Agents spending their own money, see Edward Miller, Bryan, November 27, 1867, AC, LR, 1867–1869, reel 13; William Longworth, Sutherland Springs, to [E. M. Gregory], March 17, 1866, AC, LR, 1866–1867, reel 6; P. B. Johnson, Woodville, to J. T. Kirkman, A.A.A.G., June 7, 1867, AC, LR, 1866–1867, reel 6; Charles C. Culver, Cotton Gin, to J. T. Kirkman, A.A.A.G., August 10, 1867, Records of the Superintendent of Education for the State of Texas, Bureau of Refugees, Freedmen, and

Abandoned Lands, 1865–1870, Letters Received, 1866–1867, National Archives and Records Administration, Washington, D.C., M822, reel 3 (hereafter cited SUP); and William H. Howard, Huntsville, to J. J. Reynolds, September 21, 1868, AC, LR, 1867–1869, reel 12.

14. Samuel I. Wright, A.Q.M., to William Longworth, Sutherland Springs May 10, 1866, SAC, PCLS, December 1865–October 1866, reel 1; Charles Garretson, A.A.Q.M., to William G. Kirkman, Boston, August 24, 1867, SAC, RLS, July 1867–September 1868, reel 13; Charles Garretson, A.A.Q.M., to A. H. Mayer, Liberty, June 8, 1867, SAC, PCLS, reel 1; Charles Garretson, A.A.A.G, A.A.Q.M, to Hamilton C. Peterson, Lockhart, September 25, 1867, SAC, PCLS, July 1867–October 1867, reel 2; Bureau of Refugees, Freedmen, and Abandoned Lands, *Officers' Manual* (Washington, D.C.: Government Printing Office, 1866), 28-E–28-F (hereafter cited *Officers' Manual*).

15. William H. Sinclair, Inspector, to J. T. Kirkman, A.A.A.G., March 1, 1867, AC, LR, 1866–1867, reel 8; Endorsement of letter from David L. Montgomery, Tyler, to Charles Garretson, A.A.A.G., August 26, 1867, AC, ES, March 1867–May 1869, reel 2.

16. David L. Montgomery, Tyler, to Charles Garretson, A.A.A.G.,A.A.Q.M., October 9, 1867, AC, ULR, 1867–1869 and Undated, reel 18; Charles Garretson, A.A.A.G.,A.A.Q.M., to J. J. Reynolds, October 23, 1867, AC, ULR, 1867–1869 and Undated, reel 18; Charles Garretson, A.A.A.G, A.A.Q.M., to J. J. Reynolds, October 23, 1867, AC, LS, March 1867–May 1869, reel 1.

17. Hahn, et al., eds., *Freedom: A Documentary History of Emancipation*, 1861–1867, 397; John T. Raper, Columbus, to E. M. Gregory, November 29, 1865, AC, ULR, 1865–1866, reel 17; Thomas Wagstaff, "Call Your Old Master–'Master': Southern Political Leaders and Negro Labor During Presidential Reconstruction," *Labor History* 10 (Summer 1969): 344; Circular letter from O. O. Howard, November 11, 1865, AC, ULR, 1865–1866, reel 17; A. H. Mayer, Liberty, to J. P. Richardson, A.A.A.G., February 18, 1868, AC, LR, 1867–1869, reel 13; Circular No. 13, July 28, 1865, AC, LR, 1865–1866, reel 5; Martin Abbott, "Free Land, Free Labor, and the Freedmen's Bureau," *Agricultural History* 30 (October 1956): 1–8; Circular No. 1, 1 October 12, 1865, AC, IRB, October 1865–April 1869, reel 19. For problems in Texas immediately following the war, see Jacob C. DeGress, Houston, to [Headquarters], December 1, 1865, AC, ULR, 1865–1866, reel 17; James Oakes, Austin, to J. T. Kirkman, A.A.A.G., July 31, 1867, Barry Crouch Collection, Victoria Regional History Center, Victoria College, Victoria, Texas, Box 8-A (hereafter cited as Crouch Collection–Victoria); S. J. W. Mintzer, Surgeon in Chief, to [E. M. Gregory], December 1, 1865, AC, Received and Retained Reports Relating to Rations, Lands, and Bureau Personnel, 1865–1866, reel 29 (hereafter RRR); 1st Lt. Hugh D. Bowker to Provost Marshal, 3rd District, Corpus Christi, December 6, 1865, AC, ULR, 1865–1866, reel 17; and Ronnie Tyler and Lawrence R. Murphy, eds., *The Slave Narratives of Texas* (Austin: The Encino Press, 1974), 115, 121, 123.

18. *La Grange True Issue*, June 17, 1865; C. B. Stewart to A. J. Hamilton, November 17, 1865, Incoming Correspondence, Governor Andrew Jackson Hamilton Records (RG 301), Archives Division–Texas State Library and Archives Commission (hereafter cited Governor Correspondences); [Citizens of Jackson County] to A. J. Hamilton, November 1865, Hamilton Governor Correspondences; J. O. Thally to A. J. Hamilton, November 6, 1865, Hamilton Governor Correspondences; Sallie M. Lentz, "Highlights of

Early Harrison County," *Southwestern Historical Quarterly* 61 (October 1957): 254;
F. W. Grassmeyer to A. J. Hamilton, November 22 1865, Hamilton Governor Correspondences; J. W. Throckmorton to [J. B.] Kiddoo, November 13, 1866, AC, LR, 1866–
1867, reel 9. For examinations of the Christmas scare, see Steven Hahn, "'Extravagant
Expectations of Freedom': Rumor, Political Struggle, and the Christmas Insurrection
Scare of 1865 in the American South," *Past and Present* 157 (November 1997): 122–158;
and Dan T. Carter, "The Anatomy of Fear: The Christmas Day Insurrection Scare of
1865," *Journal of Southern History* 42 (August 1976): 345–364.

19. Jeffrey R. Kerr-Ritchie, *Freedpeople in the Tobacco South: Virginia, 1860–1900*
(Chapel Hill: University of North Carolina Press, 1999), 37. For works on free labor ideology, see Eric Foner, *Free Soil, Free Labor, Free Men: The Ideology of the Republican
Party Before the Civil War* (New York: Oxford University Press, 1970); Eric Foner, *Poli-
tics and Ideology in the Age of the Civil War* (New York: Oxford University Press, 1980);
Lawrence N. Powell, "The American Land Company and Agency: John A. Andrew and
the Northernization of the South," *Civil War History* 21 (December 1975): 293–308; Bar-
bara J. Fields and Leslie S. Rowland, "Free Labor Ideology and Its Exponents in the
South During the Civil War and Reconstruction" (paper delivered at Organization of
American Historians Annual Meeting, 1984); Heather C. Richardson, *The Death of
Reconstruction: Race, Labor, and Politics in the Post–Civil War North, 1865–1901* (Cam-
bridge: Harvard University Press, 2001); Ira Berlin, et al,, eds., *The Wartime Genesis of
Free Labor: The Lower South* (Cambridge: Oxford University Press, 1990); Gerald D.
Jaynes, *Branches without Roots: Genesis of the Black Working Class in the American
South, 1862–1882* (New York: Oxford University Press, 1986); Barbara J. Fields, *Slavery
and Freedom on the Middle Ground: Maryland During the Nineteenth Century* (New
Haven: Yale University Press, 1985); Joseph P. Reidy, *From Slavery to Agrarian Capital-
ism in the Cotton Plantation South: Central Georgia, 1800–1880* (Chapel Hill: University
of North Carolina Press, 1992); and Nancy Cohen-Lack, "A Struggle for Sovereignty:
National Consolidation, Emancipation, and Free Labor in Texas, 1865," *Journal of
Southern History* 58 (February 1992): 57–98.

20. Howard, *Autobiography*, 2:212–225, 247; William Cohen, "Black Immobility
and Free Labor: The Freedmen's Bureau and the Relocation of Black Labor, 1865–1868,"
Civil War History 30 (September 1984): 234; James C. Devine, Inspector, to J. T. Kirkman, A.A.A.G., July 22, 1867, AC, LR, 1866–1867, reel 5; *Dallas Herald*, November 17,
1866. For precedents during the war, see J. Thomas May, "Continuity and Change in
the Labor Program of the Union Army and the Freedmen's Bureau," *Civil War History*
17 (September 1971): 245–254; and Willie Lee Rose, *Rehearsal for Reconstruction: The
Port Royal Experiment* (Indianapolis: Bobbs-Merrill, 1964).

21. E. M. Gregory to Benjamin G. Harris, January 20, 1866, SAC, LS, October 1865–
March 1867, reel 1; Circular letter from E. M. Gregory, October 17, 1865, AC, LS, Sep-
tember 1865–March 1867, reel 1; E. M. Gregory to O. O. Howard, April 18, 1866, AC, LS,
September 1865–March 1867, reel 1; Roger L. Ransom and Richard Sutch, *One Kind of
Freedom: The Economic Consequences of Emancipation* (Cambridge: Cambridge Uni-
versity Press, 2001), 15; Cohen-Lack, "A Struggle for Sovereignty," 61, 97–98; James M.
Smallwood, *Time of Hope, Time of Despair: Black Texans During Reconstruction* (Port
Washington: Kennikat Press, 1981), 44; Robert Higgs, *Competition and Coercion:*

Blacks in the American Economy, 1865–1914 (Cambridge: Cambridge University Press, 1977), 80–100; Alwyn Barr, *Black Texans: A History of African Americans in Texas, 1528–1995* (Norman: University of Oklahoma Press, 1995), 54–55; Campbell, *Southern Community in Crisis*, 264. For paternalism and labor contract, see Laura F. Edwards, "The Problem of Dependency: African Americans, Labor Relations, and the Law in the Nineteenth-Century South," *Agricultural History* 72 (Spring 1998): 313–340; David S. Leventhal, "'Freedom to Work, Nothing More Nor Less': The Freedmen's Bureau, White Planters, and Black Contract Labor in Tennessee, 1865–1868," *Journal of East Tennessee* 78 (2006): 23–49; and Lee J. Alston and Joseph P. Ferrie, "Paternalism in Agricultural Labor Contracts in the U.S. South: Implications for the Growth of the Welfare State," *The American Economic Review* 83 (September 1993): 852–876.

22. Eugene Smith, Waco, to William H. Sinclair, A.A.G., May 1, 1866, AC, LR, 1866–1867, reel 8; [Speech by A. H. Mayer, December 26, 1866], AC, LR, 1866–1867, reel 7; William H. Sinclair, A.A.G., to John R. Sanford, February 17, 1866, AC, LS, September 1865–March 1867, reel 1; James L. Roark, *Masters Without Slaves: Southern Planters in the Civil War and Reconstruction* (New York: W. W. Norton & Company, 1977), 139; E. M. Gregory to O. O. Howard, October 31, 1865, AC, Letters Sent, September 1865–March 1867, reel 1.

23. William H. Sinclair, Inspector, J. T. Kirkman, A.A.A.G., February 26, 1867, AC, LR, 1866–1867, reel 8; Steven Hahn, et al., eds., *Freedom: A Documentary History of Emancipation, 1861–1867,* 309; Amy Dru Stanley, "Beggars Can't Be Choosers: Compulsion and Contract in Postbellum America," *Journal of American History* 78 (March 1992): 1283; [Speech by unknown agent], date unknown, AC, LR, 1866–1867, reel 1; Samuel C. Sloan, Richmond, to Chauncey C. Morse, A.A.A.G, January 16, 1866, AC, LR, 1866–1867, reel 8; Chauncey C. Morse, A.A.A.G, to Samuel C. Sloan, Richmond, January 22, 1866, AC, LS, September 1865–March 1867, reel 1.

24. Isaac Johnson, La Grange, to E. M. Gregory, March 10, 1866, AC, ULR, 1865–1866, reel 17; William H. Sinclair, Inspector, J. T. Kirkman, A.A.A.G., February 26, 1867, AC, LR, 1866–1867, reel 8; Edward Miller, Victoria, to William H. Sinclair, A.A.G., July 10, 1866, AC, LR, 1866–1867, reel 7; Cohen-Lack, "Struggle for Sovereignty," 79; Jacob C. DeGress, Houston, to E. M. Gregory, November 3, 1865, AC, RRR, 1865–1866, reel 29. For freedmen contracting, see Jacob C. DeGress, Houston, to [E. M] Gregory, November 1, 1865, AC, RRR, 1865–1866, reel 29; John T. Raper, Columbus, to E. M. Gregory, November 29, 1865, AC, ULR, 1865–1866, reel 17; George C. Abbott, Hempstead, to E. M. Gregory, December 16, 1865, AC, ULR, 1865–1866, reel 17; Eli W. Green, Columbus, to Chauncey C. Morse, A.A.A.G, October 24, 1865, AC, ULR, 1865–1866, reel 17; and Chauncey C. Morse, A.A.I.G., to William H. Sinclair, A.A.G, April 18, 1866, AC, LR, 1866–1867, reel 7. According to Randolph B. Campbell, approximately 5 to 6 percent left their former masters, the rest remained and worked (see *An Empire for Slavery: The Peculiar Institution in Texas, 1821–1865* [Baton Rouge: Louisiana State University Press, 1989], 250–251). Students note the ambiguities of contract labor. Of these, many castigate the contract: it precluded choice and economic freedom or pacified the workforce and reestablished the old system under "unreconstructed" former masters. For more positive—or at least contextualized—works on contracts, see Hahn, et al., eds., *Freedom: A Documentary History of Emancipation, 1861–1867,* chapter 3; Rebecca

Edwards, *Angels in the Machinery: Gender in American Party Politics from the Civil War to the Progressive Era* (New York: Oxford University Press, 1997); Amy Dru Stanley, *From Bondage to Contract: Wage Labor, Marriage, and the Market in the Age of Slave Emancipation* (New York: Cambridge University Press, 1998); and Charles H. Wesley, *Negro Labor in the United States, 1850–1925* (New York: Russell & Russell, 1967). For critical works on the contract, see Lewis Nicholas Wynne, *The Continuity of Cotton: Planter Politics in Georgia, 1865–1892* (Macon: Mercer University Press, 1986), 11–17; Lewis C. Chartock, "A History and Analysis of Labor Contracts Administered by the Bureau of Refugees, Freedmen, and Abandoned Lands in Edgefield, Abbeville and Anderson Counties, South Carolina, 1865–1868" (Ph.D. diss., Bryn Mawr College, 1974); and Steven Engerrand, "Now Scratch or Die: The Genesis of Capitalistic Agricultural Labor in Georgia, 1865–1880" (Ph.D. diss., University of Georgia, 1981). For concern about verbal contracts, see E. M. Gregory to O. O. Howard, December 9, 1865, AC, LS, September 1865–March 1867, reel 1; and S. J. W. Mintzer, Surgeon in Chief, to [E. M. Gregory], December 1, 1865, RRR, 1865–1866, reel 29. Northern racial beliefs are in David Roediger, *The Wages of Whiteness: Race and the Making of the American Working Class* (New York: Verso, 1991); Kenneth C. White, "Wager Swayne: Racist or Realist," *Alabama Review* 31 (April 1978): 92–109; and George M. Fredrickson, *The Black Image in the White Mind* (New York: Harper & Row, Publishers, 1971). To examine the different racial views of agents and white planters, see Thomas D. Morris, "Equality, 'Extraordinary,' and Criminal Justice: The South Carolina Experience, 1865–1866," *South Carolina Historical Magazine* 83 (January 1982): 31–32; William F. Messner, *Freedmen and the Ideology of Free Labor: Louisiana 1862–1865* (Lafayette: University of Southwestern Louisiana, 1978), 186; Frank V. Vandiver, "Some Problems Involved in Writing Confederate History," *Journal of Southern History* 36 (August 1970): 409; and Roberta Sue Anderson, "Presidential Reconstruction: Ideology and Change," in *The Facts of Reconstruction: Essays in Honor of John Hope Franklin*, ed. Eric Anderson and Alfred A. Ross, Jr. (Baton Rouge: Louisiana State University Press, 1991), 35. For the paradoxes and limitations of free labor and dissimilar visions of what freedom meant, see Eric Foner, "The Meaning of Freedom in the Age of Emancipation," *Journal of American History* 81 (September 1994): 454–460; James D. Schmidt, *Free to Work: Labor Law, Emancipation, and Reconstruction, 1815–1860* (Athens: University of Georgia Press, 1998); and Nancy Fraser and Linda Gordon, "A Genealogy of 'Dependency': Tracing a Keyword of the US Welfare State," *Signs* 19 (Winter 1994): 309–336. Contract resistance is in Ralph Shlomowitz, "The Transition from Slave to Freeman Labor Arrangements in Southern Agriculture, 1865–1870" (Ph.D. diss., University of Chicago, 1979), 31–35.

25. Chauncey C. Morse, A.A.I., to William H. Sinclair, Inspector, April 6, 1866, AC, LR, 1866–1867, reel 7; Philip Howard, Meridian, to E. M. Gregory, March 22, 1866, AC, LR, 1866–1867, reel 6; Joe M. Richardson, "An Evaluation of the Freedmen's Bureau in Florida," *Florida Historical Quarterly* 41 (January 1963): 227; Elizabeth Bethel, "The Freedmen's Bureau in Alabama," *Journal of Southern History* 24 (February 1948): 56; H. S. Johnson, Sumpter, to [Headquarters, 1867], AC, Letters Received, 1866–1867, reel 6.

26. Samuel C. Sloan, Richmond, to Chauncey C. Morse, A.A.A.G., February 28, 1866, AC, ULR, 1865–1866, reel 17; Mortimer H. Goddin, Livingston, to J. T. Kirkman,

A.A.A.G., July 20, 1867, AC, LR, 1866–1867, reel 5; Stanton Weaver to Sub Assistant Commissioner, Jefferson, April 5, 1867, AC, LR, 1866–1867, reel 9; Thomas Affleck to Charles Griffin, August 26, 1867, AC, LR, 1866–1867, reel 4; J. B. Kiddoo to [O. O. Howard], January 11, 1866, AC, LS, September 1865–March 1867, reel 1. Examples of compliant planters are Philip Howard, Meridian, to J. B. Kiddoo, September 19, 1866, AC, LR, 1866–1867, reel 6; William H. Sinclair, Inspector, to J. T. Kirkman, A.A.A.G., February 26, 1867, AC, LR, 1866–1867, reel 8; J. Bates to James F. Hutchison, Columbia, July 5, 1866, SAC, LR, January 1866–December 1868, reel 15; Aaron Coffee to James F. Hutchison, Columbia, September 2, 1866, SAC, LR, January 1866–December 1868, reel 15; and Charles Power to E. M. Gregory, October 1865, AC, ULR, 1865–1866, reel 17.

27. O. O. Howard to E. M. Gregory, November 3, 1866, M742C, LS, May 16–December 1865, reel 1; Chad Alan Goldberg, *Citizens and Paupers: Relief, Rights, and Race, from the Freedmen's Bureau to Workfare* (Chicago: University of Chicago Press, 2008), 40–41); S. J. W. Mintzer, Surgeon in Chief, to [E. M. Gregory], December 1, 1865, AC, RRR, 1865–1866, reel 29; William H. Sinclair, A.A.G., to F. D. Inge, Leona, March 27, 1866, AC, LS, September 1865–March 1867, reel 1; George C. Abbott, Hempstead, to E. M. Gregory, November 22, 1865, AC, ULR, 1865–1866, reel 17; Dan T. Carter, *When the War Was Over: The Failure of Self-Reconstruction in the South, 1865–1867* (Baton Rouge: Louisiana State University Press, 1985), 83; A. P. Delano, Marlin Falls, to Chauncey C. Morse, A.A.I.G., February 14, 1866, AC, LR, 1866–1867, reel 5. Planters noticing benefits of fair treatment, see W. H. Williams to E. M. Gregory, December 9, 1865, AC, ULR, 1865–1866, reel 17; P. H. Webster to [E. M.] Gregory, February 5, 1866, AC, ULR, 1865–1866, reel 17.

28. Stanton Weaver, Crockett, to Chauncey C. Morse, A.A.A.G., January 27, 1866, AC, ULR, 1865–1866, reel 17; William H. Sinclair, Inspector, to J. T. Kirkman, A.A.A.G., March 1, 1867, AC, LR, 1866–1867, reel 8; William H. Sinclair, Inspector, Galveston, to Henry A. Ellis, A.A.A.G., November 30, 1866, AC, ULR, 1865–1866, reel 17; William H. Rock, Richmond, to William H. Sinclair, A.A.G., August 9, 1866, AC, LR, 1866–1867, reel 7; George C. Abbott, Hempstead, to E. M. Gregory, December 16, 1865, AC, ULR, 1865–1866, reel 17; George C. Abbott, Hempstead, to E. M. Gregory, January 16, 1866, AC, ULR, 1865–1866, reel 17; Litwack, *Been in the Storm So Long*, 418.

29. Carpenter, "Agents of the Freedmen's Bureau," 27; William Longworth, Sutherland Springs, to Captain, January 15, 1866, AC, ULR, 1865–1866, reel 17; May, "Freedmen's Bureau at the Local Level," 17; Lynda J. Morgan, *Emancipation in Virginia Tobacco's Belt, 1850–1870* (Athens: University of Georgia Press, 1992), 134; Chauncey C. Morse, A.A.A.G., to Stanton Weaver, Crockett, January 15, 1866, AC, LR, 1865–1866, reel 1; Stanton Weaver, Crockett, to Chauncey C. Morse, A.A.A.G., January 17, 1866, AC, ULR, 1865–1866, reel 17; Stanton Weaver, Crockett, to Chauncey C. Morse, A.A.A.G., February 13, 1866, AC, ULR, 1865–1866, reel 17; Byron Porter, A.A.G., to John T. Scott, Victoria, December 9, 1865, AC, LR, 1865–1866, reel 1; B. J. Arnold, Brenham, to E. M. Gregory, October 30, 1865, AC, ULR, 1865–1866, reel 17; Joseph Ferguson, San Antonio, to William H. Sinclair, A.A.G., April 28, 1866, AC, LR, 1866–1867, reel 5; Byron Porter, Austin, to J. T. Kirkman, A.A.A.G., February 8, 1867, AC, Reports of Operations and Conditions, December 1866–May 1867, reel 20 (hereafter ROC); John T. Raper, Columbus, to E. M. Gregory, November 29, 1865, AC, ULR, 1865–1866, reel 17.

More examples are Eugene Smith, Indianola, to [E. M. Gregory], December 24, 1865, AC, ULR, 1865–1866, reel 17; Johnathan T. Whiteside, Courtney, to [E. M. Gregory], November 30, 1865, AC, ULR, 1865–1866, reel 17; Willis A. Bledsoe, Lancaster, to Charles A. Vernou, A.A.A.G., June 30, 1868, AC, ROC, May–July, 1868, reel 26; George C. Abbott, Hempstead, to E. M. Gregory, December 16, 1865, AC, ULR, 1865–1866, reel 17; and Hiram Seymour Hall, Marshall, to E. M. Gregory, December 9, 1865, AC, ULR, 1865–1866, reel 17.

30. Eli W. Green, Columbus, to Chauncey C. Morse, A.A.A.G., October 24, 1865, AC, LR, 1865–1866, reel 17; Byron Porter, Austin, to Henry A. Ellis, A.A.A.G., November 2, 1866, AC, LR, 1866–1867, reel 7; John T. Scott, Victoria, to [E. M. Gregory], November 12, 1865, AC, ULR, 1865–1866, reel 17; J. P. Richardson, A.A.A.G., to Albert Evans, Edinburgh, December 9, 1867, SAC, PCLS, October 1867–February 1868, reel 2. More instances of confusion are William Longworth, Sutherland Springs, to Captain, January 15, 1866, ULR, 1865–1866, reel 17; Philip Howard, Meridian, to E. M. Gregory, April 1, 1866, AC, LR, 1866–1867, reel 6; and John T. Raper, Columbus, to E. M. Gregory, November 29, 1865, AC, ULR, 1865–1866, reel 17. Agents hiring unauthorized help are Hiram Seymour Hall, Marshall, December 9, 1865, AC, ULR, 1865–1866, reel 17; Christopher B. Bean, "'A Most Singular and Interesting Attempt': The Freedmen's Bureau at Marshall, Texas," *Southwestern Historical Quarterly* 110 (April 2007): 468; John M. Barbour to Charles Griffin, February 2, 1867, AC, LR, 1866–1867, reel 4; Chauncey C. Morse, A.A.A.G, to Fred E. Miller, January 17, 1866, AC, LR, 1865–1866, reel 1; and Chauncey C. Morse, A.A.A.G., to William H. Farner, Millican, January 22, 1866, AC, LS, September 1865–March 1867, reel 1.

31. Johnathan T. Whiteside, Courtney, to [E. M. Gregory], December 8, 1865, AC, ULR, 1865–1866, reel 17; Johnathan T. Whiteside, Courtney, to [J. B. Kiddoo], April 24, 1866, AC, LR, 1866–1867, reel 9; William H. Sinclair, A.A.A.G., to Johnathan T. Whiteside, Courtney, April 28, 1866, AC, LS, September 1865–March 1867, reel 1; DeWitt C. Brown, Navasota, to [J. T. Kirkman, A.A.A.G.], March 7, 1867, AC, ROC, December 1866–May 1867, reel 20.

32. Chauncey C. Morse, A.A.I.G., to William H. Sinclair, A.I.G., April 6, 1866, AC, LR, 1866–1867, reel 7; Richter, *Overreached on All Sides*, 52, 49–54. Numbers came from the Roster of Officers and Civilians from January 1866 through March 1866 and Special Orders. The approximate 32 percent is noticeably lower than the 50 percent claimed by William L. Richter (see Richter, *Overreached on All Sides*, 49).

33. Endorsement of letter from Samuel Thomas to J. B. Kiddoo, August 20, 1866, AC, ES, April 1866–September 1867, reel 2; Carpenter, *Sword and Olive Branch*, 101.

34. Special Orders No. 46, O. O. Howard, March 30 1866, AC, IRB, October 1865–April 1869, reel 19; Crouch, *Freedmen's Bureau and Black Texans*, 19–20; Special Orders No. 48, O. O. Howard, April 2, 1866, AC, IRB, October 1865–April 1869, reel 19.

3. Conservative Phoenix: The J. B. Kiddoo Era, May 1866–Summer 1866

1. Otis, ed., *Medical and Surgical History of the War*, 3:234; David A. Murdoch, "Profiles in Leadership: Allegheny County's Lawyer-Generals in the Civil War," *Pittsburgh History* 81 (Winter 1998): 182; Richter, *Overreached on All Sides*, 79–80; Boatner,

Civil War Dictionary, 458–459; Francis B. Heitman, *Historical Register and Dictionary of the United States Army, From Its Organization, September 29, 1789, to March 2, 1903*, 2 vols. (Washington, D.C.: Government Printing Office, 1988), 1:596; Tyler, ed., *New Handbook of Texas*, 3:1091; William H. Powell, comp., *List of Officers of the Army of the United States From 1779 to 1900* (New York: L. R. Hamersley and Company, 1900), 413; Donald Bounds Kiddoo, "The Life of General Joseph Kiddoo," *Heritage Library News* 8 (Fall 2004): 4–8; National Rifle Association, *The National Rifle Association, 1873: Address, Annual Reports, and Regulations for Rifle Practice* (New York: Reynolds & Whelpey, 1877), 155–156; J. B. Kiddoo to O. O. Howard, October 25, 1866, O. O. Howard Papers, 1833–1912 Correspondences, Freedmen's Bureau Period, M91, Box 4, Bowdoin College, Brunswick, Maine (hereafter cited Howard Papers–Bowdoin); Samuel P. Bates, *History of Pennsylvania Volunteers, 1861–1865* (Harrisburg, PA: B. Singerly, State Publisher, 1869–1871), 4:337; Donald Scott, Sr., *Camp William Penn, 1863–1865: America's First Federal African American Soldiers' Fight for Freedom* (Altgen, PA: Schiffer Publishing, 2012), 198, 210–211; *New York Times*, October 11, 1877. There are conflicting accounts concerning Kiddoo's age. Many sources have him born in 1840 and dying at 40; while a few have him born in 1837 and dying at 43. Those that have him deceased at 43 are *New York Times*, August 24, 1880, and Samuel P. Bates, *Martial Deeds of Pennsylvania* (Philadelphia: T. H. Davis & Co., 1876), 941.

2. J. B. Kiddoo to O. O. Howard, May 14, 1866, AC, LS, September 1865–March 1867, reel 1; Samuel C. Sloan, Richmond, to Chauncey C. Morse, A.A.A.G., January 16, 1866, AC, ULR, 1865–1866, reel 17; *New York Herald*, July 30, 1866. For further problems with the state's labor situation, see J. W. McConaughey, Wharton, to [E. M. Gregory], January 11, 1866, AC, ULR, 1865–1866, reel 17; Champ Carter, Sterling, to [Headquarters], May 21, 1866, AC, LR, 1866–1867, reel 4; and Stanton Weaver, Crockett, to Chauncey C. Morse, A.A.A.G., January 31, 1866, AC, ULR, 1865–1866, reel 17.

3. J. B. Kiddoo to O. O. Howard, May 28, 1866, AC, LR, 1865–1866, reel 1; Circular No. 14, May 15, 1866, AC, IRB, October 1865–April 1869, reel 19; Richter, *Overreached on All Sides*, 81; Richardson, *Death of Reconstruction*, xiv.

4. Circular No. 14, May 15, 1866, AC, IRB, October 1865–April 1869, reel 19; Roark, *Masters Without Slaves*, 136; Endorsement of letter from L. S. Barnes, Crockett, to William H. Sinclair, A.A.G., June 21, 1866, AC, ES, April 1866–September 1867, reel 2; Endorsement of letter from J. B. Moore, Seguin, to William H. Sinclair, A.A.G., July 25, 1866, AC, ES, April 1866–September 1867, reel 2; Schmidt, *Free to Work*, 128; Circular No. 14, May 15, 1866, AC, IRB, October 1865–April 1869, reel 19.

5. J. Ernest Goodman, Columbus, to William H. Sinclair, A.A.G., July 31, 1866, AC, LR, 1866–1867, reel 5; James A. Hogue, Livingston, to J. B. Kiddoo, July 13, 1866, AC, LR, 1866–1867, reel 6; James A. Hogue, Livingston, to J. B. Kiddoo, July 18, 1866, AC, LR, 1866–1867, reel 6; Alex B. Coggeshall, Bastrop, to William Sinclair, A.A.I., July 2, 1866, AC, LR, 1866–1867, reel 4. Comments on immense workload are L. S. Barnes, Crockett, to Henry A. Ellis, A.A.A.G., October 20, 1866, AC, LR, 1866–1867, reel 4; Circular No. 17, June 19, 1866, AC, IRB, October 1865–April 1869, reel 19; William H. Rock, Richmond, to Lemuel K. Morton, A.A.A.G., September 19, 1866, AC, LR, 1866–1867, reel 7; Special Orders No. 100, August 16, 1866, AC, IRB, October 1865–April 1869, reel 19; and Endorsement of letter from L. S. Barnes to Henry A. Ellis, A.A.A.G., October

13, 1866, AC, ES, April 1866–September 1867, reel 2. For reports of better relations, see J. Ernest Goodman, Columbus, to William H. Sinclair, A.A.G., July 31, 1866, LR, 1866–1867, reel 5; L. S. Barnes, Crockett, to William H. Sinclair, A.A.G., June 30, 1866, LR, 1866–1867, reel 4; and Fred Cole, "Texas Career of Thomas Affleck" (Ph.D. diss., Louisiana State University, 1942). Reports following Kiddoo's issuance of Circular No. 14 are H. W. Allen, Hempstead, to William H. Sinclair, A.A.G., July 12, 1866, AC, LR, 1866–1867, reel 4; Albert A. Metzner, Clinton, to William H. Sinclair, A.A.G., August 14, 1866, AC, LR, 1866–1867, reel 7; L. S. Barnes, Crockett, to William H. Sinclair, A.A.G., June 30, 1866, AC, LR, 1866–1867, reel 4; Samuel C. Sloan, Richmond, to William H. Sinclair, A.A.G., June 27, 1866, AC, LR, 1866–1867, reel 8; Special Orders No. 51, March 12, 1866, AC, IRB, October 1865–April 1869, reel 19; Byron Porter, Houston, to William H. Sinclair, A.A.G., June 8, 1866, AC, LR, 1866–1867, reel 7; Charles P. Russell, Gonzales, to [William H.] Sinclair, A.A.G., August 4, 1866, AC, LR, 1866–1867, reel 7; J. B. Kiddoo to O. O. Howard, August 29, 1866, AC, LS, September 1865–March 1867, reel 1; Albert A. Metzner, Clinton, to William H. Sinclair, A.A.G., August 14, 1866, AC, LR, 1866–1867, reel 7; Johnathan F. Brown, Anderson, to William H. Sinclair, A.A.G., July 25, 1866, AC, LR, 1866–1867, reel 4; and Carl Moneyhon, *Texas After the Civil War: The Struggle of Reconstruction* (College Station: Texas A&M University Press, 2004), 56.

6. J. W. McConaughey, Wharton, to William H. Sinclair, A.A.G., March 28, 1866, AC, LR, 1866–1867, reel 7; L. S. Barnes, Crockett, to William H. Sinclair, A.A.G., June 14, 1866, LR, 1866–1867, reel 4; H. W. Allen, Hempstead, to William H. Sinclair, A.A.G., July 12, 1866, AC, LR, 1866–1867, reel 4; J. Orville Shelby, Liberty, to J. B. Kiddoo, July 8, 1866, AC, ULR, 1865–1866, reel 17; J. Orville Shelby, Liberty, to J. B. Kiddoo, July 18, 1866, AC, ULR, 1865–1866, reel 17; Endorsement of letter from Louis H. Jacobs, Millican, to William H. Sinclair, A.A.G., July 15, 1866, AC, ES, April 1866–September 1867, reel 2; J. Orville Shelby, Liberty, to J. B. Kiddoo, July 18, 1866, AC, ULR, 1865–1866, reel 17; Richard Cole to J. B. Kiddoo, June 26, 1866, AC, ULR, 1865–1866, reel 17; William H. Sinclair, A.A.G., to J. Orville Shelby, Liberty, July 25, 1866, LS, September 1865–March 1867, reel 1; J. Orville Shelby, Liberty, to J. B. Kiddoo, July 8, 1866, AC, LR, 1866–1867, reel 8; Special Orders No. 98, July 10, 1866, AC, IRB, October 1865–April 1869, reel 19; William H. Sinclair, A.A.G., to J. Orville Shelby, Liberty, August 16, 1866, AC, LS, September 1865–March 1867, reel 1; Endorsement of letter from J. Orville Shelby to J. T. Kirkman, A.A.A.G., April 9, 1867, LR, 1866–1867, reel 2. For planter discontent, see Statement of W. B. Anderson, May 30, 1866, AC, ULR, 1865–1866, reel 17; and Endorsement of letter from J. Bates to Henry A. Ellis, A.A.A.G., October 25, 1866, AC, ES, April 1866–September 1867, reel 2. For instances of excessive punishment for labor violations, see Champ Carter, Marlin Falls, to [Headquarters], April 19, 1866, AC, LR, 1866–1867, reel 4; Charles Harrison to Colonel, May 5, 1866, AC, ULR, 1865–1866, reel 17; Robert Singleton, "William Gilmore Simms, Woodlands, and the Freedmen's Bureau," *Mississippi Quarterly* 50 (Winter 1996): 18–36; Benjamin J. Brisbane, Chaplain 2nd Wisconsin Volunteer Cavalry, Hempstead, to Thomas W. Conway, Superintendent of Freedmen, Department of Gulf, September 14, 1865, AC, ULR, 1865–1866, reel 17; Fred W. Reinhard, Centreville, to [Headquarters], November 16, 1866, AC, LR, 1866–1867, reel 9; Frank Holsinger, Beaumont, to William H. Sinclair, A.A.G., April 5, 1866, AC, LR, 1866–1867, reel 6; J. B. Kiddoo to O. O. Howard, June 26, 1866, Correspon-

dences, Freedmen's Bureau Period, M912, Box 4, Howard papers–Bowdoin; Champ
Carter, Seguin, to [J. B. Kiddoo], June 7, 1866, SAC, LS, January 1867–March 1868 and
June–September 1868, reel 26; Statement of W. B. Anderson, May 30, 1866, AC, ULR,
1865–1866, reel 17; Robert McClermont to O. O. Howard, August 4, 1866, Correspon-
dences, Freedmen's Bureau Period, Howard papers–Bowdoin, M91, Box; and Harry
Wilcox Pfanz, "Soldiering in the South During the Reconstruction Period, 1865–1877"
(Ph.D. diss., Ohio State University, 1958), 74–82.

    7. A. H. Mayer, Liberty, to S. H. Lathrop, A.A.A.G., December 23, 1866, AC, LR,
1866–1867, reel 7; Circular No. 19, August 20, 1866; Circular No. 21, October 1, 1866,
Circular No. 23, November 1, 1866, and Circular No. 25, December 21, 1866, AC (all in
IRB, October 1865–April 1869, reel 19). For agents' suspicion toward planters, see Lemuel K. Morton, Sterling, to J. B. Kiddoo, September 30, 1866, AC, LR, 1866–1867, reel 7;
Samuel C. Sloan, Richmond, to William H. Sinclair, A.A.G., May 31, 1866, AC, LR,
1866–1867, reel 8; and George C. Abbott, Hempstead, to [E. M.] Gregory, October 31,
1865, AC, ULR, 1865–1866, reel 17.

    8. For the problem of seizures, see Jacob C. DeGress, Houston, to Henry A. Ellis,
A.A.A.G., November 5, 1866, LR, 1866–1867, reel 5; A. H. Mayer, Liberty, to William H.
Sinclair, Inspector, Galveston, December 31, 1866, AC, LR, 1866–1867, reel 7; William
H. Sinclair, Inspector, to Henry A. Ellis, A.A.A.G., December 4, 1866, AC, LR, 1866–
1867, reel 8; William H. Sinclair, Inspector, to Henry A. Ellis, A.A.A.G., December 2,
1866, AC, LR, 1866–1867, reel 8; and J. B. Kiddoo to Jacob C. DeGress, Houston,
December 1, 1866, AC, LS, September 1865–March 1867, reel 1. For lack of responsibility
with free labor compared to slavery, see Eugene D. Genovese, *Roll, Jordan, Roll: The
World the Slaves Made* (New York: Pantheon Books, 1972), 74; J. Thomas May, "The
Medical Care of Blacks in Louisiana During the Occupation and Reconstruction,
1862–1868: Its Social and Political Background" (Ph.D. diss., Tulane University, 1972),
169–170; and Anne Barber Harris, "The South as Seen by Travelers, 1865–1880" (Ph.D.
diss., University of North Carolina, 1971), 15. For vagrancy, see W. E. B. DuBois, *The
Philadelphia Negro: A Social Study* (New York: Benjamin Bloom, 1899); Nathan Glazer
and Daniel Patrick Moynihan, *Beyond the Melting Pot* (Cambridge: M.I.T. Press, 1963);
E. Franklin Frazier, *The Negro in the United States* (New York: The MacMillan Company, 1971); and Genovese, *Roll, Jordan, Roll*. In Texas, care for the indigent, unlike
other states, was not pressing (see Elaine Cutler Everly, "The Freedmen's Bureau in the
National Capital" (Ph.D. diss., George Washington University, 1971), 101, 83; J. B. Kiddoo to Generals, January 11, 1866, AC, LS, September 1865–March 1867, reel 1; Robert
H. Bremner, *The Public Good: Philanthropy and Welfare in the Civil War Era* (New
York: Alfred A. Knopf, 1980), 113–126; Mary Farmer-Kaiser, "'Are they not in some
sorts vagrants': Gender and the Efforts of the Freedmen's Bureau to Combat Vagrancy
in the Reconstruction South," *Georgia Historical Quarterly* 88 (Spring 2004): 25–49;
Mary J. Farmer, "Freedwomen and the Freedmen's Bureau: Race, Gender, and Public
Policy in the Age of Emancipation" (Ph.D. diss., Bowling Green State University,
2000), 87–90; Mary Farmer-Kaiser, *Freedwomen and the Freedmen's Bureau* (New
York: Fordham University Press, 2010), chapters 1–3; Robert C. Lieberman, "The
Freedmen's Bureau and the Politics of Institutional Structure," *Social Sciences History*
18 (Autumn 1994): 406, 427; Fredrickson, *Black Image*, 178–179; Foner, *Reconstruction*,

152; Olds, "Freedmen's Bureau as a Social Agency," 2; Richard Paul Fuke, "A Reform Mentality: Federal Policy Toward Black Marylanders, 1864–1868," *Civil War History* 22 (September 1976): 214–226; Chad Alan Goldberg, "The Freedmen's Bureau and Civil War Pensions: Race and Policy Feedback in America's Nineteenth-Century Welfare State" (paper delivered at American Sociological Association Annual Meeting, 2006.

9. Circular No. 16, June 18, 1866, AC, IRB, October 1865–April 1869, reel 19; J. D. O'Connell, Houston, to [Headquarters], June 22, 1867, AC, LR, 1866–1867, reel 7; O. Hendrick to [J. W.] Throckmorton, March 25, 1867, Incoming Correspondence, Governor J. W. Throckmorton Records (RG 301), Archives Division–Texas State Library, Austin, Texas (hereafter cited Governor Correspondences); O. Hendrick to [J. W.] Throckmorton, March 15, 1867, Throckmorton Governor Correspondences; Charles F. Rand, Marshall, to O. Hendrick, March 31, 1867, AC, LR, 1866–1867, reel 9; J. W. Throckmorton to Maj. Gen. Charles Griffin, Commander, District of Texas, March 4, 1867, AC, LR, 1866–1867, reel 9; J. W. Throckmorton to Maj. Gen. Charles Griffin, Commander, District of Texas, April 10, 1867, AC, LR, 1866–1867, reel 9. Resistance are in John E. George to Maj. Gen. [Charles] Griffin, May 8, 1867, AC, LR, 1866–1867, reel 5; James Lowrie, Jasper, to J. T. Kirkman, A.A.A.G., July 31, 1867, AC, ROC, June–August, 1867, reel 21; A. S. Gardner to J. W. Throckmorton, April 3, 1867, AC, LR, 1866–1867, reel 9; and Samuel A. Craig, Brenham, to William H. Sinclair, A.A.G., August 2, 1866, AC, LR, 1866–1867, reel 4.

10. J. W. Throckmorton to J. B. Kiddoo, August 30, 1866, AC, LR, 1866–1867, reel 9; J. W. Throckmorton to Louis T. Wigfall, December 30, 1866, James W. Throckmorton Papers, Letterbook, 1866–1867, Center for American History, Austin, Texas (hereafter cited Throckmorton papers–Center for American History); Philip H. Sheridan, *Personal Memoirs of Philip Sheridan* (London: Chatto and Windus Peccadilly, 1888), 232.

11. Endorsement of letter from H. W. Allen, Hempstead, to William H. Sinclair, A.A.G., June 2, 1866, AC, ES, April 1866–September 1867, reel 2; Stanton Weaver, Crockett, to Judge Cooper, February 28, 1867, AC, ULR, 1865–1866, reel 17; Byron Porter, Houston, to Lemuel K. Morton, A.A.A.G., September 12, 1866, AC, LR, 1866–1867, reel 7; Jacob C. DeGress, Houston, to Henry A. Ellis, A.A.A.G., December 14, 1866, AC, LR, 1866–1867, reel 5.

12. William Longworth to Secretary of the Freedmen's Bureau for the State of Texas, June 30, 1865, AC, LR, September 1865–March 1867, reel 7; William Longworth, Sutherland Springs, to [E. M. Gregory], January 15, 1866, AC, ULR, 1865–1866, reel 17; Tyler, ed., *New Handbook of Texas*, 3:458–459; Special Orders No. 18, December 28, 1865, AC, IRB, October 1865–April 1869, reel 19; William Longworth to A. J. Hamilton, October 9, 1865, Hamilton Governor Correspondences; William Longworth to A. J. Hamilton, October 10, 1865, Hamilton Governor Correspondences.

13. Litwack, *Been in the Storm So Long*, 237; Mary Farmer-Kaiser, "With a Weight of Circumstances Like Millstones About Their Necks: Freedwomen, Federal Relief, and the Benevolent Guardianship of the Freedmen's Bureau," *Virginia Magazine of History and Biography* 115 (2007): 431; William Longworth, Sutherland Springs, to [E. M. Gregory], March 9, 1866, LR, 1866–1867, reel 6; James L. Dial to [J. B.] Kiddoo, June 6, 1866, AC, LR, 1866–1867, reel 5; William H. Sinclair, A.A.G., to William Longworth, Sutherland Springs, March 23, 1866, AC, LS, September 1865–March 1867, reel 1; James

L. Dial to E. M. Gregory, February 10, 1866, AC, LR, 1866–1867, reel 5; R. H. Brahan to [Headquarters], May 8, 1866, AC, LR, 1866–1867, reel 6; William H. Sinclair, A.A.G., to James L. Dial, March 19, 1866, AC, LS, September 1865–March 1867, reel 1.

14. William Longworth, Seguin, to [Headquarters], May 25, 1866, AC, LR, 1866–1867, reel 6; William Longworth, Seguin, to W. C. Wiseman, May 21, 1866, AC, LR, 1866–1867, reel 6; William Longworth, Seguin, to William H. Sinclair, A.A.G., June 25, 1866, AC, LR, 1866–1867, reel 6; William Longworth, Seguin, to William H. Sinclair, A.A.G., May 30, 1866, AC, LR, 1866–1867, reel 6.

15. William H. Sinclair, A.A.G., to William Longworth, Seguin, June 9, 1866, AC, LS, September 1865–March 1867, reel 1; William Longworth, Seguin, to J. B. Kiddoo, June 21, 1866, LR, 1866–1867, reel 6; William H. Sinclair, A.A.G., to William Longworth, Seguin, July 27, 1866, LS, September 1865–March 1867, reel 1; Special Orders No. 95, AC, IRB, October 1865–April 1869, reel 19. Information on Longworth's successor is in Henry A. Ellis, A.A.A.G., to Maj. Gen. Philip Sheridan, Commander, Department of the Gulf, November 10, 1866, AC, LS, September 1865–March 1867, reel 1; William H. Sinclair, Inspector, to Henry Ellis, A.A.A.G., October 7, 1866, AC, LR, 1866–1867, reel 5; and Special Orders No. 126, October 24, 1866, AC, IRB, October 1865–April 1869, reel 19.

16. Edwin Bohne, "The History of the *Brenham Banner Press*" (Master's Thesis, Sam Houston State University, 1950), 2; Craig, "Memoirs," 81; Special Orders No. 69, 1866, AC, IRB, October 1865–April 1869, reel 19; William H. Sinclair, A.A.G., to Samuel A. Craig, Brenham, July 19, 1866, AC, ES, April 1866–September 1867, reel 2; Tyler, ed., *New Handbook of Texas*, 4:401.

17. Craig, "Memoirs," 81; William H. Sinclair, A.A.G., to Samuel A. Craig, Brenham, August 8, 1866, LS, September 1865–March 1867, reel 1; Endorsement of letter from Samuel A. Craig, Brenham, to William H. Sinclair, A.A.G., July 16, 1866, AC, ES, April 1866–September 1867, reel 2; *Galveston Tri Weekly News*, September 7, 1866; Samuel A. Craig, Brenham, to William H. Sinclair, A.A.G., August 12, 1866, AC, LR, 1866–1867, reel 4; Samuel A. Craig, Brenham, to William H. Sinclair, A.A.G., August 14, 1866, AC, LR, 1866–1867, reel 4; Samuel A. Craig, Brenham, to William H. Sinclair, A.A.G., August 21, 1866, AC, LR, 1866–1867, reel 4; Samuel A. Craig, Brenham, to William H. Sinclair, A.A.G., August 27, 1866, AC, LR, 1866–1867, reel 4; J. B. Kiddoo to Samuel A. Craig, Brenham, August 14, 1866, AC, LS, September 1865–March 1867, reel 1; J. B. Kiddoo to Brvt. Gen. Horatio G. Wright, Commander, District of Texas, July 21, 1866, ES, April 1866–September 1867, reel 2.

18. Craig, "Memoirs," 81; J. B. Kiddoo to Samuel A. Craig, Brenham, August 30, 1866, AC, LS, September 1865–March 1867, reel 1; Samuel A. Craig, Brenham, to William H. Sinclair, A.A.G., August 12, 1866, LR, 1866–1867, reel 4; Samuel A. Craig, Brenham, to William H. Sinclair, A.A.G., August 23, 1866, LR, 1866–1867, reel 4.

19. J. W. Throckmorton to Charles R. Breedlove, December 21, 1866, Throckmorton papers–Center for American History; J. W. Throckmorton to [J. B.] Kiddoo, September 18, 1866, AC, LR, 1866–1867, reel 9; J. B. Kiddoo to J. W. Throckmorton, September 13, 1866, AC, LS, September 1865–March 1867, reel 1; Ernest Wallace, *Texas in Turmoil: The Saga of Texas, 1849–1875* (Austin: Steck-Vaughn Company, 1965), 158; Telegram from Samuel A. Craig, Seguin, to William H. Sinclair, A.A.G., August 15, 1866, AC, LR,

1866–1867, reel 4; William H. Sinclair, A.A.G., to Samuel A. Craig, Brenham, September 2, 1866, LS, September 1865–March 1867, reel 1; J. W. Throckmorton to J. B. Kiddoo, August 20, 1866, AC, LR, 1866–1867, reel 9; Telegram from J. W. Throckmorton to O. O. Howard, August 22, 1866, M752C, LR, March–May 1866, reel 30; J. B. Kiddoo to O. O. Howard, September 17, 1866, AC, LS, September 1865–March 1867, reel 1; Telegram from O. O. Howard to J. B. Kiddoo, August 29, 1866, AC, LR, 1866–1867, reel 6; O. O. Howard to J. B. Kiddoo, August 23, 1866, M742C, LS, January 1–December 1866, reel 2; Special Orders No. 113, September 19, 1866, AC, IRB, October 1865–April 1869, reel 19.

20. Jerry D. Thompson, *Civil War to the Bloody End: The Life and Times of Major General Samuel P. Heintzelman* (College Station: Texas A&M University Press, 2006), 336; William Longworth to [J. B.] Kiddoo, November 12, 1866, AC, LR, 1866–1867, reel 6; Henry A. Ellis, A.A.A.G, to William Longworth, September 19, 1866, LS, September 1865–March 1867, reel 1; Endorsement of letter from William Longworth to J. B. Kiddoo, September 17, 1866, AC, ES, April 1866–September 1867, reel 2; J. B. Kiddoo to William Longworth, September 21, 1866, LS, September 1865–March 1867, reel 1; Henry A. Ellis, A.A.A.G., to Samuel A. Craig, Seguin, September 28, 1866, LS, September 1865–March 1867, reel 1.

21. W. Goodrich to J. W. Throckmorton, October 8, 1866, Throckmorton Governor Correspondences; Samuel A. Craig, Seguin, to William H. Sinclair, A.A.G., October 21, 1866, AC, LR, 1866–1867, reel 4; George C. Potwin to Brvt. Maj. Gen. Samuel P. Heintzelman, Commander, District of Texas, September 29, 1866, AC, LR, 1866–1867, reel 7; Samuel A. Craig, Seguin, to Henry A. Ellis, A.A.A.G., October 8, 1866, AC, LR, 1866–1867, reel 4; J. W. Throckmorton to J. B. Kiddoo, October 13, 1866, AC, LR, 1866–1867, reel 9.

22. James B. Moore, Seguin, to Colonel, August 6, 1866, AC, LR, 1866–1867, reel 7; Craig, "Memoirs," 89–91; William H. Sinclair, Inspector, to J. T. Kirkman, A.A.A.G., May 29, 1867, AC, LR, 1866–1867, reel 7; Samuel A. Craig, Seguin, to William H. Sinclair, A.A.G., October 21, 1866, AC, LR, 1866–1867, reel 4; Tyler, ed., *New Handbook of Texas*, 3:867; Samuel A. Craig, Seguin, to Henry A. Ellis, A.A.G., December 6, 8, and 11, 1866, AC, LR, 1866–1867, reel 4; Thompson, *Civil War to the Bloody End*, 335; Endorsement of letter from T. S. Leason to J. B. Kiddoo, December 21, 1866, AC, ES, April 1866–September 1867, reel 2; Special Orders No. 148, December 14, 1866, AC, IRB, October 1865–April 1869, reel 19; Special Orders No. 154, December 25, 1866, AC, IRB, October 1865–April 1869, reel 19.

23. Endorsement of letter from J. B. Kiddoo to Brvt. Maj. Gen. Horatio G. Wright, Commander, District of Texas, June 9, 1866, AC, ES, April 1866–September 1867, reel 2.

24. Endorsement of letter from Samuel A. Craig, Seguin, to Henry A. Ellis, A.A.A.G., November 10, 1866, AC, ES, April 1866–September 1867, reel 2; O. O. Howard to J. B. Kiddoo, August 23, 1866, M742C, LS, January 1–December 29, 1866, reel 2. An instance from Louisiana where an agent caused problems for his successors is in Solomon K. Smith, "'Better to not look at a place, than send an unsupported man there as Agent:' Chaplain Thomas Callahan, and the arrival of the Freedmen's Bureau in Shreveport," *North Louisiana History* 36 (2005): 154–166.

25. Richter, "Who Was the Real Head of the Texas Freedmen's Bureau?," 121; Bentley, *History of Freedmen's Bureau*, 105; A. P. Delano, Marlin Falls, to F. B. Sturgis,

Waco, January 10, 1867, AC, ULR, 1867–1869 and Undated, reel 18; Samuel C. Sloan, Richmond, to William H. Sinclair, A.A.G., May 31, 1866, AC, LR, 1866–1867, reel 8; Philip Howard, Meridian, to E. M. Gregory, March 22, 1866, LR, 1866–1867, reel 6; Charles C. Hardenbrook, Beaumont, to William H. Sinclair, A.A.G., May 7, 1866, AC, LR, 1866–1867, reel 6; Charles C. Hardenbrook, Beaumont, to William H. Sinclair, A.A.G., May 10, 1866, AC, LR, 1866–1867, reel 6; Charles C. Hardenbrook, Beaumont, to William H. Sinclair, A.A.G., June 18, 1866, AC, LR, 1866–1867, reel 6; Charles C. Hardenbrook File, Pension Record; Endorsement of letter from Charles C. Hardenbrook, Beaumont, to William H. Sinclair, A.A.G., May 1, 1866, AC, LR, 1866–1867, reel 6; Endorsement of letter from J. B. Kiddoo to Brvt. Maj. Gen. Horatio G. Wright, Commander, District of Texas, June 4, 1866, AC, ES, April 1866–September 1867, reel 2; *Flake's Daily Bulletin*, April 30, 1866; Charles C. Hardenbrook, Beaumont, to William H. Sinclair, July 8, 1866, AC, LR, 1866–1867, reel 6; Crouch, "Freedmen's Bureau in Beaumont," (Part One) 14–18; Charles C. Hardenbrook, Houston, to Henry A. Ellis, A.A.A.G., November 22, 1866, AC, LR, 1866–1867, reel 6; Special Orders No. 63, April 16, 1866, AC, IRB, October 1865–April 1869, reel 19; Special Orders No. 149, December 17, 1866, AC, IRB, October 1865–April 1869, reel 19; Special Orders No. 122, October 16, 1866, AC, IRB, October 1865–April 1869, reel 19; Special Orders No. 150, December 19, 1866, AC, IRB, October 1865–April 1869, reel 19; Foner, *Politics and Ideology*, 101; J. B. Kiddoo to Brvt. Maj. Gen. Horatio G. Wright, Commander, Department of Texas, May 29, 1866, AC, LS, September 1865–March 1867, reel 1; J. B. Kiddoo to Brvt. Maj. Gen. Horatio G. Wright, Commander, District of Texas, May 30, 1866, AC, LS, September 1865–March 1867, reel 1. Further complaints of violence are William H. Horton, Wharton, to J. B. Kiddoo, January 1, 1866, AC, LR, 1866–1867, reel 6; Charles C. Hardenbrook, Richmond, to Henry A. Ellis, A.A.A.G., November 17, 1866, AC, LR, 1866–1867, reel 7; Samuel C. Sloan, Richmond, to William H. Sinclair, A.A.G., June 30, 1866, AC, LR, 1866–1867, reel 8; Ira P. Pedigo, Woodville, to J. B. Kiddoo, August 6, 1866, AC, LR, 1866–1867, reel 7; *Dallas Herald*, April 28 and May 5, 1866; W. D. Wood, *Reminiscences of Reconstruction in Texas and Reminiscences of Texas and Texans Fifty Years Ago* (n.p, 1902), 15; A. B. Newsom et al., to [Headquarters], July 23, 1866, AC, LR, 1866–1867, reel 7; and Gilles Vandal, "'Bloody Caddoo': White Violence Against Blacks in a Louisiana Parish, 1865–1876," *Journal of Social History* 25 (Winter 1991): 373–388.

26. Philip Howard, Meridian, to E. M. Gregory, March 22, 1866, AC, LR, 1866–1867, reel 6; Philip Howard, Meridian, to [J. B. Kiddoo], July 31, 1866, LR, 1866–1867, reel 6; Camp Carter, Sterling, to [J. B. Kiddoo], May 21, 1866, AC, LR, 1866–1867, reel 4; William Longworth, Sutherland Springs, to William H. Sinclair, May 1, 1866, AC, LR, 1866–1867, reel 6; William Longworth, Sutherland Springs, to General, March 9, 1866, AC, LR, 1866–1867, reel 6. Examples of violence are Byron Porter, Houston, to William H. Sinclair, A.A.G., May 3, 1866, AC, LR, 1866–1867, reel 7; F. D. Inge, Leona, to [E. M.] Gregory, March 22, 1866, AC, LR, 1866–1867, reel 6; John H. Archer, Hempstead, to J. B. Kiddoo, January 10, 1867, AC, LR, December 1866–May 1867, reel 20; James D. Richardson, ed., *A Compilation of the Messages and Papers of the Presidents, 1789–1897*, 10 vols. (Washington, D.C.: Government Printing Office, 1897), 6:398–405, 422–426; O. O. Howard to General, February 23, 1866, AC, ULR, 1865–1866, reel 17; Circular No. 7, March 6, 1866, AC, IRB, October 1865–April 1869, reel 19; and E. D. Townsend, A.A.G.,

to Brvt. Maj. Gen. P. M. Brannan, Commander, Department of Georgia, April 9, 1866, AC, IRB, reel 19. For the showdown between President Johnson and Radical Republicans, see LaWanda Cox and John H. Cox, *Politics, Principle, and Prejudice 1865–1866: Dilemma of Reconstruction America* (London: The Free Press of Glencoe, 1963). For other opinions about President Johnson, see William F. Mugleston, ed., "The Freedmen's Bureau and Reconstruction in Virginia: The Diary of Marcus Sterling Hopkins, a Union Officer," *Virginia Magazine of History and Biography* 86 (January 1978): 49.

27. Donald G. Nieman, "Andrew Johnson, the Freedmen's Bureau, and the Problem of Equal Rights, 1865–1866," *Journal of Southern History* 44 (August 1978): 420; Cox and Cox, "General Howard and 'Misrepresented Bureau,'" 437; F. B. Sturgis, La Grange, to Henry A. Ellis, A.A.A.G., November 19, 1866, AC, LR, 1866–1867, reel 8; Richter, "Revolver Rules the Day!," 325; Paul David Philips, "Freedmen's Bureau in Tennessee" (Ph.D. diss., Vanderbilt University, 1966), 324; Telegram from James C. Devine, Huntsville, to Henry A. Ellis, A.A.A.G., October 22, 1866, AC, LR, 1866–1867, reel 5; James C. Devine, Huntsville, to Henry A. Ellis, A.A.A.G., October 24, 1866, AC, LR, 1866–1867, reel 4; Croushore and Potter, eds., *A Union Officer in the Reconstruction*, 110–112.

28. Thomas H. Baker, Lockhart, to Charles A. Vernou, A.A.A.G., May 31, 1868, AC, ROC, May–July, 1868, reel 25; Thomas H. Baker, Lockhart, to Charles A. Vernou, A.A.A.G., June 30, 1868, AC, ROC, May–July, 1868, reel 25; Thomas H. Baker, Lockhart, to Charles A. Vernou, A.A.A.G., July 31, 1868, AC, ROC, May–July, 1868, reel 26; Louis W. Stevenson, Columbus, to Charles A. Vernou, A.A.A.G., November 30, 1868, AC, ROC, November–December, 1868, reel 28; Louis W. Stevenson, Columbus, to Charles A. Vernou, A.A.A.G., December, 31, 1868, AC, ROC, November–December, 1868, reel 28; James P. Butler, Huntsville, to J. P. Richardson, A.A.A.G., March 1, 1868, AC, ROC, March-August, 1868, reel 25; James P. Butler, Huntsville, to J. P. Richardson, A.A.A.G., May 2, 1868, AC, ROC, March-April, 1868, reel 25; James P. Butler, to J. P. Richardson, A.A.A.G., May 31, 1868, AC, ROC, May–July, 1868, reel 26; James C. Devine, Huntsville, to Henry A. Ellis, A.A.A.G., October 22, 1866, AC, LR, 1866–1867, reel 4. Thomas H. Baker's reports are Thomas H. Baker, Lockhart, to Charles S. Morse, A.A.A.G., August, 31, 1868, AC; Thomas H. Baker, Lockhart, to C. S. Roberts, A.A.A.G., September 5, 1868, AC; Thomas H. Baker, Lockhart, to C. S. Roberts, A.A.A.G., October, 31, 1868, AC; Thomas H. Baker, Lockhart, to Charles A. Vernou, A.A.A.G., November 30, 1868, AC; and Thomas H. Baker, Lockhart, to Charles A. Vernou, A.A.A.G., December 31, 1868, AC (all in ROC, reel 27–28). James P. Butler's are James P. Butler, Huntsville, to J. P. Richardson, A.A.A.G., AC, ROC, January–February, 1868, reel 24; and James P. Butler, Huntsville, to J. P. Richardson, A.A.A.G., February 29, 1868, AC, ROC, January–February, 1868, reel 24.

29. Philip Howard, Meridian, to [E. M.] Gregory, April 1, 1866, AC, LR, 1866–1867, reel 6; Philip Howard, Meridian, to [J. B. Kiddoo], July 10, 1866, AC, LR, 1866–1867, reel 6; Philip Howard, Meridian, to [J. B. Kiddoo], July 10, 1866, AC, LR, 1866–1867, reel 6; Philip Howard, Meridian, to William H. Sinclair, A.A.G., August 22, 1866, AC, LR, 1866–1867, reel 6; Special Orders No. 128, October 27, 1866, AC, IRB, October 1865–April 1869; Special Orders No. 96, October 31, 1867, AC, IRB, October 1865–April 1869, reel 19; Special Orders No. 6, January 25, 1868, AC, IRB, October 1865–April 1869, reel 19.

4. Bureau Expansion, Bureau Courts, and the Black Code: The J. B. Kiddoo Era, Summer 1866–November 1866

1. *Statutes at Large*, 14:173–177; Circular Letter from O. O. Howard, August 1, 1867, AC, LR, 1866–1867, reel 6. Nonpayment as a punishment is in Special Orders No. 323, June 25, 1867, AC, LR, 1866–1867, reel 6.

2. William H. Heistand, Hallettsville, to Henry A. Ellis, A.A.A.G., November 13, 1866, AC, LR, 1866–1867, reel 6; *Report of the Joint Committee on Reconstruction*, 39th Congress, 1st Session, Report No. 30 (Washington, D.C.: Government Printing Office, 1866), 46 (hereafter cited *Joint Committee*); Robert Smith, District Tax Commissioner, to [J. B.] Kiddoo, AC, LR, 1866–1867, reel 8; William Prissick to J. B. Kiddoo, September 23, 1866, AC, LR, 1866–1867, reel 7; Rebecca A. Kosary, "Regression to Barbarism in Reconstruction Texas: An Analysis of White Violence Against African-Americans from the Texas Freedmen's Bureau Records, 1865–1868" (Master's Thesis, Southwest Texas State, 1999), 69. Even Kiddoo experienced the adverse conditions in the interior (See J. B. Kiddoo to O. O. Howard, August 8, 1866, M742C, LR, May–August, 1866, reel 36).

3. Paul A. Cimbala, "Lining up to Serve: Wounded and Sick Union Officers from the Veteran Reserve Corps during Civil War/Reconstruction," *Prologue* 35 (Spring 2003): 40; Endorsement of letter from Isaac M. Beebe, Marshall, to J. B. Kiddoo, August 14, 1866, AC, ES, April 1866–September 1867, reel 2; William H. Sinclair, Inspector, to Henry A. Ellis, A.A.A.G., November 30, 1866, AC, ULR, 1866–1867, reel 17; Special Orders No. 105, December 24, 1867, AC, IRB, October 1865–April 1869, reel 19; C. H. Whittelsey, A.A.A.G., to J. J. Reynolds, January 7, 1868, AC, LR, 1867–1869, reel 16; Special Orders No. 65, April 18, 1866, AC, IRB, October 1865–April 1869, reel 19; Special Orders No. 62, October 18, 1868, AC, IRB, October 1865–April 1869, reel 19; Paul A. Cimbala, "Soldiering on the Home Front: The Veteran Reserve Corps and the Northern People," in *Union Soldiers and the Northern Home Front: Wartime Experiences, Postwar Adjustments*, ed. Paul A. Cimbala and Randall M. Miller (New York: Fordham University Press, 2002), 183; Cimbala, *Under the Guardianship of the Nation*, 271–272; Carpenter, "Agents of the Freedmen's Bureau," 303. Numbers and appointments are in Roster of Officers and Civilians, AC, Received and Retained Reports Relating to Rations, Lands, and Bureau Personnel, reels 29–31.

4. James P. Hutchison, Columbia, to William H. Sinclair, A.A.G., January 3, 1867, AC, LR, 1866–1867, reel 6; James P. Hutchison, Columbia, to Charles Griffin, January 31, 1867, AC, ROC, December 1866–May 1867, reel 20; James P. Hutchison, Columbia, to J. B. Kiddoo, January 19, 1867, AC, LR, 1866–1867, reel 8; William H. Sinclair, Inspector, to Henry A. Ellis, A.A.A.G., November 30, 1866, AC, ULR, 1866–1867, reel 17; L. J. Warner, Inspector, to Henry A. Ellis, A.A.A.G., December 6, 1866, AC, LR, 1866–1867, reel 9; William H. Sinclair, A.A.G., to James P. Hutchison, Columbia, January 10, 1867, AC, LR, 1866–1867, reel 8; James P. Hutchison, Columbia, to Charles Griffin, January 31, 1867, AC, ROC, December 1866–May 1867, reel 20.

5. James P. Hutchison, Columbia, to J. B. Kiddoo, January 19, 1866, AC, LR, 1866–1867, reel 6; James P. Hutchison, Columbia, to J. T. Kirkman, A.A.A.G., May 1, 1867, LR, 1866–1867, reel 6; Special Orders No. 57, May 26, 1867, AC, IRB, October 1865–April 1869, reel 19.

6. J. Ernest Goodman to William H. Sinclair, A.A.G., September 22, 1866, AC, LR, 1866–1867, reel 5; *Field Record of Officers of the Veteran Reserve Corps, from the Commencement to the Close of the Rebellion* (Washington, D.C.: Scriver & Swing, n.d.), 28, 35; J. Ernest Goodman File, Pension Record; Special Orders No. 67, April 23, 1866, AC, IRB, October 1865–April 1869, reel 19; J. Ernest Goodman, Columbus, to William H. Sinclair, A.A.G., July 31, 1866, AC, LR, 1866–1867, reel 5; William H. Sinclair, A.A.G., to J. Ernest Goodman, Columbus, July 19, 1866, AC, LS, April 1866–1867, reel 2; William H. Sinclair, A.A.G., to J. Ernest Goodman, Columbus, July 19, 1866, AC, LS, April 1866–1867, reel 2; Special Orders No. 101, August 18, 1866, AC, IRB, October 1865–April 1869, reel 19; C. A. Dempsey, 17th Infantry, A.A.Q.M., to L. H. Lathrop, Commander, Post of Houston, August 29, 1866, AC, LR, 1866–1867, reel 5; Richter, *Overreached on All Sides*, 107. For information on Metzner, Eddleson, and Horton, see William H. Sinclair, Inspector, to Charles A. Vernou, A.A.A.G., July 13, 1868, AC, LR, 1867–1869, reel 15; Special Orders No. 63, April 16, 1866, AC, IRB, October 1865–April 1869, reel 19; Special Orders No. 44, July 31, 1868, AC, IRB, October 1865–April 1869, reel 19; J. J. Reynolds to O. O. Howard, July 31, 1868, AC, IRB, October 1865–April 1869, reel 16; William H. Horton File, Pension Record; William H. Horton, Bastrop, to J. P. Richardson, A.A.A.G., May 2, 1868, AC, LR, 1867–1869, reel 10; Henry H. Eddleson File, Pension Record; Special Orders No. 20, February 18, 1867, AC, IRB, October 1865–April 1869, reel 19; William H. Horton, Bastrop, to [C. S.] Roberts, A.A.A.G., September 22, 1868, AC, LR, 1867–1869, reel 11; Special Orders No. 55, September 19, 1868, AC, IRB, October 1865–April 1869, reel 19; Perry S. Taylor to John J. Good, August 24, 1868, AC, LR, 1867–1869, reel 16; G. T. Kendall to J. J. Reynolds, April 10, 1868, AC, LR, 1867–1869, reel 13; William H. Horton to Charles A. Vernou, A.A.A.G., October 28, 1868, AC, LR, 1867–1869, reel 12; William H. Horton, Dallas, to J. P. Richardson, A.A.A.G., [February 1868], AC, LR, 1867–1869, reel 12; William H. Horton to Charles A. Vernou, A.A.A.G., October 30, 1868, AC, LR, 1867–1869, reel 12; and Charles A. Vernou, A.A.A.G., to William H. Horton, November 4, 1868, AC, LS, March 1867–May 1869, reel 2.

7. Charles Griffin to O. O. Howard, June 15, 1867, AC, Unregistered LR, 1867–1869 and Undated, reel 18; Alfred T. Manning, Waco, to J. T. Kirkman, A.A.A.G., February 28, 1867, AC, LR, 1866–1867, reel 7; Alfred T. Manning, Waco, to J. B. Kiddoo, January 20, 1867, AC, LR, 1866–1867, reel 7; Special Orders No. 91, July 17, 1866, AC, IRB, October 1865–April 1869, reel 19; Alfred T. Manning, Waco, to [J. B. Kiddoo], October 18, 1866, AC, LR, 1866–1867, reel 7; *Field Record of Officers of the Veteran Reserve Corps*, 28; Barry A. Crouch, "Spirit of Lawlessness: White Violence, Texas Blacks, 1865–1868," *Journal of Social History* 48 (Winter 1984): 225.

8. Charles B Pearce to J. W. Throckmorton, February 6, 1867, AC, LR, 1866–1867, reel 7; J. W. Throckmorton to Charles Griffin, January 28, AC, LR, 1866–1867, reel 9; J. W. Throckmorton to Charles Griffin, February 8, 1867, AC, LR, 1866–1867, reel 9; William L. Richter, *The Army in Texas During Reconstruction, 1865–1870* (College Station: Texas A&M University Press, 1987), 90; Special Orders No. 38, April 1, 1867, AC, IRB, October 1865–April 1869, reel 19; Alfred T. Manning, Cotton Gin, to J. T. Kirkman, A.A.A.G., May 30, 1867, AC, LR, 1866–1867, reel 7; J. T. Kirkman, A.A.A.G., to Alfred T. Manning, Cotton Gin, May 28, 1867, AC, LS, September 1865–March 1867, reel 1; Endorsement of letter from Charles E. Culver, Cotton Gin, to J. T. Kirkman, A.A.A.G.,

June 28, 1867, AC, ES, April 1866–September 1867, reel 2; Charles E. Culver, Cotton Gin, to J. T. Kirkman, A.A.A.G., July 31, 1867, AC, LR, 1866–1867, reel 4; E. A. McCrackin to J. T. Kirkman, A.A.A.G., June 25, 1867, AC, LR, 1866–1867, reel 7; Glenn R. Waters, et al, to [Headquarters], June 1867, AC, LR, 1866–1867, reel 9; Charles Dabian to Charles Garretson, A.A.A.G., July 9, 1867, AC, LR, 1866–1867, reel 5; Special Orders, No. 85, August 7, 1867, AC, IRB, October 1865–April 1869, reel 19.

9. Louis W. Stevenson, Columbus, to Charles A. Vernou, A.A.A.G., May 31, 1868, AC, ROC, May–July, 1868, reel 26; Richter, *Overreached on All Sides*, 40; Richter, *Army in Texas During Reconstruction*, 11–31; Robert W. Shook, "Federal Occupation and Administration of Texas, 1865–1870" (Ph.D. diss., North Texas State University, 1972), 218–219, 247; Pfanz, "Soldiering in the South During the Reconstruction Period," 10, 17–20; Endorsement of letter from Isaac M. Beebe, Marshall, to William H. Sinclair, A.A.G., May 26, 1866, AC, ES, April 1866–September 1867, reel 2; Endorsement of letter from L. S. Barnes, Crockett, to J. B. Kiddoo, August 7, 1866, AC, ES, April 1866–September 1867, reel 2; Endorsement of letter from A. G. Malloy, Marshall, to J. T. Kirkman, A.A.A.G., May 8, 1867, AC, ES, April 1866–September 1867, reel 2. A few examples of requests for cavalry are Arthur B. Homer, Columbia, to J. P. Richardson, A.A.A.G., January 31, 1868, AC, ROC, January–February, 1868, reel 24; John Dix, Corpus Christi, to J. T. Kirkman, A.A.A.G., [August 1867], AC, ROC, June–August, 1867, reel 21; T. M. K. Smith, Nacogdoches, to Charles Garretson, October, 5, 1867, AC, ROC, September–October, 1867, reel 22; and David L. Montgomery, Tyler, to J. P. Richardson, A.A.A.G., February 1, 1868, AC, ROC, January–February, 1868, reel 24.

10. L. S. Barnes, Crockett, to William H. Sinclair, A.A.G., May 29, 1866, AC, LR, 1866–1867, reel 4; Endorsement of letter from L. S. Barnes, Crockett, to William H. Sinclair, A.A.G., May 29, 1866, AC, ES: April 1866–September 1867, reel 2; Endorsement of letter from L. S. Barnes, Crockett, to William H. Sinclair, A.A.G., August 7, 1866, AC, ES: April 1866–September 1867, reel 2; L. S. Barnes, Crockett, to William H. Sinclair, A.A.G., March 26, 1866, AC, LR, 1866–1867, reel 4; L. S. Barnes, Crockett, to William H. Sinclair, A.A.G., April 25, 1866, AC, LR, 1866–1867, reel 4; L. S. Barnes, Crockett, to William H. Sinclair, A.A.G., May 6, 1866, AC, LR, 1866–1867, reel 4; L. S. Barnes, Crockett, to William H. Sinclair, A.A.G., September 1, 1866, AC, LR, 1866–1867, reel 4; L. S. Barnes, Crockett, to William H. Sinclair, A.A.G., May 6, 1866, AC, LR, 1866–1867, reel 4; L. S. Barnes, Crockett, to Henry A. Ellis, A.A.A.G., October 20, 1866, AC, LR, 1866–1867, reel 4; Special Orders No. 134, November 9, 1866, AC, IRB, September 1865–April 1869, reel 19; James E. Sefton, *The United States Army and Reconstruction, 1865-1877* (Baton Rouge: Louisiana State University Press, 1967), 95; Craig, "Memoirs," 85; William L. Richter, "The Brenham Fire of 1866: A Texas Reconstruction Atrocity," *Louisiana Studies* 14 (Fall 1975): 299–312; J. J. Reynolds to O. O. Howard, April 14, 1868, M752C, LR, January–June, 1868, reel 56. For instances of U.S. troops unnecessarily causing problems for agents after 1866, see Edward Miller, Millican, to J. P. Richardson, A.A.A.G., November 27, 1867, AC, LR, 1867–1869, reel 13; F. B. Sturgis, La Grange, to Henry A. Ellis, A.A.A.G., October 29, 1866, SAC, LR, 1866–1867, reel 8; N. H. Randlett, Bryan, to J. P. Richardson, A.A.A.G., May 6, 1868, AC, ROC, March–April, 1868, reel 25; Otto F. Steinberg, Columbia, to C. S. Roberts, A.A.A.G., October 15, 1868, SAC, Letters Sent and Register of Letters Received, October 1868, reel 21

(hereafter LSR); and William H. Heistand, Hallettsville, to Commanding Officer, 35th U.S. Infantry, March 11, 1867, SAC, LS, May–June 1866 and October 1866–March 1868, reel 21. Agents requesting troops, despite problems they caused, is in *Galveston Daily News*, June 9, 1865; Hiram Seymour Hall, Marshall, to E. M. Gregory, December 26, 1865, AC, ULR, 1865–1866, reel 17; Oliver H. Swingley, Austin, to E. M. Gregory, February 28, 1866, AC, ULR, 1865–1866, reel 17; *Bellville Countryman*, August 18, 1865; *Galveston Weekly News*, January 31, 1866; and David Work, "United States Colored Troops in Texas During Reconstruction, 1865–1867," *Southwestern Historical Quarterly* 109 (January 2006): 348–350. Other examples of SACs in Texas complaining about the actions, disposition, and attitudes of U.S. troops are Byron Porter, Houston, to Chauncey C. Morse, A.A.A.G., March 3, 1866, AC, ULR, 1865–1866, reel 17; Edward Collins, Brenham, to [J. T. Kirkman, A.A.A.G.], June 30, 1867, AC, LR, 1866–1867, reel 4; *Brownsville Ranchero*, November 13, 1866; Frank Holsinger, Beaumont, to William H. Sinclair, A.A.G., April 5, 1866, AC, LR, 1866–1867, reel 6; Hiram Seymour Hall, Marshall, to E. M. Gregory, December 26, 1865, AC, ULR, 1865–1866, reel 17; Ira P. Pedigo, Woodville, to [E. M.] Gregory, March 1, 1866, AC, ULR, 1865–1866, reel 17; and Capt. E. Pratt to D. S. Proudfit, A.A.A.G., Eastern District of Texas, April 7, 1866, AC, ULR, 1865–1866, reel 17.

11. W. E. B. DuBois, *The Souls of Black Folk* (New York: Penguin Books, 1969), 72; Tunnell, ed., *Carpetbagger from Vermont*, 92; Max Woodhull, A.A.G., to E. M. Gregory, November 24, 1865, M742C, LS, May 16–December 30, 1865, reel 1; *Statutes at Large*, 14:173–177; A. P. Ketchum, A.A.A.G., to [E. M. Gregory], September 19, 1865, AC, LR, 1866–1867, reel 6; Max Woodhull, A.A.G., to E. M. Gregory, November 24, 1865, AC, ULR, 1865–1866, reel 17; James Oakes, "A Failure of a Vision: The Collapse of the Freedmen's Bureau Courts," *Civil War History* 25 (March 1979): 69; Diane Neal and Thomas W. Kremm, "'What Shall We Do With the Negro?': The Freedmen's Bureau in Texas," *East Texas Historical Journal* 27 (Fall 1989): 25. Sloan's punishment for offenders is in Bryan, SAC, ROC, 1866–1969, reel 14. The importance of color-blind judicial proceedings is in James Forman, Jr., "Juries and Race in the Nineteenth Century," *Yale Law Journal* 113 (January 2004): 895–938; and Wayne K. Durrill, "Political Legitimacy and Local Courts: 'Politicks at Such a Rage' in a Southern Community During Reconstruction," *Journal of Southern History* 70 (August 2004): 577–602.

12. Stanton Weaver, Crockett, to Chauncey C. Morse, A.A.A.G., February 13, 1866, AC, ULR, 1865–1866, reel 17.

13. Carpenter, "Agents of the Freedmen's Bureau," 40; Endorsement of letter from Chauncey C. Morse, A.A.A.G., to Byron Porter, Houston, January 26, 1866, AC, ES, September 1865–March 1867, reel 2; Nora Estelle Owens, "Presidential Reconstruction in Texas: A Case Study" (Ph.D., diss., Auburn University, 1983), 265; Endorsement of letter from J. Albert Saylor, Hallettsville, to William H. Sinclair, A.A.G., May 21, 1866, AC, ES, September 1865–March 1867, reel 1; Fred W. Reinhard, Crockett, to [Headquarters], November 13, 1867, AC, LR, 1867–1869, reel 15; Donald G. Nieman, *To Set the Law in Motion: The Freedmen's Bureau and the Legal Rights of Blacks, 1865–1868* (Millwood: KTO Press, 1979), 5; Howard, *Autobiography*, 2:223. For the importance of the Civil Rights Act of 1866 and later Fourteenth Amendment, see Alfred Avins, "The Right to

Be a Witness and the Fourteenth Amendment," *Missouri Law Review* 31 (Fall 1966): 471–504.

14. I compiled the data for the courts from the Records of the Field Offices (M1912), not the Records of the Assistant Commissioner (M821). Where all offenses for the latter are on reel 32, those for the field offices are located in the categories of Register of Complaints, Letters Sent, Register of Contracts, Register of Letters Received, and Letters Sent and Registers of Letters Received with Endorsements. All the court cases from the field offices are located from reel 12 to reel 28. The advantage is the agents compiled this information in real time and chronologically. For example, Greg Cantrell found 1,390 in his study of Reconstruction violence, while Crouch used 1,524 cases. Rebecca Kosary had 2,214. Besides the aforementioned, a further reason for the disparity between the total numbers in this study compared to others is those three students looked exclusively at "criminal" (those considered violent) offenses, probably dismissing everything else that did not meet such standards. (See Gregg Cantrell, "Racial Violence and Reconstruction Politics in Texas, 1867–1868," *Southwestern Historical Quarterly* 93 [January 1990]: 343; Crouch, "Spirit of Lawlessness," 220; and Rebecca Kosary, "To Degrade and Control: White Violence and the Maintenance of Racial and Gender Boundaries in Reconstruction Texas, 1865–1868" [Ph.D. diss., Texas A&M University, 2006], chapter 3 and Appendix B).

15. For the cases involving bestiality and black gun rights, see Case of James Haynes (fm) vs. Fletcher Burnet (wm), July 11, 1867, Austin, SAC, ROC, June 1867–December 1868, reel 12; and Case of Washington Thomas (fm) vs. Mr. Symersman (wm), July 6, 1868, Houston, SAC, ROC, December 1865–December 1868, reel 22.

16. Samuel Spencer (fm) vs. Primus Dickes, October 3, 1868, SAC, Gonzales, ROC, October 1868, reel 21.

17. Abner Doubleday, Galveston, to J. T. Kirkman, A.A.A.G., March 1, 1867, AC, ROC, December 1866–May 1867, reel 20; George C. Abbott, Hempstead, to E. M. Gregory, November 23, 1865, AC, ULR, 1865–1866, reel 17; William H. Sinclair, Inspector, to Henry A. Ellis, A.A.A.G., October 7, 1866, AC, LR, 1866–1867, reel 8; Mortimer H. Goddin, Livingston, to J. T. Kirkman, A.A.A.G., July 20, 1866, AC, LR, 1866–1867, reel 5; William Garretson, Matagorda, to J. T. Kirkman, A.A.A.G., May 31, 1867, AC, ROC, December 1866–May 1867, reel 20; Nieman, *To Set the Law in Motion*, 173; Richter, *Overreached on All Sides*, 137; Sara Rapport, "The Freedmen's Bureau as a Legal Agent for Black Men and Women in Georgia, 1865–1868," *Georgia Historical Quarterly* 73 (Spring 1989): 26–29.

18. F. D. Inge, Leona, to Colonel, July 30, 1866, AC, LR, 1866–1867, reel 6; Abbott, *Freedmen's Bureau in South Carolina*, 105; Jacob C. DeGress, Houston, to Colonel, December 6, 1866, AC, LR, 1866–1867, reel 5; Arthur H. Edey to J. B. Kiddoo, August 18, 1866, AC, LR, 1866–1867, reel 5; Philip Howard, Meridian, to [E. M.] Gregory, April 30, 1866, AC, LR, 1866–1867, reel 6; Albert Evans, Sherman, to Henry A. Ellis, A.A.A.G., October 31, 1866, AC, LR, 1866–1867, reel 5; George C. Abbott, Hempstead, to [E. M.] Gregory, October 31, 1865, AC, ULR, 1865–1866, reel 17; Jacob C. DeGress, Houston, to [Maj. Gen. Joseph Anthony Mower, Commander, District of Eastern Texas], November 13, 1865, AC, LR, 1866–1867, reel 5; William Garretson, Matagorda, to J. T. Kirkman, A.A.A.G., June 14, 1867, AC, LR, 1866–1867, reel 5); Eliza (fw) vs. John

Pulty (fm), June 14, 1867, Bryan, SAC, ROC, 1866–1868, reel 14; J. J. Reynolds to A. Bledsoe, April 20, 1868, AC, LS, March 1867–May 1869, reel 1; J. P. Richardson, A.A.A.G., to F. P. Wood, Brenham, March 18, 1868, AC, LS, March 1867–May 1869, reel 1; General Orders, No. 5, February 2, 1867, AC, IRB, October 186–April 1869, reel 19; Charles Griffin to O. O. Howard, July 1, 1867, AC, LS, March 1867–May 1869, reel 1; Endorsement of letter from N. H. Randlett, Courtney, to William H. Sinclair, A.A.G., August 8, 1866, AC, ES, April 1866–September 1867, reel 2; Nieman, *To Set the Law in Motion*, 9.

19. The numbers for black vs. white are: settlement (547), money (2,584), and contract (189). Those for white vs. black are: settlement (60), money (176), and contract (251). Those for black vs. black are: settlement (30), money (532), and contract (17).

20. Charles Haughn, Waco, to J. P. Richardson, A.A.A.G., April 4, 1868, AC, ROC, March–April, 1868, reel 25; Nesbit B. Jenkins, Wharton, to J. P. Richardson, A.A.A.G., March 31, 1868, AC, ROC, March–April, 1868, reel 25; Case of Zillah Rodgers (fw) vs. John Rodgers (wm), September 5, 1868, Austin, SAC, ROC, February 1867–December 1868, reel 12; John F. Stokes, Columbia, to W. L. Perry, May 21, 1867, SAC, Letters Sent and Registers of Letters Received with Endorsements, April 1867–November 1868, reel 15 (hereafter LSRE); Patrick F. Duggan, Columbia, to J. T. Kirkman, A.A.A.G., June 24, 1867, SAC, LSRE, April 1867–November 1868, reel 15. Case breakdowns are in the records for the subdistricts of Liberty, August 1866 to December 1868, and Marshall, November 1868 to December 1868: 74 for contract; 8 for stealing and loss of property; 15 for assault and battery; and 9 cases classified as other. For Marshall it was: 65 for contract; 5 loss of property; 13 for assault and theft; 4 threats; and 3 cases under other. (See Liberty, SAC, ROC, August 1866–December 1868, reel 23 and Marshall, SAC, ROC, February 1866–November 1867, reel 24.) For other courses in judicial matters, see J. P. Richardson, ASAC, Austin, to J. T. Kirkman, A.A.A.G., March 31, 1867, SAC, LS, October 1866–May 1867, reel 12; Henry Sweeney, Jefferson, to Post Adjutant, Post of Jefferson, December 14, 1868, SAC, LS, October–December 1868, reel 23; A. H. Mayer, Liberty, to Henry A. Ellis, A.A.A.G., September 30, 1866, AC, LR, 1866–1867, reel 7; A. H. Mayer, Liberty, to Charles Garretson, A.A.A.G., October 1, 1867, AC, ROC, September–October, 1867, reel 22; George C. Abbott, Hempstead, to [E. M. Gregory], October 25, 1865, AC, ULR, 1865–1866, reel 17.

21. Owens, "Presidential Reconstruction," 270; Max Woodhull, A.A.G., to E. M. Gregory, November 24, 1865, AC, ULR, 1865–1866, reel 17; Endorsement of letter from H. W. Allen, Hempstead, to William H. Sinclair, A.A.G., June 3, 1866, AC, ES, April 1866–September 1867, reel 2; Endorsement of letter from H. W. Allen, Hempstead, to William H. Sinclair, A.A.G., June 2, 1866, AC, ES, September 1865–March 1868, reel 2; Hardin Hart, Greenville, to A. H. M. Taylor, A.A.A.G., May 31, 1866, AC, ROC, December 1866–May 1867, reel 20; Jacob C. DeGress, Houston, to Henry A. Ellis, A.A.A.G., November 19, 1866, AC, LR, 1866–1867, reel 5; *Joint Committee*, 39th Congress, 1st Session, 146; Endorsement of letter from L. S. Barnes, Crockett, to William H. Sinclair, A.A.G., June 21, 1866, AC, ES, April 1866–September 1867, reel 2. For agents observing civil tribunals, see A. H. Mayer, Liberty, to J. B. Kiddoo, January 9, 1867, AC, ROC, December 1866–May 1867, reel 20; George C. Abbott, Hempstead, to Chauncey C. Morse, A.A.A.G., February 19, 1866, AC, ULR, 1865–1866, reel 17; Endorsement of

letter from Isaac Johnson, La Grange, to William H. Sinclair, A.A.G., July 28, 1866, AC, ES, April 1866–September 1867, reel 2; Charles W. Ramsdell, *Reconstruction in Texas* (Austin: University of Texas Press, 1910), 76–77; and E. Merton Coulter, *Georgia: A Short History* (Chapel Hill: University of North Carolina Press, 1947), 349–350.

22. William H. Sinclair, Inspector, to Henry A. Ellis, A.A.A.G., November 30, 1866, AC, ULR, 1865–1866, reel 17; Samuel C. Sloan, Richmond, to William H. Sinclair, A.A.G., June 30, 1866, AC, LR, 1866–1867, reel 8; Stanton Weaver, Crockett, to Chauncey C. Morse, A.A.A.G., February 21, 1866, AC, ULR, 1865–1866, reel 17; and Stanton Weaver, Crockett, to Chauncey C. Morse, A.A.A.G., February 28, 1866, AC, ULR, 1865–1866, reel 17; Rapport, "Freedmen's Bureau as a Legal Agent," 46. Cases involving J. Ernest Goodman are Colorado County District Court Records, Criminal Cause File Nos. 570, 591, 603, and 611, Criminal Minute Book D., Colorado County Courthouse, Colorado County, Texas, pp. 114, 126, 185, 226.

23. Jacob C. DeGress, Houston, to Henry A. Ellis, A.A.A.G., December 4, 1866, AC, LR, 1866–1867, reel 5; Nieman, *To Set the Law in Motion*, 117, 136–137, 142–144; J. B. Kiddoo to O. O. Howard, May 23, 1866, AC, LS, September 1865–March 1867, reel 1; Low, "Freedmen's Bureau and Civil Rights in Maryland," 239; Endorsement of letter from Edward Miller, Victoria, to S. H. Lathrop, A.A.A.G., December 6, 1866, AC, ES, April 1866–September 1867, reel 2.

24. Belz, *A New Birth of Freedom*, 158; Robert J. Kaczorowski, *The Politics of Judicial Interpretation: The Federal Courts, Department of Justice and Civil Rights, 1866–1876* (New York: Oceana Publications, Inc., 1985), 27, 36, 117–119; Nieman, *To Set the Law in Motion*, 105; Foner, *Reconstruction*, 149; Donald G. Nieman, "The Freedmen's Bureau and the Mississippi Black Code," *Journal of Mississippi History* 40 (May 1978): 92; Cohen-Lack, "Struggle for Sovereignty," 81–82; David J. Flanigan, "The Criminal Law of Slavery and Freedom, 1800–1868" (Ph.D. diss., Rice University, 1973), 399–400; Richardson, ed., *Compilation of the Messages and Papers of the Presidents*, 6:429–431, 434–438. On the belief about civil rights and federalism, see Robert J. Kaczorowski, "To Begin the Nation Anew: Congress, Citizenship, and Civil Rights After the Civil War," *American Historical Review* 92 (February 1987): 45–68; Charles Fairman, *Reconstruction and Reunion, 1864–1868* (New York: The Macmillan Company, 1971), 1228–1229; Harold Hyman, *A More Perfect Union: The Impact of the Civil War and Reconstruction on the Constitution* (New York: Alfred K. Knopf, 1973); Michael Les Benedict, *A Compromise of Principle: Congressional Republicans and Reconstruction* (New York: W.W. Norton & Company, 1974), 27, 41, 48, 56–69, 122–126, 147–149, 170; Michael Les Benedict, "Preserving the Constitution: The Conservative Basis of Radical Reconstruction," *Journal of American History* 61 (June 1974): 65–90; and Phillip S. Paludan, *A Covenant with Death: The Constitution, Law, and Equality in the Civil War Era* (Urbana: University of Illinois Press, 1975), 58, 261, 274–275.

25. William H. Sinclair, Inspector, to J. B. Kiddoo, December 23, 1866, AC, LR, 1866–1867, reel 8; J. B. Kiddoo to O. O. Howard June 26, 1866, AC, LS, September 1865–March 1867, reel 1; J. B. Kiddoo to O. O. Howard, May 26, 1866, AC, LS, September 1865–March 1867, reel 1; A. P. Ketchum, A.A.A.G., to J. B. Kiddoo, June 7, 1866, M742C, LS, January 1–December 19, 1866, reel 2; Telegram from O. O. Howard to J. B. Kiddoo, July 10, 1866, AC, LR, 1866–1867, reel 6.

26. L. S. Barnes, Crockett, to A.A.A.G., September 11, 1866, AC, LR, 1866–1867, reel 4; A. P. Ketchum, A.A.A.G., to J. B. Kiddoo, September 19, 1866, AC, LR, 1866–1867, reel 6.

27. Anthony M. Bryant, Sherman, to J. T. Kirkman, A.A.A.G., June 30, 1867, AC, ROC, June–August, 1867, reel 21; Nesbit B. Jenkins, Wharton, to Charles A. Vernou, A.A.A.G., May 31, 1868, AC, ROC, May–July, 1868, reel 26; Craig, "Memoirs," 79; Foner, *Reconstruction*, 150; Oliver H. Swingley, Austin, to E. M. Gregory, November 1, 1865, AC, ULR, 1865–1866, reel 17; Stanton Weaver, Crockett, to Chauncey C. Morse, A.A.A.G., February 21, 1866, AC, ULR, 1865–1866, reel 17; Endorsement of letter from Isaac Johnson, La Grange, to William H. Sinclair, A.A.G., September 6, 1866, AC, ES, April 1866–September 1867, reel 2; William S. McFeely, "The Freedmen's Bureau: A Study in Betrayal" (Ph.D. diss., Yale University, 1966), 255; O. O. Howard to [Assistant Commissioners], September 6, 1865, AC, ULR, 1865–1866, reel 17; J. B. Kiddoo to O. O. Howard, June 26, 1866, M752C, LR, May–August, 1866, reel 36; J. Ernest Goodman, Columbus, to William H. Sinclair, A.A.A.G., May 22, 1866, SAC, LS, April–July and November 1866, reel 16; Oakes, "Failure of a Vision," 66; Jacob C. DeGress, Houston, to [E. M. Gregory], December 1, 1865, AC, ULR, 1865–1866, reel 17; George C. Abbott, Hempstead, to E. M. Gregory, October 31, 1865, AC, ULR, 1865–1866, reel 17; Cohen-Lack, "Struggle for Sovereignty," 82; Cimbala and Miller, eds., *Freedmen's Bureau and Reconstruction*, 17–21; Endorsement of letter from Champ Carter, Sterling, to William H. Sinclair, A.A.G., June 2, 1866, AC, ES, April 1866–September 1867, reel 2. Other instances of agents confused about their judicial jurisdiction, see Endorsement of letter from Samuel C. Sloan, Richmond, to William H. Sinclair, A.A.G., May 22, 1866, AC; Endorsement of letter from J. Ernest Goodman, Columbus, to William H. Sinclair, A.A.G., May 22, 1866, AC; Endorsement of letter from Samuel A. Craig, Brenham, to William H. Sinclair, A.A.G., May 26, 1866, AC (all in ES, April 1866–September 1867, reel 2). Works critical of Bureau courts are Harry August Volz III, "The Administration of Justice by the Freedmen's Bureau in Kentucky, South Carolina, and Virginia" (Master Thesis, University of Virginia, 1975), 52; Kaczorowski, *Politics of Judicial Interpretation*, 43; Oakes, "Failure of a Vision," 66–76; Rapport, "Freedmen's Bureau as a Legal Agent," 46, 52–53; Barry A. Crouch, "Black Dreams and White Justice," *Prologue* 6 (Winter 1974): 264; Neal and Kremm, "What Shall We Do With the Negro?," 25; and Nieman, *To Set the Law in Motion*, 146. Bureau men's confusion caused by the numerous, and at times contradictory, policies are Stanton Weaver, Crockett, to Chauncey C. Morse, A.A.A.G., February 21, 1866, AC, ULR, 1865–1866, reel 17; Endorsement of letter from Isaac Johnson, La Grange, to William H. Sinclair, A.A.G., September 6, 1866, AC, ES, April 1866–September 1867, reel 2; William S. McFeely, "The Freedmen's Bureau: A Study in Betrayal" (Ph.D. diss., Yale University, 1966), 255; O. O. Howard to [Assistant Commissioners], September 6, 1865, AC, ULR, 1865–1866, reel 17; J. B. Kiddoo to O. O. Howard, June 26, 1866, M752C, LR, May–August, 1866, reel 36; J. Ernest Goodman, Columbus, to William H. Sinclair, A.A.A.G., May 22, 1866, SAC, LS, April–July and November 1866, reel 16; Endorsement of letter from Champ Carter, Sterling, to William H. Sinclair, A.A.G., June 2, 1866, AC, ES, April 1866–September 1867, reel 2.

28. Oakes, "A Failure of a Vision," 74; Nieman, "Andrew Johnson, the Freedmen's Bureau," 420; Nieman, *To Set the Law in Motion*, 113–114. Civil courts evading their

responsibilities are in Charles Griffin to O. O. Howard, February 12, 1867, M752C, LR, January–May, 1867, reel 44; James P. Butler, Huntsville, to J. P. Richardson, A.A.A.G., May 2, 1868, AC, ROC, March–April, 1868, reel 25; Nesbit B. Jenkins, Wharton, to Charles A. Vernou, A.A.A.G., June 30, 1868, AC, ROC, May–July, 1868, reel 26; Arthur B. Homer, Columbia, to J. P. Richardson, A.A.A.G., July 27, 1868, AC, LR, 1867–1869, reel 12; and E. M. Pease to J. J. Reynolds, February 27, 1868, AC, LR, 1867–1869, reel 12.

29. Tyler, ed., *New Handbook of Texas*, 1:562–563; Winnell Albrecht, "The Texas Black Codes" (Master's Thesis, Southwest Texas State University, 1969), 84–102.

30. Barry Crouch, "'All the Vile Passions': The Texas Black Codes of 1866," *Southwestern Historical Quarterly* 97 (July 1993), 23–24; H. P. N. Gammel, *The Laws of Texas, 1822–1897* ... 10 vols. (Austin: The Gammel Book Company, 1898), 5:995–996.

31. Farmer-Kaiser, *Freedwomen and the Freedmen's Bureau*, 213; Gammel, *The Laws of Texas*, 5:979; Schmidt, *Free to Work*, 62–63; Karin Zipf, *Labor of Innocents: Forced Apprenticeship in North Carolina, 1715–1919* (Baton Rouge: Louisianan State University Press, 2005), 40–41; Crouch, "All the Vile Passions," 26; J. Michael Rhyne, "'Conduct ... Inexcusable and Unjustifiable': Bound Children, Battered Freedwomen, and the Limits of Emancipation in Kentucky's Bluegrass Region," *Journal of Social History* 42 (Winter 2008): 324; Endorsement of letter from J. Albert Saylor, Hallettsville, to William H. Sinclair, A.A.G., May 7, 1866, AC, Endorsements Sent, April 1866–March 1867, reel 2; Michael Grossberg, *Governing the Hearth: Law and the Family in Nineteenth-Century America* (Chapel Hill: University of North Carolina Press, 1985), 259.

32. William H. Sinclair, A.A.G., to Stanton Weaver, Crockett, January 23, 1866, AC, LS, September 1865–March 1867, reel 1; Endorsement of letter from J. Orville Shelby, Liberty, to William H. Sinclair, A.A.G., May 1, 1866, AC, ES, April 1866–September 1867, reel 2; Byron Porter, Austin, to John Bremond, November 20, 1866, SAC, LS, July 1866–May 1867, reel 12; Endorsement of letter from J. F. Hutchison, Columbia, to William H. Sinclair, A.A.G., May 8, 1866, AC, ES, April 1866–September 1867, reel 2; William H. Sinclair, A.A.G., to J. W. McConaughey, Richmond, February 5, 1866, SAC, LS, March 1867–May 1869, reel 1; Eugene Smith, Waco, to Chauncey C. Morse, A.A.A.G., February 23, 1866, AC, ULR, 1865–1886, reel 17; Endorsement of letter from Phineas Stevens, Hallettsville, to Charles Griffin, August 27, 1867, AC, ES, March 1867–May 1869, reel 2; W. A. Low, "The Freedmen's Bureau and Civil Rights in Maryland," *Journal of Negro History* 37 (July 1952): 232; B. J. Arnold, Brenham, to Chauncey C. Morse, A.A.A.G., October 28, 1865, AC, ULR, 1865–1866, reel 17; J. B. Kiddoo to M. L. Dunn, August 20, 1866, AC, LS, September 1865–March 1867, reel 1.

33. J. B. Kiddoo to M. L. Dunn, August 20, 1866, AC, LS, September 1865–March 1867, reel 1; Oliver H. Swingley, Austin, to E. M. Gregory, November 25, 1865, AC, RRR, 1865–1866, reel 29; Oliver H. Swingley, Waco, to E. M. Gregory, December 8, 1865, AC, ULR, 1865–1866, reel 17; Ira P. Pedigo, Woodville, to E. M. Gregory, March 1, 1866, AC, LR, 1866–1867, reel 7; John T. Raper, Columbus, to E. M. Gregory, November 29, 1865, AC, ULR, 185–1866, reel 17; Chauncey C. Morse, A.A.A.G., to John T. Raper, Columbus, November 29, 1865, AC, LS, September 1865–March 1867, reel 1; Hiram Seymour Hall, Marshall, to E. M. Gregory, November 6, 1865, AC, ULR, 1865–1866, reel 17; Endorsement of letter from E. M. McCullugh to J. T. Kirkman, A.A.A.G., August 20,

1867, AC, ES, April 1866–September 1867, reel 2. For the similarities in apprentice policy, see Farmer-Kaiser, *Freedwomen and the Freedmen's Bureau*, 56–57.

34. William J. Neely, Victoria, to Captain, August 20, 1868, AC, LR, 1867–1869, reel 14; F. P. Wood, Brenham, to Charles A. Vernou, A.A.A.G., August 8, 1868, AC, LR, 1867–1869, reel 16.

35. David S. Beath, Cotton Gin, to [J. J. Reynolds], September 18, 1868, AC, LR, 1867–1869, reel 10; LaVonne Roberts Jackson, "'Family and Freedom': The Freedmen's Bureau and African-American Women in Texas in the Reconstruction Era, 1865–1869" (Ph.D. diss., Howard University, 1996), 128, 126; James C. Devine, Huntsville, to James Hentiss, March 6, 1867, SAC, PCLS, January 1867–March 1868, reel 22. Other examples of oversight of apprentice contracts are Alex B. Coggeshall, Bastrop, to J. T. Kirkman, A.A.A.G., February 5, 1867, AC, LR, 1866–1867, reel 4; Case of Mary Warren (fw) vs. James Finnie, November 12, 1866, Hallettsville, SAC, ROC, October 1866–January 1867 and October–December 1868, reel 21; and Endorsement of letter from Walter B. Pease, Houston, to J. T. Kirkman, A.A.A.G., March 12, 1867, AC, ES, April 1866–September 1867, reel 2.

36. Endorsement of letter from J. P. Jones, citizen, to William H. Sinclair, A.A.G., June 1, 1866, SAC, ES, April 1866–September 1867, reel 2.

37. Samuel C. Sloan, Richmond, to Chauncey C. Morse, A.A.A.G., January 27, 1866, AC, ULR, 1865–1866, reel 17; Charles C. Culver, Cotton Gin, to J. T. Kirkman, A.A.A.G., July 24, 1867, AC, LR, 1866–1867, reel 4; Case of Sandy Mungoe (fw) to Ed. Brunnells, November 6, 1867, Boston, SAC, ROC, July 1867–June 1868, reel 13; Endorsement of letter from Walter B. Pease, Houston, to J. T. Kirkman, A.A.A.G., February 16, 1867, AC, ES, April 1866–September 1867, reel 2; Gregory Barrett, Tyler, to Charles A. Vernou, A.A.A.G., June 30, 1868, AC, ROC, May–July, 1868, reel 26; Case of Charlotte Duckett (fw) vs. Levinia E. Lucas, July 8, 1867, Boston, SAC, ROC, July 1867–June 1868, reel 13; Jones, "Soldiers of Light and Love," 47; Jackson, "Family and Freedom," 119; Barry A. Crouch and Larry Madaras, "Reconstructing Black Families: Perspectives from the Texas Freedmen's Bureau Records," *Prologue* 18 (Summer 1986): 116–117; Case of Charles Leigh (fm) vs. Charles Rock, November 5, 1867, Boston, SAC, ROC, July 1867–June 1868, reel 13; Karin L. Zipf, "Reconstructing 'Free Woman': African-American Women, Apprenticeship, and Custody Rights during Reconstruction," *Journal of Women's History* 12 (Spring 2000): 25. For the effect of free labor domesticity, apprenticeship, and gender relations, see Farmer-Kaiser, *Freedwomen and the Freedmen' Bureau*. For works arguing freedwomen were distrustful of the Bureau, believing it unresponsive to their needs, narrow in its expectations, preoccupied with restoring order, divergent in its definition of womanhood, ignorant to gender/racial disparities, compromising to freedpeople's freedom, inadequate in its help, and coercive and racist in its practices, see Catherine Clinton, "Reconstructing Freedwomen," in *Divided Houses: Gender and the Civil War*, ed. Catherine Clinton and Nina Silber (New York: Oxford University Press, 1992), 306–319; Leslie A. Schwalm, *A Hard Fight for We: Women's Transition from Slavery to Freedom in South Carolina* (Urbana: University of Illinois Press, 1997), especially chapter 5; Nancy Cott, *Public Vows: A History of Marriage and the Nation* (Cambridge: Harvard University Press, 2000), 84–94; Laura F. Edwards, *Scarlett Doesn't Live Here Anymore: Southern Women in the Civil War Era*

(Urbana: University of Illinois Press, 2004), 84–94, 133; Tera W. Hunter, *To 'Joy My Freedom: Southern Black Women's Lives and Labors After the Civil War* (Cambridge: Harvard University Press, 1997), 23–24; Linda Kerber, *No Constitutional Right to be Ladies: Women and the Obligations of Citizenship* (New York: Hill and Wang, 1998), 68; Zipf, *Labor of Innocents*, 90–91; and Susan E. O'Donovan, *Becoming Free in the Cotton South* (Cambridge: Harvard University Press, 2007), 166–170, 220–221, 267.

38. Case of George Turner (fm) vs. Hall (wm), November 10, 1866, Hallettsville, SAC, LS, May–June 1866 and October 1866–March 1868, reel 21; James Oakes, Austin, to J. T. Kirkman, A.A.A.G., May 30, 1867, SAC, LS, May 1867–December 1868, reel 12. Other examples of agents approaching apprenticed contracts case-by-case include Case of Dinah Wren (fw) vs. Dr. Hartridge, June 18, 1867, Houston, SAC, ROC, December 1865–December 1868, reel 22; Endorsement of letter from Charles E. Culver, Cotton Gin, to Charles Griffin, July 24, 1867, AC, ES, April 1866–September 1867, reel 2; Louis W. Stevenson, Columbus, to James Gillette, Bryan, November 19, 1868, SAC, Letters Received and Receipts, October–December, 1868, reel 14 (hereafter LRR); J. P. Richardson, A.A.A.G., to J. D. Vernay, Goliad, June 3, 1867, SAC, LS, May 1867–December 1868, reel 12; and J. W. McConaughey, Wharton, to Captain, February 24, 1866, AC, LR, 1866–1867, reel 9.

39. Farmer, "Freedwomen and the Freedmen's Bureau," 91; Case of May (fw) vs. Frank (fm), June 28, 1867, Bryan, SAC, ROC, 1866–1868, reel 14; Henry Young, Austin, to C. S. Roberts, A.A.A.G., September 11, 1868, AC, LR, 1867–1869, reel 16; Herbert G. Gutman, *The Black Family in Slavery and Freedom, 1750–1925* (New York: Pantheon Books, 1976), 392; Farmer-Kaiser, "With a Weight of Circumstances Like Millstones About Their Necks," 420–421, 425; Farmer-Kaiser, *Freedwomen and the Freedmen's Bureau*, 153. For the intricacies of the government's entry into dependency, see Katherine M. Franke, "Taking Care," *Chicago-Kent Law Review* 76 (2001): 1541–1555.

40. Endorsement of letter from William Longworth, Seguin, to William H. Sinclair, A.A.G., May 17, 1866, AC, ES, April 1866–September 1867, reel 2; Anthony M. Bryant, Sherman, to Charles Garretson, A.A.A.G., October 31, 1867, AC, ROC, September–October, 1867, reel 22; Anthony M. Bryant, Sherman, to Charles Garretson, A.A.A.G., September 30, 1867, AC, ROC, September–October, 1867, reel 22; John Dix, Corpus Christi, to J. P. Richardson, A.A.A.G., February 29, 1868, AC, ROC, January–February, 1868, reel 24; Isaac Johnson, La Grange, to J. P. Richardson, A.A.A.G., November 30, 1867, AC, ROC, November–December, 1867, reel 23; Charles Haughn, Waco, to Charles A. Vernou, A.A.A.G., December 31, 1868, AC, ROC, November–December, 1868, reel 28; Endorsement of letter from J. Orville Shelby, Liberty, to William H. Sinclair, A.A.G., May 8, 1866, AC, ES, April 1866–September, 1867, reel 2; Endorsement of letter from B. A. Brown to William H. Sinclair, A.A.G., July 22, 1866, AC, ES, April 1866–September 1867, reel 2; Endorsement of letter from Martha Watt to William H. Sinclair, A.A.G., [Summer 1866], AC, ES, April 1866–September 1867, reel 2.

41. Farmer-Kaiser, *Freedwomen and the Freedmen's Bureau*, 107–108, 112–113; Laura Edwards, *Gendered Strife and Confusion: The Political Culture of Reconstruction* (Urbana: University of Illinois Press, 1997), 50; Noralee Frankel, *Freedom's Women: Black Women and Family in Civil War Era Mississippi* (Bloomington: Indiana University Press,

1999), 136; Rapport, "Freedmen's Bureau as a Legal Agent," 39; Rebecca Scott, "The Battle Over the Child: Child Apprenticeship and the Freedmen's Bureau in North Carolina," *Prologue* 10 (Summer 1978): 102.

42. Kosay, "To Degrade and Control," 73.

43. Scott, "Battle Over the Child," 110; W. A. Low, "The Freedmen's Bureau in the Border States," in *Radicalism, Racism, and Party Realignment: The Border States During Reconstruction*, ed. Richard Curry (Baltimore: Johns Hopkins University Press, 1969), 247; Richard Paul Fuke, "Planters, Apprenticeship, and Forced Labor: The Black Family Under Pressure in Post-Emancipation Maryland," *Agricultural History* 62 (Fall 1988): 72–73; Troy Lee Kickler, "Black Children and Northern Missionaries: Freedmen's Bureau Agents, Southern Whites in Reconstruction Tennessee, 1865–1869" (Ph.D. diss., University of Tennessee, 2003), 150–151; Farmer-Kaiser, "With a Weight of Circumstances Like Millstones About Their Necks," 429; Rapport, "Freedmen's Bureau as a Legal Agent," 39; Kosary, "To Degrade and Control," 73; Edwards, *Gendered Strife and Confusion*, 50; Morgan, *Emancipation in Virginia's Tobacco Belt*, 139, 173; Schwalm, *A Hard Fight for We*, 251, 254; Farmer-Kaiser, *Freedwomen and the Freedmen's Bureau*, 128; Zipf, "Reconstructing 'Free Woman,'" 25. More works that criticize Bureau agents for apprenticing black children are Kickler, "Black Children and Northern Missionaries," 174; Litwack, *Been in the Storm So Long*, 237; Famer-Kaiser, "With a Weight of Circumstances Like Millstones About Their Necks," 431; and Scott, "Battle Over the Child," 101–113.

44. John H. Morrison, Palestine, to J. P. Richardson, A.A.A.G., January 31, 1868, AC, ROC, January–February, 1868, reel 24.

5. The Bureau's Highwater Mark: The J. B. Kiddoo Era, November 1866–January 1867

1. Circular No. 9, March 23, 1866, AC, IRB, October 1865–1869, reel 19; Circular Letter from O. O. Howard, March 2, 1866, AC, Letters Received, 1866–1867, reel 6; Barry A. Crouch, "The 'Chords of Love': Legalizing Black Marital and Family Rights in Postwar Texas," *Journal of Negro History* 79 (Autumn 1994): 334, 338.

2. Circular Letter from O. O. Howard, March 2, 1866, AC, LR, 1866–1867, reel 6; Circular No. 9, March 23, 1866, AC, IRB, October 1865–April 1869, reel 19; Franke, "Taking Care," 1545; Grossberg, *Governing the Hearth*, 130; Endorsement of letter from L. S. Barnes, Crockett, to William H. Sinclair, A.A.G., June 21, 1866, AC, ES, April 1866–September 1867, reel 2.

3. A. P. Delano, Marlin Falls, to Chauncey C. Morse, A.A.G., March 26, 1866, AC, LR, 1866–1867, reel 5; A. P. Delano, Marlin Falls, to J. B. Kiddoo, December 31, 1866, AC, ROC, December 1866–May 1867, reel 20. For freedpeople marriages, see William J. Neely, Victoria, to Captain, August 20, 1868, AC, LR, 1867–1869, reel 14; C. S. Roberts, A.A.A.G., to William J. Neely, Victoria, August 25, 1868, AC, LS, March 1867–May 1669, reel 1; and J. W. McConaughey, Wharton, to William H. Sinclair, A.A.G., May 1, 1866, AC, LR, 1866–1867, reel 7.

4. Case of Sally King (fw) vs. Bob King (fm), December 21, 1868, Brenham, SAC, ROC, April–December 1868, reel 14. For cases where the defendant was male, see Case

of John Adams (fm) vs. Catherine (fw), May 26, 1868, Houston, SAC, ROC, December 1865–December 1868, reel 22; Case of John Adams (fm) vs. Woody Hunter (fm), May 26, 1868, Houston, SAC, ROC, December 1865–December 1868; Case of George Lewis (fm) vs. Nellie Lewis (fw), May 23, 1868, Houston, SAC, ROC, December 1865–December 1868. Other cases of divorce/separation are Case of Fansy Edgar (fw) vs. Bob Edgar (fm), November 1867, Galveston, SAC, LS, January 1867–June 1868, reel 19; Case of Margaret Aaron (fw) vs. Dennis Aaron (fm), November 6, 1867, Galveston, SAC, LS, January 1867–June 1868, reel 19; Case of John Coleman (fm) vs. Mary Coleman (fw), October 21, 1868, Brenham, SAC, ROC, April–December 1868, reel 14; and Case of Lucinda (fw) vs. Charly Reed (fm), August 22, 1868, Houston, SAC, ROC, June 1867–September 1868, reel 22.

   5. David S. Beath, Cotton Gin, to Charles A. Vernou, A.A.A.G., September 26, 1868, AC, LR, 1867–1869, reel 10; John Dix, Corpus Christi, to Charles A. Vernou, A.A.A.G., [September 1868], AC, ROC, August–October, 1868, reel 27; Case of Common Decency vs. Bevy of Young Women, June 24, 1867, SAC, Houston, ROC, December 1865–December 1868, reel 22; B. J. Arnold, Brenham, to E. M. Gregory, October 30, 1865, AC, ULR, 1865–1866, reel 17; Ruthe Winegarten, ed., *Black Texas Women: 150 Years of Trial and Triumph* (Austin: University of Texas Press, 1995), 57; Crouch, "Chords of Love," 346.

   6. Samuel C. Sloan, Richmond, to Chauncey C. Morse, A.A.A.G., January 27, 1866, AC, ULR, 1865–1866, reel 17; Case of Sheania Crawford (fw) vs. Allec Warren (fm), August 20, 1866, Houston, SAC, ROC, December 1865–December 1868, reel 22; James P. Butler, Huntsville, to J. T. Kirkman, A.A.A.G., May 31, 1867, AC, ROC, December 1866–May 1867, reel 20; Franke, "Taking Care," 1548; James T. Downs, "Diagnosing Reconstruction: Sickness, Dependency, and the Medical Division of the Freedmen's Bureau, 1861–1870" (Ph.D. diss., Columbia University, 2005), 175–176; Farmer-Kaiser, *Freedwomen and the Freedmen's Bureau*, 50. For works on nineteenth-century attitudes about marriage and gender roles, see Stanley, *From Bondage to Contract*, 58–59; Franklin, *Ensuring Inequality*, 31, 42; and Elizabeth A. Regosin, *Freedom's Promise: Ex-Slave Families and Citizenship in the Age of Emancipation* (Charlottesville: University of Virginia Press, 2002), 148–157. Agents had leeway in concerning marriage because Bureau regulations were quite broad. (See Suzanne Stone Johnson, ed., *Bitter Freedom: William Stone's Record of Service in the Freedmen's Bureau* [Columbia: University of South Carolina Press, 2010]: 9.)

   7. Farmer-Kaiser, *Freedwomen and the Freedmen's Bureau*, 157; A. P. Wiley to E. M. Gregory, February 20, 1866, AC, ULR, 1865–1866, reel 17; Patrick F. Duggan, Columbia, to J. T. Kirkman, A.A.A.G., June 24, 1867, SAC, LSRE, April 1867–November 1868, reel 15; Case of Emma Hatfield (fw) vs. Lacy McKenzie (wm), Austin June, 4, 1867, Austin, SAC, ROC, June 1867–December 1868, reel 12; Patrick F. Duggan, Columbia, to J. T. Kirkman, A.A.A.G., June 24, 1867, SAC, LSRE, April 1867–November 1868, reel 15. Custody dealings are Case of Maria Scoggs vs. Campbell Trigg, April 4, 1867, Bastrop, SAC, ROC, February 1867–December 1868, reel 12; Endorsement of letter from Jacob C. DeGress, Houston, to D. F. Meyers, December 13, 1865, AC, ES, September 1865–March 1867, reel 2; Peter W. Bardaglio, "Challenging Parental Custody Rights: The Legal Reconstruction of Parenthood in the Nineteenth-Century

American South," *Continuity and Change* 4 (August 1989): 270–280; Jesse Rigdom, (fm), to [Headquarters], January 10, 1866, AC, ULR, 1865–1866, reel 17; Case of Joanna (fw) vs. Charles Bowden and Jim Smith (fm), July 10, 1867, Bryan, SAC, ROC, 1866–1868, reel 14; and Walter B. Pease, Houston, to James P. Hutchison, Columbia, [March 1867], SAC, LR, January 1866–December 1868, reel 15. For cases of excess against freedmen, see Champ Carter, Sterling, to Colonel, April 19, 1866, AC, LR, 1866–1867, reel 4; and William H. Sinclair, A.A.G., to Champ Carter, Sterling, April 25, 1866, AC, LS, September 1865–March 1867, reel 1.

 8. Rhyne, "'Conduct . . . Inexcusable and Unjustifiable,'" 331; Case of Mariah Random (fw) vs. Lorenzo Random (fm), May 27, 1867, Richmond, SAC, ES, August 1866–December 1868, reel 25.

 9. Hannah Rosen, *Terror in the Heartland: Citizenship, Sexual Violence, and the Meaning of Race in the Postemancipation South* (Chapel Hill: University of North Carolina Press, 2009), 225; William H. Rock, Richmond, to J. T. Kirkman, July 4, 1867, AC, ROC, June–August, 1867, reel 21; Complaint of Dr. John Donaldson (fm), June 5, 1867, Austin, SAC, ROC, June 1867–December 1868, reel 12; Farmer-Kaiser, *Freedwomen and the Freedmen's Bureau*, 78–79; Schwalm, *Hard Fight for We*, 242–243; and Stanley, *From Bondage to Contract*, 37. SACs protecting against white male violence are Case of Tony Hubert (fw), stepdaughter (fc) vs. John P. Cox, October 28, 1867, Centreville, SAC, ROC, July–October 1867, reel 14; Case of Jackson (fm) vs. Russell, October 3, 1868, Houston, SAC, ROC, December 1865–December 1868, reel 22; Lisa Cardyn, "Sexualized Racism/Gendered Violence: Outraging the Body Politics in the Reconstruction South," *Michigan Law Review* 100 (February 2006): 687; Bell Hooks, *Ain't I a Woman: Black Women and Feminism* (Boston: South End Press, 1981), 56–57; Gerda Lerner, ed., *Black Women in White America: A Documentary History* (New York: Random House, Inc., 1972), 149; and Case of L. Wolfrom vs. Mary Ann Hodge (fw), October 6, 1866, Galveston, SAC, ROC, June 1866–July 1868, reel 19.

 10. Case of Jennette Le Claire (fw) vs. Julia Johnson (fw), March 27, 1867, Galveston, SAC, LS, January 1867–June 1868, reel 19; Case of Arica Ward (fw) vs. Dick Grey (fm), December 2, 1866, Hallettsville, SAC, LS, May–June 1866 and October 1866–March 1868. For antagonism toward prostitutes, see Catherine Clinton, "'Public Women' and Sexual Politics During the American Civil War," in *Battle Scars: Gender and Sexuality in the American Civil War*, ed. Catherine Clinton and Nina Silber (New York: Oxford University Press, 2006), 61–77.

 11. Smallwood, *Time of Hope, Time of Despair*, 94, 6–7; J. B. Kiddoo to O. O. Howard, May 15, 1866, AC, LS, September 1865–March 1867, reel 1; Nehemiah McKinley Christopher, "The History of Negro Public Education in Texas, 1865–1900" (Ph.D. diss., University of Pittsburgh, 1948), 24; E. M. Gregory to O. O. Howard, April 18, 1866, AC, LS, September 1865–March 1867, reel 1; Sandra Eileen Small, "The Yankee Schoolmarm in Southern Freedmen's Schools, 1861–187: The Career of a Stereotype" (Ph.D. diss., Washington State University, 1976), 27–28; William Frank Troost, "Accomplishment and Abandonment: A History of the Freedmen's Bureau School" (Ph.D. diss., University of California Irvine, 2007), 25–48; Joe M. Richardson, *Christian Reconstruction: The American Missionary Association and Southern Blacks, 1861–1890* (Athens: University of Georgia, 1986), 44; Jacqueline Jones, *Soldiers of Light and Love: Northern Teach-*

ers and Georgia Blacks, 1865–1873 (Chapel Hill: University of North Carolina Press, 1980), 9–14; John L. Bell, "Samuel Stanford Ashley, Carpetbagger and Educator," *The North Carolina Historical Review* 72 (Winter 1995): 461–472; Frank M. Hodgson, "Northern Missionary Aid Societies, the Freedmen's Bureau and Their Effect on Education in Montgomery County, Tennessee, 1862–1870," *The West Tennessee Historical Society Papers* 43 (1989): 33; Ronald E. Butchart, *Northern Schools, Southern Blacks, and Reconstruction: Freedmen's Education, 1862–1875* (Westport: Greenwood Press, 1980), 138–143; Ronald E. Butchart, "'We Best Can Instruct Our Own People': New York African Americans in the Freedmen's Schools, 1861–1875," *Afro-Americans in New York Life and History* 12 (1988): 27–49; Heather Andrea Williams, "'Clothing Themselves in Intelligence': The Freedpeople, Schooling, and Northern Teachers, 1861–1871," *Journal of African American History* 87 (Autumn 2002): 372–389; Luther P. Jackson, "The Educational Efforts of the Freedmen's Bureau and Freedmen's Aid Societies in South Carolina, 1862–1872," *The Journal of Negro History* 8 (January 1923): 1–40; John B. Myers, "The Education of the Alabama Freedmen During Presidential Reconstruction, 1865–1867," *Journal of Negro Education* 40 (Spring 1971): 163–171; Ronald E. Butchart and Amy F. Bolleri, "Iowa Teachers Among the Freedpeople of the South, 1862–1876," *The Annals of Iowa* 62 (Winter 2003): 1–29; Joseph Browne, "'To Bring Out the Intellect of the Race': An African American Freedmen's Bureau Agent in Maryland," *Maryland Historical Magazine* 104 (Winter 2008): 374–401; Henry Allen Bullock, *A History of Negro Education in the South: From 1619 to the Present* (Cambridge: Harvard University Press, 1967), 23; Robert C. Morris, *Reading, 'Riting, and Reconstruction: The Education of Freedmen in the South, 1861–1870* (Chicago: University of Chicago Press, 1981), xi. For the focus on moral uplift, see "Education of the Colored Man," Speech by O. O. Howard, date unknown, Oliver Otis Howard Papers, Moorland-Spingarn Research Center, Howard University, Box 53–2, Folder 88, Washington, D.C.; F. P. Wood, Brenham, to Joseph Welch, Superintendent of Education, December 31, 1868, SUP, LR, 1868–1870, reel 9; James C. Devine, Jasper, to J. T. Kirkman, A.A.A.G., July 30, 1867, AC, ROC, June–August 1867, reel 21; William H. Sinclair, A.A.A.G., to John F. Brown, Grimes, March 8, 1866, AC, LS, September 1865–March 1867, reel 1; O. O. Howard to J. W. McKim, March 11, 1867, AC, LR, 1866–1867, reel 6; George T. Ruby, Traveling Agent, to J. T. Kirkman, A.A.A.G., Superintendent of Schools, August 12, 1867, SUP, LR, 1866–1867, reel 4; J. W. McConaughey, Wharton, to J. T. Kirkman, A.A.A.G., April 3, 1867, AC, ROC, December 1866–May 1867, reel 20; and Circular Letter from O. O. Howard, May 15, 1867, AC, LR, 1866–1867, reel 6. Unlike operations in other states, such as Louisiana, the assistant commissioners in Texas did not enact a tax or fee on contracts or wages to fund educational efforts (see Susan E. Dollar, *The Freedmen's Bureau Schools of Natchitoches Parish Louisiana, 1865–1868* [Natcitoches, LA: Northwestern State University Press, 1998], 10).

12. Circular Letter No. 20, August 31, 1866, AC, IRB, October 1865–April 1869, reel 19; James D. Anderson, *The Education of Blacks in the South, 1860–1935* (Chapel Hill: University of North Carolina Press, 1988), 5; Circular No. 4, March 29, 1867, AC, IRB, October 1865–Arpil 1869, reel 19; Charles Griffin to O. O. Howard, July 1, 1867, AC, IRB, October 1865–April 1869, reel 19; Patrick F. Duggan, Columbia, to J. T. Kirkman, A.A.A.G., Superintendent of Schools, August 23, 1867, SUP, LR, 1866–1867, reel 3;

Edwin Miller, Millican, to J. T. Kirkman, A.A.A.G., Superintendent of Schools, March 30, 1867, SUP, LR, 1866–1867, reel 4; O. E. Pratt, Austin, to [Headquarters], September 15, 1866, AC, LR, 1866–1867, reel 7; William H. Rock, Richmond, to J. T. Kirkman, A.A.A.G., AC, ROC, December 1866–May 1867, reel 20; Louis W. Stevenson, Columbus, to J. P. Richardson, A.A.A.G., April 23, 1868, AC, LR, 1867–1869, reel 15; Alex Coggeshall, Bastrop, to E. M. Wheelock, Superintendent of Schools, January 9, 1867, SUP, LR, 1866–1867, reel 3; James C. Devine, Huntsville, to E. M. Wheelock, Superintendent of Schools, March 1, 1867, SUP, LR, 1866–1867, reel 3; James P. Butler, Brownsville, to E. M. Wheelock, Superintendent of Schools, February 28, 1867, LR, 1866–1867, reel 3; Patrick F. Duggan, Columbia, to J. T. Kirkman, A.A.A.G., June 25, 1867, AC, LS, 1866–1867, reel 5; Mortimer H. Goddin, Livingston, to [Charles Griffin], April 19, 1867, AC, LR, 1866–1867, reel 5; Charles Haughn, Waco, to [J. J. Reynolds], September 16, 1868, AC, LR, 1867–1869, reel 12. Charles Griffin's requirements toward education can be found in Circular letter from [Charles Griffin], February 7, 1867, AC, IRB, October 1865–April 1869, reel 19.

13. *Austin Weekly Southern Intelligencer*, February 22, 1868; Frederick Eby, *The Development of Education in Texas* (New York: The Macmillan Company, 1925), 157; Hardin Hart, Greenville, to Charles Garretson, A.A.A.G., September 25, 1867, LR, 1866–1867, reel 3; Alex B. Coggeshall, Bastrop, to E. M. Gregory, Superintendent of Schools, January 12, 1867, LR, 1866–1867, reel 3; John H. Archer, Beaumont, to J. P. Richardson, A.A.A.G., November 1867, SUP, LR, 1866–1867, reel 3; Barry Crouch, "The Freedmen's Bureau in Beaumont," *Texas Gulf Historical and Biographical Record* (Part Two) 29 (1993): 24; Barbara J. Hayward, "Winning the Race: Education of Texas Freedmen Immediately After the Civil War" (Ph.D. diss., University of Houston, 1999), 212; Mahlon E. Davis, Houston, to C. S. Roberts, A.A.A.G., October 1, 1868, AC, ROC, August–October, 1868, reel 27; L. S. Barnes, Crockett, to E. M. Wheelock, Superintendent of Schools, February 22, 1866, ULR, 1866–1867 and 1869–1870, reel 10; D. T. Allen, Assistant Superintendent of Schools, to J. T. Kirkman, A.A.A.G., June 1, 1867, SUP, LR, 1866–1867, reel 4; Henry Sweeney, Marshall, to Joseph Welch, Superintendent of Education, September 25, 1868, SUP, LR, 1868–1870, reel 8; Alfred T. Manning, Waco, to E. M. Wheelock, Superintendent of Schools, January 1, 1866, SUP, LR, 1866–1867, reel 4; Joshua L. Randall, Sterling, to J. T. Kirkman, A.A.A.G., August 31, 1867, AC, ROC, June–August, 1867, reel 21; Isaac M. Beebe, Marshall, to E. M. Wheelock, Superintendent of Schools, June 21, 1866, SUP, ULR, 1866–1867 and 1869–1870, reel 10; Ira H. Evans, Wharton, to J. T. Kirkman, A.A.A.G., Superintendent of Schools, July 31, 1867, SUP, LR, 1866–1867, reel 3; David L. Montgomery, Tyler, to J. T. Kirkman, A.A.A.G., Superintendent of Schools, June 14, 1867, SUP, LR, 1866–1867, reel 4; Crouch, "Black Education in Civil War and Reconstruction Louisiana," 287–308; Charles Kassel, "Educating the Slave—A Forgotten Chapter of Civil War History," *Open Court* 40 (1927): 239–256; Joshua L. Randall, Sterling, to J. P. Richardson, A.A.A.G., [October 1867], AC, ROC, September–October, 1867, reel 22.

14. H. S. Howe, Round Top, to J. P. Richardson, A.A.A.G., November 30, 1867, SUP, LR, 1866–1867, reel 3; John H. Archer, Hempstead, to E. M. Wheelock, Superintendent of Schools, SUP, LR, 1866–1867, reel 3; J. H. Bradford, Centreville, to Charles Garretson, A.A.A.G., AC, ROC, September–October, 1867, reel 22; Nesbit B. Jenkins, Whar-

ton, to Joseph Welch, Superintendent of Education, December 31, 1868, SUP, LR, 1868–1870, reel 6; Anthony M. Bryant, Sherman, to J. P. Richardson, A.A.A.G., October 31, 1867, SUP, LR, 1866–1867, reel 3; A. H. Cox, Liberty, to Charles A. Vernou, A.A.A.G., December 1868, AC, ROC, November–December, 1868, reel 28. For freedmen apathy toward education, see S. H. Starr, Mount Pleasant, to Charles Garretson, A.A.A.G., October 4, 1867, SUP, LR, 1866–1867, reel 4. For problems, such as lack of funds for tuition, see James P. Butler, Huntsville, to J. P. Richardson, A.A.A.G., November 30, 1867, SUP, LR, 1866–1867, reel 3; Edward Collins, Brenham, to [J. T. Kirkman, A.A.G., Superintendent of Schools], April 1, 1867, SUP, LR, 1866–1867, reel 3; J. R. Fitch, Indianola, to [J. T. Kirkman, A.A.G., Superintendent of Schools], May 7, 1867, LR, 1866–1867, reel 3; C. Stuart McGehee, "E. O. Trade, Freedmen's Education, and the Failure of Reconstruction in Tennessee," *Tennessee Historical Quarterly* 43 (1984): 376–389; and Whittington B. Johnson, "A Black Teacher and Her School in Reconstruction Darien: The Correspondence of Hettie Sabattie and J. Murray Hoag, 1868–1869," *The Georgia Historical Quarterly* 75 (Spring 1991): 90–105. The frustration and doubt concerning the "experiment" of black education was even evident with Freedmen's Bureau teachers (see Samuel L. Horst, ed., *The Fire of Liberty in Their Hearts: The Diary of Jacob E. Yoder of the Freedmen's Bureau School, Lynchburg, Virginia, 1866–1870* [Richmond: The Library of Virginia, 1996], xix).

15. Small, "The Yankee Schoolmarm in Southern Freedmen's Schools," 29; William H. Rock, Richmond, to Charles A. Vernou, A.A.A.G., November 8, 1868, SUP, LR, 1868–1870, reel 7; Charles Haughn, Waco, to [Headquarters], September 30, 1868, SUP, LR, 1868–1870, reel 6; Nesbit B. Jenkins, Wharton, to Joseph Welch, Superintendent of Education, December 31, 1868, SUP, LR, 1868–1870, reel 6; Thomas Bayley, Marshall, to E. M. Wheelock, Superintendent of Schools, September 20, 1866, SUP, ULR, 1866–1867 and 1869–1870, reel 10; Jackson, "Family and Freedom," 96–97, 101–102; Henry Lee Swint, *The Northern Teacher in the South, 1862–1870* (Nashville: Vanderbilt University Press, 1941), 35–68, 82–83, 92–95, 136; Abbott, *Freedmen's Bureau in South Carolina,* 122–123, 129; Martin Abbott, "The Freedmen's Bureau and Negro Schooling in South Carolina," *South Carolina Historical Magazine* 56 (Spring 1956): 75; Alton Hornsby, Jr., "The Freedmen's Bureau Schools in Texas, 1865–1870," *Southwestern Historical Quarterly* 76 (July 1972-April 193): 398; *Flake's Daily Bulletin,* February 10, 1867. Complaints in obtaining lodging for white women teachers are in Edwin Miller, Millican, to J. T. Kirkman, A.A.A.G., Superintendent of Schools, April 30, 1867, SUP, LR, 1866–1867, reel 4; and Charles E. Culver, Cotton Gin, to J. T. Kirkman, A.A.A.G., Superintendent of Schools, September 7, 1868, SUP, LR, 1866–1867, reel 3.

16. James Jay Emerson, Waco, to J. T. Kirkman, A.A.A.G., Superintendent of Schools, May 31, 1867, SUP, LR, 1866–1867, reel 3; Morris, *Reading, 'Riting, and Reconstruction,* 133; Hayward, "Winning the Race," 80; William H. Sinclair, A.A.G., to J. Ernest Goodman, Columbus, July 19, 1866, AC, LS, September 1865–March 1867, reel 1; Louis W. Stevenson, Columbus, to J. P. Richardson, A.A.A.G., April 30, 1868, SUP, LR, 1868–1870, reel 7; Charles F. Rand, Marshall, to E. M. Wheelock, Superintendent of Schools, March 4, 1867, SUP, LR, 1866–1867, reel 4. For run-ins between agents and teachers, see Charles F. Rand, Marshall, to Edwin M. Wheelock, Superintendent of Schools, March 4, 1867, SAC, LS, December 1866–December 1868, reel 21; C. E. Coleman

to [E. M.] Gregory, April 25, 1866, AC, LR, 1866–1867, reel 4; L. H. Sanger, Woodville, to A.A.A.G., District of Texas, August 4, 1867, SAC, LR, 1866–1867, reel 8; and DeWitt C. Brown, Paris, to J. P. Richardson, A.A.A.G., May 20, 1868, AC, LR, 1867–1869, reel 10; and Bill Stein, "Consider the Lily: The Ungilded History of Colorado County, Texas," *Nesbitt Memorial Library Journal* 9 (January 2000): 13.

17. John H. Morrison, San Antonio, to [Charles] Griffin, July 8, 1867, AC, LR, 1866–1867, reel 7; Patrick F. Duggan, Columbia, to J. T. Kirkman, A.A.A.G., August 8, 1867, SUP, LR, 1866–1867, reel 3.

18. Richter, *Overreached on All Sides*, 157; Robert Harrison, "Welfare and Employment Policies of the Freedmen's Bureau in the District of Columbia," *Journal of Southern History* 77 (February 2006): 108; De Forest, *Union in Reconstruction*, 87–88; Cox and Cox, "General Howard and 'Misrepresented Bureau,'" 429–430; Olds, "Freedmen's Bureau as a Social Agency," 127; Everly, "Freedmen's Bureau in the National Capital," 19; White, "Black Lives, Red Tape," 242; Carpenter, "Agents of the Freedmen's Bureau," 30.

19. Alex B. Coggeshall, Bastrop, to [J. B. Kiddoo], October 2, 1866, AC, LR, 1866–1867, reel 4; Cox and Cox, "General Howard and 'Misrepresented Bureau,'" 430; Byron Porter, Austin, to J. B. Kiddoo, January 25, 1867, AC, LR, 1866–1867, reel 7; *Galveston Daily News*, January 13, 1867; Byron Porter, Bastrop, to J. R. Kirkman, A.A.A.G., June 3, 1867, AC, ROC, June–August, 1867, reel 21; Alex B. Coggeshall, Bastrop, to Chauncey C. Morse, A.A.A.G., February 25, 1867, AC, LR, 1866–1867, reel 4; Alex B. Coggeshall, Bastrop, to William H. Sinclair, A.A.G., January 18, 1867, AC, LR, 1866–1867, reel 4; Julius Schultz to J. B. Kiddoo, January 22, 1867, AC, LR, 1866–1867, reel 8; Special Orders No. 6, January 11, 1867, AC, IRB, October 1865–April 1869, reel 19; C. V. Shafer, et al., to [J. T. Kirkman], A.A.A.G., [1867], AC, LR, 1866–1867, reel 8; Julius Schultze, et al., to Chauncey C. Morse, A.A.A.G., [1865], AC, ULR, 1865–1866, reel 17; William H. Sinclair, A.A.G., to Alex B. Coggeshall, Bastrop, January 15, 1867, LS, April 1866–September 1867, reel 2; William H. Sinclair, A.A.G., to Alex B. Coggeshall, Bastrop, February 18, 1867, AC, LS, April 1866–September 1867, reel 2; Special Orders No. 15, February 13, 1867, AC, IRB, October 1865–April 1869, reel 19; Special Orders No. 22, February 20, 1867, AC, IRB, October 1865–April 1869, reel 19; Special Orders No. 42, July 13, 1868, AC, IRB, October 1865–April 1869.

20. William H. Sinclair, Inspector, to C. S. Roberts, A.A.A.G., September 7, 1868, AC, LR, 1867–1869, reel 15; William Longworth, Sutherland Springs, to [Headquarters], April 16, 1866, AC, LR, 1866–1867, reel 6; A. H. Mayer, Liberty, to Henry A. Ellis, A.A.A.G., September 30, 1866, AC, LR, 1866–1867, reel 7; Charles Garretson, A.A.Q.M., to Fred W. Reinhard, Centreville, July 15, 1867, SAC, PCLS, July–October, 1867, reel 2; Endorsement of letter from Charles E. Culver, Cotton Gin, to Charles Garretson, A.A.A.G., October 2, 1867, AC, ES, March 1867–May 1869, reel 2; Charles Garretson, A.A.Q.M., to Chief Quartermaster of Bureau, October 26, 1867, SAC, PCLS, October 1867–February 1868, reel 2; Charles Garretson, A.A.Q.M., to William G. Kirkman, Boston, October 15, 1867, SAC, PCLS, July–October 1867, reel 2.

21. Walter B. Pease, Houston, to J. P. Richardson, A.A.A.G., February 1, 1868, AC, ROC, January–February, 1868, reel 24. Another example of such double-duty is

Edward W. Whittemore, Seguin, to A. H. M. Taylor, A.A.A.G., District of Texas, February 1, 1867, AC, Letters Received, 1866–1867, reel 9.

22. Hardin Hart, Greenville, to A. H. M. Taylor, A.A.A.G., District of Texas, May 31, 1866, AC, ROC, December 1866–May 1867, reel 20; Endorsement of letter from William G. Kirkman, Boston, to Charles Garretson, A.A.A.G., September 16, 1867, AC, ES, March 1867–May 1869, reel 2. For agents taking offense, see George C. Abbott, Hempstead, to Chauncey C. Morse, A.A.A.G., February 19, 1866, AC, ULR, 1865–1866, reel 17, A. H. N. Rolfe, Columbia, to J. P. Richardson, A.A.A.G., AC, LR, 1867–1869, reel 14; A. F. N. Rolfe, Columbia, to J. P. Richardson, A.A.A.G., February 11, 1868, AC, LR, 1867–1869, reel 14; and B. J. Arnold, Brenham, to Chauncey C. Morse, A.A.A.G., December 2, 1865, AC, ULR, 1865–1866, reel 17. William G. Kirkman's paperwork returned is in SAC, Register of Letters Received and Endorsements, July 1867–September 1868 (hereafter RLE), Registered Letters Received, July 1867–September 1868 (hereafter RLR), and LR, August 1867–August 1868, reel 13.

23. A. H. Mayer, Liberty, to J. T. Kirkman, A.A.A.G., February 3, 1867, AC, LR, 1866–1867, reel 6; A. H. Mayer, Liberty, to J. B. Kiddoo, January 25, 1867, AC, LR, 1866–1867, reel 7. More instances are Byron Porter, Austin, to J. B. Kiddoo, January 25, 1867, AC, LR, 1866–1867, reel 7; Charles Garretson, A.A.Q.M., to James P. Butler, Huntsville, May 11, 1867, SAC, PCLS, July–October 1867, reel 1; Charles Garretson, A.A.Q.M., to Anthony M. Bryant, Sherman, July 18, 1867, SAC, PCLS, July–October 1867, reel 2; and Endorsement of letter from William H. Rock, Richmond, to Henry A. Ellis, A.A.A.G., October 1, 1866, AC, ES, April 1866–September 1867, reel 2.

24. S. J. W. Mintzer, Surgeon in Chief, to [E. M. Gregory], December 1, 1865, AC, RRR, 1865–1866, reel 29; J. B. Kiddoo to O. O. Howard, July 23, 1866, AC, LS, September 1865–March 1867, reel 1. Examples of requests for leaves of absence or resignations are Frank Holsinger, Beaumont, to William H. Sinclair, A.A.G., April 29, 1866, AC, LR, 1866–1867, reel 6; Special Orders No. 39, February 15, 1866, AC, IRB, October 1865–April 1869, reel 19; Frank Holsinger File, Pension Record; Special Orders No. 63, April 16, 1866, AC, IRB, October 1865–April 1869, reel 19; Frederick H. Dyer, comp., *A Compendium of the War of the Rebellion* (New York: Thomas Yoseloff, 1959), 3:1726–1727; J. Orville Shelby, Liberty, to [J. B.] Kiddoo, July 26, 1866, AC, LR, 1866–1867, reel 8; Special Orders No. 98, July 10, 1866, AC, IRB, October 1865–April 1869, reel 19; James A. Hogue, Cold Springs, to J. B. Kiddoo, July 18, 1866, AC, LR, 1866–1867, reel 6; Special Orders No. 100, August 16, 1866, AC, IRB, October 1865–April 1869, reel 19. Charles C. Hardenbrook and J. Ernest Goodman wanted to remain with the Bureau, just in another state. For these two men, particularly Goodman, headquarters was more than willing to accommodate them (see Endorsement of letter from Brvt. Brig. Gen. F. E. Trotter to J. B. Kiddoo, July 27, 1866, AC, ES, April 1866–September 1867, reel 2; and Endorsement of letter J. Ernest Goodman, Columbus, to J. B. Kiddoo, June 4, 1866, AC, ES, April 1866–September 1867, reel 2). For instances being denied, see Endorsement of letter from O. O. Howard to J. B. Kiddoo, October 3, 1866, AC, ES, April 1866–September 1867, reel 2; Endorsement of letter from Isaac Johnson, La Grange, to William H. Sinclair, A.A.G., August 6, 1866, AC, ES, April 1866–September 1867, reel 2; Endorsement of letter from John H. Morrison, Palestine, to C. S. Roberts, A.A.A.G., September

15, 1868, AC, ES, April 1866–September 1867, reel 2; Endorsement of letter from [David] R. Porter, San Antonio, to J. B. Kiddoo, October 2, 1866, AC, ES, April 1866–September 1867, reel 2; and Isaac Johnson, La Grange, to C. H. Whittelsey, A.A.G., September 4, 1866, AC, LR, 1866–1867, 6.

25. William H. Sinclair, A.A.G., to William Longworth, Seguin, June 20, 1866, AC, ES, April 1866–September 1867, reel 2; Alex B. Coggeshall, Bastrop, to [Headquarters], October 2, 1866, AC, LR, 1866–1867, reel 4; Alex B. Coggeshall, Bastrop, to J. T. Kirkman, A.A.A.G., February 5, 1867, AC, LR, 1866–1867, reel 4; Albert A. Metzner, San Augustine, to J. T. Kirkman, A.A.A.G., June 30, 1867, AC, ROC, June–August, 1867, reel 21; William H. Rock, Richmond, to J. T. Kirkman, A.A.A.G., February 2, 1867, AC, ROC, December 1866–May 1867, reel 20; Arthur B. Homer, Columbia, to Charles A. Vernou, A.A.A.G., November 30, 1868, AC, ROC, November–December, 1868, reel 28. Agents also saw that when planters had a bad crop, which reduced their income, violence against the freedmen increased (see Ira H. Evans, Wharton, to Charles Garretson, A.A.A.G., October 1, 1867, AC, ROC, September–October, 1867, reel 22; and Edward Collins, Brenham, to J. P. Richardson, A.A.A.G., February 1, 1868, AC, ROC, January–February, 1868, reel 24). For works on antebellum attempts to transplant free labor into the slaveholding South, see Otis K. Rice, "Eli Thayer and the Friendly Invasion of Virginia," *Journal of Southern History* 37 (November 1971): 575–596; Sara T. Philips, "Antebellum Agricultural Reform, Republican Ideology, and Sectional Tension," *Agricultural History* 74 (Autumn 2000): 799–822; George Winston Smith, "Ante-Bellum Attempts of Northern Business Interests to 'Redeem' the Upper South," *Journal of Southern History* 11 (May 1945): 177–213; and Patricia P. Hickin, "John Curtis Underwood and the Antislavery Crusade, 1809–1860" (Master's Thesis, University of Virginia, 1961).

26. Edward Miller, Victoria, to A. H. M. Taylor, A.A.A.G., District of Texas, January 31, 1867, AC, ROC, December 1866–May 1867, reel 20; Jacob C. DeGress, Houston, to Henry A. Ellis, A.A.A.G., October 15, 1866, AC, LR, 1866–1867, reel 5; Endorsement of letter from Jacob C. DeGress, Houston, to Henry A. Ellis, A.A.A.G., December 6, 1866, AC, ES, April 1866–September 1867, reel 2; Samuel A. Craig, Brenham, to William H. Sinclair, A.A.G., August 2, 1866, AC, LR, 1866–1867, reel 4. For more examples of better race relations due to competition, see Lemuel K. Morton, Sterling, to [J. B. Kiddoo], November 6, 1866, AC, LR, 1866–1867, reel 7; William H. Sinclair, Inspector, to C. S. Roberts, A.A.A.G., August 18, 1868, AC, LR, 1867–1869, reel 15; Edward Collins, Brenham, to J. T. Kirkman, A.A.A.G., August 3, 1867, AC, ROC, June–August, 1867, reel 21; DeWitt C. Brown, Wharton, to J. T. Kirkman, A.A.A.G., April 3, 1867, AC, ROC, December 1866–May 1867, reel 20; and L. J. Warner, Inspector, to Henry A. Ellis, A.A.A.G., December 6, 1866, AC, LR, 1866–1867, reel 9. Studies finding competition and profits to protect the former slaves are Higgs, *Competition and Coercion*, ix; and Roark, *Master Without Slaves*, 134–155; and Joe M. Richardson, "The Freedmen's Bureau and Negro Labor in Florida," *Florida Historical Quarterly* 39 (October 1960): 167–174.

27. James P. Hutchison, Columbus, to William H. Sinclair, A.A.G., August 14, 1866, AC, LR, 1866–1867, reel 6; Albert A. Metzner, Clinton, to William H. Sinclair, A.A.G., August 14, 1866, AC, LR, 1866–1867, reel 7; Joshua L. Randall, Sterling, to J. T. Kirkman,

A.A.A.G., April 30, 1867, AC, ROC, December 1866–May 1867, reel 20; L. S Barnes, Crockett, to William H. Sinclair, A.A.G., June 14, 1866, AC, LR, 1866–1867, reel 4.

28. A. H. Mayer, Liberty, to J. B. Kiddoo, January 9, 1867, AC, ROC, December 1866–May 1867, reel 20; Albert A. Metzner, San Augustine, to J. T. Kirkman, A.A.A.G., September 1, 1867, AC, ROC, June–August, 1867, reel 21; Circular Order No. 1, February 2, 1867, AC, IRB, October 1865–April 1869, reel 19; Lemuel K. Morton, Sterling, to J. B. Kiddoo, September 30, 1866, AC, LR, 1866–1867, reel 7; A. G. Malloy, Marshall, to J. P. Richardson, A.A.A.G., November 30, 1867, AC, ROC, November–December, 1867, reel 23; A. H. Mayer, Liberty, to J. T. Kirkman, A.A.A.G., May 1, 1867, AC, ROC, December 1866–May 1867, reel 20; Charles H. Morse, Brownsville, to J. T. Kirkman, A.A.A.G., June 1, 1867, AC, ROC, December 1866–May 1867, reel 23.

29. William Heistand, Hallettsville, to Henry A. Ellis, A.A.A.G., November 23, 1866, AC, LS, June 1868–January 1869, reel 21. Studies finding simultaneous advocating for sharecropping and wages are in Daniel R. Weinfeld, "'More Courage Than Discretion': Charles M. Hamilton in Reconstruction-Era Florida," *Florida Historical Quarterly* 84 (Spring 1984): 482–484; and Ralph Shlomowitz, "'Bound' or "Free"? Black Labor in Cotton and Sugarcane Farming, 1865–1880," *Journal of Southern History* 50 (November 1984): 369–596.

30. Works indicting the agency for the rise of sharecropping are Wiener, *Social Origins of the New South*; Novak, *Wheel of Servitude*, chapter 2; and Franklin, *Ensuring Inequality*, chapter 2.

31. Albert A. Metzner, San Augustine, to [Headquarters], November 23, 1867, AC, LR, 1867–1869, reel 14; Albert A. Metzner, San Augustine, to [Headquarters], November 23, 1867, AC, LR, 1867–1869, reel 14; William H. Sinclair, Inspector, to Charles A. Vernou, A.A.A.G., July 13, 1868, AC, LR, 1867–1868, reel 15; William Philips, et al, to [Headquarters], October 16, 1867, AC, LR, 1867–1869, reel 14; Jacob Omerod to J. P. Richardson, A.A.A.G., December 6, 1867, AC, LR, 1867–1869, reel 14; S. W. Blount to [Headquarters], November 23, 1867, AC, LR, 1867–1869, reel 14. For more examples of agents having their performance questioned, see Samuel I. Wright, A.Q.M., Disbursing Officer, to [William H.] Sinclair, Special Duty, October 22, 1866, AC, LR, 1866–1867, reel 9; William H. Sinclair, Inspector, to J. T. Kirkman, A.A.A.G., April 1, 1867, AC, LR 1866–1867, reel 8; John Williamson to J. T. Kirkman, A.A.A.G., March 8, 1866, AC, LR, 1866–1867, reel 9; Special Orders No. 104, August 21, 1866, AC, IRB, October 1865–April, 1868, reel 19.

32. Mahlon E. Davis, Brenham, to William H. Sinclair, Special Duty, Galveston, January 17, 1867, AC, LR, 1866–1867, reel 5; William H. Sinclair, A.A.G., to Mahlon E. Davis, Brenham, January 3, 1867, AC, LS, September 1865–March 1867, reel 1; Special Orders No. 112, September 17, 1866, AC, IRB, October 1865–April 1869, reel 19.

33. Mahlon E. Davis, Brenham, to William H. Sinclair, Special Duty, Galveston, January 17, 1867, AC, LR, 1866–1867, reel 5.

34. Special Orders No. 15, February 7, 1867, AC, IRB, 1867–1869, reel 19; Special Orders No. 20, February 18, 1867, AC, IRB, 1867–1869, reel 19; Special Orders No. 28, March 7, 1867, AC, IRB, 1867–1869, reel 19; J. J. Reynolds to O. O. Howard, May 14, 1868, AC, LR, 1867–1869, reel 16; Special Orders No. 33, May 22, 1868, AC, IRB, October 1865–April 1869, reel 19.

NOTES TO PAGES 107–109

35. Cap. W. H. Redman to E. M. Gregory, May 1, 1866, AC, LR, 1866–1867, reel 7; Cap. W. H. Redman to E. M. Gregory, May 1, 1866, AC, LR, 1866–1867, reel 7; O. A. McGinnis to J. B. Kiddoo, August 22, 1866, AC, LR, 1866–1867, reel 7; Special Orders No. 100, August 16, 1866, AC, IRB, October 1865–April 1867, reel 19.

36. William H. Sinclair, Inspector, to Henry A. Ellis, A.A.A.G., December 10, 1866, AC, LR, 1866–1867, reel 8; Champ Carter, Sterling, to [J. B. Kiddoo], June 6, 1866, AC, LR, 1866–1867, reel 4; A. P. Delano, Marlin Falls, to J. B. Kiddoo, December 31, 1866, ROC, December 1866–May 1867, reel 20; Special Orders No. 20, December 30, 1865, AC, IRB, October 1865–April 1869, reel 19; William H. Sinclair, Inspector, to J. B. Kiddoo, December 23, 1866, AC, LR, 1866–1867, reel 8; *Flake's Daily Bulletin*, May 9, 1866; Special Orders No. 3, January 8, 1867, AC, IRB, October 1865–April 1869, reel 19. For Delano's post-Bureau problems, see A. G. Perry to Charles Griffin, July 16, 1867, AC, ULB, 1867–1869 and Undated, reel 18; F. B. Sturgis, Marlin, to [Charles Griffin], June 30, 1867, AC, ROC, December 1866–May 1867, reel 20; F. B. Sturgis, Marlin Falls, to J. J. Emerson, August 22, 1867, AC, LR, 1866–1867, reel 8; John Love, et al., to [J. J.] Reynolds, November [1867], AC, LR, 1867–1869, reel 14; George T. Ruby, Traveling Agent, to J. T. Kirkman, A.A.A.G., July 27, 1867, AC, LR, 1866–1867, reel 8; and H. N. Dubb, Attorney, to [Charles Griffin], July 6, 1867, AC, LR, 1866–1867, reel 5.

37. Richter, "Who Was the Real Head of the Texas Freedmen's Bureau?" 125–126, 129; William H. Sinclair, Inspector, Galveston, to Henry A. Ellis, A.A.A.G., November 30, 1866, AC, ULR, 1865–1866, reel 17; *Flake's Daily Bulletin*, May 23, 1866; Richter, "Who Was the Real Head of the Texas Freedmen's Bureau?," 132–134; Special Orders No. 123, October 17, 1866, AC, IRB, October 1865–April 1869, reel 19; Special Orders No. 139, November 19, 1866, AC, IRB, October 1865–April 1869, reel 19; William H. Sinclair, Inspector, to Henry A. Ellis, A.A.A.G., December 4, 1866, AC, LR, 1866–1867, reel 8; William H. Sinclair, Inspector, to Henry A. Ellis, A.A.A.G., December 10, 1866, AC, LR, 1866–1867, reel 8. For similar problems with agents in the cotton trade in other states, see Howard A. White, *The Freedmen's Bureau in Louisiana* (Baton Rouge: Louisiana State University Press, 1970), 34–37. Reported labor problems are in F. B. Sturgis, La Grange, to Lemuel K. Morton, A.A.A.G., September 18, 1866, AC, LR, 1866–1867, reel 8; J. W. McConaughey, Wharton, to [Headquarters], July 8, 1866, AC, LR, 1866–1867, reel 7; Albert A. Metzner, Clinton, to William H. Sinclair, A.A.G., August 14, 1866, AC, LR, 1866–1867, reel 7; and Byron Porter, Austin, to Henry A. Ellis, A.A.A.G., November 1, 1866, SAC, LS, October 1866–May 1867, reel 12. Reports of satisfactory conditions are James F. Hutchison, Columbus, to William H. Sinclair, A.A.G., August 14, 1866, AC, LR, 6; Ira P. Pedigo, Woodville, to Henry A. Ellis, A.A.A.G., November 19, 1866, AC, LR, 1866–1867, reel 7; Alex B. Coggeshall, Bastrop, to [Headquarters], October 2, 1866, AC, LR, 1866–1867, reel 4; and Fred W. Reinhard, Centreville, to [Headquarters], November 12, 1866, AC, LR, 1866–1867, reel 7.

38. William H. Sinclair, Inspector, to Henry A. Ellis, A.A.A.G., December 10, 1866, AC, LR, 1866–1867, reel 8; William H. Sinclair, Inspector, to Henry A. Ellis, A.A.A.G., November 30, 1866, AC, ULR, 1865–1866, reel 17; L. J. Warner, Inspector, to Henry A. Ellis, A.A.A.G., December 6, 1866, AC, LR, 1866–1867, reel 9; William H. Sinclair, Inspector, to Henry A. Ellis, A.A.A.G., December 23, 1866, AC, LR, 1868–1870.

39. J. B. Kiddoo to O. O. Howard, December 24, 1866, M752C, LR, January–May, 187, reel 44; Charles Griffin to O. O. Howard, [February 1867], M742C, LR, January–May 1867, reel 44; Circular No. 25, December 21, 1866, AC, IRB, October 1865–April 1869, reel 19; Circular letter from J. B. Kiddoo, December 31, 1866, AC, IRB, October 1865–April 1869, reel 19; Charles Griffin to O. O. Howard, February 7, 1867, Correspondence, M91, Box 4, Howard Papers–Bowdoin; O. O. Howard to J. B. Kiddoo, November 27, 1866, Manuscript Volume Folio, M91, Box 7, Howard Papers–Bowdoin; O. O. Howard to Charles Griffin, Letters Sent, January 14, 1867, M742C, LS, January 2–September 20, 1867, reel 3; A. P. Ketchum, A.A.A.G., to J. B. Kiddoo, January 14, 1867, M742C, LS, January 2–September 20, 1867, reel 3. In the months between Kiddoo's dismissal and Griffin's succession there were three interim Bureau chiefs in Texas: Henry Ashfield Ellis, Abner Doubleday, and Solon H. Lathrop. (See Thompson, *Civil War to the Bloody End*, 333; and Richter, *Overreached on All Sides*, 143.)

40. *Galveston Daily News*, February 5, 1867.

6. "They must vote with the party that shed their blood . . . in giving them liberty": Bureau Agents, Politics, and the Bureau's New Order: The Charles Griffin Era, January 1867–Summer 1867

1. Buell, The Cannoneer, 320; Richter, *Overreached on All Sides*, 150; Heitman, *Historical Register and Dictionary of the United States Army*, 1:478; George W. Cullum, *Biographical Register of the Officers and Graduates of the U.S. Military Academy at West Point, New York, from Its Establishment March 16, 1802, to the Army Reorganization of 1866–1867*, 2 vols. (New York: D. Van Nostrand, 1868), 2:196–197; Tyler, ed., *New Handbook of Texas*, 3:337; 5:1018–1019; John E. Eicher and David J. Eicher, *Civil War High Commands* (Stanford, CA: Stanford University Press, 2001), 269, 701,707, 712, 722; William L. Richter, "Tyrant and Reformer: General Griffin Reconstructs Texas, 1865–1866," *Prologue* 10 (Winter 1978): 226, 229; Boatner, *Civil War Dictionary*, 360–361.

2. General Orders No. 5, February 2, 1867, TxAGO, Box 401–861, Folder 861–26; Richter, "Tyrant and Reformer," 230; J. T. Kirkman, A.A.A.G., to J. R. Fitch, Indianola, March 18, 1867, AC, LS, September 1865–March 1867, reel 1; General Orders No. 9, February 12, 1867, AC, IRB, October 1865–April 1869, reel 19; General Orders No. 1, January 1, 1867, AC, IRB, October 1865–April 1869; General Orders No. 3, January 29, 1867, AC, IRB, October 1865–April 1869, reel 19; Charles Griffin to O. O. Howard, July 15, 1867, M752C, LR, June–August, 1867, reel 48; O. O. Howard to [Charles Griffin], January 24, 1867, AC, LR, 1866–1867, reel 6; Edward Miller, Victoria, to J. T. Kirkman, A.A.A.G., January 24, 1867, AC, LR, 1866–1867, reel 7. The correspondence from Griffin and Kiddoo to Howard are in Box 5, folders for December 1866 through February 1867, Correspondences, Freedmen's Bureau Period, Howard Papers–Bowdoin.

3. Endorsement of letter from Chilton and Branch to Charles Griffin, February 4, 1867, AC, ES, April 1866–September 1867, reel 2; Charles Griffin to O. O. Howard, February 18, 1867, M752C, LR, January–May 1867, reel 44; General Orders No. 4, January 30, 1867, AC, IRB, October 1865–April 1869, reel 19. Concern about Griffin's policies is in Charles F. Rand, Marshall, to J. T. Kirkman, A.A.A.G., February 26, 1867, AC, LR, 1866–1867, reel 7.

4. J. T. Kirkman, A.A.A.G., to all Subassistant Commissioners, June 21, 1867, AC, LS, March 1867–May 1869, reel 2; Circular No. 1, February 2, 1867, AC, IRB, October 1865–April 1869, reel 19.

5. Richter, *Overreached on All Sides*, 158; General Orders No. 4, January 30, 1867, AC, IRB, October 1865–April 1869, reel 19; Charles Griffin to O. O. Howard, July 1, 1867, AC, LS, March 1867–May 1869, reel 1; Charles Griffin to O. O. Howard, July 15, 1867, M752C, LR, June–August, 1867, reel 48; Claude Elliot, "The Freedmen's Bureau in Texas," *Southwestern Historical Quarterly* 56 (July 1952): 14; Richter, *Army in Texas During Reconstruction*, 74.

6. Statutes at Large, 14:428–429.

7. Richter, *Overreached on All Sides*, 204–207; Richter, "Tyrant and Reformer," 245; *Statutes at Large*, 14:429; 15:2–4; Lieberman, "Freedmen's Bureau and the Politics of Institutional Structure," 429; Randolph B. Campbell, *Gone to Texas: A History of the Lone Star State* (New York: Oxford University Press, 2003), 276; Owens, "Presidential Reconstruction," 180.

8. Endorsement of letter from Charles E. Culver, Cotton Gin, to J. P. Richardson, A.A.A.G., November 2, 1867, AC, ES, September 1867–May 1869, reel 2; Charles Griffin to O. O. Howard, June 17, 1867, M752C, LR, June–August, 1867, reel 48; *Statutes at Large*, 14:428; William R. Richter, "'Devil Take Them All': Military Rule in Texas, 1862–1870," *Southern Studies* 25 (Spring 1986): 17; J. T. Kirkman, A.A.A.G., to Subassistant Commissioners, March 30, 1867, AC, LS, September 1865–March 1867, reel 1.

9. Carpenter, *Sword and Olive Branch*, 135, 139; *House Miscellaneous Document*, 41st Congress, 2nd Session, No. 154, pp. 35, 38; Cox and Cox, "General Howard and 'Misrepresented Bureau,'" 442–443, 447–450; Engelsman, "Freedmen's Bureau in Louisiana," 164; Richard L. Hume, "The Freedmen's Bureau and the Freedmen's Vote in the Reconstruction of Southern Alabama: An Account by Agent Samuel S. Gardner," *Alabama Historical Quarterly* 37 (Fall 1975): 219.

10. J. W. Wilbarger, *Indian Depredations in Texas* (Austin: Steck Company, 1935), 128.

11. C. S. Roberts, Clarksville, Special Duty, to J. T. Kirkman, A.A.A.G., August 14, 1867, AC, LR, 1866–1867, reel 7; Richter, "Tyrant and Reformer," 235–239. Duties regarding registration are Patrick F. Duggan, Columbia, to J. T. Kirkman, A.A.A.G., August 6, 1867, SAC, LSRE, April 1867–November 1868, reel 15; P. B. Johnson, Woodville, to J. T. Kirkman, A.A.A.G., July 31, 1867, AC, ROC, June–August 1867, reel 21; John Dix, Corpus Christi, to J. T. Kirkman, A.A.A.G., April 23, 1867, AC, LR, 1866–1867, reel 5; J. T. Kirkman, A.A.A.G., to [SACs], July 10, 1867, AC, LS, March 1867–May 1869, reel 1; William H. Sinclair, Inspector, to N. Prime, Secretary, Office of Civil Affairs, June 22, 1867, LR, April 1867–May 1869, Correspondences of the Office of Civil Affairs of the District of Texas, the 5th Military District, and the Department of Texas, 1867–1870, Record Group 393, National Archives and Records Administration, Washington, D.C. (Microfilm M1188, reel 7), hereafter cited as OCA; Mathew Young, Belton, to J. T. Kirkman, A.A.A.G., July 16, 1867, SAC, LS, July–December 1867, reel 13; Randolph B. Campbell, *Grass-Roots Reconstruction, 1865–1880* (Baton Rouge: Louisiana State University Press, 1997), 39; Byron Porter, Bastrop, to J. T. Kirkman, A.A.A.G., May 21, 1867, SAC, LS, February 1867–February 1868, reel 13; William A. Russ, Jr., "Registration and Dis-

franchisement Under Radical Reconstruction," *Mississippi Valley Historical Review* 21 (September 1934): 171–172; J. P. Richardson, Austin, to J. T. Kirkman, A.A.A.G., SAC, LS, October 1866–May 1867, reel 12; William Garretson, Matagorda, to N. Prime, Secretary, Office of Civil Affairs, July 1, 1867, SAC, LR, May–September 1867, reel 24; E. M. Pease to J. J. Reynolds, February 27, 1868, AC, LR, 1867–1869, reel 12; Arthur B. Homer, Columbia, to J. P. Richardson, A.A.A.G., March 17, 1868, AC, LR, 1867–1869, reel 12; and Arthur B. Homer, Columbia, to J. P. Richardson, A.A.A.G., July 27, 1868, AC, LR, 1867–1869, reel 12. An example an agent had in finding adequate replacements is Gregory Barrett, Tyler, to Charles A. Vernou, A.A.A.G., June 2, 1868, AC, Letters Received, 1867–1869, reel 10. Those agents who entered politics shortly after their tenure were Champ Carter, William Garretson, John Dix, A. K. Foster, A. H. Cox, Jacob C. DeGress, Johnathan T. Whiteside, William H. Sinclair, Byron Porter, J. P. Richardson, George T. Ruby, Albert H. Latimer, Hardin Hart, F. P. Wood, John H. Archer, Edwin Finch, Alex B. Coggeshall, E. M. Wheelock, P. B. Johnson, James P. Butler, Ira H. Evans, Thomas H. Baker, Oscar F. Hunsaker, D. S. Hunsaker, Charles Haughn, John H. Morrison, Fred W. Reinhard, William J. Neely, Thomas C. Griffin, John C. Conner, Mortimer H. Goddin, A. G. Malloy, B. J. Arnold, Samuel A. Craig, and Anthony M. Bryant. William D. Price was nominated as Texas state treasurer but refused to run.

12. Richter, "Who Was the Real Head of the Texas Freedmen's Bureau?," 152–155; Tyler, ed., *New Handbook of Texas*, 2:565–566; W. C. Nunn, *Texas Under the Carpetbaggers* (Austin: University of Texas Press, 1962), 127; Carl H. Moneyhon, *Republicanism in Reconstruction Texas* (Austin: University of Texas Press, 1980), 158; Paul D. Casdorph, *A History of the Republican Party in Texas, 1865–1965* (Austin: Pemberton Press, 1965), 51, 7, 47, 249; *Biographical Directory of the American Congress, 1774–1949* (Washington, D.C.: Government Printing Office, 1950), 415. For other agents turned politicians, see R. J. Denny, et al., to Charles Griffin, June 5, 1867, AC, LR, 1866–1867, reel 5; Randolph B. Campbell, "Scalawag District Judges: The E. J. Davis Appointees, 1870–1873," *Houston Review* 14 (Fall 1992): 81; Randolph B. Campbell, *Grass-Roots Reconstruction in Texas, 1865–1880* (Baton Rouge: Louisiana State University Press, 1997), 90; *Digest of Contested Elections*, 45th Congress, 2nd Session, No. 52, 221; John Y. Simon, et al., eds., *The Papers of Ulysses S. Grant*, 31 vols. (Carbondale: Southern Illinois University Press, 1991), 18:248; Ernest William Winkler, ed., *Platforms of Political Parties in Texas* (Austin: University of Texas Press, 1916), 128; Thomas William Herringshaw, ed., *Herringshaw's Encyclopedia of American Biography of the Nineteenth Century* (Chicago: American Publishers' Association, 1901), 259; Tyler, ed., *New Handbook of Texas*, 2:657; E. J. Davis to J. T. Kirkman, A.A.A.G., August 2, 1867, AC, Letters Received, 1866–1867, reel 5. For a few with Democratic leanings, see Carpenter, "Agents of the Freedmen's Bureau," 226; Thomas H. Baker, Lockhart, to E. M. Pease, July 14, 1868, AC, LR, 1867–1869, 15; Winker, ed., *Platforms of Political Parties*, 128; Tyler, ed., *New Handbook of Texas*, 2:274; and *Biographical Directory of the American Congress, 1774–1949* (Washington, D.C.: Government Printing Office, 1950), 1010–1011.

13. Mortimer H. Goddin to [Charles Griffin], April 19, 1867, AC, LR, 1866–1867, reel 5; Mortimer H. Goddin, Livingston, to J. T. Kirkman, A.A.A.G., April 15, 1867, AC, LR, 1866–1867, reel 5; Mortimer H. Goddin, Livingston, to J. T. Kirkman, A.A.A.G., May 31, 1867, AC, ROC, December 1866–May 1867, reel 20; J. T. Kirkman,

A.A.A.G., to Mortimer H. Goddin, Livingston, March 26, 1867, AC, LS, October 1865–
September 1867, reel 2; Mortimer H. Goddin, Livingston, to [Charles Griffin], April 1,
1867, AC, LR, 1866–1867, reel 5; Tyler, ed., *New Handbook of Texas*, 3:196–197; Mortimer H. Goddin, Livingston, to Charles Garretson, A.A.A.G., September 25, 1867,
AC, LR, 1867–1869, reel 11; Mortimer H. Goddin to [Charles Griffin], April 1, 1867, AC,
LR, 1866–1867, reel 5; Special Orders No. 35, March 25, 1867, AC, IRB, October 1865–
April 1869, reel 19; Mortimer H. Goddin to [Charles Griffin], April 19, 1867, AC, LR,
1866–1867, reel 5. For examples of the actions of P. B. Johnson and William Garretson,
see James C. Devine, Inspector, to J. T. Kirkman, A.A.A.G., July 22, 1867, AC, LR,
1867–1869, reel 15; William Garretson, Matagorda, to J. T. Kirkman, A.A.A.G., May 18,
1867, AC, LR, 1866–1867, reel 5; William Garretson, Matagorda, to J. T. Kirkman,
A.A.A.G., May 21, AC, LR, 1866–1867, reel 5; J. T. Kirkman, A.A.A.G., to William Garretson, Matagorda, May 23, 1867, AC, LS, March 1867–May 1869, reel 1; William Garretson, Matagorda, to J. T. Kirkman, A.A.A.G., June 6, 1867, AC, LR, 1866–1867, reel 5;
William Garretson, Matagorda, to J. T. Kirkman, A.A.A.G., June 14, 1867, AC, LR,
1866–1867, reel 5; William Garretson, Matagorda, to J. T. Kirkman, A.A.A.G., June 30,
1867, AC, ROC, June–August, 1867, reel 21; William Garretson, Matagorda, to J. T.
Kirkman, A.A.A.G., July 31, 1867, AC, ROC, June–August, 1867, reel 21; J. T. Kirkman,
A.A.A.G., to A. P. Ketchum, A.A.A.G., District of Texas, August 24, 1867, AC, LS,
March 1867–May 1869, reel 2; and Election Registers 1838–1972: Appointments to
Office under Provisional Government, August 1866–1870 and Election and Appointment of State and County Officials, 1866–1870, Texas State Archives and Library, Aus-
tin, Texas, reel 4, pg. 68 (hereafter cited as Election Registers).

14. Mortimer H. Goddin, Livingston, to [Charles Griffin], April 15, 1867, AC, LR,
1866–1867, reel 5; Mortimer H. Goddin, Livingston, to [Charles Griffin], June 3, 1867,
AC, LR, 1866–1867, reel 5; Brvt. Maj. L. H. Sanger, Post of Livingston, Commander, to
A. H. M. Taylor, A.A.A.G., District of Texas, August 5, 1867, AC, LR, 1866–1867, reel 8;
Mortimer H. Goddin, Livingston, to J. T. Kirkman, A.A.A.G., July 31, 1867, AC, ROC,
June–August 1867, reel 21; L. H. Sanger, Woodville, to J. T. Kirkman, A.A.A.G., September 10, 1867, AC, LR, 1867–1869, reel 15; Mortimer H. Goddin, Livingston, to [Head-
quarters], June 22, 1867, AC, ROC, June–August, 1867, reel 21; Mortimer H. Goddin,
Livingston, to J. T. Kirkman, A.A.A.G., July 24, 1867, AC, LR, 1866–1867, reel 5; Mor-
timer H. Goddin, Livingston, to [Headquarters], September 10, 1867, AC, LR, 1867–
1869, reel 11; Mortimer H. Goddin, Livingston, to J. T. Kirkman, A.A.A.G., September
9, 1867, AC, LR, 1867–1869, reel 11; Mortimer H. Goddin, Livingston, to [Headquarters],
August 31, 1867, AC, LR, 1867–1869, reel 11; Mortimer H. Goddin, Livingston, to J. T.
Kirkman, A.A.A.G., September 30, 1867, AC, ROC, September–October 1867, reel 22;
Mortimer H. Goddin, Livingston, to J. A. Potter, A.A.A.G., August 31, 1867, AC, ROC,
June–August 1867, reel 21.

15. L. H. Sanger, Woodville, to J. T. Kirkman, A.A.A.G., September 10, 1867, AC,
LR, 1867–1869, reel 16; Tyler, ed., *New Handbook of Texas*, 3:197; Mortimer H. Goddin,
Livingston, to [Headquarters], n.d., AC, LR, 1867–1869, reel 11; Mortimer, H. Goddin,
Livingston, to J. T. Kirkman, A.A.A.G., July 31, 1867, AC, ROC, June–August 1867, reel
21; Special Orders No. 90, September 28, 1867, AC, IRB, October 1865–April 1869, reel
19; L. H. Sanger, Livingston, to Charles Garretson, A.A.A.G., AC, LR, 1867–1869, reel

15; James Lowrie, Jasper, to J. J. Reynolds, October 13, 1867, AC, ULR, 1867–1869, reel 18; James Lowrie, Jasper, to J. J. Reynolds, October 22, 1867, AC, ULR, 1867–1869, reel 18; James P. Butler, Huntsville, to J. P. Richardson, A.A.A.G., November 30, 1867, AC, ROC, November–December, 1867, reel 23. For the dispute with William H. Howard find William H. Howard, Huntsville, to Charles A. Vernou, A.A.A.G., December 25, 1868, AC, LR, 1867–1869, reel 12; and William H. Howard, Huntsville, to Charles A. Vernou, A.A.A.G., February 3, 1869, AC, LR, 1867–1869, reel 12.

16. Edward Guthridge, U.S. Attorney, Eastern District of Texas, to Benjamin Harris Brewster, Attorney General, July 24, 1883, Crouch Collection–Victoria.

17. Cimbala, *Under the Guardianship of the Nation*, 67, 220; Carpenter, "Agents of the Freedmen's Bureau," 280; Alfred T. Manning to Charles A. Vernou, A.A.A.G., June 26, 1868, AC, LR, 1867–1869, reel 13; Smallwood, "Charles E. Culver, A Reconstruction Agent in Texas," 358; Moneyhon, "George T. Ruby," 368; Michael W. Fitzgerald, *The Union League Movement in the Deep South: Politics and Agricultural Change During Reconstruction* (Baton Rouge: Louisiana State University Press, 1989), 2. For works that find Bureau political activity, but are less certain about its extent, see Lee W. Formwalt, "The Origins of African-American Politics in Southwest Georgia: A Case Study of Black Political Organization During Presidential Reconstruction, 1865–1867," *Journal of Negro History* 77 (Autumn 1992): 211–222; Weymouth T. Jordan, "The Freedmen's Bureau in Tennessee," *East Tennessee Historical Society's Publications* 11 (1939): 58; Carpenter, *Sword and Olive Branch*, 143–144; Abbott, *Freedmen's Bureau in South Carolina*, 29–36; and Joel Williamson, *After Slavery: The Negro in South Carolina During Reconstruction, 1861–1877* (Chapel Hill: University of North Carolina Press, 1965), 364–365. For works concluding the agency as politically partisan, see James Marten, "'What is to become of the Negro?' White Reaction to Emancipation in Texas," *Mid-America: An Historical Review* 73 (April–July 1991): 122–123; Weinfeld, "More Courage Than Discretion," 491–492; White, *Freedmen's Bureau in Louisiana*, 27–30; Randolph B. Campbell, "The Burden of Local Black Leadership During Reconstruction: A Research Note," *Civil War History* 39 (June 1993): 148–153; Bentley, *History of the Freedmen's Bureau*, 195, 214; George R. Bentley, "The Political Activity of the Freedmen's Bureau in Georgia," *Florida Historical Quarterly* 28 (July 1948): 28–37; White, *Freedmen's Bureau in Louisiana*, 39; Staples, *Reconstruction in Arkansas*, 216; James G. Randall and David Donald, *The Civil War and Reconstruction* (Boston: D. C. Heath and Company, 1961), 576–577; Charles Hubert Coleman, *Election of 1868: The Democratic Effort to Regain Control* (New York: Columbia University Press, 1933), 369–370; Nunn, *Texas Under the Carpetbaggers*, 246; Claude Oubre, *Forty Acres and a Mule* (Baton Rouge: Louisiana State University Press, 1978), 192; Paul Skeels Pierce, *The Freedmen's Bureau, A Chapter in the History of Reconstruction* (Iowa City: University of Iowa, 1904), 168; Philips, "Freedmen's Bureau in Tennessee," 337; James A Baggett, "Birth of the Texas Republican Party," *Southwestern Historical Quarterly* 78 (July 1974–April 1975): 1–20; James A. Baggett, "Origins of Early Texas Republican Party Leadership," *Journal of Southern History* 40 (August 1974): 441–454; Richard G. Lowe, "The Freedmen's Bureau and Local Black Leadership," *Journal of American History* 80 (December 1993): 989–998; Lowe, "Freedmen's Bureau and Local White Leaders in Virginia," 455–472; Mugleston, ed., "The Freedmen's Bureau and Reconstruction in Virginia," 47; and Thompson, *Reconstruction in Georgia*, 53.

18. Mathew Young, Belton, to Dr. Powell, et al., September 9, 1867, SAC, LS, July–December 1867, reel 13; Albert A. Metzner, San Augustine, to James C. Devine, Galveston, August 14, 1867, AC, LR, 1866–1867, reel 7; Charles E. Culver, Cotton Gin, to [J. T.], Kirkman, A.A.A.G., July 5, 1867, AC, LR, 1866–1867, reel 4; F. B. Sturgis, Marlin Falls, to J. T. Kirkman, A.A.A.G., July 16, 1867, AC, LR, 1866–1867, reel 8.

19. Joshua L. Randall, Sterling, to J. T. Kirkman, A.A.A.G., May 31, 1867, AC, ROC, December 1866–May 1867, reel 20; Joshua L. Randall, Sterling, to J. T. Kirkman, A.A.A.G., April 30, 1867, AC, ROC, December 1866–May 1867, reel 20.

20. Charles Haughn, Waco, to C. S. Roberts, A.A.A.G., September 5, 1868, AC, ROC, August–October, 1868, reel 27; Thomas H. Baker, Lockhart, to Charles S. Morse, A.A.A.G., August 31, 1868, AC, ROC, August–October, 1868, reel 27; Charles Schmidt, Sumpter, to Charles A. Vernou, A.A.A.G., September 1, 1868, AC, ROC, August–October, 1868, reel 27; John Dix, Corpus Christi, to Charles A. Vernou, A.A.A.G., August 31, 1868, AC, ROC, August–October, 1868, reel 27; Joshua L. Randall, Sterling, to Charles A. Vernou, A.A.A.G., August 31, 1868, AC, ROC, August–October, 1868, reel 27; F. P. Wood, Brenham, to Charles A. Vernou, A.A.A.G., August 31, 1868, AC, ROC, June–August, 1867, reel 21; Carpenter, *Sword and Olive Branch*, 143–144.

21. William H. Sinclair, Inspector, to J. T. Kirkman, A.A.A.G., April 1, 1867, AC, LR, 1866–1867, reel 8.

22. Anthony M. Bryant, Sherman, to Charles Garretson, A.A.A.G., October 31, 1867, AC, ROC, September–October, 1867, reel 22; Philip Howard, Meridian, to Charles Garretson, A.A.A.G., September 30, 1867, AC, LR, 1866–1867, reel 6; Alex Ferguson, Nacogdoches, to J. P. Richardson, A.A.A.G., April 15, 1868, AC, LR, 1867–1869, reel 11; Alex Ferguson, Nacogdoches, to J. P. Richardson, A.A.A.G., May 1, 1868, AC, LR, 1867–1869, reel 11; John Hope Franklin, *Reconstruction: After the Civil War* (Chicago: University of Chicago, 1961), 86.

23. Joseph A. Wright to O. O. Howard, October 3, 1867, AC, LR, 1867–1869, reel 16; Excerpt of *Crockett Sentinel*, October 24, 1867, AC, ULR, 1867–1869 and Undated, reel 18; J. H. Bradford, Centerville, to Charles Garretson, A.A.A.G., October 3, 1867, AC, LR, 1867–1869, reel 12; Charles Griffin to O. O. Howard, August 17, 1867, AC, LS, March 1867–May 1869, reel 1; Special Orders No. 87, August 19, 1867, AC, IRB, October 1865–April 1869, reel 19; D. S. Hunsaker, Crockett, to Charles Garretson, A.A.A.G., October 3, 1867, AC, LR, 1867–1869, reel 18; D. S. Hunsaker, Crockett, to AAAG, n.d., AC, LR, 1867–1869, reel 18; Special Orders No. 90, September 28, 1867, AC, IRB, October 1865–April 1869, reel 19. Men remaining as agents, despite not being able to take the required ironclad oath, is in John H. Lippard to Charles Griffin, August 31, 1867, AC, LR, 1867–1869, reel 13; Alvin Wright to Charles Garretson, A.A.A.G., October 18, 1867, AC, LR, 1867–1869, reel 16; Edwin Finch, Milford, to Charles Garretson, A.A.A.G., October 9, 1867, AC, LR, 1867–1869, reel 11; Edwin Finch, Milford, to Charles Garretson, A.A.A.G., October 22, 1867, AC, LR, 1867–1869, reel 11; and Charles Garretson, A.A.A.G., to Edwin Finch, Milford, October 19, 1867, AC, LS, March 1867–May 1869, reel 2. For examples being removed or not being appointed because of past activities with the Confederacy or discovery of misdeeds, see J. J. Reynolds to O. O. Howard, June 2, 1868, AC, LS, March 1867–May 1869, reel 2; Excerpt of *Crockett Sentinel*, October 23, 1867, AC, ULR, 1867–1869 and Undated, reel 18; William H. Sinclair, Inspector, to J. P. Rich-

ardson, A.A.A.G., December 13, 1867, AC, LR, 1867–1869, reel 15; James Burke to [E. M.] Pease, May 29, 1868, Incoming Correspondence, Governor Elisha M. Pease Records (RG 301), Archives Division–Texas State Library, Austin, Texas (hereafter cited as Governor Correspondences); James Burke to E. M. Pease, June 1, 1868, Pease Governor Correspondences; J. T. Kirkman, A.A.A.G., to H. S. Johnson, March 26, 1867, AC, LS, September 1865–March 1867, reel 2; J. H. Bradford, Centerville, to J. P. Richardson, A.A.A.G., November 2, 1867, AC, LR, 1867–1869, reel 10; O. A. McGinnis, November 15, 1867, AC, LR, 1867–1869, reel 13; J. H. Bradford, Centreville, to J. P. Richardson, A.A.A.G., November 8, 1867, AC, ROC, September–October, 1867, reel 22; J. P. Richardson, A.A.A.G., to S. F. Robb, December 10, 1867, AC, LS, March 1867–May 1869, reel 1; Telegram from William H. Sinclair, Inspector, to J. P. Richardson, A.A.A.G., December 7, 1867, LR, 1867–1869, reel 15; William H. Sinclair, Inspector, to [Post Commander], Sumpter, December 7, 1867, AC, LR, 1867–1869, reel 15; William H. Sinclair, Inspector, to J. P. Richardson, A.A.A.G., January 10, 1868, AC, LR, 1867–1869, reel 15; and Special Orders No. 3, January 11, 1869, AC, IRB, October 1865–April 1869, reel 19.

24. R. J. Denny, et al., to Charles Griffin, June 5, 1867, AC, LR, 1866–1867, reel 5.

25. Anthony M. Bryant, Sherman, to [Charles Griffin], June 5, 1867, AC, LR, 1866–1867, reel 4; J. P. Richardson, A.A.A.G., to Anthony M. Bryant, Sherman, June 14, 1867, AC, LS, April 1866–September 1867, reel 2; Special Orders No. 35, March 25, 1867, AC, IRB, October 1865–April 1869, reel 19; Election Registers, pp. 45, 264; Special Orders No. 96, October 31, 1867, AC, IRB, October 1865–April 1869, reel 19.

26. Richter, *Overreached on All Sides*, 203; Charles Griffin to Philip H. Sheridan, Commander, Fifth Military District, May 29, 1867, Papers of Philip H. Sheridan, Library of Congress, Washington, D.C., reel 3 (hereafter cited Philip H. Sheridan papers); Harold Hyman, *Era of the Oath: Northern Loyalty Tests During the Civil War and Reconstruction* (Philadelphia: University of Pennsylvania Press, 1954), 158; John Pressley Carrier, "A Political History of Texas During the Reconstruction, 1865–1874" (Ph.D. diss., Vanderbilt University Press, 1971), 159.

27. Charles E. Culver, Cotton Gin, to J. T. Kirkman, A.A.A.G., September 4, 1867, AC, LR, 1867–1869, reel 10; A. H. Mayer, Liberty, to J. T. Kirkman, A.A.A.G., July 1, 1867, AC, ROC, June–August, 1867, reel 21; Gregory Barrett, Tyler, to [Charles] A. Vernou, A.A.A.G., June 6, 1868, AC, LR, 1867–1869, reel 10; Byron Porter, Bastrop, to J. T. Kirkman, A.A.A.G., July 5, 1867, SAC, LS, February 1867–February 1868, reel 13; Dale Baum, *Counterfeit Justice: The Judicial Odyssey of Texas Freedwoman Azeline Hearne* (Baton Rouge: Louisiana State University Press, 2009), 96; A. H. Mayer, Liberty, to Charles Griffin, June 29, 1867, AC, LR, 1866–1867, reel 7; W. D. Ector to J. W. Throckmorton, May 10, 1867, Throckmorton Governor Correspondences; John J. Good to [J. W. Throckmorton], May 21, 1867, Throckmorton Governor Correspondences; John J. Good to J. W. Throckmorton, May 14, 1867, Throckmorton Governor Correspondences; Campbell, *Grass-Roots Reconstruction*, 73. Regarding agents' expressing confusion and resistance about Griffin's are General Orders No. 13, see Mortimer H. Goddin, Livingston, to [Charles Griffin], May 13, 1867, AC, LR, 1866–1867, reel 5; Byron Porter, Bastrop, to J. T. Kirkman, A.A.A.G., June 3, 1867, SAC, LS, February 1867–February 1868, reel 13; M. S. Hunson to Andrew Johnson, April 30, 1867, Andrew Johnson Papers, National Archives and Records Administration, Washington, D.C., Series 1, reel 27

(hereafter cited Andrew Johnson papers); Byron Porter, Austin, to J. T. Kirkman, A.A.A.G., February 8, 1867, AC, ROC, December 1866–May 1867, reel 20; Charles Griffin to Brig. Gen. James W. Forsythe, June 10, 1867, Philip H. Sheridan papers, reel 3; Philip H. Sheridan, Commander, Fifth Military District, to Ulysses S. Grant, General of the Army of the U.S., May 22, 1867, Papers of Ulysses S. Grant, Library of Congress, Washington, D.C., reel 24; John E. George to [Charles] Griffin, May 8, 1867, AC, LR, 1866–1867, reel 5; Thomas Affleck to [Charles] Griffin, August 26, 1867, AC, LR, 1866–1867, reel 4; A. H. Shanks to Andrew Johnson, May 8, 1867, Andrew Johnson Papers, Series 1, reel 27; J. W. Throckmorton to Andrew Johnson, May 20, 1867, Andrew Johnson papers, Series 1, reel 27; *Brownsville Daily Ranchero*, May 11, 1867; and *Houston Telegraph*, April 30 and May 1, 1867.

28. John M. Morrison, Palestine, to J. P. Richardson, A.A.A.G., February 29, 1868, AC, AC, ROC, January–February, 1868, reel 24; John H. Morrison, Palestine, to J. P. Richardson, A.A.A.G., March 31, 1868, AC, ROC, March–April, 1868, reel 25; James Oakes, Austin, to J. T. Kirkman, A.A.A.G., SAC, June 30, 1867, LS, May 1867–December 1868, reel 12; Walter B. Pease, Houston, to J. T. Kirkman, A.A.A.G., March 6, 1867, AC, ROC, December 1866–May 1867, reel 20; J. P. Richardson, ASAC, Austin, to James Oakes, Austin, September 26, 1867, SAC, LS, May 1867–December 1868, reel 12. For Howard's concern, see O. O. Howard to Charles Griffin, February 9, 1867, AC, LR, 1866–1867, reel 6; Charles Griffin to O. O. Howard, February 18, 1867, M752C, LR, January–May, 1867, reel 44; Charles Griffin to O. O. Howard, February 12, 1867, AC, LS, September 1865–March 1867, reel 1.

29. James C. Devine, Huntsville, to James Hentiss, March 6, 1867, SAC, PCLS, January 1867–March 1868, reel 22; James C. Devine, Huntsville, to J. T. Kirkman, A.A.A.G., February 3, 1867, AC, ROC, December 1866–May 1867, reel 20; Enon M. Harris, Columbus, to J. T. Kirkman, A.A.A.G., May 1, 1867, AC, ROC, December 1866–May 1867, reel 20; Enon M. Harris, Columbus, to J. T. Kirkman, A.A.A.G., August 3, 1867, AC, ROC, June–August, 1867, reel 21; Patrick F. Duggan, Columbia, to J. T. Kirkman, A.A.A.G., June 30, 1867, AC, ROC, June–August 1867, reel 21. Other examples of the beneficial effects are James Oakes, Austin, to J. T. Kirkman, A.A.A.G., March 31, 1867, AC, ROC, December 1866–May 1867, reel 20; William Garretson, Matagorda, to J. T. Kirkman, A.A.A.G., May 31, 1867, AC, ROC, December 1866–May 1876, reel 20; William Garretson, Matagorda, to J. T. Kirkman, A.A.A.G., June 30, 1867, AC, ROC, June–August, 1867, reel 21; Fred W. Reinhard, Centreville, to J. T. Kirkman, A.A.A.G., July 31, 1867, AC, ROC, June–August, 1867, reel 21; J. J. Reynolds, Brownsville, to J. T. Kirkman, A.A.A.G., September 3, 1867, AC, ROC, June–August, 1867, reel 21; P. B. Johnson, Woodville, to J. T. Kirkman, A.A.A.G., July 31, 1867, AC, ROC, June–August 1867, reel 21; Hamilton C. Peterson, Lockhart, to Charles Garretson, A.A.A.G., February 29, 1868, AC, ROC, January–February, 1868, reel 24; Charles F. Rand, Marshall, to Henry A. Ellis, A.A.A.G., January 24, 1867, SAC, LS, December 1866–December 1868, reel 24; Hamilton C. Peterson, Lockhart, to Charles Garretson, A.A.A.G., AC, ROC, September–October, reel 22; Hamilton C. Peterson, Lockhart, to J. P. Richardson, A.A.A.G., AC, November 30, 1867, AC, ROC, November–December, reel 23; Hamilton C. Peterson, Lockhart, to C. S. Roberts, A.A.A.G., December 31, 1867, AC, ROC, November–December, 1867, reel 23; Edward Collins, Goliad, to [J. T. Kirkman, A.A.A.G.], April 10, 1867, AC, LR, 1866–1867,

reel 4; H. S. Johnson, Sumpter, to J. B. Kiddoo, March 17, 1867, AC, LR, 1866–1867, reel 6; P. E. Holcomb, Goliad, to [J. T. Kirkman, A.A.A.G.], April 10, 1867, AC, LR, 1866–1867, reel 6; P. E. Holcomb, Goliad, to [J. T. Kirkman, A.A.A.G.], June 3, 1867, AC, ROC, June–August, 1867, reel 21; A. G. Malloy, Marshall, to J. T. Kirkman, A.A.A.G., May 31, 1867. AC, ROC, December 1866–May 1867, reel 20; Mortimer H. Goddin, Livingston, to [Charles Griffin], May 13, 1867, AC, LR, 1866–1867, reel 5; H. S. Johnson, Sumpter, to J. T. Kirkman, A.A.A.G., July 1, 1867, AC, ROC, June–August, 1867, reel 21; P. E. Holcomb, Goliad, to [J. T. Kirkman, A.A.A.G.], August 31, 1867, AC, ROC, June–August, 1867, reel 21; Charles F. Rand, Marshall, to J. T. Kirkman, A.A.A.G., March 4, 1867, AC, ROC, December 1866–May 1867, reel 20; and A. G. Malloy, Marshall, to J. T. Kirkman, A.A.A.G., June 30, 1867, AC, ROC, June–August, 1867, reel 21.

30. Race relations were so good, a few agents admitted there was no need for the Bureau along the border. This was partly because whites needed the black population to help protect the frontier and partly because there were so few freedpeople (see Lewis G. Brown, Rio Grande City, to J. T. Kirkman, A.A.A.G., June 6, 1867, AC, LR, 1866–1867, reel 4; Charles C. Cresson, San Antonio, to Charles A. Vernou, A.A.A.G., September 2, 1868, AC, ROC, August–October, 1868, reel 27; John W. Eckles, San Antonio, to Charles A. Vernou, A.A.A.G., September 30, 1868, AC, ROC, August–October, 1868, reel 27; J. R. Fitch, San Antonio, to Charles A. Vernou, A.A.A.G., November 30, 1868, AC, ROC, November–December, 1868, reel 28; P. E. Holcomb, Goliad, to [Headquarters], July 15, 1867, AC, LR, 1866–1867, reel 6; Ranald S. Macken-zie, Brownsville, to J. P. Richardson, A.A.A.G., December 20, 1867, AC, ROC, Novem-ber–December, 1867, reel 23; S. B. Hayman, Fort Griffin, to Charles A. Vernou, July 3, 1868, AC, ROC, May–July, 1868, reel 26; Charles Steelhammer, Weatherford, to J. P. Richardson, A.A.A.G., February 1, 1868, AC, ROC, January–February, 1868, reel 24; A. M. Randol, Brownsville, to J. P. Richardson, A.A.A.G., January 7, 1868, AC, ROC, November–December, 1867, reel 23; A. M. D. McCook, Brownsville, to Charles A. Ver-nou, A.A.A.G., August 31, 1868, AC, ROC, August–October, 1868, reel 27; George C. Cram, Camp Verde, to J. P. Richardson, A.A.A.G., February 8, 1868, AC, ROC, Janu-ary–February, 1868, reel 24; and P. E. Holcomb, Fort Mason, to J. P. Richardson, A.A.A.G., May 1, 1868, AC, ROC, March–April, 1868, reel 25).

31. J. R. Fitch, Refugio, to J. P. Richardson, A.A.A.G., January 31, 1867, AC, ROC, January–February, 1868, reel 24; A. H. Mayer, Liberty, to J. T. Kirkman, A.A.A.G., May 1, 1867, AC, ROC, December 1866–May 1867, reel 20; William H. Rock, Richmond, to J. T. Kirkman, A.A.A.G., March 6, 1867, AC, ROC, December 1866–May 1867, reel 20; William H. Rock, Richmond, to Charles A. Vernou, A.A.A.G., July 15, 1868, AC, ROC, May–July, 1868, reel 26; William H. Rock, Richmond, to Charles A. Vernou, A.A.A.G., November 8, 1868, AC, ROC, August–October, 1868, reel 27; J. R. Fitch, Refugio, to J. T. Kirkman, A.A.A.G., August 31, 1867, AC, ROC, June–August, 1867, reel 21; J. R. Fitch, Refugio, to Charles Garretson, A.A.A.G., October 1, 1867, AC, ROC, September–Octo-ber, 1867, reel 1867, reel 22; J. R. Fitch, Refugio, to Charles Garretson, A.A.A.G., November 1, 1867, AC, ROC, November–December, 1867, reel 23; J. R. Fitch, Refugio, to J. P. Richardson, A.A.A.G., December 1, 1867, AC, ROC, November–December, 1867, reel 23; A. H. Mayer, Liberty, to J. T. Kirkman, A.A.A.G., June 2, 1867, AC, ROC, December 1866–May 1867, reel 20.

32. Hiram Clark, Clinton, to [J. T. Kirkman, A.A.A.G.], July 5, 1867, AC, ROC, June–August, 1867, reel 21; P. E. Holcomb, Goliad, to J. T. Kirkman, A.A.A.G., August 21, 1867, AC, ROC, June–August, 1867, reel 21; Isaac Johnson, La Grange, to J. T. Kirkman, A.A.A.G., September 3, 1867, AC, ROC, December 1866–May 1867, reel 20; Edward Miller, Millican, to J. T. Kirkman, A.A.A.G., March 31, 1867, AC, ROC, December 1866–May 1867, reel 20; Edward Miller, Bryan City, to J. P. Richardson, A.A.A.G., November 30, 1867, AC, ROC, November–December, 1867, reel 23; Hiram Clark, Clinton, to [J. T. Kirkman, A.A.A.G.], May 28, 1867, AC, ROC, December 1866–May 1867, reel 20; Hiram Clark, Clinton, to Charles Garretson, A.A.A.G., September 30, 1867, AC, ROC, September–October, 1867, reel 22; Hiram Clark, Clinton, to J. P. Richardson, A.A.A.G., October 31, 1867, AC, ROC, September–October, 1867, reel 22; Hiram Clark, Clinton, to J. P. Richardson, A.A.A.G., [December 1867], AC, ROC, November–December, 1867, reel 23; Edward Miller, Millican, to J. T. Kirkman, A.A.A.G., May 31, 1867, AC, ROC, December 1866–May 1867, reel 20. More examples are Charles F. Rand, ASAC, Gilmer, to Charles Garretson, A.A.A.G., October 31, 1867, AC, LR, 1867–1869, reel 14; Charles F. Rand, ASAC, Gilmer, to J. P. Richardson, A.A.A.G., November 30, 1867, AC, ROC, November–December 1867, reel 23; Charles F. Rand, ASAC, Gilmer, to J. T. Kirkman, A.A.A.G., July 1, 1867, AC, LR, 1866–1867, reel 7; Charles F. Rand, ASAC, Gilmer, to J. T. Kirkman, A.A.A.G., September 1, 1867, AC, ROC, June–August, 1867, reel 21; Charles F. Rand, ASAC, Gilmer, to Charles Garretson, A.A.A.G., October 1, 1867, AC, ROC, September–October 1867, reel 22; Patrick F. Duggan, Columbia, to J. T. Kirkman, A.A.A.G., August, 1, 1867, AC, ROC, June–August, 1867, reel 21; Patrick F. Duggan, Columbia, to J. T. Kirkman, A.A.A.G., September 1, 1867, AC, ROC, June–August, 1867, reel 21; and N. H. Randlett, Anderson, to J. T. Kirkman, A.A.A.G., May 3, 1867, AC, Reports of Operations and Conditions, December 1866–May 1867, reel 20.

33. Crouch, "Freedmen's Bureau in Beaumont," (Part One) 22; James P. Butler, Huntsville, to J. T. Kirkman, A.A.A.G., May 31, 1867, AC, ROC, December 1866–May 1867, reel 20; Philip Howard, Meridian, to [Headquarters], June 30, 1867, AC, ROC, June–August, 1867, reel 21; Philip Howard, Meridian, to J. P. Richardson, A.A.A.G., November 30, 1867, AC, ROC, September–October, 1867, reel 22; James P. Butler, Huntsville, to J. T. Kirkman, A.A.A.G., May 25, 1867, AC, ROC, December 1866–May 1867, reel 20; James P. Butler, Huntsville, to J. T. Kirkman, A.A.A.G., June 30, 1867, AC, ROC, June–August, 1867, reel 21; John H. Archer, Beaumont, to J. T. Kirkman, A.A.A.G., AC, ROC, December 1866–May 1867, reel 22; John H. Archer, Beaumont, to J. P. Richardson, A.A.A.G., November 1, 1867, AC, ROC, September–October, 1867, reel 22; Philip Howard, Meridian, to J. T. Kirkman, A.A.A.G., August 31, 1867, AC, ROC, June–August, 1867, reel 21; Philip Howard, Meridian, to Charles Garretson, A.A.A.G., October 31, 1867, AC, ROC, September–October, 1867, reel 22; Philip Howard, Meridian, to J. P. Richardson, A.A.A.G., December 31, 1867, AC, ROC, November–December, 1867, reel 23; Philip Howard, Meridian, to Charles Garretson, A.A.A.G., September 30, 1867, AC, ROC, September–October, 1867, reel 22.

34. A. K. Foster, Hallettsville, to Charles A. Vernou, A.A.A.G., July 31, 1868, AC, ROC, May–July, 1868, reel 26; Hamilton C. Peterson, Lockhart, to J. P. Richardson, A.A.A.G., March 31, 1868, AC, ROC, March–April, 1868, reel 25; Louis W. Stevenson,

Columbus, to Charles A. Vernou, A.A.A.G., May 31, 1868, AC, ROC, May–July, 1868, reel 26; Fred W. Reinhard, Centreville, to Charles A. Vernou, A.A.A.G., July 10, 1868, AC, ROC, May–July, 1868, reel 26; Hiram Clark, Clinton, to Charles A. Vernou, A.A.A.G., July 2, 1868, AC, ROC, May–July, 1868, reel 26; William Holt, La Grange, to C. S. Roberts, A.A.A.G., October, 31, 1868, AC, ROC, August–October, 1868, reel 27; A. K. Foster, Hallettsville, to Charles A. Vernou, A.A.A.G., May 31, 1868, AC, ROC, May–July, 1868, reel 26; A. K. Foster, Hallettsville, to Charles A. Vernou, A.A.A.G., July 1, 1868, AC, ROC, May–July, 1868, reel 26; A. K. Foster, Hallettsville, to Charles A. Vernou, A.A.A.G., August 31, 1868, AC, ROC, August–October, 1868, reel 27; A. K. Foster, Hallettsville, to Charles A. Vernou, A.A.A.G., September 30, 1868, AC, ROC, August–October, 1868, reel 27; A. K. Foster, Hallettsville, to Charles A. Vernou, A.A.A.G., October 31, 1868, AC, ROC, August–October, 1868, reel 27; A. K. Foster, Hallettsville, to Charles A. Vernou, A.A.A.G., November 30, 1868, AC, ROC, November–December, 1868, reel 28; A. K. Foster, Hallettsville, to Charles A. Vernou, A.A.A.G., December 2, 1868, AC, ROC, November–December, 1868, reel 28; Hamilton C. Peterson, Lockhart, to J. P. Richardson, A.A.A.G., April 30, 1868, AC, ROC, March–April, 1868, reel 25; Louis W. Stevenson, Columbus, to J. P. Richardson, A.A.A.G., April 30, 1868, AC, ROC, March–April, 1868, reel 25; Louis W. Stevenson, Columbus, to Charles A. Vernou, A.A.A.G., June 30, 1868, AC, ROC, May–July, 1868, reel 26; Louis W. Stevenson, Columbus, to Charles A. Vernou, A.A.A.G., July 31, 1868, AC, ROC, May–July, 1868, reel 26; Hiram Clark, Clinton, to J. P. Richardson, A.A.A.G., January 2, 1868, AC, ROC, November–December, 1867, reel 23; Hiram Clark, Clinton, to J. P. Richardson, A.A.A.G, March 3, 1868, AC, ROC, January–February, 1868, reel 24; Hiram Clark, Clinton, to Charles A. Vernou, A.A.A.G., September 2, 1868, AC, ROC, August–October, 1868, reel 27; William Holt, La Grange, to C. S. Roberts, A.A.A.G., September 30, 1868, AC, ROC, August–October, 1868, reel 27; Thomas H. Baker, Lockhart, to Charles A. Vernou, A.A.A.G., July 31, 1868, AC, ROC, May–July, 1868, reel 26; Thomas H. Baker, Lockhart, to Charles S. Morse, A.A.A.G., August 31, 1868, AC, ROC, August–October, 1868, reel 27; Thomas H. Baker, Lockhart, to C. S. Roberts, A.A.A.G., October 31, 1868, AC, ROC, August–October, 1868, reel 27; Thomas H. Baker, Lockhart, to C. S. Roberts, A.A.A.G., September 30, 1868, AC, ROC, August–October, 1868, reel 27; Thomas H. Baker, Lockhart, to Charles A. Vernou, A.A.A.G., November 30, 1868, AC, ROC, November–December, 1868, reel 28; Thomas H. Baker, Lockhart, to Charles A. Vernou, A.A.A.G., December 31, 1868, AC, ROC, November–December, 1868, reel 28; Thomas C. Griffin, Kaufman, to Charles A. Vernou, A.A.A.G., December 1, 1868, AC, ROC, November–December, 1868, reel 28; William J. Neely, Victoria, to C. S. Roberts, A.A.A.G., October 1, 1868, AC, ROC, August–October, 1868, reel 27; William J. Neely, Victoria, to Charles A. Vernou, A.A.A.G., October 20, 1868, AC, ROC, August–October, 1868, reel 27; Hiram Clark, Victoria, to [Charles A. Vernou, A.A.A.G.], November 3, 1868, AC, ROC, August–October, 1868, reel 27; [P. E. Holcomb], Goliad, to J. P. Richardson, A.A.A.G., December 1, 1868, AC, ROC, November–December, 1868, reel 23; [P. E. Holcomb], Goliad, to J. P. Richardson, A.A.A.G., January 21, 1868, AC, ROC, November–December, 1867, reel 23; P. E. Holcomb, Goliad, to J. P. Richardson, A.A.A.G., January 31, 1868, AC, ROC, January–February, 1868, reel 24; J. W. Wham, Goliad, to J. P. Richardson, A.A.A.G., March 1, 1868, AC, ROC, January–February,

1868, reel 24; [Julius A. Hayden], Goliad, to J. P. Richardson, A.A.A.G., March 30, 1868, AC, ROC, March–April, 1868, reel 25.

    35. Carpenter, "Agents of the Freedmen's Bureau," 118–119.

    36. Mugleston, ed., "The Freedmen's Bureau and Reconstruction in Virginia," 49.

    37. DeWitt C. Brown, Wharton, to J. T. Kirkman, A.A.A.G., May 31, 1867, AC, ROC, December 1866–May1867, reel 20.

7. Violence, Frustration, and Yellow Fever: The Charles Griffin Era, Summer–Fall 1867

    1. Kathleen Davis, "Year of Crucifixion: Galveston, Texas," *Texana* 8 (1970): 140–153. The agents who died while in Bureau service were Isaac M. Beebe (died in 1866), Augustus B. Bonnaffon (1867), George F. Eber (1868), Charles E. Culver (1867), James C. Devine (1867), L. H. Warren (1867), Patrick F. Duggan (1867), David L. Montgomery (1868), Ira W. Claflin (1867), John A. Thompson (1867), Sam W. Black (1867), J. D. O'Connell (1867), William G. Kirkman (1868), and John Williamson (1868). Samuel P. Voris, William Garretson, and Thomas Murray Tolman died in 1867, but their deaths occurred after they had left the Freedmen's Bureau.

    2. James Lowrie, Jasper, to J. J. Reynolds, October 22, 1867, AC, ULR, 1867–1869, reel 18; Mortimer H. Goddin, Livingston, to [Headquarters], August 31, 1867, AC, LR, 1867–1869, reel 1; John Dix, Corpus Christi, to [J. T. Kirkman, A.A.A.G.], September 1867, AC, ROC, September–October, 1867, reel 22; A. H. Mayer, Liberty, to J. T. Kirkman, A.A.A.G., July 30, 1867, AC, LR, 1866–1867, reel 7; C. S. Roberts, A.A.A.G., to Henry C. Lacy, Crockett, September 25, 1867, SAC, LS, May–November, 1867 and September–November 1868, reel 19. Examples of registration violence are Oscar F. Hunsaker, Sterling, to J. T. Kirkman, A.A.A.G., July 16, 1867, AC, LR, 1866–1867, reel 6; Albert A. Metzner, San Augustine, to Charles Garretson, A.A.A.G., October 31, 1867, AC, ROC, September–October, 1867, reel 22; James Lowrie, Jasper, to J. T. Kirkman, A.A.A.G., September 13, 1867, AC, LR, 1867–1869, reel 13; Billy D. Ledbetter, "White Texans' Attitudes Toward the Political Equality of Negroes, 1865–1870," *Phylon* 40 (September 1979): 253–263; *Flake's Daily Bulletin*, August 16, 1867; P. B. Johnson, Woodville, to J. T. Kirkman, A.A.A.G., July 31, 1867, AC, ROC, June–August, 1867, reel 21; A. G. Malloy, Marshall, to J. T. Kirkman, A.A.A.G., September 31, 1867, AC, ROC, June–August, 1867, reel 21; Special Orders No. 137, November 18, 1866, AC, IRB, October 1865–April–1869, reel 19; George W. Smith, Seguin, to J. T. Kirkman, A.A.A.G., July 4, 1867, AC, ROC, June–August, 1867, reel 21; Albert Evans, Kaufman, to J. T. Kirkman, A.A.A.G., June 30, 1867, AC, ROC, June–August, 1867, reel 21; S. H. Lincoln, Kaufman, to J. P. Richardson, A.A.A.G., November 30, 1867, AC, ROC, November–December, 1867, reel 23; [E. M. Wheelock], Galveston, to J. P. Richardson, A.A.A.G., October 31, 1867, AC, ROC, September–October, 1867, reel 22; William G. Kirkman, Boston, to Charles Garretson, A.A.A.G., July 31, 1867, AC, ROC, June–August, 1867, reel 21; William G. Kirkman, Boston, to J. T. Kirkman, A.A.A.G., September, 4, 1867, AC, LR, 1867–1869, reel 16; and *Flake's Daily Bulletin*, July 12, 1867. Examples of smooth registration are Phineas Stevens, Hallettsville, to J. T. Kirkman, A.A.A.G., ROC, July 1, 1867, and August 1, 1867, AC, ROC, June–August, 1867, reel 21;

and A. G. Malloy, Marshall, to J. T. Kirkman, A.A.A.G., June 1, 1867, AC, LR, 1866–1867, reel 7.

3. Albert Evans, Sherman, to S. H. Lathrop, A.A.A.G., February 14, 1867, AC, ROC, December 1866–May 1867, reel 20; H. S. Johnson, Sumpter, to J. T. Kirkman, A.A.A.G., August 20, 1867, AC, LR, 1866–1867, reel 6; H. S. Johnson, Sumpter, to J. T. Kirkman, A.A.A.G., May 8, 1867, AC, LR, 1866–1867, reel 6; Albert A. Metzner, San Augustine, to J. T. Kirkman, A.A.A.G., July 31, 1867, AC, June–August, 1867, reel 21; Albert Evans, Sherman, to J. T. Kirkman, A.A.A.G., February 28, 1867, December 1866–May 1867, reel 20; Thomas M. Tolman, Sherman, to [Headquarters], March 31, 1867, ROC, December 1866–May 1867, reel 20.

4. Ira H. Evans, Wharton, to J. T. Kirkman, A.A.A.G., August 14, 1867, AC, LR, 1866–1867, reel 5; Ira H. Evans, Wharton, to J. T. Kirkman, A.A.A.G., August 14, 1867, AC, LR, 1866–1867, reel 5; Endorsement of letter from Ira H. Evans, Wharton, to J. T. Kirkman, August 16, 1867, AC, ES, April– 1866–September 1867, reel 2.

5. Joshua L. Randall, Sterling, to J. T. Kirkman, A.A.A.G., June 7, 1867, AC, LR, 1866–1867, reel 7; E. H. Mitchell to Charles Griffin, May 28, 1867, AC, LR, 1866–1867, reel 7; Joshua L. Randall, Sterling, to J. T. Kirkman, A.A.A.G., May 11, 1867, AC, LR, 1866–1867, reel 7.

6. Joshua L. Randall, Sterling, to J. T. Kirkman, A.A.A.G., June 7, 1867, AC, LR, 1866–1867, reel 7; Joshua L. Randall, Sterling, to J. T. Kirkman, A.A.A.G., July 19, 1867, AC, LR, 1866–1867, reel 7; Andrew J. Torget, "Carpetbagger on the Brazos: The Texas Freedmen's Bureau in Robertson County," *Agora: An Online Undergraduate Journal of the Humanities* 1 (Winter 2000): 12; George E. Durant to J. P. Richardson, A.A.A.G., AC, LR, 1867–1869, reel 11; J. T. Kirkman, A.A.A.G., to Joshua L. Randall, Sterling, June 1, 1867, AC, LS, March 1867–May 1869, reel 2; J. P. Richardson, A.A.A.G., to Joshua L. Randall, Sterling, January 27, 1867, AC, LS, September 1865–March 1867, reel 2. For Joshua L. Randall's reports, see Joshua L. Randall, Sterling, to J. P. Richardson, A.A.A.G., January 31, 1867 and February 29, 1867, AC, ROC, January–February, 1868, reel 24; Joshua L. Randall, Sterling, to J. P. Richardson, A.A.A.G., March 31, 1867, and April– 30, 1868, AC, ROC, March–April–, 1868, reel 25; Joshua L. Randall, Sterling, to Charles A. Vernou, A.A.A.G., May 31, 1868, June 30, 1868, and July 31, 1868, AC, ROC, May–July 1868, reel 26; Joshua L. Randall, Sterling, to Charles A. Vernou, A.A.A.G., September 30, 1868, and October 31, 1868, AC, ROC, August–October, 1868, reel 27; and Joshua L. Randall, Sterling, to Charles A. Vernou, A.A.A.G., November 30, 1868, and December 30, 1868, AC, ROC, November–December, 1868, reel 28.

7. Byron Porter, Bastrop, to J. T. Kirkman, A.A.A.G., April– 20, 1867, AC, LR, 1866–1867, reel 7; Byron Porter, Bastrop, to J. P. Richardson, A.A.A.G., November 17, 1867, AC, LR, 1867–1869, reel 14; Byron Porter, Bastrop, to J. P. Richardson, A.A.A.G., November 17, 1867, AC, LR, 1867–1869, reel 14; Byron Porter, Bastrop, to J. T. Kirkman, A.A.A.G., April– 18, 1867, SAC, LS, February 1867–February 1868, reel 13; Byron Porter, Bastrop, to J. T. Kirkman, A.A.A.G., August 28, 1867, AC, LR, 1867–1869, reel 14; Byron Porter, Bastrop, to J. P. Richardson, A.A.A.G., February 7, 1868, AC, LR, 1867–1869, reel 7; Byron Porter, Bastrop, to J. T. Kirkman, A.A.A.G., May 1, 1867, AC, LR, December 1866–May 1867, reel 20; Byron, Porter, Bastrop, to J. T. Kirkman, A.A.A.G., April– 2, 1867, AC, LR, 1866–1867, reel 7.

8. Byron Porter, Bastrop, to J. P. Richardson, A.A.A.G., November 17, 1867, AC, LR, 1867–1869, reel 14; Byron Porter, Bastrop, to J. P. Richardson, A.A.A.G., February 7, 1868, AC, LR, 1867–1869, reel 14; William T. Allen, et. al, to [Headquarters], n.d., AC, LR, 1867–1869, reel 14; Byron Porter, Bastrop, to J. P. Richardson, A.A.A.G., January 4, 1868, SAC, LS, February 1867–February 1868, reel 13; Byron Porter, Bastrop, to J. P. Richardson, A.A.A.G., January 4, 1868, AC, ROC, November–December, 1868, reel 23; Byron Porter, Bastrop, to J. P. Richardson, A.A.A.G., February 10, 1868, AC, LR, 1867–1869, reel 14; Byron Porter, Bastrop, to J. P. Richardson, A.A.A.G., March 28, 1868, AC, LR, 1867–1869, reel 14; Byron Porter, Bastrop, to J. P. Richardson, A.A.A.G., March 28, 1868, SAC, LS, March–December 1868, reel 13; Byron Porter, Bastrop, to J. P. Richardson, A.A.A.G., April 1, 1868, AC, ROC, March–April–, 1868, reel 25; Byron Porter, Bastrop, to J. P. Richardson, A.A.A.G., February 24, 1868, AC, LR, 1867–1869, reel 14; Byron Porter, Bastrop, to J. P. Richardson, A.A.A.G., February 20, 1868, AC, LR, 1867–1869, reel 14.

9. James Lowrie, Jasper, to Charles Garretson, A.A.A.G., September 30, 1867, AC, ROC, September–October, 1867, reel 22; John H. Archer, Beaumont, to J. T. Kirkman, A.A.A.G., August 14, 1867, AC, LR, 1866–1867, reel 4; James Lowrie, Jasper, to J. T. Kirkman, A.A.A.G., August 31, 1867, AC, ROC, June–August, 1867, reel 21; James Lowrie, Jasper, to J. T. Kirkman, A.A.A.G., July 31, 1867, AC, ROC, June–August, 1867, reel 21; James Lowrie, Jasper, to J. J. Reynolds, October 22, 1867, AC, ULR, 1867–1869, reel 18.

10. William H. Sinclair, Inspector, to Charles A. Vernou, A.A.A.G., July 23, 1868, AC, LR, 1867–1869, reel 15; Special Orders No. 44, July 31, 1868, AC, IRB, October 1865–April–1869, reel 19.

11. Charles E. Culver, Cotton Gin, to Charles Garretson, A.A.A.G., October 10, 1867, AC, LR, 1867–1869, reel 10; Charles E. Culver, Cotton Gin, to J. T. Kirkman, A.A.A.G., July 24, 1867, AC, LR, 1866–1867, reel 4; Charles E. Culver, Cotton Gin, to Charles Garretson, A.A.A.G., October 25, 1867, AC, ROC, September–October, 1867, reel 22; John Bruce, et. al, to Brig. Gen. James Oakes, Commander, Post of Austin, September 27, 1867, AC, LR, 1867–1869, reel 14; Charles E. Culver, Corsicana, to J. T. Kirkman, A.A.A.G., July 22, 1867, AC, LR, 1866–1867, reel 4.

12. Charles E. Culver, Cotton Gin, to J. T. Kirkman, A.A.A.G., June 26, 1867, AC, LR, 1866–1867, reel 4; Smallwood, "Charles E. Culver, A Reconstruction Agent in Texas," 357–358, 360–361; William H. Horton, Dallas, to J. P. Richardson, A.A.A.G., December 31, 1867, AC, ROC, November–December, 1867, reel 23; Charles E. Culver, Cotton Gin, to J. T. Kirkman, A.A.A.G., June 30, 1867, AC, ROC, June–August, 1867, reel 21; Charles E. Culver, Cotton Gin, to Charles Garretson, A.A.A.G., September 20, 1867, AC, ROC, September–October, 1867, reel 22; Charles E. Culver, Cotton Gin, to Charles Garretson, A.A.A.G., November 1, 1867, AC, ROC, September–October, 1867, reel 22; Endorsement of letter from William H. Horton, Wharton, to J. B. Kiddoo, January 7, 1867, AC, ES, April 1866–September 1867, reel 2. For examples of agents being problems in their districts, see William H. Rock, Richmond, to J. T. Kirkman, A.A.A.G., August 12, 1867, AC, ROC, June–August, 1867, reel 21; William H. Rock, Richmond, to J. D. O'Connell, Houston, August 30, 1867, AC, LR, 1867–1869, reel 14; Charles Griffin to O. O. Howard, June 15, 1867, AC, ULR, 1867–1869, reel 18; William H.

Rock, Richmond, to Charles Garretson, A.A.A.G., September 20, 1867, AC, ROC, June–August, 1867, reel 21; and *Field Record of Officers of the Veteran Reserve Corps*, 28.

13. William H. Sinclair, Inspector, [J. T.] Kirkman, A.A.A.G., July 2, 1867, AC, LR, 1866–1867, reel 8; Tyler, ed., *New Handbook of Texas*, 4:102; Richter, "This Blood-Thirsty Hole," 54–56; C. S. Roberts, Special Duty, to J. T. Kirkman, A.A.A.G., August 6, 1867, AC, LR, 1866–1867, reel 7.

14. William H. Sinclair, Inspector, to J. T. Kirkman, A.A.A.G., June 21, 1867, AC, LR, 1866–1867, reel 8; Charles F. Rand, Matagorda, to William H. Sinclair, A.A.A.G., July 27, 1866, AC, LR, 1866–1867, reel 7; Charles F. Rand, Clarksville, to Charles A. Vernou, A.A.A.G., AC, May 31, 1868, ROC, May–June, 1868, reel 26; Charles F. Rand, Clarksville, to Charles A. Vernou, A.A.A.G., July 1, 1868, AC, ROC, May–July, 1868, reel 26. For Rand's assignments to various places around the state, see Special Orders No. 64, April 17, 1866, AC, IRB, October 1865–April– 1869, reel 19; Special Orders No. 128, October 27, 1866, AC, IRB, October 1865–April– 1869, reel 19; Special Orders No. 145, December 9, 1866, AC, IRB, October 1865–April– 1869, reel 19; Special Orders No. 45, April– 17, 1867, AC, IRB, October 1865–April– 1869, reel 19; Special Orders No. 70, July 1, 1867, AC, IRB, October 1865–April 1869, reel 19; Special Orders No. 81, July 31, 1867, AC, IRB, October 1865–April 1869, reel 19; Special Orders No. 100, November 21, 1867, AC, IRB, October 1865–April 1869, reel 19; Special Orders No. 54, September 12, 1868, AC, IRB, October 1865–April 1869, reel 19; and Special Orders No. 53, September 8, 1868, AC, IRB, October 1866–April 1869, reel 19.

15. DeWitt C. Brown, Paris, to J. P. Richardson, A.A.A.G., December 1, 1867, AC, ROC, November–December, 1867, reel 23; J. P. Richardson, A.A.A.G., to Charles F. Rand, Clarksville, February 14, 1868, AC, LS, March 1867–May 1869, reel 1; C. S. Roberts, A.A.A.G., to Gregory Barrett, Tyler, August 28, 1868, AC, LS, March 1867–May 1869, reel 1; Charles F. Rand, Clarksville, to J. P. Richardson, A.A.A.G., February 4, 1868, AC, LR, 1867–1869, reel 14; Richter, "This Blood-Thirsty Hole," 64–66; Charles F. Rand, Clarksville, to C. S. Roberts, A.A.A.G., April 20, 1868, AC, LR, 1867–1868, reel 14; Charles F. Rand, Clarksville, to C. S. Roberts, A.A.A.G., April 30, 1868, AC, ROC, March–April 1868, reel 25. For other examples of firearms orders countermanded, see Endorsement of letter from Edward Miller, Millican, to J. T. Kirkman, A.A.A.G., June 14, 1867, AC, ES, April 1867–September 1867, reel 2; and Endorsement of letter from James P. Butler, Huntsville, to J. T. Kirkman, A.A.A.G., June 17, 1867, AC, ES, April– 1866–September 1867, reel 2.

16. Richter, "This Blood-Thirsty Hole," 66–70; Charles F. Rand, Clarksville, to Charles A. Vernou, A.A.A.G., July 21, 1868, M752C, LR, July–August, 1868, reel 60; Charles F. Rand, Clarksville, to Charles A. Vernou, A.A.A.G., August 2, 1868, M752C, LR, July–December, 1868, reel 60; Charles F. Rand, Clarksville, to Charles A. Vernou, A.A.A.G., July 31, 1868, AC, ROC, May–July, 1868, reel 26; Richter, "Revolver Rules the Day," 317–319; Charles F. Rand, Clarksville, to Charles A. Vernou, A.A.A.G., July 18, 1868, M752C, LR, July–December, 1868, reel 60; Endorsement of letter from DeWitt C. Brown, Paris, to J. P. Richardson, A.A.A.G., December 2, 1867, AC, ES, September 1867–May 1869, reel 2; William L. Richter, "'Oh God, Let Us Have Revenge': Ben Griffith and His Family During the Civil War and Reconstruction," *Arkansas Historical Quarterly* 57 (Autumn 1998): 274; Charles F. Rand, Marshall, to E. D. Morgan, U.S.

Senator, September 11, 1868, AC, LR, 1867–1869, reel 13; Tyler, ed., *New Handbook of Texas*, 5:496; Julius Hayden, Marshall, to Charles A. Vernou, A.A.A.G., September 2, 1868, AC, LR, 1867–1869, reel 12.

17. For examples of advice, see Endorsement of letter from A. G. Malloy, Marshall, to J. T. Kirkman, A.A.A.G., May 8, 1867, AC, ES, April 1866–September 1867, reel 2. A few examples of requests for cavalry are Endorsement of letter from Thomas Bailey, Marshall, to William H. Sinclair, A.A.G., May 16, 1866, SAC, ES, April 1866–September 1867, reel 2; and Endorsement of letter from J. B. Kiddoo to Maj. Gen. Absalom Baird, June 6, 1866, SAC, ES, April– 1866–September 1867, reel 2; Arthur B. Homer, Columbia, to J. P. Richardson, A.A.A.G., January 31, 1868, AC, ROC, January–February, 1868, reel 24; John Dix, Corpus Christi, to J. T. Kirkman, A.A.A.G., [August 1867], AC, ROC, June–August, 1867, reel 21; and T. M. K. Smith, Nacogdoches, to Charles Garretson, October, 5, 1867, AC, ROC, September–October, 1867, reel 22.

18. Patrick F. Duggan, Columbia, to J. T. Kirkman, A.A.A.G., September 1, 1867, AC, ROC, September–October, 1867, reel 22; Anthony M. Bryant, Sherman, to Charles Garretson, A.A.A.G., September 30, 1867, AC, ROC, September–October, 1867, reel 22. To see other suggestions, see James C. Devine, Inspector, to J. T. Kirkman, A.A.A.G., July 22, 1867, AC, LR, 1866–1867, reel 5; William Tweed Hartz, Tyler, to Charles A. Vernou, A.A.A.G., November 10, 1868, AC, ROC, November–December, 1868, reel 28; Phineas Stevens, Hallettsville, to J. T. Kirkman, A.A.A.G., ROC, June 1, 1867, December 1866–May 1867, reel 20; N. H. Randlett, Anderson, to J. P. Richardson, A.A.A.G., December 4, 1867, AC, ROC, November–December, 1867, reel 23; Charles E. Culver, Cotton Gin, to J. T. Kirkman, A.A.A.G., September 1, 1867, AC, ROC, June–August, 1867, reel 21; Byron Porter, Bastrop, to J. P. Richardson, A.A.A.G., November 2, 1867, AC, ROC, September–October, 1867, reel 22; John M. Morrison, Palestine, to J. T. Kirkman, A.A.A.G., August 31, 1867, AC, ROC, June–August, 1867, reel 21; E. C. Hentig, Sherman, to C. S. Roberts, A.A.A.G., October 1, 1868, AC, ROC, August–October, 1868, reel 27; Charles F. Rand, Marlin, to Charles A. Vernou, A.A.A.G., October 31, 1868, AC, ROC, August–October 1868, reel 27; and Horace Jewett, Tyler, to Charles A. Vernou, A.A.A.G., December 1, 1868, AC, ROC, November–December, 1868, reel 28.

19. General Orders No. 4, January 30, 1867, AC, IRB, October 1865–April– 1869, reel 19.

20. Charles Griffin to O. O. Howard, July 1, 1867, AC, IRB, October 1865–Apirl 1869, reel 19; Charles Griffin to O. O. Howard, February 18, 1867, M752C, LR, January–May, 1867, reel 44; General Orders No. 5, February 2, 1867, AC, IRB, October 1865–April 1869, reel 19; Charles Griffin to O. O. Howard, February 9, 1867, M752C, LR, January–May, 1867, reel 42; Richter, "Who Was the Real Head of the Texas Freedmen's Bureau?," 151; Foner, *Reconstruction*, 166.

21. William Garretson, Matagorda, to J. T. Kirkman, A.A.A.G., June 26, 1867, AC, Letters Received, 1866–1867, reel 5; Byron Porter, Bastrop, to J. T. Kirkman, A.A.A.G., September 5, 1867, AC, Reports of Operations and Conditions, June–August, 1867, reel 21; Phineas Stevens, Hallettsville, to Charles Garretson, A.A.A.G., September 2, 1867, AC, June–August, 1867, reel 21; J. T. Kirkman, A.A.A.G., to [All SACs], June 21, 1867, AC, Letters Sent, March 1867–May 1869, reel 1; L. H. Warren, Houston, to Alfred T. Manning, Unassigned, March 1, 1867, AC, Letters Received, 1866–1867, reel 9.

22. General Orders No. 11, July 8, 1867, AC, IRB, October 1865–April 1869, reel 19; Circular No. 7, September 3, 1867, AC, IRB, October 1865–April 1869, reel 19; Charles Griffin to O. O. Howard, June 12, 1867, M752C, LR, June–August, 1867, reel 46; Charles Griffin to O. O. Howard, June 17, 1867, M752C, LR, June–August, 1867, reel 48; General Orders No. 18, November 7, 1867, AC, IRB, October 1865–April 1869, reel 19.

23. Charles E. Culver, Cotton Gin, to Charles Garretson, A.A.A.G., AC, ROC, September–October, 1867, reel 22; Thomas Affleck to Charles Griffin, August 26, 1867, AC, LR, 1866–1867, reel 4; Edwin Finch, Milford, to J. T. Kirkman, A.A.A.G., September 2, 1867, AC, ROC, June–August, 1867, reel 21; John Dix, Corpus Christi, to J. P. Richardson, A.A.A.G., November 30, 1867, AC, ROC, November–December, 1867, reel 23; Edward Collins, Brenham, to J. P. Richardson, A.A.A.G., February 1, 1868, AC, ROC, January–February, 1868, reel 24; Endorsement of letter from Edward W. Whittemore, Seguin, to J. T. Kirkman, A.A.A.G., November 2, 1867, AC, ES, September 1867–May 1869, reel 2; Charles E. Culver, Cotton Gin, Charles Garretson, A.A.A.G., October 26, 1867, AC, LR, 1867–1869, reel 10; O. O. Howard to Charles Griffin, June 25, 1867, AC, LR, 1866–1867, reel 6; O. O. Howard to Charles Griffin, July 2, 1867, M742C, LS, January 2–September 30, 1867, reel 3; O. O. Howard to Charles Griffin, July 6, 1867, AC, LR, 1866–1867, reel 6; Endorsement of letter from J. H. Bradford, Centreville, to Charles Garretson, A.A.A.G., September 11, 1867, AC, ES, April 1866–September 1867, reel 2; J. H. Bradford, Centreville, to J. T. Kirkman, A.A.A.G., September 11, 1867, AC, LR, 1866–1867, reel 5. For more problems, see Edward Collins, Brenham, to J. T. Kirkman, A.A.A.G., August 3, 1867, AC, ROC, June–August, 1867, reel 21; Edward Collins, Brenham, to J. T. Kirkman, A.A.A.G., December 2, 1867, AC, ROC, November–December, 1867, reel 23; Edward Collins, Brenham, to [Charles Griffin], June 30, 1867, AC, ROC, June–August, 1867, reel 21; and William G. Kirkman, Boston, to J. P. Richardson, A.A.A.G., November 14, 1867, AC, LR, 1867–1869, reel 13.

24. J. H. Bradford, Centreville, to Charles Garretson, A.A.A.G., October 7, 1867, AC, ROC, September–October, 1867, reel 22; Anthony M. Bryant, Sherman, to Charles Garretson, A.A.A.G., October 31, 1867, AC, ROC, September–October, 1867, reel 22; Anthony M. Bryant, Sherman, to J. T. Kirkman, A.A.A.G., August 31, 1867, AC, ROC, June–August, 1867, reel 21; Anthony M. Bryant, Sherman, to J. T. Kirkman, A.A.A.G., September 11, 1867, AC, LR, 1867–1869, reel 10; Richter, "This Blood-Thirsty Hole," 54–56. For other examples of an agent notifying headquarters about an agent fulfilling his duties, see C. S. Roberts, Special Duty, to J. T. Kirkman, A.A.A.G., August 31, 1867, AC, LR, 1867–1869, reel 1; and Ira W. Claflin File, Pension Record.

25. James P. Butler, Huntsville, to J. T. Kirkman, A.A.A.G., [August 1867] AC, ROC, June–August, 1867, reel 21; A. H. Mayer, Liberty, to J. B. Kiddoo, December 27, 1866, AC, LR, 1866–1867, reel 7; A. H. Mayer, Liberty, to J. B. Kiddoo, January 2, 1867, AC, LR, 1866–1867, reel 7; Statement of A. H. Mayer, July 31, 1867, AC, LR, 1866–1867, reel 7; Special Orders No. 98, July 10, 1866, AC, IRB, October 1865–April 1869, reel 19. The previous two agents also disputed. Hiram Clark replaced William J. Neely in late 1868. This greatly angered Neely, who wrote to Bureau headquarters accusing Clark of being "a mere *cipher* as agent" (see William J. Neely to [Charles A. Vernou, A.A.A.G.], October 20, 1868, AC, LR, 1867–1869, reel 14). Accusations against Reinhard are in John Williamson, Centreville, to J. T. Kirkman, A.A.A.G., March 19, 1867, AC, LR,

1866–1867, reel 9; John Williamson, Centreville, to J. T. Kirkman, A.A.A.G., April 3, 1867, LR, 1866–1867, reel 9; John L. Miller to [Headquarters], May 29, 1867, AC, LR, 1866–1867, reel 7; Edward Miller, Millican, to J. T. Kirkman, A.A.A.G., June 15, 1867, AC, LR, 1866–1867, reel 7; and Charles Griffin to O. O. Howard, June 15, 1867, AC, LS, March 1867–May 1869, reel 1.

26. A. H. Mayer, Liberty, to J. T. Kirkman, July 30, 1867, AC, LR, 1866–1867, reel 7; Ira P. Pedigo to N. Prime, Secretary, Office of Civil Affairs, August 20, 1867, AC, LR, 1867–1869, reel 14; A. H. Mayer, Liberty, to J. P. Richardson, A.A.A.G., December 2, 1867, AC, LR, 1867–1869, reel 14; Special Orders No. 9, February 17, 1868, AC, IRB, October 1865–April 1869, reel 19; Special Orders No. 13, July 29, 1867, AC, LR, 1866–1867, reel 7.

27. William G. Kirkman, Boston, to Charles Garretson, A.A.A.G., October 26, 1867, AC, LR, 1867–1869, reel 13. For cooperation with agents in Arkansas, see Richter, "A Dear Little Job," 193; and Richter, "Revolver Rules the Day!," 316–317.

28. William M. Van Horn, Houston, to J. P. Richardson, A.A.A.G., November, 26, 1867, AC, ROC, September–October, 1867, reel 22; George Lancaster, Hempstead, to J. T. Kirkman, A.A.A.G.,[September 1867], AC, ROC, June–August, 1867, reel 21; George Lancaster, Hempstead, to Charles Garretson, A.A.A.G., October 31, 1867, AC, ROC, June–August, 1867, reel 21; George Lancaster, Hempstead, to J. P. Richardson, A.A.A.G., November 30, 1867, AC, ROC, June–August, 1867, reel 21; Edward Miller, Bryan City, to Charles Garretson, A.A.A.G., October 5, 1867, AC, ROC, September–October, 1867, reel 22; Edward Miller, Bryan City, to William H. Sinclair, A.A.G., September 23, 1867, AC, LR, 1867–1869; Special Orders No. 101, August 18, 1866, AC, IRB, October 1865–April 1869, reel 19; James P. Butler, Huntsville, to Charles Garretson, A.A.A.G., September 30, 1867, AC, ROC, September–October, 1867, reel 22; E. M. Wheelock, Galveston, to Charles Garretson, A.A.A.G., September 30, 1867, AC, ROC, September–October, 1867, reel 22; E. M. Wheelock, Galveston, to J. P. Richardson, A.A.A.G., October 31, 1867, SUP, LR, 1866–1867, reel 4; N. H. Randlett, Anderson, to Charles Garretson, A.A.A.G., September 28, 1867, AC, LR, 1867–1869, reel 14; Anne L. Buckhorn, "The Yellow Fever Epidemic of 1867 in Galveston," (Master's Thesis, University of Houston, 1962), vi, 43–44, 47–49; Isaac Johnson, La Grange, to J. P. Richardson, A.A.A.G., November 4, 1867, AC, ROC, September–October, 1867, reel 22; *Flake's Daily Bulletin*, September 20, 1867; A. H. Mayer, Liberty, to J. D. O'Connell, Houston, September 1, 1867, AC, LR, 1867–1869, reel 13.

29. William H. Sinclair, Inspector, to J. P. Richardson, A.A.A.G., December 8, 1867, AC, LR, 1867–1869, reel 15; William H. Sinclair, Inspector, to J. P. Richardson, A.A.A.G., January 30, 1868, AC, LR, 1867–1869, reel 15; William H. Sinclair, A.A.G., to O. O. Howard, September 18, 1867, AC, LR, 1867–1869, reel 15; Richter, "Who Was the Real Head of the Texas Freedmen's Bureau?" 143–144.

30. William H. Sinclair, A.A.G., to J. P. Richardson, A.A.A.G., December 8, 1867, AC, LR, 1867–1869, reel 15; Sinclair, "Who Was the Real Head of the Freedmen's Bureau?," 144; Stein, "Consider the Lily," 13; Louis W. Stevenson, Columbus, to J. P. Richardson, A.A.A.G., March 20, 1868, AC, LR, 1867–1869, reel 15; William H. Sinclair, Inspector, to J. P. Richardson, A.A.A.G., December 5, 1867, AC, LR, 1867–1869, reel 15; William H. Sinclair, Inspector, to O. O. Howard, April- 1, 1868, M752C, LR, January–

June, 1868, reel 56; Endorsement of letter from Enon M. Harris, Columbus, to J. P. Richardson, A.A.A.G., November 21, 1867, AC, ES, March 1867–May 1869, reel 2; Special Orders No. 8, February 1, 1868, AC, IRB, October 1865–April 1869, reel 19.

31. Richter, "Who Was the Real Head of the Texas Freedmen's Bureau?," 144–145; J. J. Reynolds to O. O. Howard, April 14, 1868, M752C, LR, January–June, 1868, reel 56; William H. Sinclair, Inspector, to E. M. Pease, April– 14, 1868, M752C, LR, January–June, 1868, reel 56.

32. James P. Butler, Huntsville, to N. Prime, Secretary, Office of Civil Affairs, October 18, 1867, OCA, LR, April 1867–May 1869, reel 5; *Flakes' Daily Bulletin*, September 17 and October 17, 1867; J. D. O'Connell File, Pension Record; Augustus B. Bonnaffon File, Pension Record; L. H. Warrant File, Pension Record; E. D. Townsend, A.A.A.G., to Winfield Scott Hancock, Commander, Fifth Military District, September 29, 1867, 5th Military District, Box 3; Acting Assistant Surgeon, Galveston, to [Headquarters], District of Texas, September 30, 1867, 5th Military District, Box 1.

33. T. J. Krutz, Galveston, to J. G. Williams, Mayor of Galveston, August 20, 1867, SAC, LS, January 1867–June 1868, reel 19; [T. J. Krutz], Galveston, to L. M. Hosten, August 20, 1867, SAC, LS, January 1867–June 1868, reel 19; [T. J. Krutz], Houston, to L. M. Hosten, [August 6, 1867], SAC, LS, January 1867–June 1868, reel 19; [T. J. Krutz], Galveston, to P. H. Rowe, Assistant Surgeon, August 17, 1867, SAC, LS, January 1867–June 1868, reel 19; Katherine Masur, "Reconstructing the Nation's Capital: The Politics of Race and Citizenship in the District of Columbia, 1862–1878" (Ph.D. diss.: University of Michigan, 2001): 84. For another instance dealing with the disease, see William Garretson, Matagorda, to J. T. Kirkman, A.A.A.G., June 30, 1867, SAC, LR, May–December 1867, reel 24. For previous policies toward the health of the freedmen and sanitation, see General Orders No. 16, April 14, 1866, General Orders and Circulars, August 1865–April 1870, 5th Military District; Walter B. Pease, Houston, to Alex McGovern, February 21, 1867, Post Houston, Letters Sent, November 1866–April 1868, 5th Military District; Edward Miller, Victoria, to William H. Sinclair, A.A.G., July 10, 1866, AC, LR, 1866–1867, reel 7; S. J. W. Mintzer, Surgeon in Chief, to [J. B. Kiddoo], February 28, 1866, AC, LR, 1866–1867, reel 6; *Galveston Daily News*, May 28, 1866; Byron Porter, Houston, William H. Sinclair, A.A.G., September 1866, AC, LR, 1866–1867, reel 7; A. H. Mayer, Liberty, to Henry A. Ellis, A.A.A.G., September 30, 1866, AC, LR, 1866–1867, reel 7; Randy Finley, "In War's Wake: Health Care and Arkansas Freedmen, 1863–1868," *Arkansas Historical Quarterly* 51 (Summer 1992): 135–163; Harrison, "Welfare and Employment Policies of the Freedmen's Bureau in the District of Columbia," 81–82; Gaines M. Foster, "The Limitations of Federal Health Care for Freedmen, 1862–1868," *Journal of Southern History* 48 (August 1982): 349–372; Alan Raphael, "Health and Social Welfare of Kentucky Black People, 1865–1870," *Societas* 2 (Spring 1972): 143–157; Todd L. Savitt, "Politics in Medicine: The Georgia Freedmen's Bureau and the Organization of Health Care, 1865–1868," *Civil War History* 28 (March 1982): 45–64; May, "19th Century Medical Care Program For Blacks," 160–171; Reggie L. Pearson, "'There Are Many Sick, Feeble, and Suffering Freedmen': The Freedmen's Bureau's Health Care Activities during Reconstruction in North Carolina, 1865–1868," *North Carolina Historical Review* 79 (April– 2002): 141–181; J. Thomas May, "The Louisiana Negro in Transition: An Appraisal of the Medical Activities of the Freedmen's

Bureau," *Bulletin of the Tulane Medical Faculty* 26 (February 1967): 29–36; and Gail S. Hasson, "Health and Welfare of Freedmen in Reconstruction Alabama," *Alabama Review* 35 (April 1982): 94–110.

34. Tyler, ed., *New Handbook of Texas*, 3:337; Crouch, *Freedmen's Bureau and Black Texans*, 31.

8. General Orders No. 40 and the Freedmen's Bureau's End: The J. J. Reynolds Era, September 1867–December 1868

1. Warner, *Generals in Blue*, 397–398; Patricia L. Faust, ed., *Historical Times Illustrated: Encyclopedia of the Civil War* (New York: Harper & Row, Publishers, 1986), 626; Heitman, *Historical Register*, 1:825; Boatner, *Civil War Dictionary*, 694–695; Tyler, ed., *New Handbook of Texas*, 5:556–557.

2. J. J. Reynolds to O. O. Howard, January 3, 1868, AC, LS, March 1867–May 1869, reel 1; General Orders No. 14, September 21, 1867, AC, IRB, October 1865–April 1969, reel 19; General Orders No. 23, October 23, 1867, AC, IRB, October 1865–April 1869, reel 19; J. J. Reynolds to O. O. Howard, December 3, 1867, AC, LS, reel 1; J. P. Richardson, A.A.A.G., to O. O. Howard, December 9, 1867, AC, LS, March 1867–May 1869, reel 1; Ulysses S. Grant to J. J. Reynolds, December 10, 1867, AC, LR, 1867–1869, reel 11; O. O. Howard to J. J. Reynolds, January 7, 1868, AC, LR, 1867–1869, reel 12; Circular Letter from O. O. Howard, November 28, 1867, M742C, Circulars Issued, May 15, 1865–June 19, 1869 and Special Orders Issued, May 22, 1865–June 27, 1872, reel 7; Circular Letter from O. O. Howard, December 18, 1867, M742C, LS, October 1, 1867–August 31, 1868, reel 4.

3. General Orders No. 17, October 29, 1867, AC, IRB, October 1865–April 1869, reel 19; General Orders No. 18, November 17, 1867, AC, IRB, October 1865–April 1869, reel 19; General Orders No. 20, November 27, 1867, AC, IRB, October 1865–April 1869, reel 19; J. J. Reynolds to O. O. Howard, December 3, 1867, M752C, LR, September–December, 1867, reel 51.

4. Tyler, ed., *New Handbook of Texas*, 3:439; J. J. Reynolds to O. O. Howard, December 17, 1867, AC, LS, March 1867–May 1869, reel 1; Richter, *Overreached on All Sides*, 223.

5. J. J. Reynolds to O. O. Howard, December 17, 1867, AC, LS, March 1867–May 1869, reel 1; Winfield Scott Hancock, Commander, Fifth Military District, to J. J. Reynolds, February 24, 1868, AC, LR, 1867–1869, reel 12; Joseph G. Dawson, III, *Army Generals and Reconstruction: Louisiana, 1862–1877* (Baton Rouge: Louisiana State University Press, 1982), 69; J. J. Reynolds to O. O. Howard, December 31, 1867, M752C, LR, July–December 1868, reel 60; David M. Jordan, *Winfield Scott Hancock: A Soldier's Life* (Bloomington: Indiana University Press, 1988), 318, 207; Perry D. Jamieson, *Winfield Scott Hancock: Gettysburg Hero* (Abilene: McWhiney Foundation Press, 2003), 152–153.

6. A. H. Mayer, Liberty, to J. J. Reynolds, January 24, 1868, AC, LR, 1867–1869, reel 13; A. H. Mayer, Liberty, to J. J. Reynolds, January 15, 1868, AC, LR, 1867–1869, reel 13; James P. Butler, Huntsville, to J. P. Richardson, A.A.A.G., January 31, 1868, AC, ROC, January–February, 1868, reel 24; William H. Rock, Richmond, to J. P. Richardson, A.A.A.G., February 1, 1868, AC, ROC, January–February, 1868, reel 24; William H.

Rock, Richmond, to J. P. Richardson, A.A.A.G., January 10, 1868, AC, LR, 1867–1869, reel 14; J. P. Richardson, A.A.A.G., to William H. Rock, Richmond, January 27, 1868, AC, LS, March 1867–May 1869, reel 1; C. C. Clark to D. F. Stiles, Waco, December 12, 1867, AC, LR, 1867–1869, reel 15. Further examples of Hancock's policies, effects are Byron Porter, Bastrop, to J. P. Richardson, A.A.A.G., January 4, 1868, AC, ROC, November–December, 1867, reel 23; Byron Porter, Bastrop, to J. P. Richardson, A.A.A.G., February 1, 1868, AC, ROC, January–February, 1868, reel 24; DeWitt C. Brown, Paris, to J. P. Richardson, A.A.A.G., January 31, 1868, AC, ROC, January–February, 1868, reel 24; A. H. Cox, Liberty, to Charles A. Vernou, A.A.A.G., May 31, 1868, AC, ROC, May–July, 1868, reel 26; F. P. Wood, Brenham, to Charles A. Vernou, A.A.A.G., May 1, 1868, AC, ROC, May–July, 1868, reel 25; Richter, "Revolver Rules the Day!" 323–324; and Gregory Barrett, Tyler, to J. P. Richardson, A.A.A.G., March 31, 1868, AC, ROC, March–April 1868, reel 25.

7. John H. Morrison, Palestine, to Charles A. Vernou, A.A.A.G., August 10, 1868, AC, LR, 1867–1869, reel 13; Endorsement of letter from John H. Morrison, Palestine, to C. S. Roberts, A.A.A.G., August 17, 1868, AC, ES, April 1866–September 1867, reel 2; James P. Butler, Huntsville, to J. P. Richardson, A.A.A.G., December 31, 1867, AC, ROC, November–December, 1867, reel 23; William H. Sinclair, Inspector, to J. P. Richardson, A.A.A.G., March 7, 1868, AC, LR, 1867–1869, reel 15.

8. R. Chandler, Assistant Secretary of Civil Affairs, to J. J. Reynolds, February 4, 1868, LR, 1867–1869, reel 12; Winfield Scott Hancock, Commander, Fifth Military District, to O. O. Howard, February 24, 1868, AC, LR, 1867–1869, reel 12; J. J. Reynolds to R. Chandler, Assistant Secretary of Civil Affairs, February 12, 1868, AC, LS, March 1867–May 1869, reel 1.

9. R. Chandler, Assistant Secretary of Civil Affairs, to J. J. Reynolds, February 27, 1868, LR, 1867–1869, reel 12; R. Chandler, Assistant Secretary of Civil Affairs, March 3, 1868, AC, LR, 1867–1869, reel 12.

10. J. J. Reynolds to George S. Hartsuff, A.A.A.G., Fifth Military District, February 20, 1868, AC, LR, 1867–1869, reel 12; J. J. Reynolds to R. Chandler, Assistant Secretary of Civil Affairs, March 11, 1868, AC, LS, September 1865–March 1867, reel 1; Richter, *Overreached on All Sides*, 225–228; Brvt. Lt. Col. G. Norman Lieber to [Winfield Scott Hancock, Commander, Fifth Military District], May 8, 1868, AC, LR, 1867–1869, reel 14.

11. Jordan, *Winfield Scott Hancock*, 211; General Orders No. 4, April 7, 1868, AC, IRB, October 1865–April 1869, reel 19; Endorsement of letter from John H. Morrison, Palestine, to J. P. Richardson, A.A.A.G., August 16, 1868, AC, ES, April 1866–September 1867, reel 2; Endorsement of letter from John H. Morrison, Palestine, to J. P. Richardson, A.A.A.G., April 16, 1867, AC, ES, April 1866–September 1867, reel 2; Endorsement of letter from William H. Rock, Richmond, to J. P. Richardson, A.A.A.G., April 20, 1867, AC, ES, April 1865–September 1867, reel 2.

12. T. M. K. Smith, Marshall, to Charles A. Vernou, A.A.A.G., June 25, 1868, AC, LR, 1867–1869, reel 15; F. P. Wood, Brenham, to J. J. Reynolds, April 27, 1868, AC, LR, 1867–1869, reel 16; William H. Sinclair, Inspector, to Charles A. Vernou, A.A.A.G., July 23, 1868, AC, LR, 1867–1869, reel 15; William H. Sinclair, Inspector, to C. S. Roberts, A.A.A.G., August 24, 1868, AC, LR, 1867–1869, reel 15; William G. Kirkman, to C. S.

Roberts, A.A.A.G., May 1, 1868, AC, LS, April–December, 1868, reel 14; William H. Rock, Richmond, to J. P. Richardson, A.A.A.G., April 16, 1868, AC, LR, January 1866–November 1868, reel 25; William H. Rock, Richmond, to J. P. Richardson, A.A.A.G., April 20, 1868, AC, LR, January–November 1868, reel 25; William H. Sinclair, Inspector, to Charles A. Vernou, A.A.A.G., August 10, 1868, AC, LR, 1867–1869, reel 15.

13. William H. Sinclair, Inspector, to C. S. Roberts, A.A.A.G., August 24, 1868, AC, LR, 1867–1869, reel 15; Richter, "Who Was the Real Head of the Texas Freedmen's Bureau?" 151.

14. Ibid.

15. These numbers came from the pretyped monthly reports from agents in each subdistrict. These reports are more like questionnaires so headquarters can succinctly obtain answers/data to the most important issues. There is a section in each questionnaire that asks the Bureau agent to describe the attitude of the white population. When an agent listed the attitude of whites as "good," "improving," or "indifferent," I considered it "good." If an agent described the opinion as "bad," "hostile," or "worsening," I listed it as "bad." The following are the numbers from October 1867 to December 1868: October 1867: 15 "good" and 23 "bad"; November 1867: 19 "good" and 19 "bad"; December 1867: 18 "good" and 15 "bad"; January 1868: 17 "good" and 16 "bad"; February 1868: 12 "good" and 18 "bad"; March 1868: 11 "good" and 15 "bad"; April 1868: 8 "good" and 16 "bad"; May 1868: 10 "good" and 19 "bad"; June 1868: 10 "good" and 20 "bad"; July 1868: 11 "good" and 18 "bad"; August 1868: 10 "good" and 17 "bad"; September 1868: 19 "good" and 15 "bad"; October 1868: 14 "good" and 15 "bad"; November 1868: 16 "good" and 15 "bad"; and December 1868: 9 "good" and 13 "bad."

16. C. C. Raymond, Seguin, to Charles A. Vernou, A.A.A.G., August 29, 1868, AC, ROC, August–October, 1868, reel 27; Charles Haughn, Waco, to Charles A. Vernou, A.A.A.G., August 1, 1868, AC, ROC, May–July, 1868, reel 26; Gregory Barrett, Tyler, to Charles A. Vernou, A.A.A.G., AC, June 30, 1868, AC, ROC, May–July, 1868, reel 26; Charles F. Rand, Marlin, to Charles A. Vernou, A.A.A.G., September 30, 1868, AC, ROC, August–October, 1868, reel 27; Charles F. Rand, Marlin, to Charles A. Vernou, A.A.A.G., October 31, 1868, AC, ROC, August–October, 1868, reel 21; Charles F. Rand, Marlin, to Charles A. Vernou, A.A.A.G., November 30, 1868, AC, ROC, November–December, 1868, reel 28; Charles F. Rand, Marlin, to Charles A. Vernou, A.A.A.G., December 31, 1868, AC, ROC, November–December, 1868, reel 28. For the reports Raymond claimed not needing troops, see C. C. Raymond, Seguin, to Charles A. Vernou, A.A.A.G., May 28, 1868, AC; C. C. Raymond, Seguin, to Charles A. Vernou, A.A.A.G., June 30, 1868, AC; C. C. Raymond, Seguin, to Charles A. Vernou, A.A.A.G., July 30, 1868, AC; and C. C. Raymond, Seguin, to Charles A. Vernou, A.A.A.G., September 30, 1868, AC, all in ROC, reels 26–27. For a good work on the deteriorated situation agents faced in Central Texas in 1868, see William D. Carrigan, *The Making of a Lynching Culture: Violence and Vigilantism in Central Texas, 1836–1916* (Urbana: University of Illinois, 2004), particularly chapter 5. For examples of violence, see William H. Howard, Huntsville, to Charles A. Vernou, A.A.A.G., December 23, 1868, AC, ROC, November–December, 1868, reel 28; Charles A. Vernou, A.A.A.G., to William H. Howard, Huntsville, October 2, 1868, AC, LS, March 1867–May 1869, reel 1; William H. Howard, Huntsville, to Charles A. Vernou, A.A.A.G., August 28, 1867, AC, LR, 1867–

1869, reel 12; William H. Howard, Huntsville, to Charles A. Vernou, A.A.A.G., November 6, 1868, AC, LR, 1867–1869, reel 12; Telegram from William H. Howard, Huntsville, to J. J. Reynolds, July 30, 1868, AC, LR, 1867–1869, reel 12; J. J. Reynolds to William H. Howard, Huntsville, July 31, 1868, AC, LS, March 1867–May 1869, reel 1; Charles A. Vernou, A.A.A.G., to William H. Howard, Huntsville, July 18, 1868, AC, LS, March 1867–May 1869, reel 1; Telegram from William H. Howard, Huntsville, to J. J. Reynolds, August 12, 1868, AC, LR, 1867–1869, reel 12; William H. Howard, Huntsville, to Charles A. Vernou, A.A.A.G., September 17, 1868, AC, LR, 1867–1869, reel 12; William H. Howard, Huntsville, to Charles A. Vernou, A.A.A.G., October 1, 1868, AC, LR, 1867–1869, reel 12; C. S. Roberts, A.A.A.G., to William H. Howard, Huntsville, August 29, 1868, AC, LS, March 1867–May 1869, reel 1; Charles A. Vernou, A.A.A.G., to William H. Howard, Huntsville, September 26, 1868, AC, LS, March 1867–May 1869, reel 1; William H. Howard, Huntsville, to Charles A. Vernou, A.A.A.G., September 21, 1868, AC, LR, 1867–1869, reel 12; Alex Ferguson, Nacogdoches, to Charles A. Vernou, A.A.A.G., December 1, 1868, AC, LR, 1867–1869, reel 11; Alex Ferguson, Nacogdoches, to Charles A. Vernou, A.A.A.G., December 7, 1868, AC, LR, 1867–1869, reel 11; Alex Ferguson, Nacogdoches, to [Headquarters], April 21, 1868, AC, LR, 1867–1869, reel 11; William H. Howard, Huntsville, to Charles A. Vernou, A.A.A.G., October 6, 1868, AC, LR, 1867–1869, reel 12; Arthur B. Homer, Columbia, to J. P. Richardson, A.A.A.G., February 24, 1868, AC, LR, 1867–1869, reel 12; Gregory Barrett, Tyler, to [Charles] A. Vernou, A.A.A.G., June 6, 1868, AC, LR, 1867–1869, reel 10; DeWitt C. Brown, Paris, to J. J. Reynolds, October 28, 1868, AC, LR, 1867–1869, reel 10; Joshua L. Randall, Sterling, to Charles A. Vernou, A.A.A.G., November 13, 1868, AC, LR 1867–1869, reel 14; Charles Schmidt, Sumpter, to J. P. Richardson, A.A.A.G., April 30, 1868, AC, LR, 1867–1869, reel 15; James Smallwood, "When the Klan Rode: White Terror in Reconstruction Texas," *Journal of the West* 25 (October 1986): 12; Cantrell, "Racial Violence and Reconstruction Politics," 348–349; Telegram from William H. Howard, Huntsville, to J. J. Reynolds, July 30, 1868, AC, LR, 1867–1869, reel 12; and William H. Howard, Moscow, to Charles A. Vernou, A.A.A.G., November 6, 1868, AC, LR, 1867–1869, reel 12.

17. John Dix, Corpus Christi, to Charles A. Vernou, A.A.A.G., May 31, 1868, AC, ROC, May–July, 1868, reel 26; T. M. K. Smith, Marshall, to Charles A. Vernou, A.A.A.G., June 30, 1868, AC, ROC, May–July, 1868, reel 26; Arthur B. Homer, Columbia, to Charles A. Vernou, A.A.A.G., August 31, 1868, AC, ROC, August–October, 1868, reel 27; Arthur B. Homer, Columbia, to Charles A. Vernou, A.A.A.G., November 2, 1868, AC, ROC, August–October, 1868, reel 27; John Dix, Corpus Christi, to Charles A. Vernou, A.A.A.G., June 30, 1867, AC, ROC, May–July, 1868, reel 26; John Dix, Corpus Christi, to Charles A. Vernou, A.A.A.G., [July 1868], AC, ROC, May–July, 1868, reel 26; John Dix, Corpus Christi, to Charles A. Vernou, A.A.A.G., [November 1868], AC, ROC, November–December, 1868, reel 28. White hostility due to the problems in Washington are DeWitt C. Brown, Paris, to J. P. Richardson, A.A.A.G., February 29, 1868, AC, ROC, January–February, 1868, reel 24; Mahlon E. Davis, Houston, to Charles A. Vernou, A.A.A.G., July 31, 1868, AC, ROC, May–July, 1868, reel 26; S. H. Starr, Mount Pleasant, to J. P. Richardson, A.A.A.G., March 5, 1868, AC, LR, 1867–1869, reel 15; Byron Porter, Bastrop, to J. P. Richardson, A.A.A.G., March 2, 1868, AC, ROC, January–February, 1868, reel 24; and Byron Porter, Bastrop, to J. P. Richardson, A.A.A.G.,

April 1, 1868, AC, ROC, March–April, 1868, reel 25. Other agents attributing the increased violence to politics are Alex Ferguson, Nacogdoches, to C. S. Roberts, A.A.A.G., October 4, 1868, AC, ROC, August–October, 1868, reel 27; Gregory Barrett, Tyler, to Charles A. Vernou, A.A.A.G., August 31, 1868, AC, ROC, August–October, 1868, reel 27; Henry C. Lacy, Crockett, to C. S. Roberts, A.A.A.G., September 15, 1868, AC, LR, 1867–1869, reel 13; Clarence Mauck, Austin, to Charles A. Vernou, A.A.A.G., May 31, 1868, AC, ROC, May–July, 1868, 26; John H. Morrison, Palestine, to Charles A. Vernou, A.A.A.G., AC, ROC, August–October, 1868, reel 27; William H. Rock, Richmond, to Charles A. Vernou, A.A.A.G., August 8, 1868, AC, LR, 1867–1869, reel 14; and C. S. Roberts, A.A.A.G., to William H. Rock, Richmond, August 17, 1868, AC, LS, September 1867–May 1869, reel 1.

18. F. P. Wood, Brenham, to Charles A. Vernou, A.A.A.G., July 6, 1868, AC, LR, 1867–1869, reel 16; D. Abrenbreck, Mayor of Hempstead, to J. J. Reynolds, June 26, 1868, AC, LR, 1867–1869, reel 10; F. P. Wood, Brenham, to Charles A. Vernou, A.A.A.G., July 6, 1868, AC, LR, 1867–1869, reel 16; William H. Sinclair, Inspector, to Charles A. Vernou, A.A.A.G., July 6, 1868, AC, LR, 1867–1869, reel 15; F. P. Wood, Brenham, to J. P. Richardson, A.A.A.G., March 23, 1868, AC, LR, 1867–1869, reel 16; Alex B. Coggeshall, Hempstead, to Charles A. Vernou, A.A.A.G., AC, ROC, August through December, 1868, reels 27 and 28. Detailed examinations of Klan violence in Texas are Barbara Leah Clayton, "The Lone Star Conspiracy: Racial Violence and Ku Klux Klan Terror in Post–Civil War Texas," 1865–1877 (Master's Thesis, Oklahoma State University, 1986), particularly chapters 2–4; and Douglas Hale, Hales, Douglas. "Violence Perpetrated Against African Americans by Whites in Texas During Reconstruction, 1865–1868" (Master's Thesis, Texas Tech University, 1994), particularly chapters 2–3.

19. N. H. Randlett, Bryan, to Charles A. Vernou, A.A.A.G., July 23, 1868, AC, LR, 1867–1869, reel 14; O. E. Taylor, et al., to J. J. Reynolds, June 26, 1868, AC, LR, 1867–1869, reel 16; N. H. Randlett, Bryan, to Charles A. Vernou, A.A.A.G., July 9, 1868, AC, ROC, May–July, 1868, reel 26; N. H. Randlett, Bryan, to Charles A. Vernou, A.A.A.G., June 8, 1868, AC, ROC, May–July, 1868, reel 26. For Randlett's changing story, see N. H. Randlett, Millican, to Charles A. Vernou, A.A.A.G., August 4, 1868, AC, LR, 1867–1869, reel 14 (also in M752C, Letters Received, July–December, 1868, reel 60).

20. N. H. Randlett, Millican, to Charles A. Vernou, A.A.A.G., July 23, 1868, AC, LR, 1867–1869, reel 14; Captain W. T. Gentry to C. H. Whittelsey, A.A.A.G., July 27, 1868, M752C, LR, July–December, 1868, reel 60; N. H. Randlett, Bryan, to Charles A. Vernou, A.A.A.G., August 30, 1868, AC, LR, 1867–1869, reel 14; DeWitt C. Brown, Paris, to Charles A. Vernou, A.A.A.G., September 5, 1868, AC, LR, 1867–1869, ree10; O. O. Howard to J. J. Reynolds, July 20, 1868, M742C, LS, October 1, 1867–August 31, 1868, reel 4; Special Orders No. 62, October 18, 1868, AC, IRB, October 1865–April 1869, reel 19.

21. DeWitt C. Brown, Paris, to C. S. Roberts, A.A.A.G., September 30, 1868, AC, ROC, August–October, reel 27; DeWitt C. Brown, Paris, to Charles A. Vernou, A.A.A.G., September 5, 1868, AC, LR, 1867–1869, reel 10; DeWitt C. Brown, Paris, to Charles A. Vernou, A.A.A.G., November 13, 1868, AC, LR, 1867–1869, reel 10; Richter, "Revolver Rules the Day!," 319; Dewitt C. Brown, Paris, to Charles A. Vernou, A.A.A.G., August 31, 1868, AC, ROC, August–October, 1868, reel 27; Alex Ferguson,

Nacogdoches, to J. P. Richardson, A.A.A.G., April 15, 1868, AC, LR, 1867–1869, reel 11; DeWitt C. Brown, Paris, to J. P. Richardson, A.A.A.G., November 30, 1867, AC, ROC, November–December, 1867, reel 23; DeWitt C. Brown, Paris, to C. S. Roberts, A.A.A.G., October, 31, 1868, AC, ROC, August–October, 1868, reel 27. Deteriorating conditions are in David S. Beath, Bastrop, to Charles A. Vernou, A.A.A.G., December 13, 1868, AC, LR, 1867–1869, reel 10; Excerpt of *Austin Republican*, [n.d.], AC, LR, 1867–1869, reel 13; Special Orders No. 46, August 7, 1868, AC, IRB, October 1865–April 1869, reel 19; B. Twigg to [Headquarters], January 4, 1869, AC, LR, 1867–1869, reel 16; Affidavit of Henry Spencer (fm), December 27, 1868, AC, LR, 1867–1869, reel 15; David S. Beath, Bastrop, to Charles A. Vernou, A.A.A.G., December 12, 1868, SAC, LS, March–December 1868, reel 13; David S. Beath, Bastrop, to Charles A. Vernou, A.A.A.G., December 17, 1868, AC, LR, 1867–1869, reel 10; David S. Beath, Bastrop, to Charles A. Vernou, December 13, 1868, AC, LR, 1867–1869, reel 10; David S. Beath, Bastrop, to Charles A. Vernou, December 18, 1868, AC, LR, 1867–1869, reel 10; Thomas C. Griffin, Kaufman, to Charles A. Vernou, A.A.A.G., August 31, 1868, AC, ROC, August–October, 1868, reel 27; Gregory Barrett, Tyler, to Charles A. Vernou, A.A.A.G., August 14, 1868, AC, LR, 1867–1869, reel 10; Ebenezer Gay, Austin, to Charles A. Vernou, A.A.A.G., October 31, 1868, AC, ROC, August–October, 1868, reel 27; William H. Howard, Huntsville, to Charles A. Vernou, A.A.A.G., October 1868, AC, LR, 1867–1869, reel 12; Charles A. Vernou, A.A.A.G., to Fred W. Reinhard, A.A.A.G., May 28, 1868, AC, LS, March 1867–May 1869, reel 1; and J. A. Wright to O. O. Howard, April 3, 1868, AC, LR, 1867–1869, reel 16.

22. Nesbit B. Jenkins, Wharton, to J. J. Reynolds, February 13, 1868, AC, LR, 1867–1869, reel 13; Nesbit B. Jenkins, Wharton, to Charles A. Vernou, A.A.A.G., August 31, 1868, AC, ROC, August–December, 1868, reel 27; Statement of Gray Shanks, July 25, 1868, AC, LR, 1867–1869, reel 13; L. S. Barnes, Inspector, to [Headquarters], July 25, 1868, AC, LR, 1867–1869, reel 13; Nesbit B. Jenkins, Wharton, to J. P. Richardson, A.A.A.G., March 4, 1868, AC, LR, 1867–1869, reel 13.

23. Nesbit B. Jenkins, Wharton, to [J. J. Reynolds], October 7, 1868, AC, LR, 1867–1869, reel 13.

24. Nesbit B. Jenkins, Wharton, to [J. J. Reynolds], October 7, 1868, AC, LR, 1867–1869, reel 13; Wells Thompson to J. J Reynolds, September 23, 1868, AC, LR, 1867–1869, reel 16; Nesbit Jenkins, Wharton, to Sheriff, September 12, 1868, AC, LR, 1867–1869, reel 16.

25. For a more detailed account of the events that night, see Stockade Trial Transcript, Records of the Office of the Judge Advocate General–Army Court Martial Case Files 1809–1894, Record Group 94, Records of the Adjutant General's Office, 1780–1917, National Archives, Washington, D.C., Case PP 629, Box 2582; and Christopher B. Bean, "Death of a Carpetbagger: The George Washington Smith Murder and Stockade Trial in Jefferson, Texas, 1868–1869," *Southwestern Historical Quarterly* 112 (January 2009): 263–292.

26. Ibid.

27. William G. Kirkman, Boston, to C. S. Roberts, A.A.A.G., September 18, 1868, AC, LR, 1867–1869, reel 13; N. B. Anderson to [J. J. Reynolds], September 13, 1868, AC, LR, 1867–1869, reel 13; Richter, "This Blood-Thirsty Hole," 71; George S. Shorkley,

Clarksville, to C. S. Roberts, A.A.A.G., October 15, 1868, AC, LR, 1867–1869, reel 15;
James M. Smallwood, "The Freedmen's Bureau Reconsidered: Local Agents and the
Black Community," *Texana* 11 (Fall 1973): 313–317; Thomas C. Griffin, Kaufman, to J. P.
Richardson, A.A.A.G., April 11, 1868, AC, LR, 1867–1869, reel 11; J. J. Reynolds to O. O.
Howard, March 21, 1868, AC, LR, 1867–1869, reel 16; J. J. Reynolds to O. O. Howard,
September 18, 1868, AC, LR, 1867–1869, reel 16.

28. Charles Haughn, Waco, to [Headquarters], October 2, 1868, AC, LR, 1867–1869,
reel 12; Charles Haughn, Waco, to [J. J. Reynolds], November 14, 1868, AC, LR, 1867–
1869, reel 12; Charles Haughn, Waco, to C. S. Roberts, A.A.A.G., [October 1868], AC,
ROC, August–October, 1868, reel 22; Gregory Barrett, Tyler, to Charles A. Vernou,
A.A.A.G., August 14, 1868, AC, LR, 1867–1869, reel 10; S. P. Donly to [Headquarters],
August 10, 1868, AC, LR, 1867–1869, reel 11; C. S. Roberts, A.A.A.G., to Gregory Barrett,
Tyler, August 28, 1868, AC, LS, March 1867–May 1869, reel 1; Gregory Barrett, Tyler, to
Charles A. Vernou, September 8, 1868, AC, LR, 1867–1869, reel 10. For more on remov-
ing the freedpeople as punishment, see H. S. Starr, Mount Pleasant, to J. P. Richardson,
A.A.A.G., March 5, 1868, AC, LR, 1867–1869, reel 15; C. H. Whittelsey, A.A.A.G., to J. J.
Reynolds, August 5, 1868, M742C, LS, October 1, 1867–August 31, 1868, reel 4; and
Gregory Barrett, Tyler, to Charles A. Vernou, A.A.A.G., June 6, 1868, AC, LR, 1868, reel
10; and William H. Rock, Richmond, to J. P. Richardson, A.A.A.G., May 24, 1868, AC,
ROC, May–July, 1868, reel 25. Agents believing headquarters policy more than suffi-
cient are William Holt, La Grange, to Charles A. Vernou, A.A.A.G., November 30,
1868, AC, ROC, November–December, 1868, reel 28; Thomas H. Baker, Lockhart, to C.
S. Roberts, A.A.A.G., August 31, 1868, AC, ROC, August–October, 1868, reel 27; and
Thomas H. Baker, Lockhart, to Charles A. Vernou, A.A.A.G., July 31, 1868, AC, ROC,
May–July, 1868, reel 26.

29. William H. Sinclair, Inspector, to Charles A. Vernou, A.A.A.G., July 5, 1868,
AC, LR, 1867–1869, reel 15; William H. Sinclair, Inspector, to Charles A. Vernou,
A.A.A.G., July 7, 1868, AC, LR, 1867–1869, reel 15; Special Orders No. 36, June 10, 1868,
AC, IRB, October 1865–April 1869, reel 19; R. M. Bankhead, et al., to J. J. Reynolds,
June 20, 1868, AC, LR, 1867–1869, reel 10; J. J. Reynolds to O. O. Howard, June 10, 1868,
AC, LS, Mach 1867–May 1869, reel 1; J. J. Reynolds to O. O. Howard, July 13, 1868, AC,
LS, March 1867–May 1869, reel 1; William H. Sinclair, Inspector, to AAAG, July 13,
1868, AC, LR, 1867–1869, reel 15; William H. Stewart, Huntsville, to Charles A. Vernou,
A.A.A.G., July 5, 1868, AC, LR, 1867–1869, reel 15; Special Orders No. 42, July 13, 1868,
AC, IRB, October 1865–April 1869, reel 19.

30. Hennell Stevens to [J. J. Reynolds], December 17, 1867, AC, LR, 1867–1869, reel
15; William H. Sinclair, Inspector, to J. P. Richardson, A.A.A.G., January 9, 1868, AC,
LR, 1867–1869, reel 15; A. H. M. Taylor, A.A.A.G., District of Texas, to J. P. Richardson,
A.A.A.G., February 28, 1868, AC, LR, 1867–1869, reel 16; C. H. Whittelsey, A.A.A.G., to
J. J. Reynolds, October 14, 1868, M742C, LS, October 1, 1867–August 31, 1868, reel 4;
General Orders No. 8, August 7, 1868, AC, IRB, October 1865–April 1869, reel 19; William H. Sinclair, Inspector, to J. P. Richardson, A.A.A.G., January 2, 1868, AC, LR,
1867–1869, reel 15; Special Orders No. 2, January 10, 1868, AC, IRB, October 1865–April
1869, reel 19; J. P. Richardson, A.A.A.G., to O. O. Howard, March 25, 1868, AC, LR,
1867–1869, reel 16; William H. Rock, Richmond, to William H. Sinclair, Inspector, Jan-

uary 25, 1868, AC, LR, 1867–1869, reel 15; Arthur B. Homer, Columbia, to J. P. Richardson, A.A.A.G., January 18, 1868, AC, LR, 1867–1869, reel 12; J. P. Richardson, A.A.A.G.,
to A. H. M. Taylor, A.A.A.G., District of Texas, February 20, 1868, AC, LS, March
1867–May 1869, reel 1; Major Fred Ledergerber to [Headquarters], October 18, 1868, AC,
LR, 1867–1869, reel 16; Special Orders No. 59, September 28, 1868, AC, IRB, October
1865–April 1869, reel 19; Special Orders No. 65, November 2, 1868, AC, IRB, October
1865–April 1869, reel 19; C. S. Roberts, A.A.A.G. to William H. Sinclair, Inspector,
October 2, 1868, AC, LS, March 1867–May 1869, reel 1; C. S. Roberts, A.A.A.G., to Otto
F. Steinberg, Gonzales, October 24, 1868, AC, LS, March 1867–May 1869, reel 1; J. J.
Reynolds to O. O. Howard, October 1, November 6, 1868, AC, LS, March 1867–May
1869, reel 1; J. J. Reynolds to O. O. Howard, October 1, 1868, AC, ES, September 1867–
May 1869, reel 2; Otto F. Steinberg to [Charles A. Vernou], A.A.A.G., October 30, 1868,
AC, LR, 1867–1869, reel 15.

31. Nesbit B. Jenkins, Wharton, to Charles A. Vernou, A.A.A.G., December, 31,
1868, AC, ROC, November–December, 1868, reel 28; David S. Beath, Bastrop, to
Charles A. Vernou, A.A.A.G., December, 1, 1868, AC, ROC, November–December,
1868, reel 28; James Gillette, Bryan, to Charles A. Vernou, A.A.A.G., November 5, 1868,
AC, ROC, August–October, 1868, reel 25; James Gillette, Bryan, to Charles A. Vernou,
A.A.A.G., December 10, 1868, AC, ROC, November–December, 1868, reel 28; Edward
C. Henshaw, Marshall, to C. S. Roberts, A.A.A.G., November 25, 1868, AC, LR, 1867–
1869, reel 12; Circular letter from J. J. Reynolds, December 8, 1868, AC, IRB, October
1865–April 1869, reel 19; Circular No. 10, November 17, 1868, AC, IRB, October 1865–
April 1869, reel 19; David S. Beath, Bastrop, to Charles A. Vernou, A.A.A.G., October
31, 1868, AC, ROC, August–October, 1868, reel 27.

32. For a few works on the conservative attitude of Americans during Reconstruction, see Les Benedict, *Compromise of Principle*; and William Gillette, *Retreat from
Reconstruction 1869–1879* (Baton Rouge: Louisiana State University Press, 1979).

Conclusion: The Subassistant Commissioners in Texas

1. Carpenter, *Sword and Olive Branch*, 156.

2. William H. Heistand, Hallettsville, to A. H. Lathrop, A.A.A.G., December 31,
1866, SAC, LS, May–June, 1866 and October 1866–March 1868, reel 21; Samuel C.
Sloan, Richmond, to Chauncey C. Morse, A.A.A.G., February 28, 1866, AC, ULR,
1865–1866, reel 17; George C. Abbott, Hempstead, to E. M. Gregory, October 31, 1865,
AC, ULR, 1865–1866, reel 17; A. H. Cox, Liberty, to Charles A. Vernou, A.A.A.G., July
31, 1868, AC, ROC, May–July, 1868, reel 26.

3. A work that criticizes the lack of troops during Reconstruction is Richter, *Overreached on All Sides*, 295, 300, 302–305.

4. George C. Abbott, Hempstead, to E. M. Gregory, November 23, 1865, AC, ULR,
1865–1866, reel 17.

5. DeWitt C. Brown, Wharton, to J. T. Kirkman, A.A.A.G., April 3, 1867, AC, ROC,
December 1866–May 1867, reel 20.

6. James P. Hutchison, Columbus, to William H. Sinclair, A.A.G., August 14, 1866,
AC, LR, 1866–1867, reel 6.

7. William H. Sinclair, Inspector, to J. T. Kirkman, A.A.A.G., April 1, 1867, AC, LR, 1866–1867, reel 8; Albert A. Metzner, San Augustine, to James C. Devine, Galveston, August 14, 1867, AC, LR, 1866–1867, reel 7.

8. Alex B. Coggeshall, Bastrop, to J. T. Kirkman, A.A.A.G., February 5, 1867, AC, LR, 1866–1867, reel 4; Farmer-Kaiser, 95, 116.

9. Franke, "Becoming a Citizen," 254.

10. Samuel C. Sloan, Richmond, to Chauncey C. Morse, A.A.A.G., January 27, 1866, AC, ULR, 1865–1866, reel 17; Franke, "Becoming a Citizen," 275; John Dix, Corpus Christi, to J. P. Richardson, A.A.A.G., March 26, 1868, AC, LR, 1867–1869, reel 11.

11. Endorsement of letter from William H. Sinclair, Galveston, J. B. Kiddoo, April 20, 1866, AC, ES, April 1866–September 1867, reel 2.

12. Craig, "Memoirs," 79–80.

13. P. B. Johnson, Woodville, to J. T. Kirkman, A.A.A.G., June 1, 1867, AC, LR, 1866–1867, reel 6.

14. William H. Sinclair, Inspector, to J. T. Kirkman, A.A.A.G., March 1, 1867, AC, LR, 1866–1867, reel 8; William H. Sinclair, Inspector, to Henry A. Ellis, A.A.A.G., November 30, 1866, AC, ULR, 1865–1867, reel 17; William H. Sinclair, Inspector, to J. B. Kiddoo, December 23, 1866, AC, LR, 1866–1867, reel 8.

15. Thomas H. Baker, Lockhart, to Charles A. Vernou, A.A.A.G., July 31, 1868, AC, ROC, May-July 1868, reel 26.

16. Howard, *Autobiography*, 2:363; John T. Raper, Columbus, to E. M. Gregory, November 29, 1865, AC, ULR, 1865–1866, reel 17.

17. E. M. Gregory to Benjamin Harris, January 20, 1866, AC, LS, September 1865–March 1867, reel 1; E. M. Gregory to O. O. Howard, June 18, 1866, M752C, LR, May–August, 1866, reel 32; Richter, *Overreached on All Sides*, 288; Crouch, *Freedmen's Bureau and Black Texans*, 20.

18. J. B. Kiddoo to O. O. Howard, July 23, 1866, AC, LS, April 1866–September 1867, reel 1.

19. Charles Griffin to O. O. Howard, February 18, 1867, M752C, LR, January–May, 1867, reel 44.

20. J. J. Reynolds to O. O. Howard, October 20, 1868, AC, LS, March 1867–March 1869, reel 1.

21. J. J. Reynolds to O. O. Howard, October 20, 1868, AC, LS, March 1867–May 1869, reel 1; W. H. Cundiff to [J. J.] Reynolds, August 24, 1868, AC, LR, 1867–1869, reel 10; A. T. Munroe, et al., to Chauncey E. Morse, A.A.A.G., August 17, 1868, AC, LR, 1867–1869, reel 13; A. T. Munroe to [Charles A.] Vernou, A.A.A.G., August 20, 1868, AC, LR, 1867–1869, reel 13; J. R. R. Lynch, et al., to Edwin Turnock, Commander, Post of Centreville, February 28, 1868, AC, LR, 1867–1869, reel 13; J. P. Richardson, A.A.A.G., to Fred W. Reinhard, Crockett, March 24, 1868, AC, LS, March 1867–May 1869, reel 1; J. P. Richardson, A.A.A.G., to Fred W. Reinhard, Crockett, February 12, 1868, AC, LS, March 1867–May 1869, reel 1; Charles A. Vernou, A.A.A.G., to W. H. Cundiff, October 22, 1868, AC, LS, March 1867–May 1869, reel 1.

22. Cimbala and Miller, eds., *Freedmen's Bureau and Reconstruction*, 346. For agents' racial beliefs and conservatism, see Michael Les Benedict, *Compromise of Prin-*

ciple; Perman, *Retreat from Reconstruction*; and White, "Black Lives, Red Tape," 241–258.

23. Charles Gray, "The Freedmen's Bureau: A Missing Chapter in Social Welfare History" (Ph.D., D.S.W., Yeshiva University, 1994), 1; Campbell, *Grass-Roots Recon-struction*, 108; *Dallas Herald*, November 25, 1865; Rable, *But There Was No Peace*, 25; David H. Donald, *Liberty and Union: The Crisis of Popular Government, 1830–1890* (Boston: Little Brown, 1978), 175–182.

24. William G. Kirkman, Boston, to J. P. Richardson, A.A.A.G., AC, ROC, Janu-ary–February, 1868, reel 24; William G. Kirkman, A.A.A.G., September 30, 1867, AC, ROC, September–October, 1867, reel 22.

25. Richter, Army in Texas During Reconstruction, 146–147; Richter, Overreached on All Sides, 299–300.

26. For the counterfactual, see William Blair, "The Use of Military Force to Protect the Gains of Reconstruction," *Civil War History* 51 (December 2005): 388–402.

27. Brooks Simpson, *The Reconstruction Presidents* (Lawrence: University Press of Kansas, 1998), 4. For the counterfactual arguments, see Heather Cox Richardson, "A Marshall Plan for the South? The Failure of Republican and Democratic Ideology dur-ing Reconstruction," *Civil War History* 51 (December 2005): 378–387; Robert F. Engs, "The Missing Catalyst: In Response to Essays on Reconstructions That Might Have Been," *Civil War History* 51 (December 2005): 427–431; James L. Huston, "Reconstruc-tion as It Should Have Been: An Exercise in Counterfactual History," *Civil War History* 51 (December 2005): 358–363; Blair, "Use of Military Force to Protect the Gains of Reconstruction," 388–402; Michael Vorenberg, "Imagining a Different Reconstruction Constitution," *Civil War History* 51 (December 2005): 416–426; Roger L. Ransom, "Reconstructing Reconstruction: Options and Limitations to Federal Policies on Land Distribution in 1866–1867," *Civil War History* 51 (December 2005): 364–377; and James L. Huston, "An Alternative to the Tragic Era: Applying the Virtues of Bureaucracy to the Reconstruction Dilemma," *Civil War History* 51 (December 2005): 403–415.

28. Richardson, "An Evaluation of the Freedmen's Bureau in Florida," 237.

29. Willie Lee Rose, "Blacks Without Masters: Protagonists and Issue," in *Slavery and Freedom*, ed. William W. Freehling (New York: Oxford University Press, 1982), 93; Higgs, *Competition and Coercion*, 131; Finley, *From Slavery to Uncertain Freedom*, 169.

Bibliography

Primary Sources

Manuscripts

Bowdoin College, Brunswick, Maine
    Howard, Oliver Otis. Papers.
Center for American History, University of Texas at Austin
    Evans, Ira Hobart. Vertical File.
    Throckmorton, James W. Papers.
    Wheelock, Edwin Miller Papers.
Howard University, Washington, D.C.
    Howard, Oliver Otis. Papers.
Library of Congress (Manuscripts Division), Washington, D.C.
    Grant, Ulysses S. Papers.
    Sheridan, Philip H. Papers.
National Archives and Records Administration, Washington, D.C.
    Johnson, Andrew. Papers.
New York Public Library, New York City
    Carpenter, John A. "Agents of the Freedmen's Bureau." Unpublished Manuscript (John A. Carpenter Papers).
U.S. Army Military History Institute, Carlisle Barracks, Pennsylvania
    Craig, Samuel A. "Memoirs of Civil War and Reconstruction." Unpublished Manuscript (Civil War Times Illustrated Collection).
Victoria Regional History Center, Victoria College, Victoria, Texas
    Barry A. Crouch Collection.

Manuscript Government Documents

Colorado County Courthouse, Columbus, Texas.
Colorado County District Court Records, Criminal Minute Book.
National Archives, Washington, D.C.
Bureau of Refugees, Freedmen, and Abandoned Lands. Selected Series of Records Issued by the Commissioner of the Bureau of Refugees, Freedmen, and Abandoned Lands, 1865–1872 (Microfilm M742), Record Group 105.
Bureau of Refugees, Freedmen, and Abandoned Lands. Registers and Letters Received by the Commissioner of the Bureau of Refugees, Freedmen, and Abandoned Lands, 1865–1872 (Microfilm M752), Record Group 105.

Bureau of Refugees, Freedmen, and Abandoned Lands. Records of the Assistant Commissioner for the State of Texas, Bureau of Refugees, Freedmen, and Abandoned Lands, 1865–1869 (Microfilm M821), Record Group 105.

Bureau of Refugees, Freedmen, and Abandoned Lands. Records of the Superintendent of Education for the State of Texas, Bureau of Refugees, Freedmen, and Abandoned Lands, 1865–1870 (Microfilm M822), Record Group 105.

Bureau of Refugees, Freedmen, and Abandoned lands. Records of the Field Offices for the State of Texas, 1865–1870. Record Group 105.

Bureau of Veterans Affairs, Record Group 15.

Correspondence of the Office of Civil Affairs of the District of Texas, the 5th Military District, and the Department of Texas, 1867–1870 (Microfilm M1188), Record Group 393.

Eighth Census of the United States, 1860. Records of the Bureau of the Census (Microfilm M653, T1134), Record Group 29.

Gibson, Campbell J. and Emily Lennon, comp. "Historical Census Statistics on the Foreign-Born Population of the United States: 1850 to 1990. Unpublished Working Paper No. 29, U.S. Bureau of the Census, February 1999.

Ninth Census of the United States, 1870. Records of the Bureau of the Census (Microfilm M593, T1134), Record Group 29.

Records of the Office of the Judge Advocate General—Army Court Martial Case Files1809–1894, Records of the Adjutant General's Office, Record Group 94.

Seventh Census of the United States, 1850. Records of the Bureau of the Census (Microfilm M432, T1224), Record Group 29.

Texas State Library and Archives Commission, Austin

Election Registers 1838–1972: Appointment to Office Under Provisional Government, August 1866–1870 and Election and Appointment of State and County Officials, 1866–1870.

Governor's Records

Hamilton, Andrew Jackson. Papers.

Pease, Elisha M. Papers.

Throckmorton, James W. Papers.

Texas Adjutant General's Office (Texas Adjutant Generals Department).

Published Government Documents

Bates, Samuel P. *History of Pennsylvania Volunteers, 1861–1865.* 5 vols. Harrisburg: B. Singerly, State Publisher, 1869–1871.

———. *Martial Deeds of Pennsylvania.* Philadelphia: T. H. Davis & Co., 1876.

Bureau of Refugees, Freedmen, and Abandoned Lands. *Officers' Manual.* Washington, D.C.: Government Printing Office, 1866.

Congressional Globe, 38th Congress, 2nd Session.

Gammel, H. P. N. *The Laws of Texas, 1822–1897 . . . .* 10 vols. Austin: The Gammel Book Company, 1898.

Report of Joint Committee on Reconstruction, 39th Congress, 1st Session, Report No. 30. Washington, D.C.: Government Printing Office, 1866.

Richardson, James D., ed. *A Compilation of the Messages and Papers of the Presidents, 1789–1902*. 10 vols. New York: Bureau of National Literature and Art, 1903–1905.

Simon, John Y., et al., eds. *The Papers of Ulysses S. Grant, 1837–1885*. 31 vols. Carbondale: Southern Illinois University Press, 1967–2009.

Statutes at Large, Treaties, and Proclamations of the United States of America. 119 vols. Boston: Little, Brown and Company, 1866–1869.

United States Bureau of the Census. *The Vital Statistics of the United States . . . Compiled from the Original Returns of the Ninth Census*. 4 vols. Washington, D.C.: Government Printing Company, 1872.

United States Congress. *Digest of Election Cases*, 45th Congress, 2nd Session, No. 52.

United States Congress. *House Executive Documents*, 39th Congress, 1st Session, No. 70.

United States Government. *Biographical Directory of the American Congress, 1774–1949*. Washington, D.C.: Government Printing Office, 1950.

United States War Department. *The War of the Rebellion: A Compilation of the Official Records of the Union and Confederate Armies*. 128 vols. Washington, D.C.: Government Printing Office, 1880–1901.

Records of the Union and Confederate Armies. 128 vols. Washington, D.C.: Government Printing Office, 1880–1901.

Other Published Primary Material

Andrews, Brevet Major Gen. Christopher Columbus. *Early Steps in Reconstruction: Speeches by General C. C. Andres of Minnesota in Texas and Arkansas*. Washington, D.C.: Union Republican Congressional Committee, 1865.

Baum, Dale. *Counterfeit Justice: The Judicial Odyssey of Texas Freedwoman Azeline Hearne*. Baton Rouge: Louisiana State University Press, 2009.

Berlin, Ira, et al., ed. *Freedom: A Documentary History of Emancipation, 1861–1867*. 3 vols. Cambridge: Oxford University Press, 1985–1990.

Buell, Augustus. *The Cannoneer: Recollections of Service in the Army of the Potomac*. Washington, D.C.: The National Tribune, 1890.

Campbell, William A., ed. "A Freedmen's Bureau Diary by George Wagner." Part 1. *Georgia Historical Quarterly* 48 (June 1964): 196–214.

———, ed. "A Freedmen's Bureau Diary by George Wagner." Part 2. *Georgia Historical Quarterly* 48 (September 1964): 333–359.

Crouch, Barry A., ed. "View from Within: Letters of Gregory Barrett, Freedmen's Bureau Agent." *Chronicles of Smith County, Texas* 12 (Winter 1973): 13–26.

Hahn, Steven, et al., eds. *Freedom: A Documentary History of Emancipation, 1861–1867*. Series 3, Volume 1: Land and Labor, 1865. Chapel Hill: University of North Carolina Press, 2008.

Horst, Samuel L., ed. *The Fire of Liberty in Their Hearts: The Diary of Jacob E. Yoder of The Freedmen's Bureau School, Lynchburg, Virginia, 1866–1870*. Richmond: The Library of Virginia, 1996.

Howard, Oliver Otis. *Autobiography of Oliver Otis Howard*. 2 vols. New York: The Baker and Taylor Company, 1908.

Hume, Richard L., ed. "The Freedmen's Bureau and the Freedmen's Vote in the Reconstruction of Southern Alabama: An Account by Agent Samuel S. Gardner." *Alabama Historical Quarterly* 37 (Fall 1975): 17–24.

Johnson, Suzanne Stone, ed., *Bitter Freedom: William Stone's Record of Service in the Freedmen's Bureau.* Columbia: University of South Carolina Press, 2008.

Magdol, Edward, ed. "Document: Martin R. Delany Counsels Freedmen, July 23, 1865." *The Journal of Negro History* 56 (October 1971): 303–309.

Mugleston, William F., ed. "The Freedmen's Bureau and Reconstruction in Virginia: The Diary of Marcus Sterling Hopkins, a Union Officer." *Virginia Magazine of History and Biography* 86 (January 1978): 44–102.

National Rifle Association. *The National Rifle Association 1873: Address, Annual Reports, and Regulation for Rifle Practice.* New York: Reynolds & Whelpey, 1877.

North, Thomas. *Five Years in Texas.* Cincinnati: Elm Street Publishing Company, 1871.

Otis, George A. ed., *Medical and Surgical History of the War of the Rebellion.* 12 vols. Washington, D.C.: Government Printing Office, 1876.

Sheridan, Philip H. *Personal Memoirs of Philip H. Sheridan.* London: Chatto and Windus Piccadilly, 1888.

Tunnell, Ted., ed. *Carpetbagger from Vermont: The Autobiography of Marshall Harvey Twitchell.* Baton Rouge: Louisiana State University Press, 1989.

Tyler, Ronnie and Lawrence R. Murphy, eds. *The Slave Narratives of Texas.* Austin: The Encino Press, 1974.

Wilbarger, J. W. *Indian Depredations in Texas.* Austin: Steck Company, 1935.

Wood, W. D. *Reminiscences of Reconstruction in Texas and Reminiscences of Texas and Texans Fifty Years Ago.* n.p., 1902.

Newspapers

Austin American Statesman, 1954
Austin Weekly Southern Intelligencer, 1868
Bellville Countryman, 1865
Brownsville Ranchero, 1866–1867
Flake's Daily Bulletin, 1866–1867
Galveston Daily News, 1866–1867
Galveston Tri Weekly News, 1866
Galveston Weekly News, 1866
Houston Post, 1868, 1968
Houston Telegraph, 1867
La Grange True Issue, 1865
Dallas Herald, 1865–1866
New York Herald, 1866
New York Times, 1866, 1871, 1906
Philadelphia Inquirer, 1862
The Sandusky Clarion (OH), 1844
Washington Post, 1907

Secondary Books

Abbott, Martin. *The Freedmen's Bureau in South Carolina, 1865–1872*. Chapel Hill: University of North Carolina Press, 1967.

Anderson, Eric and Alfred A. Ross, Jr., *The Facts of Reconstruction: Essays in Honor of John Hope Franklin*. Baton Rouge: Louisiana State University Press, 1991.

Anderson, James D. *The Education of Blacks in the South, 1860–1935*. Chapel Hill: University of North Carolina Press, 1988.

Baggett, James A. *The Scalawags: Southern Dissenters in the Civil War and Reconstruction*. Baton Rouge: Louisiana State University Press, 2003.

Barr, Alwyn. *Black Texans: A History of African Americans in Texas, 1528–1995*. Norman: University of Oklahoma Press, 1995.

Belz, Herman. *A New Birth of Freedom: The Republican Party and Freedmen's Rights, 1861 to 1866*. New York: Fordham University Press, 2000.

Benedict, Michael Les. *A Compromise of Principle: Congressional Republicans and Reconstruction*. New York: W. W. Norton & Company, 1974.

Bentley, George. *A History of the Freedmen's Bureau*. Philadelphia: University of Philadelphia Press, 1955.

Boatner, Mark M, III. *The Civil War Dictionary*. New York: David McKay Company, Inc., 1959.

Bremner, Robert H. *The Public Good: Philanthropy and Welfare in the Civil War Era*. New York: Alfred A. Knopf, 1980.

Brown, Thomas J., ed. *Reconstructions: New Perspectives on the Postbellum United States*. New York: Oxford University Press, 2006.

Bullock, Henry Allen. *A History of Negro Education in the South: From 1619 to the Present*. Cambridge: Harvard University Press, 1967.

Butchart, Ronald E. *Northern Schools, Southern Blacks, and Reconstruction: Freedmen's Education, 1862–1875*. Westport: Greenwood Press, 1980.

Campbell, Randolph B. and Richard G. Lowe. *Wealth and Power in Antebellum Texas*. College Station: Texas A&M University Press, 1977.

Campbell, Randolph B. *An Empire for Slavery: The Peculiar Institution in Texas, 1821–1865*. Baton Rouge: Louisiana State University Press, 1989.

———. *Gone to Texas: A History of the Lone Star State*. New York: Oxford University Press, 2003.

———. *Grass-Roots Reconstruction in Texas, 1865–1880*. Baton Rouge: Louisiana State University Press, 1997.

———. *A Southern Community in Crisis: Harrison County, Texas, 1865–1880*. Austin: Texas State Historical Association, 1983.

Carpenter, John A. *The Sword and the Olive Branch: Oliver Otis Howard*. Pittsburgh: University of Pittsburgh Press, 1964.

Carlson, Paul H. *"Pecos Bill": A Military Biography of William R. Shafter*. College Station: Texas A&M University Press, 1989.

Carrigan, William D. *The Making of a Lynching Culture: Violence and Vigilantism in Central Texas, 1836–1916*. Urbana: University of Illinois, 2004.

Carter, Dan T. *When the War Was Over: The Failure of Self-Reconstruction in the South, 1865–1867*. Baton Rouge: Louisiana State University Press, 1985.

Carter, Susan B., et al. *Historical Statistics of the United States: Earliest Times to the Present*. 6 vols. New York: Cambridge University Press, 2006.

Casdorph, Paul D. *A History of the Republican Party in Texas, 1865–1965*. Austin: Pemberton Press, 1965.

Cimbala, Paul A. *Under the Guardianship of the Nation: The Freedmen's Bureau and the Reconstruction of Georgia, 1865–1870*. Athens: University of Georgia Press, 1997.

Cimbala, Paul A. and Randall M. Miller, eds. *The Freedmen's Bureau: Reconsiderations*. New York: Fordham University Press, 1999.

———, eds. *Union Soldiers and the Northern Home Front: Wartime Experiences, Postwar Adjustments*. New York: Fordham University Press, 2002.

Coleman, Charles Hubert. *Election of 1868: The Democratic Effort to Regain Control*. New York: Columbia University Press, 1933.

Cott, Nancy. *Public Vows: A History of Marriage and the Nation*. Cambridge: Harvard University Press, 2000.

Cox, LaWanda and John H. Cox. *Politics, Principle, and Prejudice 1865–1866: Dilemma of Reconstruction America*. London: The Free Press of Glencoe, 1963.

Coulter, E. Merton. *Georgia: A Short History*. Chapel Hill: University of North Carolina Press, 1947.

———. *The South During Reconstruction, 1865–1877*. Baton Rouge: Louisiana State University Press, 1947.

Crouch, Barry A. *The Freedmen's Bureau and Black Texans*. Austin: University of Texas Press, 1992.

Cruden, Robert. *The Negro in Reconstruction*. Englewood Cliffs: Prentice-Hall, 1969.

Cullum, George W. *Biographical Register of the Officers and Graduates of the U.S. Military Academy at West Point, New York, from Its Establishment March 16, 1802 to the Army Reorganization of 1866–1867*. 2 vols. New York: D. Van Nostrand, 1868.

Currie-McDaniel, Ruth. *Carpetbagger of Conscience: A Biography of John Emory Bryant*. New York: Fordham University Press, 1999.

Dawson, Joseph G., III. *Army Generals and Reconstruction: Louisiana, 1862–1877*. Baton Rouge: Louisiana State University Press, 1982.

De Forest, John William. *A Union Officer in Reconstruction*. Edited by James H. Croushore and David M. Potter. New Haven: Yale University Press, 1948.

Donald, David H. *Liberty and Union: The Crisis of Popular Government, 1830–1890*. Boston: Little Brown, 1978.

Dollar, Susan E. *The Freedmen's Bureau Schools of Natchitoches Parish Louisiana, 1865–1868*. Natchitoches: Northwestern State University Press, 1998.

Drago, Edmund L. *Black Politicians and Reconstruction in Georgia: A Splendid Failure*. Baton Rouge: Louisiana State University Press, 1982.

DuBois, W. E. Bugharht. *The Philadelphia Negro: A Social Study*. New York: Benjamin Bloom, 1899.

———. *The Souls of Black Folk*. New York: Penguin Books, 1969.

Duncan, Russell. *Freedom's Shore: Tunis Campbell and the Georgia Freedmen*. Athens: University of Georgia Press, 1986.

Dunning, William A. *Reconstruction, Political and Economic, 1865–1877*. New York: Harper and Row Publishers, 1907.

Dyer, Frederick H., comp. *A Compendium of the War of the Rebellion*. 3 vols. New York: Thomas Yoseloff, 1959.

Eby, Frederick. *The Development of Education in Texas*. New York: The Macmillan Company, 1925.

Edwards, Laura F. *Gendered Strife and Confusion: The Political Culture of Reconstruction*. Urbana: University of Illinois Press, 1997.

———. *Scarlett Doesn't Live Here Anymore: Southern Women in the Civil War Era*. Urbana: University of Illinois Press, 2004.

Edwards, Rebecca. *Angels in the Machinery: Gender in American Party Politics from the Civil War to the Progressive Era*. New York: Oxford University Press, 1997.

Eicher, John H. and David J. Eicher. *Civil War High Commands*. Stanford: Stanford University Press, 2001.

Engs, Robert F. *Freedom's First Generation: Black Hampton, Virginia, 1861–1890*. Philadelphia: University of Pennsylvania, 1979.

Fairman, Charles. *Reconstruction and Reunion, 1864–1888*. New York: The Macmillan Company, 1971.

Farmer-Kaiser, Mary. *Freedwomen and the Freedmen's Bureau: Race, Gender, and Public Policy in the Age of Emancipation*. New York: Fordham University Press, 2010.

Faust, Patricia L., ed. *Historical Times Illustrated: Encyclopedia of the Civil War*. New York: Harper & Row Publishers, 1986.

Ficklen, John Rose. *History of Reconstruction in Louisiana Through 1868*. Baltimore: The Johns Hopkins Press, 1910.

Field Records of Officers of the Veteran Reserve Corps, from the Commencement to the Close of the Rebellion. Washington, D.C.: Scriver & Swing, n.d.

Fields, Barbara J. *Slavery and Freedom on the Middle Ground: Maryland during the Nineteenth Century*. New Haven: Yale University Press, 1985.

Finley, Randy. *From Slavery to Uncertain Freedom: The Freedmen's Bureau in Arkansas, 1865–1869*. Fayetteville: University of Arkansas Press, 1996.

Fitzgerald, Michael W. *Splendid Failure: Postwar Reconstruction in the American South*. Chicago: Ivan R. Dee Publishers, 2007.

———. *The Union League Movement in the Deep South: Politics and Agricultural Change During Reconstruction*. Baton Rouge: Louisiana State University Press, 1989.

Foner, Eric. *Free Soil, Free Labor, Free Men: The Ideology of the Republican Party before the Civil War*. New York: Oxford University Press, 1970.

———. *Politics and Ideology in the Age of the Civil War*. New York: Oxford University Press, 1980.

———. *Reconstruction: America's Unfinished Revolution, 1863–1877*. New York: Harper & Row Publishers, 1988.

Frankel, Noralee. *Freedom's Women: Black Women and Family in Civil War Era Mississippi*. Bloomington: Indiana University Press, 1999.

Franklin, Donna L. *Ensuring Inequality: The Structural Transformation of the African American Family*. New York: Oxford University Press, 1997.

Franklin, John Hope. *Reconstruction: After the Civil War*. Chicago: University of Chicago Press, 1961.

Frazee, Jerry D. *The Magnificent Carpetbagger: The Life, the Times, and the Literature of Edwin M. Wheelock, 1829–1901*. Austin: n.p., 1976.

Frazier, Edward Franklin. *The Negro in the United States*. New York: The MacMillan Company, 1971.

Fredrickson, George M. *The Black Image in the White Mind*. New York: Harper & Row, Publishers, 1971.

Garner, James W. *Reconstruction in Mississippi*. New York: The MacMillan Company, 1901.

Genovese, Eugene D. *Roll, Jordan, Roll: The World the Slaves Made*. New York: Pantheon Books, 1972.

Gerteis, Louis. *From Contraband to Freedman: Federal Policy Toward Southern Blacks, 1861–1865*. Westport: Greenwood Press, 1973.

Gillette, William. *Retreat from Reconstruction 1869–1879*. Baton Rouge: Louisiana State University Press, 1979.

Glazer, Nathan and Daniel Patrick Moynihan. *Beyond the Melting Pot*. Cambridge: M.I.T. Press, 1963.

Goldberg, Chad Alan. *Citizens and Paupers: Relief, Rights, and Race, from the Freedmen's Bureau to Workfare*. Chicago: University of Chicago Press, 2008.

Grossberg, Michael. *Governing the Hearth: Law and Family in Nineteenth-Century America*. Chapel Hill: University of North Carolina Press, 1985.

Gutman, Herbert G. *The Black Family in Slavery and Freedom, 1750–1925*. New York: Pantheon Books, 1976.

Heitman, Francis B. *Historical Register and Dictionary of the United States Army, From Its Organization, September 29, 1789, to March 2, 1903*. 2 vols. Washington, D.C.: Government Printing Office, 1988.

Herringshaw, Thomas William, ed. *Herringshaw's Encyclopedia of American Biography of the Nineteenth Century*. Chicago: American Publishers' Association, 1901.

Hesseltine, William B. *A History of the South, 1607–1936*. New York: Prentice Hall Inc., 1936.

Higgs, Robert. *Competition and Coercion: Blacks in the American Economy, 1865–1914*. Cambridge: Cambridge University Press, 1977.

hooks, bell. *Ain't I a Woman: Black Women and Feminism*. Boston: South End Press, 1981.

Hunter, Tera W. *To 'Joy My Freedom: Southern Black Women's Lives and Labors After the Civil War*. Cambridge: Harvard University Press, 1997.

Hyman, Harold M. *Era of the Oath: Northern Loyalty Tests During the Civil War and Reconstruction*. Philadelphia: University of Pennsylvania Press, 1954.

———. *A More Perfect Union: The Impact of the Civil War and Reconstruction on the Constitution*. New York: Alfred K. Knopf, 1973.

Jamieson, Perry D. *Winfield Scott Hancock: Gettysburg Hero*. Abilene: McWhiney Foundation Press, 2003.

Jaynes, Gerald D. *Branches without Roots: Genesis of the Black Working Class in the American South, 1862–1882*. New York: Oxford University Press, 1986.

Jones, Jacqueline. *Soldiers of Light and Love: Northern Teachers and Georgia Blacks, 1865–1873*. Chapel Hill: University of North Carolina Press, 1980.

Jordan, David M. *Winfield Scott Hancock: A Soldier's Life*. Bloomington: Indiana University Press, 1988.

Kaczorowski, Robert J. *The Politics of Judicial Interpretation: The Federal Courts, Department of Justice and Civil Rights, 1866–1876*. New York: Oceana Publications, Inc., 1985.

Kerber, Linda. *No Constitutional Right to Be Ladies: Women and the Obligations of Citizenship*. New York: Hill and Wang, 1998.

Kerr-Ritchie, Jeffrey R. *Freedpeople in the Tobacco South: Virginia, 1860–1900*. Chapel Hill: University of North Carolina Press, 1999.

Lang, George, Raymond L. Collins, and Gerard F. White, comps. *Medal of Honor Recipients 1863–1994*. 2 vols. New York: Facts on File, Inc., 1995.

Lerner, Gerda, ed. *Black Women in White America: A Documentary History*. New York: Random House, Inc., 1972.

Levine, Robert S. *Martin Delany, Frederick Douglass, and the Politics of Representative Identity*. Chapel Hill: University of North Carolina Press, 1997.

Litwack, Leon. *Been in the Storm So Long: The Aftermath of Slavery*. New York: Alfred K. Knopf, 1979.

McFeely, William S. *Yankee Stepfather: General O. O. Howard and the Freedmen*. New York: W. W. Norton & Company, 1968.

McKenna, Charles F., comp. *Under the Maltese Cross, Antietam to Appomattox: The Loyal Uprising in Western Pennsylvania, 1861–1865*. Pittsburgh: The 155th Regimental Association, 1910.

Messner, William F. *Freedmen and the Ideology of Free Labor: Louisiana 1862–1865*. Lafayette: University of Southwestern Louisiana Press, 1978.

Members of the Texas Congress, 1846–2004. 2 vols. Austin: Senate Publications, 2005.

Moneyhon, Carl H. *Republicanism in Reconstruction Texas*. Austin: University of Texas Press, 1980.

———. *Texas After the Civil War: The Struggle of Reconstruction*. College Station: Texas A&M University Press, 2004.

Morgan, Lynda J. *Emancipation in Virginia's Tobacco Belt, 1850–1870*. Athens: University of Georgia Press, 1992.

Morris, Robert C. *Reading, 'Riting, and Reconstruction: The Education of Freedmen in the South, 1861–1870*. Chicago: University of Chicago Press, 1981.

Nieman, Donald G. *To Set the Law in Motion: The Freedmen's Bureau and the Legal Rights of Blacks, 1865–1868*. Millwood: KTO Press, 1979.

Novak, Daniel. *The Wheel of Servitude: Black Forced Labor After Slavery*. Lexington: University of Kentucky Press, 1979.

Nunn, W. C. *Texas Under the Carpetbaggers*. Austin: University of Texas Press, 1962.

O'Donovan, Susan E. *Becoming Free in the Cotton South*. Cambridge: Harvard University Press, 2007.

Oubre, Claude. *Forty Acres and a Mule*. Baton Rouge: Louisiana State University Press, 1978.

Paludan, Phillip S. *A Covenant with Death: The Constitution, Law, and Equality in the Civil War Era*. Urbana: University of Illinois Press, 1975.

Perman, Michael. *Emancipation and Reconstruction, 1862–1877*. New York: Harper & Row, 1988.

Michael D. Pierce. *The Most Promising Young Officer: A Life of Ranald Slidell Mackenzie*. Norman: University of Oklahoma Press, 1993.

Pierce, Paul Skeels. *The Freedmen's Bureau, A Chapter in the History of Reconstruction*. Iowa City: University of Iowa Press, 1904.

Pitre, Merline. *Through Many Dangers, Toils, and Snares: The Black Leadership of Texas, 1868–1900*. Austin: Eakin Press, 1985.

Portrait and Biographical Album of Washtenaw County, Michigan, Containing Biographical Sketches of Prominent and Representative Citizens . . . . Chicago: Biographical Publishing Company, 1891.

Powell, William H., comp. *List of Officers of the Army of the United States from 1779 to 1900*. New York: L. R. Hamersley and Company, 1900.

Ramsdell, Charles W. *Reconstruction in Texas*. Austin: University of Texas Press, 1910.

Randall, James G. and David Donald. *The Civil War and Reconstruction*. Boston: D. C. Heath and Company, 1961.

Ranson, Roger L. and Richard Sutch. *One Kind of Freedom: The Economic Consequences of Emancipation*. Cambridge: Cambridge University Press, 2001.

Regosin, Elizabeth A. *Freedom's Promise: Ex-Slave Families and Citizenship in the Age of Emancipation*. Charlottesville: University of Virginia Press, 2002.

Reidy, Joseph P. *From Slavery to Agrarian Capitalism in the Cotton Plantation South: Central Georgia, 1800–1880*. Chapel Hill: University of North Carolina Press, 1992.

Reynolds, John S. *Reconstruction in South Carolina, 1865–1877*. Columbia: The State Company Publishers, 1905.

Richardson, Heather C. *The Death of Reconstruction: Race, Labor, and Politics in the Post–Civil War North, 1865–1900*. Cambridge: Harvard University Press, 2001.

Richardson, Joe M. *Christian Reconstruction: Freedmen's Education, 1862–1875*. Westport: Greenwood Press, 1980.

Richter, William L. *The Army in Texas During Reconstruction, 1865–1870*. College Station: Texas A&M University Press, 1987.

———. *Overreached on All Sides: The Freedmen's Bureau Administrators in Texas, 1865–1868*. College Station: Texas A&M University Press, 1991.

Roark, James L. *Masters Without Slaves: Southern Planters in the Civil War and Reconstruction*. New York: W. W. Norton & Company, 1977.

Robinson, Charles, III. *Bad Hand: A Biography of General Ranald S. Mackenzie* (Austin: State House Press, 1993).

Roediger, David. *The Wages of Whiteness: Race and the Making of the American Working Class*. New York: Verso, 1991.

Rollins, Frank A. *Life and Public Services of Martin R. Delaney*. Manchester, N.H.: Ayer Company Publishers, 1970.

Rose, Willie Lee. *Rehearsal for Reconstruction: The Port Royal Experiment*. Indianapolis: Bobbs-Merrill, 1964.

Rosen, Hannah. *Terror in the Heartland: Citizenship, Sexual Violence, and the Meaning of Race in the Postemancipation South*. Chapel Hill: University of North Carolina Press, 2009.

Schmidt, James D. *Free to Work: Labor Law, Emancipation, and Reconstruction 1815–1880*. Athens: University of Georgia Press, 1998.

Schwalm, Leslie A. *A Hard Fight for We: Women's Transition from Slavery to Freedom in South Carolina*. Urbana: University of Illinois Press, 1997.

Scott, Donald, Sr. *Camp William Penn, 1863–1865: America's First Federal African American Soldiers' Fight for Freedom*. Altgen: Schiffer Publishing, 2012.

Sefton, James E. *The United States Army and Reconstruction, 1865–1877*. Baton Rouge: Louisiana State University Press, 1967.

Simpson, Brooks. *The Reconstruction Presidents*. Lawrence: University Press of Kanas, 1998.

Smallwood, James M. *Time of Hope, Time of Despair: Black Texans During Reconstruction*. Port Washington, New York: Kennikat Press, 1981.

Soltow, Lee. *Men and Wealth in the United States, 1850–1870*. New Haven: Yale University Press, 1975.

———. *Patterns in Wealthholding in Wisconsin since 1850*. Madison: University of Wisconsin Press, 1971.

Stampp, Kenneth M. and Leon Litwack, eds. *Reconstruction: An Anthology of Revisionist Writings*. Baton Rouge: Louisiana State University Press, 1969.

Stanley, Amy Dru. *From Bondage to Contract: Wage Labor, Marriage, and the Market in the Age of Slave Emancipation*. New York: Cambridge University Press, 1998.

Staples, Thomas S. *Reconstruction in Arkansas, 1862–1874*. New York: Columbia University Press, 1923.

Sterling, Dorothy. *The Making of an Afro-American: Martin Robison Delany, 1812–1885*. New York: Da Capro Press, 1996.

Strickland, Arvarh E. and Jerome R. Reich. *The Black American Experience: From Slavery Through Reconstruction*. New York: Harcourt Brace Jovanovich, 1974.

Swint, Henry Lee. *The Northern Teacher in the South, 1862–1870*. Nashville: Vanderbilt University Press, 1941.

Thompson, C. Mildred. *Reconstruction in Georgia: Economic, Social, Political, 1865- 1872*. Savannah: The Beehive Press, 1972.

Thompson, Jerry D. *Civil War to the Bloody End: The Life and Times of Major General Samuel P. Heintzelman*. College Station: Texas A&M University Press, 2006.

Tunnel, Ted. *Edge of the Sword: The Ordeal of Carpetbagger Marshall H. Twitchell in the Civil War and Reconstruction*. Baton Rouge: Louisiana State University Press, 2001.

Tyler, Ron, et al., eds. *The New Handbook of Texas*. 6 vols. Austin: Texas State Historical Association, 1996.

Wallace, Ernest. *Ranald S. Mackenzie on the Texas Frontier*. College Station: Texas A&M University Press, 1993.

———. *Texas in Turmoil: The Saga of Texas, 1849–1875*. Austin: Steck-Vaughn Company, 1965.

Warner, Ezra J. *Generals in Blue: Lives of the Union Commanders*. Baton Rouge: Louisiana State University Press, 1964.

Webster, Laura Josephine. *The Operations of the Freedmen's Bureau in South Carolina*. New York: Russell and Russell, 1970.

Wesley, Charles H. *Negro Labor in the United States, 1850–1925*. New York: Russell and Russell, 1967.

White, Howard A. *The Freedmen's Bureau in Louisiana*. Baton Rouge: Louisiana State University Press, 1970.

Wiener, Jonathan M. *Social Origins of the New South: Alabama, 1865–1885*. Baton Rouge: Louisiana State University Press, 1978.

Wiley, Bell Irvin. *The Life of Billy Yank: The Common Soldier of the Union*. Baton Rouge: Louisiana State University Press, 1971.

Williamson, Joel. *After Slavery: The Negro in South Carolina During Reconstruction, 1861–1877*. Chapel Hill: University of North Carolina Press, 1965.

Winegarten, Ruthe, ed. *Black Texas Women: 150 Years of Trial and Triumph*. Austin: University of Texas Press, 1995.

Winkler, Ernest William, ed. *Platforms of Political Parties in Texas*. Austin: University of Texas Press, 1916.

Wynne, Lewis Nicholas. *The Continuity of Cotton: Planter Politics in Georgia, 1865–1892*. Macon: Mercer University Press, 1986.

Zimmerman, Warren. *First Great Triumph: How Five Americans Made Their Country a World Power*. Farrar, Straus and Giroux, 2002.

Zipf, Karin. *Labor of Innocents: Forced Apprenticeship in North Carolina, 1715–1919*. Baton Rouge: Louisiana State University Press, 2005.

Articles

Abbott, Martin. "The Freedmen's Bureau and Negro Schooling in South Carolina." *South Carolina Historical Magazine* 57 (Spring 1956): 65–81.

———. "Free Land, Free Labor, and the Freedmen's Bureau." *Agricultural History* 30 (October 1956): 150–156.

Alston, Lee J. and Joseph P. Ferrie. "Paternalism in Agricultural Labor Contracts in the U.S. South: Implications for the Growth of the Welfare State." *The American Economic Review* 83 (September 1993): 852–876.

Avins, Alfred. "The Right to Be a Witness and the Fourteenth Amendment." *Missouri Law Review* 31 (Fall 1966): 471–504.

Baggett, James A. "Birth of the Texas Republican Party." *Southwestern Historical Quarterly* 78 (July 1974-April 1975): 1–20.

———. "Origins of Early Texas Republican Party Leadership." *Journal of Southern History* 40 (August 1974): 441–454.

Bardaglio, Peter W. "Challenging Parental Custody Rights: The Legal Reconstruction of Parenthood in the Nineteenth-Century American South." *Continuity and Change* 4 (August 1989): 259–292.

Bean, Christopher B. "Death of a Carpetbagger: The George Washington Smith Murder and Stockade Trial in Jefferson, Texas, 1868–1869." *Southwestern Historical Quarterly* 112 (January 2009): 263–292.

———. " 'A Most Singular and Interesting Attempt': The Freedmen's Bureau at Marshall, Texas." *Southwestern Historical Quarterly* 110 (April 2007): 465–485.

Bell, John L. "Samuel Stanford Ashley, Carpetbagger and Educator." *The North Carolina Historical Review* 72 (October 1995): 456–483.

Belz, Herman. "The Freedmen's Bureau Act of 1865 and the Principle of No Discrimination According to Color." *Civil War History* 21 (September 1975): 197–217.

Benedict, Michael Les. "Preserving the Constitution: The Conservative Basis of Radical Reconstruction." *Journal of American History* 61 (June 1974): 65–90.

Bentley, George R. "The Political Activity of the Freedmen's Bureau in Georgia." *Florida Historical Quarterly* 28 (July 1949): 28–37.

Bethel, Elizabeth. "The Freedmen's Bureau in Alabama." *Journal of Southern History* 24 (February 1948): 49–92.

Blair, William. "The Use of Military Force to Protect the Gains of Reconstruction." *Civil War History* 51 (December 2005): 388–402.

Boris, Eileen and Peter Bardaglio. "The Transformation of Patriarchy: The Historical Role of the State." In *Families, Politics, and Public Policy: A Feminist Dialogue on Women and the State*, ed. Irene Diamond. New York: Longman, 1983.

Browne, Joseph. "'To Bring Out the Intellect of the Race': An African American Freedmen's Bureau Agent in Maryland." *Maryland Historical Magazine* 104 (Winter 2008): 374–401.

Butchart, Ronald E. and Amy F. Rolleri. "Iowa Teachers among the Freedpeople of the South, 1862–1876." *The Annals of Iowa* 62 (Winter 2003): 1–29.

———. "'We Best Can Instruct Our Own People': New York African Americans in the Freedmen's Schools, 1861–1875." *Afro-Americans in New York Life and History* 12 (1988): 27–49.

Campbell, Randolph B. "The Burden of Local Black Leadership During Reconstruction: A Research Note." *Civil War History* 39 (June 1993): 148–153.

———. "Scalawag District Judges: The E. J. Davis Appointees, 1870–1873." *Houston Review* 14 (Fall 1992): 75–88.

Cantrell, Greg. "Racial Violence and Reconstruction Politics in Texas, 1867–1868." *Southwestern Historical Quarterly* 93 (January 1990): 333–354.

Cardyn, Lisa. "Sexualized Racism/Gendered Violence: Outraging the Body Politics in the Reconstruction South." *Michigan Law Review* 100 (February 2002): 675–867.

Carter, Dan T. "The Anatomy of Fear: The Christmas Day Insurrection Scare of 1865." *Journal of Southern History* 42 (August 1976): 345–364.

Cimbala, Paul A. "Lining up to Serve Wounded and Sick Union Officers from Veteran Reserve Corps during Civil War/Reconstruction." *Prologue* 35 (Spring 2003): 38–49.

———. "Making Good Yankees: The Freedmen's Bureau and Education in Reconstruction Georgia, 1865–1870." *Atlanta Historical Journal* 29 (Fall 1985): 5–18.

———. "On the Front Line of Freedom: Freedmen's Bureau Officers and Agents in Reconstruction Georgia, 1865–1866." *Georgia Historical Quarterly* 76 (Fall 1992): 577–611.

———. "Soldiering on the Home Front: The Veteran Reserve Corps and the Northern People." In *Union Soldiers and the Northern Home Front: Wartime Experiences, Postwar Adjustments*, ed. Paul A. Cimbala and Randall M. Miller, 182–218. New York: Fordham University Press, 2002.

———. "The 'Talisman Power': Davis Tillson, the Freedmen's Bureau, and Free Labor in Reconstruction Georgia, 1865–1868." *Civil War History* 28 (June 1982): 153–171.

Clampitt, Brad R. "The Breakup: The Collapse of the Confederate Trans-Mississippi Army in Texas, 1865." *Southwestern Historical Quarterly* 108 (April 2005): 499–536.

Clinton, Catherine. "Reconstructing Freedwomen." In *Divided Houses: Gender in the Civil War*, ed. Catherine Clinton and Nina Silber. New York: Oxford University Press, 1992.

Clinton, Catherine. "'Public Women' and Sexual Politics During the American Civil War." In *Battle Scars: Gender and Sexuality in the American Civil War*, ed. Catherine Clinton and Nina Silber. New York: Oxford University Press, 2006.

Cohen-Lack, Nancy. "A Struggle for Sovereignty: National Consolidation, Emancipation, and Free Labor in Texas, 1865." *Journal of Southern History* 58 (February 1992): 57–98.

Cohen, William. "Black Immobility and Free Labor: The Freedmen's Bureau and the Relocation of Black Labor, 1865–1868." *Civil War History* 30 (September 1984): 221–334.

Colby, Ira C. "The Freedmen's Bureau: From Social Welfare to Segregation." *Phylon* 46 (3rd Qrt., 1985): 219–230.

Cox, John and LaWanda Cox. "General O. O. Howard and the 'Misrepresented Bureau.'" *Journal of Southern History* 19 (November 1953): 427–456.

Crouch, Barry A. "'All the Vile Passions': The Texas Black Code of 1866." *Southwestern Historical Quarterly* 97 (July 1993): 12–34.

———. "Black Dreams and White Justice." *Prologue* 6 (Winter 1974): 255–265.

———. "Black Education in Civil War and Reconstruction Louisiana: George T. Ruby, the Army, and the Freedmen's Bureau." *Louisiana History* 38 (Summer 1997): 287–308.

———. "The 'Chords of Love': Legalizing Black Marital and Family Rights in Postwar Texas." *Journal of Negro History* 79 (Autumn 1994): 334–351.

———. "The Freedmen's Bureau in Beaumont." *Texas Gulf Historical and Biographical Record* (Part One) 28 (1992): 8–27.

———. "The Freedmen's Bureau in Beaumont." *Texas Gulf Historical and Biographical Record* (Part Two) 29 (1993): 8–30.

———. "Guardian of the Freedpeople: Texas Freedmen Bureau Agents and the Black Community." *Southern Studies: An Interdisciplinary Journal of the* South (Fall 1992): 185–201.

———. "Spirit of Lawlessness: White Violence, Texas Blacks, 1865–1868." *Journal of Social History* 48 (Winter 1984): 217–232.

Crouch, Barry A. and Larry Madaras. "Reconstructing Black Families: Perspectives from the Texas Freedmen's Bureau Records." *Prologue* 18 (Summer 1986): 109–122.

Curry, Richard O. "The Abolitionists and Reconstruction: A Reappraisal." *Journal of Southern History* 34 (November 1968): 527–45.

Davis, Kathleen. "Year of Crucifixion: Galveston, Texas." *Texana* 8 (1970): 140–153.

DuBois, W. E. Burghardt. "The Freedmen's Bureau." *Atlantic Monthly* 87 (March 1901): 254–265.

Durrill, Wayne K. "Political Legitimacy and Local Courts: 'Politicks at Such a Rage' in a Southern Community during Reconstruction." *Journal of Southern History* 70 (August 2004): 577–602.

Edwards, Laura F. "The Problem of Dependency: African Americans, Labor Relations, and the Law in the Nineteenth-Century South." *Agricultural History* 72 (Spring 1998): 313–340.

Elliot, Claude. "The Freedmen's Bureau in Texas." *Southwestern Historical Quarterly* 56 (July 1952): 1–24.

Engelsman, John Cornelius. "The Freedmen's Bureau in Louisiana." *Louisiana Historical Quarterly* 32 (January 1949): 145–224.

Engs, Robert F. "The Missing Catalyst: In Response to Essays on Reconstructions That Might Have Been." *Civil War History* 51 (December 2005): 427–431.

Escott, Paul D. "Clinton A. Cilley, Yankee War Hero in the Postwar South: A Study in the Compatibility of Regional Values." *The North Carolina Historical Review* 68 (October 1991): 404–426.

Farmer-Kaiser, Mary. "'Are they not in some sorts vagrants': Gender and the Efforts of the Freedmen's Bureau to Combat Vagrancy in the Reconstruction South." *Georgia Historical Quarterly* 88 (Spring 2004): 25–49.

———. "With a Weight of Circumstances Like Millstones About Their Necks: Freedwomen, Federal Relief, and the Benevolent Guardianship of the Freedmen's Bureau." *Virginia Magazine of History and Biography* 115 (2007): 413–442.

Finley, Randy. "In War's Wake: Health Care and Arkansas Freedmen, 1863–1868." *Arkansas Historical Quarterly* 51 (Summer 1992): 135–163.

Foner, Eric. "The Meaning of Freedom in the Age of Emancipation." *Journal of American History* 81 (September 1994): 433–460.

———. "Reconstruction Revisited." *Reviews in American History* 10 (December 1982): 82–100.

Forman, James, Jr. "*Juries and Race in the Nineteenth Century*." Yale Law Journal 113 January 2004): 895–938.

Formwalt, Lee. W. "The Origins of African-American Politics in Southwest Georgia: A Case Study in Black Political Organization During Presidential Reconstruction, 1865–1867." *Journal of Negro History* 77 (Autumn 1992): 211–222.

Foster, Gaines M. "The Limitations of Federal Health Care for Freedmen, 1862–1868." *Journal of Southern History* 48 (August 1982): 349–372.

Franke, Katherine M. "Becoming a Citizen: Reconstruction Era Regulation of African American Marriages." *Yale Journal of Law & the Humanities* 11 (1999): 251–309.

———. "Taking Care." *Chicago-Kent Law Review* 76 (2001): 1541–1555.

Fraser, Nancy and Linda Gordon. "A Genealogy of 'Dependency': Tracing a Keyword of U.S. Welfare." *Signs* 19 (Winter 1994): 309–336.

Fuke, Richard Paul. "Planters, Apprenticeship, and Forced Labor: The Black Family Under Pressure in Post-Emancipation Maryland." *Agricultural History* 62 (Fall 1988): 57–74.

———. "A Reform Mentality: Federal Policy Toward Black Marylanders, 1864–1868." *Civil War History* 22 (September 1976): 214–235.

Groff, Patrick. "The Freedmen's Bureau in High School History Texts." *Journal of Negro Education* 51 (Autumn 1982): 425–433.

Hahn, Steven. "'Extravagant Expectations': Rumors, Political Struggle, and the Christmas Insurrection Scare of 1865 in the American South." *Past and Present* 157 (November 1997): 122–158.

Harrison, Robert. "New Representations of a 'Misrepresented Bureau': Reflections on Recent Scholarship on the Freedmen's Bureau." *American Nineteenth Century History* 8 (June 2007): 205–229.

———. "Welfare and Employment Policies of the Freedmen's Bureau in the District of Columbia." *Journal of Southern History* 77 (February 2006): 75–110.

Haskins, Patricia A. "The Freedmen's Bureau in the Jackson Purchase Region of Kentucky, 1866–1868." *The Register of the Kentucky Historical Society* 110 (Summer/Autumn 2012): 503–531.

Hasson, Gail S. "Health and Welfare of Freedmen in Reconstruction Alabama." *Alabama Review* 35 (April 1982): 94–110.

Hodgson, Frank. "Northern Missionary Aid Societies, the Freedmen's Bureau and Their Effect on Education in Montgomery." *The West Tennessee Historical Society Papers* 43 (1989): 28–43.

Hornsby, Alton, Jr. "The Freedmen's Bureau Schools in Texas, 1865–1870." *Southwestern Historical Quarterly* 76 (July 1972-April 1973): 397–417.

Humphrey, George D. "The Failure of the Mississippi Freedmen's Bureau in Black Labor Relations, 1865–1867." *Journal of Mississippi History* 45 (February 1983): 23–37.

Huston, James L. "An Alternative to the Tragic Era: Applying the Virtues of Bureaucracy to the Reconstruction Dilemma." *Civil War History* 51 (December 2005): 403–415.

———. "Reconstruction as It Should Have Been: An Exercise in Counterfactual History." *Civil War History* 51 (December 2005): 358–363.

Jackson, Luther P. "The Educational Efforts of the Freedmen's Bureau and Freedmen's Aid Societies in South Carolina, 1862–1872." *The Journal of Negro History* 8 (January 1923): 1–40.

Johnson, Whittington B. "A Black Teacher and Her School in Reconstruction Darien: The Correspondence of Hettie Sabattie and J. Murray Hoag, 1868–1869." *The Georgia Historical Quarterly* 75 (Spring 1991): 90–105.

Jordan, Weymouth T. "The Freedmen's Bureau in Tennessee." *East Tennessee Historical Society's Publications* 11 (1939): 47–61.

Kaczorowski, Robert J. "The Enforcement Provisions of the Civil Rights Act of 1866: A Legislative History in Light of *Runyon v. McCrary*." *Yale Law Review* 98 (January 1989): 565–595.

———. "To Begin the Nation Anew: Congress, Citizenship, and Civil Rights after the Civil War." *American Historical Review* 92 (February 1987): 45–68.

Kassel, Charles. "Educating the Slave—A Forgotten Chapter of Civil War History." *Open Court* 40 (1927): 239–256.

———. "Edwin Miller Wheelock." *The Open Court* 34 (September 1920): 564–569.

———. "Edwin Miller Wheelock: A Prophet of Civil War Times." *The Open Court* 36 (February 22): 116–124.

Kemp, Thomas R. "Community and War: The Civil War Experience of Two New Hampshire Towns." In *Toward a Social History of the American Civil War: Exploratory Essays*, ed. Maris A. Vinovskis. New York: Cambridge University Press, 1990.

Kiddoo, Donald Bounds. "Life of General Joseph Kiddoo." *Heritage Library News* 8 Fall 2004): 4–8.

Ledbetter, Billy D. "White Texans' Attitudes Toward the Political Equality of Negroes, 1865–1870." *Phylon* 40 (September 1979): 253–263.

Lentz, Sallie M. "Highlights of Early Harrison County." *Southwestern Historical Quarterly* 61 (October 1957): 240–256.

Leventhal, David S. " 'Freedom to Work, Nothing More Nor Less': The Freedmen's Bureau, White Planters, and Black Contract Labor in Postwar Tennessee, 1865–1868." *Journal of East Tennessee History* 78 (2006): 23–49.

Lieberman, Robert C. "The Freedmen's Bureau and the Politics of Institutional Structure." *Social Science History* 18 (Autumn 1994): 405–417.

Longacre, Edward. "Brave, Radical, Wild: The Contentious Career of Brigadier General Edward A. Wild." *Civil War Times Illustrated* 19 (June 1980): 8–19.

Low, W. A. "The Freedmen's Bureau and Civil Rights in Maryland." *Journal of Negro History* 37 (July 1952): 221–247.

———. "The Freedmen's Bureau in the Border States." In *Radicalism, Racism, and Party Realignment: The Border States during Reconstruction*, ed. Richard O. Curry, 245–264. Baltimore: Johns Hopkins University Press, 1969.

Lowe, Richard G. "The Freedmen's Bureau and Local Black Leadership." *Journal of American History* 80 (December 1993): 989–998.

———. "The Freedmen's Bureau and Local White Leaders in Virginia." *Journal of Southern History* 64 (August 1998): 455–472.

Lowe, Richard G. and Randolph B. Campbell. "Wealthholding and Political Power in Antebellum Texas." *Southwestern Historical Quarterly* 75 (July 1979): 21–30.

Marten, James. "What is to become of the Negro?" White Reaction to Emancipation in Texas" *Mid-America: An Historical Review* 73 (April-July 1991): 115–133.

May, J. Thomas. "A 19th Century Medical Care Program for Blacks: The Case of the Freedmen's Bureau." *Anthropological Quarterly* 46 (July 1973): 160–171.

———. "Continuity and Change in the Labor Program of the Union Army and the Freedmen's Bureau." *Civil War History* 17 (September 1971): 245–254.

———. "The Freedmen's Bureau at the Local Level: A Study of a Louisiana Agent." *Louisiana History* 9 (Winter 1968): 455–472.

———. "The Louisiana Negro in Transition: An Appraisal of the Medical Activities of the Freedmen's Bureau." *Bulletin of the Tulane Medical Faculty* 26 (February 1967): 29–36.

McGehee, C. Stuart. "E. O. Trade, Freedmen's Education, and the Failure of Reconstruction in Tennessee." *Tennessee Historical Quarterly* 43 (1984): 376–389.

Moneyhon, Carl. "George T. Ruby and the Politics of Expediency in Texas." In *Southern Black Leaders of the Reconstruction Era*, ed. Howard A. Rabinowitz, 364–378. Urbana: University of Illinois Press, 1982.

Moreno, Paul. "Racial Classifications and Reconstruction Legislation." *Journal of Southern History* 61 (May 1995): 271–304.

Morris, Thomas D. "Equality, 'Extraordinary Law,' and Criminal Justice: The South Carolina Experience, 1865–1866." *South Carolina Historical Magazine* 83 (January 1982): 15–33.

Murdoch, David A. "Profiles in Leadership: Allegheny County's Lawyer-Generals in the Civil War." *Pittsburgh History* 81 (Winter 1998): 172–185.

Myers, John B. "The Education of the Alabama Freedmen During Presidential Reconstruction, 1865–1867." *Journal of Negro Education* 40 (Spring 1971): 163–171.

Nash, Steven E. "Aiding the Southern Mountain Republicans: The Freedmen's Bureau in Buncombe County." *North Carolina Historical Review* 83 (January 2006): 1–30.

Neal, Diane and Thomas W. Kremm. "'What Shall We Do with the Negro?': The Freedmen's Bureau in Texas." *East Texas Historical Journal* 27 (Fall 1989): 23–34.

Newell, Clayton R. and Charles R. Shrader. "The U.S. Army's Transition to Peace, 1865–1866." *The Journal of Military History* 77 (July 2013): 867–894.

Nieman, Donald G. "Andrew Johnson, the Freedmen's Bureau, and the Problem of Equal Rights, 1865–1866." *Journal of Southern History* 44 (August 1978): 399–420.

———. "The Freedmen's Bureau and the Mississippi Black Code." *Journal of Mississippi History* 40 (May 1978): 91–118.

Oakes, James. "A Failure of a Vision: The Collapse of the Freedmen's Bureau Courts." *Civil War History* 25 (March 1979): 66–76.

Pearson, Reggie L. "'There Are Many Sick, Feeble, and Suffering Freedmen': The Freedmen's Bureau's Health Care Activities during Reconstruction in North Carolina, 1865–1868." *North Carolina Historical Review* 79 (April 2002): 141–181.

Philips, Sara T. "Antebellum Agricultural Reform, Republican Ideology, and Sectional Tension." *Agricultural History* 74 (Autumn 2000): 799–822.

Powell, Lawrence. "The American Land Company and Agency: John A. Andrew and the Northernization of the South." *Civil War History* 21 (December 1975): 293–308.

———. "The Politics of Livelihood: Carpetbaggers in the Deep South." In *Region, Race, and Reconstruction: Essays in Honor of C. Vann Woodward*. Edited by J. Morgan and James M. McPherson. New York: Oxford University Press, 1982.

Price, Charles L. "John C. Barnett, Freedmen's Bureau Agent in North Carolina." *Of Tar Heel Towns, Shipbuilders, Reconstructionists, and Alliancemen: Papers in North Carolina History* 5 (Autumn 1981): 51–74.

Ramsdell, Charles W. "Texas From the Fall of the Confederacy to the Beginning of Reconstruction." *Quarterly of the Texas State Historical Association* 11 (July 1907–April 1908): 199–219.

Ransom, Roger L. "Reconstructing Reconstruction: Options and Limitations to Federal Policies on Land Distribution in 1866–1867." *Civil War History* 51 (December 2005): 364–377.

Raphael, Alan. "Health and Social Welfare of Kentucky Black People, 1865–1870." *Societas* 2 (Spring 1972): 143–157. Rapport, Sara. "The Freedmen's Bureau as a Legal Agent for Black Men and Women in Georgia, 1865–1868," *Georgia Historical Quarterly* 73 (Spring 1989): 26–53.

Reed, Pamela Denise. "From the Freedmen's Bureau to FEMA: A Post-Katrina Historical, Journalistic, and Literary Analysis." 37 *Journal of Black Studies* (March 2007): 555–567.

Rhodes, Charles D. "William Rufus Shafter." *Michigan History Magazine* 16 (Fall 1932): 375–383.

Rhyne, J. Michael. "'Conduct . . . Inexcusable and Unjustifiable': Bound Children, Battered Freedwomen, and the Limits of Emancipation in Kentucky's Bluegrass Region." *Journal of Social History* 42 (Winter 2008): 319–340.

Richardson, Heather Cox. "A Marshall Plan for the South? The Failure of Republican and Democratic Ideology during Reconstruction." *Civil War History* 51 (December 2005): 378–387.

Rice, Otis K. "Eli Thayer and the Friendly Invasion of Virginia." *Journal of Southern History* 37 (November 1971): 575–596.

Richardson, Joe M. "An Evaluation of the Freedmen's Bureau in Florida." *Florida Historical Quarterly* 41 (January 1963): 223–238.

———. "The Freedmen's Bureau and Negro Labor in Florida." *Florida Historical Quarterly* 39 (October 1960): 167–174.

Richter, William L. "'A Dear Little Job': Second Lieutenant Hiram F. Willis, Freedmen's Bureau Agent in Southwestern Arkansas, 1866–1868." *Arkansas Historical Quarterly* 50 (Summer 1991): 158–200.

———. "'This Blood-Thirsty Hole': The Freedmen's Bureau Agency at Clarksville, Texas, 1867–1868." *Civil War History* 38 (March 1992): 51–77.

———. "The Brenham Fire of 1866: A Texas Reconstruction Atrocity." *Louisiana Studies* (Fall 1975): 287–314.

———. "'Devil Take Them All': Military Rule in Texas, 1862–1870." *Southern Studies* 25 (Spring 1986): 5–30.

———. "'Oh God, Let Us Have Revenge': Ben Griffith and His Family During the Civil War and Reconstruction." *Arkansas Historical Quarterly* 57 (Autumn 1998): 255–286.

———. "'The Revolver Rules the Day!': Colonel DeWitt C. Brown and the Freedmen's Bureau in Paris, Texas, 1867–1868." *Southwestern Historical Quarterly* 93 (January 1990): 302–332.

———. "Tyrant and Reformer: General Griffin Reconstructs Texas, 1865–1866." *Prologue* 10 (Winter 1978): 225–241.

———. "Who Was the Real Head of the Texas Freedmen's Bureau?: The Role of Brevet Colonel William H. Sinclair as Acting Assistant Inspector General." *Military History of the Southwest* 20 (Fall 1990): 121–156.

Rorabaugh, W. J. "Who Fought for the North in the Civil War? Concord, Massachusetts, Enlistments." *Journal of American History* 73 (December 1986): 695–701.

Rose, Willie Lee. "Blacks Without Masters: Protagonists and Issues." In *Slavery and Freedom*, ed. William W. Freehling. New York: Oxford University Press, 1982.

Russ, William A. "Registration and Disfranchisement Under Radical Reconstruction." *Mississippi Valley Historical Review* 21 (September 1934): 163–180.

Savitt, Todd L. "Politics in Medicine: The Georgia Freedmen's Bureau and the Organization of Health Care, 1865–1866." *Civil War History* 28 (March 1982): 45–64.

Scott, Rebecca. "The Battle Over the Child: Child Apprenticeship and the Freedmen's Bureau in North Carolina." *Prologue* 10 (Summer 1978): 101–133.

Shlomowitz, Ralph. "'Bound' or 'Free'? Black Labor in Cotton and Sugarcane Farming, 1865–1880." *Journal of Southern History* 50 (November 1984): 569–596.

Singleton, Robert. "William Gilmore Simms, Woodlands, and the Freedmen's Bureau." *Mississippi Quarterly* 50 (Winter 1996): 18–36.

Smallwood, James M. "Charles E. Culver, A Reconstruction Agent in Texas: The Work of Local Freedmen's Bureau Agents and the Black Community." *Civil War History* 27 (December 1981): 350–361.

———. "The Freedmen's Bureau Reconsidered: Local Agents and the Black Community." *Texana* 11 (Fall 1973): 309–320.

———. "G. T. Ruby: Galveston's Black Carpetbagger in Reconstruction Texas." *Houston Review* 5 (Winter 1983):24–33.

————. "When the Klan Rode: White Terror in Reconstruction Texas." *Journal of the West* 25 (October 1986): 4–13.

Smith, George Winston. "Ante-Bellum Attempts of Northern Business Interests to 'Redeem' the Upper South." *Journal of Southern History* 11 (May 1945): 177–213.

Smith, John David. "'The Work It Did Not Do Because It Could Not': Georgia and the 'New' Freedmen's Bureau Historiography." *Georgia Historical Quarterly* 82 (Summer 1998): 331–349.

Smith, Solomon K. "'Better to not look at a place, than send an unsupported man there as Agent': Chaplain Thomas Callahan, and the arrival of the Freedmen's Bureau in Shreveport." *North Louisiana History* 36 (2005): 154–166.

————. "The Freedmen's Bureau in Shreveport: The Struggle for Control of the Red River District." *Louisiana History* 41 (Fall 2000): 435–465.

Smith, Thomas H. "Conflict and Corruption: The Dallas Establishment vs. the Freedmen's Bureau Agent." *Legacies: A History Journal for Dallas and North Central Texas* 1 (Fall 1989): 154–171.

Stanley, Amy Dru. "Beggars Can't Be Choosers: Compulsion and Contract in Postbellum America." *Journal of American History* 78 (March 1992): 1265–1293.

Stein, Bill. "Consider the Lily: The Ungilded History of Colorado County, Texas." *Nesbitt Memorial Library Journal* 9 (January 2000): 3–39.

Stealey, John Edmund. "Reports of Freedmen's Bureau Operations in West Virginia: Agents in The Eastern Panhandle." *West Virginia History* 42 (Fall-Winter 1981): 94–129.

Sullivan, Barry. "Historical Reconstruction, Reconstruction History, and the Proper Scope of Section 1981." *Yale Law Journal* 98 (January 1989): 541–564.

Thompson, C. Mildred. "The Freedmen's Bureau in Georgia in 1865–1866: An Instrument of Reconstruction." *Georgia Historical Quarterly* 5 (March 1921): 40–49.

Torget, Andrew J. "Carpetbagger on the Brazos: The Texas Freedmen's Bureau in Robertson County." *Agora: An Online Undergraduate Journal of the Humanities* 1 (Winter 2000): 1–14.

Vandal, Gilles. "'Bloody Caddo': White Violence Against Blacks in a Louisiana Parish, 1865–1876." *Journal of Social History* 25 (Winter 1991): 373–388.

Vandiver, Frank V. "Some Problems Involved in Writing Confederate History." *Journal of Southern History* 36 (August 1970): 400–410.

Vinovskis, Maris A. "Have Social Historians Lost the Civil War? Some Preliminary Demographic Speculations." In *Toward a Social History of the American Civil War: Exploratory Essays*, ed. Maris A. Vinovskis. New York: Cambridge University Press, 1990.

Vorenberg, Michael. "Imagining a Different Reconstruction Constitution." *Civil War History* 51 (December 2005): 416–426.

Wagstaff, Thomas. "Call Your Old Master–'Master': Southern Political Leaders and Negro Labor During Presidential Reconstruction." *Labor History* 10 (Summer 1969): 323–345.

Webb, Ross A., "The Past Is Never Dead, It's Not Even Past": Benjamin P. Runkle and The Freedmen's Bureau in Kentucky, 1866–1870." *Register of the Kentucky Historical Society* 84 (Autumn 1986): 343–360.

Weinfeld, Daniel R. "'More Courage Than Discretion': Charles M. Hamilton in Reconstruction-Era Florida." *Florida Historical Quarterly* 84 (Spring 1984): 479–516.

White, Kenneth B. "Black Lives, Red Tape: The Alabama Freedmen's Bureau." *Alabama Historical Quarterly* 43 (Winter 1981): 241–258.

———. "Wager Swayne: Racist or Realist." *Alabama Review* (April 1978): 92–109.

Williams, Heather Andrea. "'Clothing Themselves in Intelligence': The Freedpeople, Schooling, and Northern Teachers, 1861–1871." *Journal of African American History* 87 (Autumn 2002): 372–389.

Woods, Randall B. "George T. Ruby: A Black Militant in the White Business Community." *Red River Valley Historical Review* 1 (August 1974): 269–280.

Work, David. "United States Colored Troops in Texas during Reconstruction, 1865–1867." *Southwestern Historical Quarterly* 109 (January 2006): 336–357.

Zipf, Karin L. "Reconstructing "Free Woman": African-American Women, Apprenticeship, and Custody Rights during Reconstruction." *Journal of Women's History* 12 (Spring 2000): 8–31.

Dissertations, Theses, and Unpublished Manuscripts

Albrecht, Winnell. "The Texas Black Codes." Master's Thesis, Southwest Texas State University, 1969.

Alderson, William T. "The Influence of Military Rule and the Freedmen's Bureau on Reconstruction Virginia, 1865–1870." Ph.D. diss., Vanderbilt University, 1952.

Ashcraft, Allan. "Texas, 1860–1866: The Lone Star State in the Civil War." Ph.D. diss., Columbia University, 1960.

Bohne, Edwin. "The History of the *Brenham Banner Press*." Master's Thesis, Sam Houston State University, 1950.

Bronson, Louis Henry. "The Freedmen's Bureau: A Public Policy Analysis." D.S.W. diss., University of Southern California, 1970.

Buckhorn, Anne L. Moore. "The Yellow Fever Epidemic of 1867 in Galveston." Master's Thesis, University of Houston, 1962.

Burks, William H. "The Freedmen's Bureau, Politics, and Stability Operations During Reconstruction in the South." Master's Thesis, U.S. Air Force Academy, 2009.

Carrier, John Pressley. "A Political History of Texas During the Reconstruction, 1865–1874." Ph.D. diss., Vanderbilt University, 1971.

Chartock, Lewis C. "A History and Analysis of Labor Contracts Administered by the Bureau of Refugees, Freedmen, and Abandoned Lands in Edgefield, Abbeville and Anderson Counties, South Carolina, 1865–1868." Ph.D. diss., Bryn Mawr College, 1974.

Christopher, Nehemiah McKinley. "The History of Negro Public Education in Texas, 1865–1900." Ph.D. diss., University of Pittsburgh, 1948.

Clayton, Barbara Leah. "The Lone Star Conspiracy: Racial Violence and Ku Klux Klan Terror in Post–Civil War Texas, 1865–1877." Master's Thesis, Oklahoma State University, 1986.

Cole, Fred. "Texas Career of Thomas Affleck." Ph.D. diss., Louisiana State University, 1942.

Downs, James T. "Diagnosing Reconstruction: Sickness, Dependency, and the Medical Division of the Freedmen's Bureau, 1861–1870." Ph.D. diss., Columbia University, 2005.

Drago, Edmund L. "Black Georgia During Reconstruction." Ph.D. diss., University of California-Berkeley, 1975.

Dudley, Ross Nathaniel. "Texas Reconstruction: The Role of the Bureau of Refugees, Freedmen and Abandoned Lands, 1865–1870, Smith County, (Tyler) Texas." Master's Thesis, Texas A&I University, 1986.

Engerrand, Steven. "Now Scratch or Die: The Genesis of Capitalistic Agricultural Labor in Georgia, 1865–1880." Ph.D. diss., University of Georgia, 1981.

Everly, Elaine Cutler. "The Freedmen's Bureau in the National Capital." Ph.D. diss., George Washington University, 1971.

Farmer, Mary J. "Freewomen and the Freedmen's Bureau: Race, Gender, and Public Policy in the Age of Emancipation." Ph.D. diss., Bowling Green State University, 2000.

Field, Barbara J., and Leslie S. Rowland. "Free Labor Ideology and Its Exponents in the South During the Civil War and Reconstruction." Paper presented at the Organization of American Historians Annual Meeting, 1984.

Flanigan, David J. "The Criminal Law of Slavery and Freedom, 1800–1868." Ph.D. diss., Rice University, 1973.

Goldberg, Chad Alan. "The Freedmen's Bureau and Civil War Pensions: Race and Policy Feedback in America's Nineteenth-Century Welfare State." Paper presented at the American Sociological Association Annual Meeting, 2006.

Gray, Charles. "The Freedmen's Bureau: A Missing Chapter in Social Welfare History." D.S.W., Ph.D. diss., Yeshiva University, 1994.

Hales, Douglas. "Violence Perpetrated Against African Americans by Whites in Texas During Reconstruction, 1865–1868." Master's Thesis, Texas Tech University, 1994.

Harper, Jr., Cecil. "Freedmen's Bureau Agents: A Profile." Paper presented at the Texas State Historical Association Annual Meeting, 1987.

Harris, Anne Barber. "The South as Seen by Travelers, 1865–1880." Ph.D. diss., University of North Carolina, 1971.

Hayward, Barbara J. "Winning the Race: Education of Texas Freedmen Immediately After the Civil War." Ph.D. diss., University of Houston, 1999.

Hickin, Patricia P. "John Curtis Underwood and the Antislavery Crusade, 1809–1860." Master's Thesis: University of Virginia, 1961.

Jackson, LaVonne Roberts. "'Family and Freedom': The Freedmen's Bureau and African-American Women in Texas in the Reconstruction Era, 1865–1872." Ph.D. diss., Howard University, 1996.

Kickler, Troy Lee. "Black Children and Northern Missionaries: Freedmen's Bureau Agents, and Southern Whites in Reconstruction Tennessee, 1865–1869." Ph.D. diss., University of Tennessee, 2003.

Kosary, Rebecca A. "Regression to Barbarism in Reconstruction Texas: An Analysis of White Violence Against African-Americans from the Texas Freedmen's Bureau Records, 1865–1868." Master's Thesis, Southwest Texas State, 1999.

―――――. "To Degrade and Control: White Violence and the Maintenance of Racial and Gender Boundaries in Reconstruction Texas, 1865–1868." Ph.D. diss., Texas A&M University, 2006.

Masur, Katherine. "Reconstructing the Nation's Capital: The Politics of Race and Citizenship in the District of Columbia, 1862–1878." Ph.D. diss., University of Michigan, 2001.

May, J. Thomas. "The Medical Care of Blacks in Louisiana During the Occupation and Reconstruction, 1862–1868: Its Social and Political Background." Ph.D. diss., Tulane University, 1972.

McFeely, William S. "The Freedmen's Bureau: A Study in Betrayal." Ph.D. diss., Yale University, 1966.

Olds, Victoria. "The Freedmen's Bureau as a Social Agency." Ph.D. diss., Columbia University, 1966.

Owens, Nora Estelle. "Presidential Reconstruction in Texas: A Case Study." Ph.D. diss., Auburn University, 1983.

Owens, James L. "The Negro in Georgia during Reconstruction, 1864–1872: A Social History." Ph.D. diss., University of Georgia, 1975.

Pfanz, Harry Wilcox. "Soldiering in the South During Reconstruction, 1865–1877." Ph.D. diss., Ohio State University, 1958.

Philips, Paul David. "The Freedmen's Bureau in Tennessee." Ph.D. diss., Vanderbilt University, 1966.

Sherman, Honorine Anne. "The Freedmen's in Louisiana." Master's Thesis, Tulane University, 1936.

Shlomowitz, Ralph. "The Transition from Slave to Freedman Labor Arrangements in Southern Agriculture, 1865–1870." Ph.D. diss., University of Chicago, 1979.

Shook, Robert W. "Federal Occupation and Administration of Texas, 1865–1870." Ph.D. diss., North Texas State University, 1972.

Small, Sandra Eileen. "The Yankee Schoolmarm in Southern Freedmen's Schools, 1861–1871: The Career of a Stereotype." Ph.D. diss., Washington State University, 1976.

Troost, William Frank. "Accomplishment and Abandonment: A History of the Freedmen's Bureau Schools." Ph.D. diss., University of California Irvine, 2007.

Volz, Harry August. "The Administration of Justice by the Freedmen's Bureau in Kentucky, South Carolina, and Virginia." Master's Thesis, University of Virginia, 1975.

Index

Hans L. Trefousse, *Impeachment of a President: Andrew Johnson, the Blacks, and Reconstruction.*

Richard Paul Fuke, *Imperfect Equality: African Americans and the Confines of White Ideology in Post-Emancipation Maryland.*

Ruth Currie-McDaniel, *Carpetbagger of Conscience: A Biography of John Emory Bryant.*

Paul A. Cimbala and Randall M. Miller, eds., *The Freedmen's Bureau and Reconstruction: Reconsiderations.*

Herman Belz, *A New Birth of Freedom: The Republican Party and Freedmen's Rights, 1861 to 1866.*

Robert Michael Goldman, *"A Free Ballot and a Fair Count": The Department of Justice and the Enforcement of Voting Rights in the South, 1877–1893.*

Ruth Douglas Currie, ed., *Emma Spaulding Bryant: Civil War Bride, Carpetbagger's Wife, Ardent Feminist—Letters, 1860–1900.*

Robert Francis Engs, *Freedom's First Generation: Black Hampton, Virginia, 1861–1890.*

Robert F. Kaczorowski, *The Politics of Judicial Interpretation: The Federal Courts, Department of Justice, and Civil Rights, 1866–1876.*

John Syrett, *The Civil War Confiscation Acts: Failing to Reconstruct the South.*

Michael Les Benedict, *Preserving the Constitution: Essays on Politics and the Constitution in the Reconstruction Era.*

Andrew L. Slap, *The Doom of Reconstruction: The Liberal Republicans in the Civil War Era.*

Edmund L. Drago, *Confederate Phoenix: Rebel Children and Their Families in South Carolina.*

Mary Farmer-Kaiser, *Freedwomen and the Freedmen's Bureau: Race, Gender, and Public Policy in the Age of Emancipation.*

Paul A. Cimbala and Randall Miller, eds., *The Great Task Remaining Before Us: Reconstruction as America's Continuing Civil War.*

John A. Casey Jr., *New Men: Reconstructing the Image of the Veteran in Late-Nineteenth-Century American Literature and Culture.*

Hilary Green, *Educational Reconstruction: African American Schools in the Urban South, 1865–1890.*

Christopher B. Bean, *Too Great a Burden to Bear: The Struggle and Failure of the Freedmen's Bureau in Texas.*